# Advances in Computer Vision and Pattern Recognition

More information about this series at http://www.springer.com/series/4205

Sébastien Marcel · Mark S. Nixon
Stan Z. Li
Editors

# Handbook of Biometric Anti-Spoofing

Trusted Biometrics under Spoofing Attacks

Springer

*Editors*
Sébastien Marcel
Idiap Research Institute
Martigny
Switzerland

Mark S. Nixon
University of Southampton
Southampton
UK

Stan Z. Li
Institute of Automation
Center for Biometrics and Security
  Research
Chinese Academy of Sciences
Beijing
China

*Founding Editor*
Sameer Singh
Rail Vision Europe Ltd.
Castle Donington
Leicestershire
UK

*Series Editor*
Sing Bing Kang
Interactive Visual Media Group
Microsoft Research
Redmond
WA
USA

ISSN 2191-6586         ISSN 2191-6594   (electronic)
ISBN 978-1-4471-6523-1     ISBN 978-1-4471-6524-8   (eBook)
DOI 10.1007/978-1-4471-6524-8

Library of Congress Control Number: 2014942635

Springer London Heidelberg New York Dordrecht

© Springer-Verlag London 2014
This work is subject to copyright. All rights are reserved by the Publisher, whether the whole or part of the material is concerned, specifically the rights of translation, reprinting, reuse of illustrations, recitation, broadcasting, reproduction on microfilms or in any other physical way, and transmission or information storage and retrieval, electronic adaptation, computer software, or by similar or dissimilar methodology now known or hereafter developed. Exempted from this legal reservation are brief excerpts in connection with reviews or scholarly analysis or material supplied specifically for the purpose of being entered and executed on a computer system, for exclusive use by the purchaser of the work. Duplication of this publication or parts thereof is permitted only under the provisions of the Copyright Law of the Publisher's location, in its current version, and permission for use must always be obtained from Springer. Permissions for use may be obtained through RightsLink at the Copyright Clearance Center. Violations are liable to prosecution under the respective Copyright Law.
The use of general descriptive names, registered names, trademarks, service marks, etc. in this publication does not imply, even in the absence of a specific statement, that such names are exempt from the relevant protective laws and regulations and therefore free for general use.
While the advice and information in this book are believed to be true and accurate at the date of publication, neither the authors nor the editors nor the publisher can accept any legal responsibility for any errors or omissions that may be made. The publisher makes no warranty, express or implied, with respect to the material contained herein.

Printed on acid-free paper

Springer is part of Springer Science+Business Media (www.springer.com)

# Foreword

Hollywood has long and richly enjoyed depicting biometric spoofing. As early as 1971, in the movie *Diamonds Are Forever*, Sean Connery's James Bond character uses a fake fingerprint attached to his fingertip to convince a woman of his assumed identity. In the movie RED, Bruce Willis' retired CIA agent character uses a custom contact lens to spoof an eye scanner and break into CIA headquarters. In the movie, the scanner is called a retinal scanner, but it clearly images the iris rather than the retina. We should not press Hollywood too much for technical accuracy! In the film *Charlie's Angels: Full Throttle*, Cameron Diaz's character uses a custom contact lens and fake fingerprints to fool a multi-modal biometric scanner and break into the bad-guy corporate headquarters. Anyone working in biometrics can probably supply several more of their favorite such biometric spoofing scenes.

In the most general sense, biometric spoofing can be defined as the deliberate attempt to create an error in a biometric system, either a false match or a false non-match. This typically involves presenting a biometric sample to the system that does not truly correspond to the person presenting it. The person committing the spoof either wants simply to avoid being recognized as their true identity, or wants to be recognized as a some specific chosen identity that is not their own. In the most general sense, then, anti-spoofing is about detecting the presence of biometric samples that are not a true representation of the person presenting the sample. The term "liveness detection" is used to refer to anti-spoofing methods that are based on determining if the sensor is imaging a "live" sample, as opposed to a gummy finger, a textured contact lens, a video of a face, or some other non-live sample.

It is easy to envy what Stan Z. Li, Mark Nixon, and Sébastien Marcel have accomplished with their *Handbook on Biometric Anti-Spoofing*. One reason is that they managed to envision a truly novel theme for their handbook. There are of course many recent books on various themes in biometrics, and more appearing all the time. After all, biometrics is a hot area for both research and application. Some of the books have a chapter devoted to spoofing attacks of one kind or another, but it is not common to have even one chapter devoted to anti-spoofing methods. And while any new spoofing attack tends to attract attention and publicity, it is the anti-spoofing methods that are more important to the "good guys." Thus, it is significant that Professors Li, Nixon, and Marcel have realized the first book devoted entirely to anti-spoofing methods in biometrics.

A second reason to envy their accomplishment is that I believe Professors Li, Nixon, and Marcel have anticipated an important emerging need. There is now a good amount of solid research on anti-spoofing methods. But it is spread out in the literature of the various biometrics modalities. It is rather difficult for one person to keep abreast of it all. And there is not yet, until this book, and attempt to pull things together and make connections and leverage commonalities between anti-spoofing concepts developed in the context of different modalities. So there is a good opportunity for a whole-is-greater-than-the-sum-of-the-parts effect in this instance.

A third reason is that I judge Professors Li, Nixon, and Marcel to have also timed the wave of need just about right. Large-scale biometric applications are being deployed in many countries around the world. And many of these applications—India's Aadhaar being a prime example—have serious implications for commerce. The old saying about the criminal Willie Sutton was that he robbed banks because that is where the money was. In the same way, as biometrics becomes the means of identity verification for commerce, we can expect the frequency and intensity of spoofing attacks to increase. A news article that appeared just this month ran with the title, "Crime of the Future—Biometric Spoofing?" [1]. Everyone working in the area of biometrics can appreciate that this title may be destined to be more true than we would like. So the biometrics research community needs to increase the amount of attention paid to anti-spoofing methods. This book will serve as the introduction to the topic for biometrics professionals who must come up to speed on the area.

A fourth reason is that the labors of Professors Li, Nixon, and Marcel have resulted in a quality product. They have well covered the breadth of biometric modalities. The depth of the material covered is state of the art, due to Professors Li, Nixon, and Marcel having solicited contributions from accomplished researchers throughout the world. The core technical contributions are placed in the broader context by additional chapters dealing with essential issues such as evaluation methodologies, databases, standards, and legal concerns.

And so the final result is the *Handbook of Biometric Anti-Spoofing*. It is the only book on this important theme. It arrives at just the time that the need for it should be apparent to all in the biometrics community. And it is a well-executed concept, collecting together chapters of quality material authored by leading experts, and covering all the major topics and issues.

As mentioned, Professors Li, Nixon, and Marcel have solicited chapters that well cover the breadth of different biometric modalities. There are two chapters on fingerprint spoofing, from the forensic viewpoint and the biometric viewpoint, by Christophe Champod and Marcela Espinoza, and by Javier Galbally and coworkers, respectively. There are also two chapters on face anti-spoofing, covering a visual approach and a multi-spectral imaging approach, by André Anjos and coworkers, and by Dong Yi and co-workers, respectively. Iris anti-spoofing is covered by Zhenan Sun and Tieniu Tan, who have done some of the pioneering work in the area. Voice anti-spoofing is covered by Nick Evans and coworkers, gait anti-spoofing by the John Bustard and coworkers, and multi-modal anti-spoofing by Giorgio Fumera and coworkers. In addition to broad coverage of anti-spoofing techniques for various major biometric modalities, this book also includes chapters on important general topics. Nesli Erdoğmus and Sébastien Marcel set the stage early in the book with a general overview of biometric spoofing attacks. Ivana Chingovska and coworkers cover the important topic of how to evaluate the effectiveness of anti-spoofing methods. Christoph Busch discusses the topic of standards related to anti-spoofing methods. Els Kindt addresses the topic of legal issues related to anti-spoofing. And, finally, Stan Z. Li summarizes the evaluation databases that are currently available.

I take it as a confirmation of the comprehensive and authoritative approach that Professors Li, Nixon, and Marcel have taken that their Handbook includes a chapter covering evaluation methodologies. In our own experience working on iris anti-spoofing methods at the University of Notre Dame, we found that coming to the right view of how to evaluate the accuracy of an anti-spoofing method can be difficult. In our initial work, we happily evaluated the accuracy of algorithms to detect textured contact lenses using a person-disjoint, ten-fold cross-validation. This is, after all, the standard approach for evaluation of biometric algorithms. Using this approach to evaluation, any of a variety of classifiers trained with local-binary-pattern feature vectors could achieve highly accurate detection of textured contact lenses. But when it occurred to us to ask what would happen if the textured lenses in the test partition were from a manufacturer whose lenses were not represented in the training data, the results were much lower on average and highly variable with the specific lens manufacturer represented in the test partition [2]. This illustrates how the area of biometric anti-spoofing is a specialized and difficult subarea of biometrics research.

The *Handbook of Biometric Anti-Spoofing* edited by Professors Li, Nixon, and Marcel is a valuable addition to the biometrics research literature. It brings a needed focus to a theme that is certain to grow in interest and importance. I predict that the *Handbook of Biometric Anti-Spoofing* will prove quite popular, and that it will not be long before several additional books imitating this theme appear.

Notre Dame, Indiana, USA, November 2013　　　　　　　　　　　Kevin W. Bowyer

# References

1. Crime of the future—biometric spoofing? (2013) http://www.zdnet.com/crime-of-the-future-biometric-spoofing-2039376855/. Accessed 11 Nov 2013
2. Doyle JS, Bowyer KW, Flynn PJ (2013) Variation in accuracy of textured contact lens detection based on iris sensor and contact lens manufacturer. In: IEEE international conference on biometrics: theory, applications and systems (BTAS 13), Sept 30–Oct 2

# Preface

In its short history, biometrics has developed very fast and is now used to enrol entire populations. As Kevin Bowyer's Foreword points out, the motivation of spoofing such systems is natural and must be expected. Under the leadership of Sébastien Marcel, the EU-funded seventh Framework Research Programme: Trusted Biometrics under Spoofing Attacks (TABULA RASA) was aimed to be the first concerted research program that addressed this issue. The TABULA RASA team was formed of an international set of researchers from Switzerland, Italy, Finland, France, UK, Spain, and China who addressed the main biometric modalities, many of which feature within the chapters that follow. The program included industrial partners and their demonstration and commercial material is less suited to inclusion with a text, though their contribution to the research program's success was enormous.

The publisher now with the largest coverage of biometrics is Springer. Those attending any of the major conferences that includes biometrics will have met Wayne Wheeler and so our gratitude remains for his early enthusiasm of this project. Of late, Simon Rees has been very patient while we reach the final stages of the book. We regret that delay appears innate to edited texts, though this can lead to greater polish in the result.

As such, with many thanks to many people: the authors, the reviewers, and the technical staff, here you will find the first consolidated text that addresses biometric anti-spoofing. It has been a great pleasure to work with the TABULA RASA teams during the past 4 years; it has been a great pleasure to work in biometrics for this is a technology that will continue to mature as it offers the solutions to many of the problems faced by modern society. As researchers in the field we trust you find this text of use as guidance and as reference in a field which will continue to inspire and challenge its many researchers.

| | |
|---|---|
| Switzerland, May 2014 | Sébastien Marcel |
| England | Mark S. Nixon |
| China | Stan Z. Li |

# Acknowledgments

The editors would like to thank the TABULA RASA (www.tabularasa-euproject.org) and BEAT projects (www.beat-eu.org) funded under the seventh Framework Programme of the European Union (EU) (grant agreement numbers 257289 and 284989) for financial support.

# Contents

1 **Introduction**..... 1
Nesli Erdoğmuş and Sébastien Marcel

2 **Forgeries of Fingerprints in Forensic Science**..... 13
Christophe Champod and Marcela Espinoza

3 **Fingerprint Anti-spoofing in Biometric Systems**..... 35
Javier Galbally, Julian Fierrez, Javier Ortega-Garcia
and Raffaele Cappelli

4 **Face Anti-spoofing: Visual Approach**..... 65
André Anjos, Jukka Komulainen, Sébastien Marcel,
Abdenour Hadid and Matti Pietikäinen

5 **Face Anti-spoofing: Multi-spectral Approach**..... 83
Dong Yi, Zhen Lei, Zhiwei Zhang and Stan Z. Li

6 **Iris Anti-spoofing**..... 103
Zhenan Sun and Tieniu Tan

7 **Speaker Recognition Anti-spoofing**..... 125
Nicholas Evans, Tomi Kinnunen, Junichi Yamagishi,
Zhizheng Wu, Federico Alegre and Phillip De Leon

8 **Gait Anti-spoofing**..... 147
John D. Bustard, Mohammad Ghahramani, John N. Carter,
Abdenour Hadid and Mark S. Nixon

9 **Multimodal Anti-spoofing in Biometric Recognition Systems**..... 165
Giorgio Fumera, Gian Luca Marcialis, Battista Biggio,
Fabio Roli and Stephanie Caswell Schuckers

| 10 | **Evaluation Methodologies** | 185 |
|---|---|---|
|    | Ivana Chingovska, André Anjos and Sébastien Marcel | |
| 11 | **Related Standards** | 205 |
|    | Christoph Busch | |
| 12 | **Legal Aspects: Biometric Data, Evidence Rules and Trusted Identities** | 217 |
|    | Els J. Kindt | |
| 13 | **Ethical Issues in Anti-spoofing** | 233 |
|    | Andrew P. Rebera | |

**Appendix A: Evaluation Databases** .......... 247

**Index** .......... 279

# Contributors

**Federico Alegre** Department of Multimedia Communications, Campus Sophia-Tech, EURECOM, Biot, France

**André Anjos** Idiap Research Institute, Martigny, Switzerland

**Battista Biggio** Department of Electrical and Electronic Engineering, University of Cagliari, Cagliari, Italy

**Christoph Busch** Fraunhofer IGD, Darmstadt, Germany

**John D. Bustard** University of Southampton, Southampton, UK

**Raffaele Cappelli** Biometric Systems Laboratory (BioLab), Universit'a di Bologna, Bologna, Italy

**John N. Carter** University of Southampton, Southampton, UK

**Christophe Champod** Faculty of Law and Criminal Justice, School of Criminal Justice, Institute of Forensic Science, University of Lausanne, Lausanne, Switzerland

**Ivana Chingovska** Idiap Research Institute, Martigny, Switzerland

**Phillip De Leon** Department 3-O, Klipsch School of Electrical and Computer Engineering, New Mexico State University, Las Cruces, NM, USA

**Nesli Erdoğmuş** Idiap Research Institute, Martigny, Switzerland

**Marcela Espinoza** Faculty of Law and Criminal Justice, School of Criminal Justice, Institute of Forensic Science, University of Lausanne, Lausanne, Switzerland

**Nicholas Evans** Department of Multimedia Communications, Campus Sophia-Tech, EURECOM, Biot, France

**Julian Fierrez** Biometric Recognition Group—ATVS, Universidad Autonoma de Madrid, Madrid, Spain

**Giorgio Fumera** Department of Electrical and Electronic Engineering, University of Cagliari, Cagliari, Italy

**Javier Galbally** Biometric Recognition Group—ATVS, Universidad Autonoma de Madrid, Madrid, Spain

**Mohammad Ghahramani** Pentti Kaiteran katu 1, Oulu, Finland

**Abdenour Hadid** Pentti Kaiteran katu 1, Oulu, Finland; Center for Machine Vision Research (CMV), Department of Computer Science and Engineering (CSE), University of Oulu, Oulu, Finland

**Els J. Kindt** KU Leuven, Leuven, Belgium

**Tomi Kinnunen** Speech and Image Processing Unit, School of Computing, University of Eastern Finland (UEF), Joensuu, Finland

**Jukka Komulainen** Center for Machine Vision Research (CMV), Department of Computer Science and Engineering (CSE), University of Oulu, Oulu, Finland

**Zhen Lei** Chinese Academy of Sciences, Institute of Automation, Beijing, China

**Stan Z. Li** Chinese Academy of Sciences, Institute of Automation, Beijing, China

**Sébastien Marcel** Idiap Research Institute, Martigny, Switzerland

**Gian Luca Marcialis** Department of Electrical and Electronic Engineering, University of Cagliari, Cagliari, Italy

**Mark S. Nixon** University of Southampton, Southampton, UK

**Javier Ortega-Garcia** Biometric Recognition Group—ATVS, Universidad Autonoma de Madrid, Madrid, Spain

**Matti Pietikäinen** Center for Machine Vision Research (CMV), Department of Computer Science and Engineering (CSE), University of Oulu, Oulu, Finland

**Andrew P. Rebera** Independent Scholar, 7, Albert Road, Keynsham, UK

**Fabio Roli** Department of Electrical and Electronic Engineering, University of Cagliari, Cagliari, Italy

**Stephanie Caswell Schuckers** Department of Electrical and Computer Engineering, Clarkson University, Potsdam, NY, USA

**Zhenan Sun** Center for Research on Intelligent Perception and Computing, National Laboratory of Pattern Recognition, Institute of Automation, Chinese Academy of Sciences, Beijing, P.R. China

**Tieniu Tan** Center for Research on Intelligent Perception and Computing, National Laboratory of Pattern Recognition, Institute of Automation, Chinese Academy of Sciences, Beijing, P.R. China

**Zhizheng Wu** Emerging Research Lab, School of Computer Engineering, Nanyang Technological University (NTU), Singapore, Singapore

**Junichi Yamagishi** National Institute of Informatics, Chiyoda-ku, Tokyo, Japan; University of Edinburgh, Edinburgh, UK

**Dong Yi** Chinese Academy of Sciences, Institute of Automation, Beijing, China

**Zhiwei Zhang** Chinese Academy of Sciences, Institute of Automation, Beijing, China

# Chapter 1
# Introduction

**Nesli Erdoğmuş and Sébastien Marcel**

In a well-designed system, biometric security ensures that only authorized persons can access to the protected facility or information, because it assesses a person's most unique physical and behavioural features that can be practically sensed by devices and interpreted by computers. It is also convenient as the users need to carry or remember identification data is eliminated. Mainly driven by the biometrics passports that are currently in use in many countries, more and more biometric-enabled applications are used in daily life. However, despite a stimulating and rapidly growing market, a crucial security issue is still to be considered by concerning parties: vulnerability to attacks, in other words, attempts to subvert and circumvent the system.

It has been shown recently that conventional biometric techniques, such as fingerprint or face recognition are prone to one of the most potent and damaging threats involving personal Data-Identity fraud, mostly known as spoofing.

Spoofing, also referred to as presentation attack, is a direct attack performed at the sensor level outside the digital limits of the system. Therefore, no digital protection mechanisms can be used against it. In an attempt to spoof a biometric system, an intruder tries to masquerade as a valid user by forging a fake biometric sample and presenting it to the biometric sensor to be captured. Anti-spoofing (or presentation attack detection) refers to the countermeasures to detect and avert these attempts. Commercial biometric authentication products without anti-spoofing modules would place personal security at high risk.

---

N. Erdoğmuş (✉) · S. Marcel
Idiap Research Institute, Rue Marconi 19, 1920 Martigny, Switzerland
e-mail: nesli.erdogmus@idiap.ch,

S. Marcel
e-mail: sebastien.marcel@idiap.ch

© Springer-Verlag London 2014
S. Marcel et al. (eds.), *Handbook of Biometric Anti-Spoofing*,
Advances in Computer Vision and Pattern Recognition,
DOI: 10.1007/978-1-4471-6524-8_1

## 1.1 The Need for Biometrics

Biometrics is a multidisciplinary field concerned with measuring and mapping specific biological traits, e.g. fingerprints, face, palm veins, etc. to be used as an individualized code for recognition. The need and the complexity of recognition of humans has never been this great in our history as it is now and biometrics is considered as an indispensable tool to overcome the difficulties being faced. In order to come to this conclusion, one needs to consider some of the demographic facts about today's societies that are related to this requirement of security and identification.

The first and most prominent change in the world today that both convolute and promote the identification problem is population growth (see Fig. 1.1). Identifying human beings is an essential element for societies to function properly, and this was very straightforward in the early days of civilization, when people lived in much smaller communities and everyone knew each other. To have a clear view of the change, we do not even have to go back further than two centuries. The identity card that was introduced for workers by Napoleon in the early 1800s, to stop them moving around without their employers' permission can be accepted as the ancestor of modern ID systems [1]. In fact, before World War I, most people did not have or need an identity document. However with continuing population growth, identity establishment started to rely on documents and soon its substantial dependence on biometrics followed. The first biometric links between the ID documents and their holders were the facial photos, which began to be attached to passports and alike in the early decades of the twentieth century, once photography became widespread and evidently, it did not stop there.

The impact of population growth on the necessity and complexity of secure identity has been elevated by a companion occurrence, that is the increasing mobility of masses of people within and across international borders. International tourist

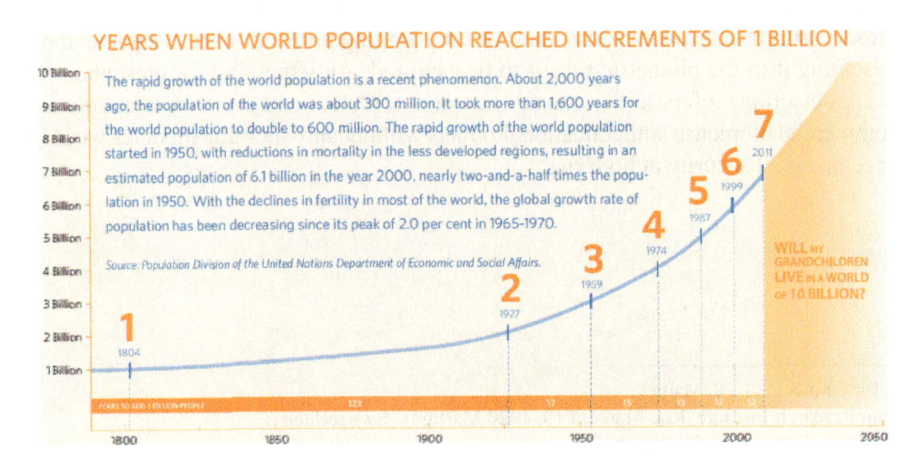

**Fig. 1.1** Years when world population reached increments of 1 billion [2]

# 1 Introduction

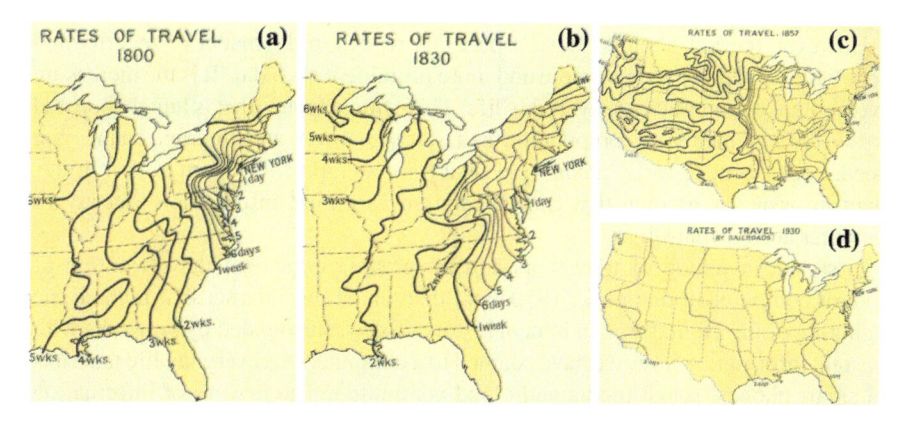

**Fig. 1.2** Rates of travel depicted by the time required to travel from New York to various locations in **a**, **b**, **c** and **d**

arrivals grew well above expectation in 2013 by 5 % and reached a new record 1,087 million arrivals worldwide. For 2014, the growth is forecast to be 4–4.5 % again [3]. Mainly reinforced by the advancements in transportation technologies, the mobility of the world population expanded enormously in the last century. The series of maps from the 1932 Atlas of the Historical Geography of the United States in Fig. 1.2 show a progressive decrease in travel time, mainly due to the introduction of railroads [4].

Today, it is possible to cover the longest distances in North America (e.g. Miami to Seattle) in less than 7 h, thanks to air transport. This convenience in travel has obliterated the notion of isolated communities where everybody and their business are known to each other or at least to an authority. Naturally, this phenomenon boosted the importance of border controls, which like identity documents started to spread just after World War I and become even more important after the horrific 9/11 attacks. Today, the need for fast and accurate identification solutions is crucial for border control points to operate smoothly and that is how biometrics come into play.

Up to this point, we have mainly discussed about how population growth accompanied by an increasing mobility plays a role in identity management problem, specifically in physical access control, for instance, to a country or a building and where biometrics come into the picture. The scope can be further extended to forensic applications through criminal identification techniques which have deep roots in the science of anthropometry. In fact, the first anthropometric system was invented back in 1879, by a French criminologist Alphonse Bertillon, as an alternative means of identification to detect repeat offenders, after the repeal of the previous system by which criminals were branded. However, the famous case of Will West in 1903 proved the fallibility of the Bertillon system. Consequently, police departments and prisons around the world switched to the fingerprint identification system developed by Sir Richard Edward Henry of Scotland Yard. Fingerprinting which was more reliable and far easier to collect took over the forensic scene and has been dominating it since.

However, there is another social aspect that relates to the matter of security and identification which becomes more and more prominent each day. It is the increasing involvement of computers in everyday life. This critical factor, that is hugely boosted by the advancements in computation and storage power and Internet connection speed, does not necessarily disturb physical (or geographical) security but it brings about an issue of its own that can be referred as digital information security or computer access control.

First, the invention of transistors and integrated circuits set the revolution of modern computer in motion in 1950s and then came the Internet that marked the beginning of the Digital Age in human history. Today, surrounded by networks with constant information flow, we have adapted to a computerized everyday life that runs via smart phones, social media and cloud computing. The density of information storage in commercially available devices has reached impressive levels, allowing us to create and store exabytes of information each day.

Naturally, these developments raise serious concerns with respect to the privacy and security issues. Digital information security is a young discipline that involves information stored in computers and it stems from early computer security studies done in mid-20th century. Currently, the majority of the access control systems, either to a laptop or an online account, relies on user passwords. In [5], it is claimed that Internet users have 25 password protected accounts in average but have an average of 6.5 different passwords, despite the common advice to avoid reusing them. Additionally, they tend to pick weak passwords that are short and simple and do not change them regularly. Consequently, biometrics-based solutions stand out as an attractive and convenient alternative that improves security over weak passwords while reducing the demand for user effort.

When we look at the whole picture, it tells us biometrics is a vital approach to identification and security application with its obvious ergonomic benefits, scalability and reliability. Biometric identifiers provide convenience and relatively equal security level to all users and they are difficult to be lost, forgotten or stolen. Biometric systems are becoming a natural component of identification and security applications, such as national ID cards, passports, online shopping and computer data security.

## 1.2 Biometric System Security and Spoofing

Being intrinsically linked to the user, biometric traits can be safely argued to have the unique advantage to truly verify that a person is in fact who he claims to be. They are not like passwords or badges that can be easily stolen and used by an intruder. On the other hand, there is an inevitable dilemma in accepting biometrics as private. We cannot claim them to be secret whilst our facial images are captured by surveillance cameras or even by ourselves to be shared on social media platforms, our voices are recorded by most phone-based services or we leave our fingerprints and DNA uncontrollably everywhere we touch.

1 Introduction

When he says "Amateurs hack systems, professionals hack people," American computer security and privacy specialist Bruce Schneier emphasizes the fact that ongoing developments in computer security technologies to prevent attackers are thwarted by the human factor. For instance, in a survey undertaken by Infosecurity Europe 2003 [6], 152 office workers at Waterloo Station in London were asked to share their passwords for a cheap pen. Strikingly, more than three quarters of the people immediately gave their password.

Although biometrics is proposed as an alternative solution for this type of issues of conventional methods, ultimately, it is still defeated by the same "hacking the people" approach, but this time in a different sense. In this new context, system users are hacked by capturing and replicating their biometric samples (most of which can be obtained rather easily) instead of working their passwords out.

An act of circumventing a biometric system by adversaries is referred as an *attack* [7]. Broadly, two types of attacks can be considered: indirect and direct attacks. Indirect attacks are performed inside the system, intruded by cyber-criminal hackers or insiders, e.g. by manipulating the feature extractor or the matcher, or by modifying the template database. This type of attacks can be prevented by numerous measures that include but not limited to firewalls, anti-virus software, intrusion detection and encryption. On the other hand, direct attacks are performed at the sensor (user interface) level outside the digital limits of the system and therefore, no digital protection mechanisms can be used against it.

In a direct attack, an impostor can either change his biometric characteristic in order to evade identification (*obfuscation*) or claim an authorized user's identity by simply posing himself (*zero-effort attack*) or by presenting a falsified biometric trait of that user (*spoofing* or *presentation attack* as detailed in 10) [8].

Spoofing is potentially the most dangerous type of attack as it does not require any advanced programming skills like indirect attacks. Contrary to zero-effort attacks, spoofing poses a serious threat to the security and the privacy of the enrolled individuals irrespective of the recognition performance, specifically false acceptance rate, of the biometric system. A spoofing attack occurs as a person tries to masquerade as a valid user by presenting this user's counterfeit biometric trait to the sensor. It has been shown that conventional biometric techniques such as fingerprint [9] and face recognition [10] are prone to this potent risk. There are also methods other than cloning a legitimate biometric. For instance, many fingerprint recognition systems can be deceived by reactivating the latent print left on the device from the last user, by dusting or breathing on the collection plate.

There is a plethora of news items concerning biometrics spoofing, which continues to grow. For instance, in 2008, a South Korean woman was caught trying to pass through the immigration screening system in Nippon, Japan by using a special tape with someone else's fingerprints on her fingers to fool the fingerprint recognition machine. Japanese officials believe many more illegal foreigners might have entered using the same technique [13].

Similarly in 2013, a Brazilian doctor was arrested in Sao Paulo for using prosthetic fingers, shown in Fig. 1.3a, to fool the biometric device that tracks employee atten-

Fig. 1.3 Examples of spoofing incidents: a Six silicone fingers recovered at the time of doctor's arrest [11]. b Cigarette vending machines using facial age verification [12]. c Banknote portraits that are used to fool the age verification system [12]

dance at the hospital she works. The following police investigation showed that about 300 public employees had been receiving pay checks without going to work [11].

The last example is again from Japan, this time about cigarette vending machine age verification system (Fig. 1.3b). Just after the Finance Ministry officially approved the use of facial age estimation technology and before the full scale deployment of the system around the country, a news reporter has confirmed that the cameras can be tricked by using magazine photos of celebrities and even using the portraits of Hideyo Noguchi and Yukichi Fukuzawa on 1,000-yen and 10,000-yen bills (Fig. 1.3c) [12].

As the given examples also indicate, artificial biometric traits such as a thin layer gelatin moulded with a fingerprint, a printed photo of a face or a recorded voice can be easily presented to the sensor to gain illegitimate access unless the security system is equipped with a spoofing detection ability that distinguish between real and fake biometric samples. Ideally, a good biometrics system should be able to determine "liveness" and should not rely on the inaccessibility of the biometric traits.

As Dorothy E. Denning says, "It's liveness, not secrecy, that counts". The biometric prints of users do not need to (and for many modalities can not) be kept secret, instead the validation process should be coupled with a liveness test to make sure that the biometric trait to be evaluated is from a real, living subject and not from a photo or a severed finger. Therefore, countermeasure modules that differentiate liveness *versus* spoof are indispensable for reliable biometric systems.

## 1.3 Biometric Anti-spoofing

It cannot be argued that since biometrics can now affect whole populations, anti-spoofing needs determined study. Biometrics experts both in academia and industry have been working on methods to deal with the spoofing threat. Referred as *anti-spoofing*, *spoof detection* or *presentation attack detection*, this task consists of differentiating between a real biometric reading from a live person and a fake one forged by the attacker. On the other hand, *liveness detection* is used to indicate the act of verifying vitality such as pulse or blood flow. In different areas of research,

1 Introduction

liveness detection is taken as either a synonym of spoof detection or a method of doing so. In this chapter, this term will be used as a subcategory of anti-spoofing methods.

Spoof detection can be implemented during the acquisition or the processing of the biometric data using three different approaches:

- Employing additional hardware: An extra sensor is utilized for anti-spoofing. This approach may be costly and may still be invalidated by presenting any real biometric trait to this sensor while using a fake one for identity verification.
- Capturing extra data with the same sensor: The information already captured by the device is further processed or accumulated over time to extract discriminating features.
- Using the biometric data: Authenticity information inherent to the captured biometric trait is utilized for spoof detection. Although being ideal for cost, computational load and user convenience, this approach is hard to substantiate.

As will be discussed in the following chapters of this book, there is a wide range of spoof detection algorithms for different biometric modalities, but all these techniques can again be classified into three main groups based on their working mechanisms. The first group of techniques makes use of intrinsic properties of real biometric samples such as shape, color or elasticity. The second group tries to detect liveness from the biometric recording via aforementioned methods, whereas the third group searches for counterfeiting clues in the contextual data.

## 1.3.1 Checking Intrinsic Properties

Biometric samples from a real living body possess certain intrinsic properties, which can be used to check their validity. These properties can be visual such as colour, shape and texture; physical such as density, stiffness and elasticity; spectral such as reflectance and absorbance; and finally electrical such as permittivity and capacitance. A commercial fingerprint recognition product that utilize this kind of approach is presented in Fig. 1.4.

Numerous anti-spoofing techniques fall into this category for different biometric systems. While some of them require additional hardware, the rest use the same biometric trait captured for recognition purposes. For instance, electric resistance of human skin can be measured with additional devices to fingerprint scanner, in order to check whether it is within a particular range. On the other hand, analysing the texture of iris images as detailed in Chap. 6 does not entail usage of extra equipment.

The examples can be expanded to face and speaker recognition as well. The texture and reflectance properties of facial skin can be utilized to detect spoofing attacks. Alternatively, the difference between the shape of a face and an attack instrument such as photo paper or mobile device screen gives a hint about the face sample's authenticity. For this purpose, either an extra device such as a depth sensor or a second camera can be used or motion of the objects in the image can be analysed.

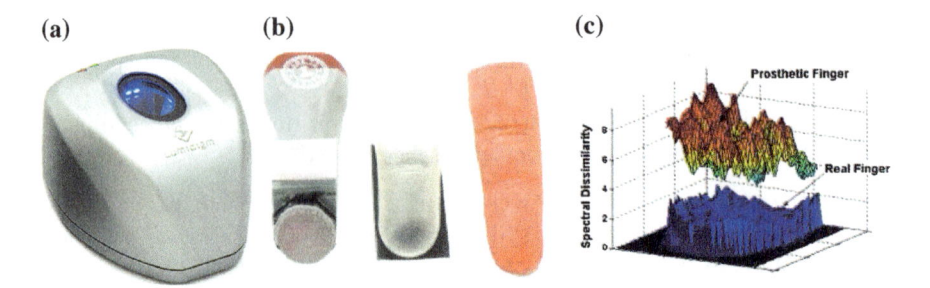

**Fig. 1.4 a** Lumidigm V-Series is a fingerprint sensor that checks intrinsic (spectral) properties of human tissue for antispoofing. **b** Example spoofing attacks. **c** Spectrographic analysis to differentiate between real fingers and fake artefacts [14]

More details are given in Chap. 4. Moreover, there can be cases like mentioned in Chap. 5 where multi-spectral face recognition systems are proven to be inherently robust to photo attacks. In other words, it is shown that photo attacks can be rendered impractical by just using the multi-spectral sensors instead of ones that work under visible light.

As for the speaker recognition systems discussed in Chap. 7, detecting acoustic differences between natural and synthesized or converted voices as a countermeasure against spoofing belongs to this group of techniques.

## 1.3.2 Detecting Liveness

Various methods to detect liveness of biometric samples have been proposed and implemented. In general, these methods make use of principally three groups of signals from a living body:

- Involuntary signals such as blood pressure, pulse and perspiration at the fingertips, hippus movement of iris and brain wave (EEG) and electrical heart signals (ECG)
- Reflexive signals such as pupillary light reflex (pupil dilation—an example study with near-infrared iris recognition system is presented in Fig. 1.5), corneal reflex (blink reflex) and patellar reflex (knee-jerk)
- Voluntary signals given unconsciously or as a response to a "challenge" such as blinking, mouth movements and facial expressions.

In Chap. 4, blinking and facial movement detection is mentioned for anti-spoofing in face recognition systems as well as challenge response precondition in which user is prompted to perform a specific action like smiling. Same approach can also be used for speaker recognition in a text-dependent scenario as detailed in Chap. 7.

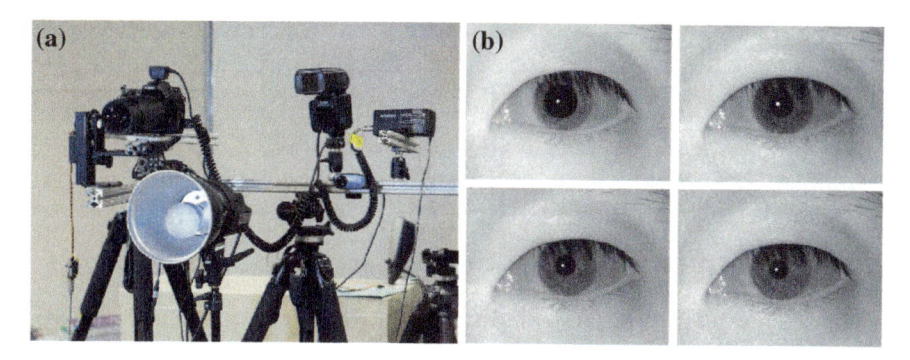

**Fig. 1.5 a** Iris image acquisition system: (1) Near infrared NFOV camera; (2) Near infrared flash; (3) WFOV video camera; (4) Controllable visible light source. **b** Size of the pupil decreasing (constriction) with increasing exposure values [15]

## 1.3.3 Detecting Counterfeit

Differently from the two previous categories, this group of methods aim to protect biometric systems by spotting clues of forgery in the collected sample instead of liveness.

In fact, this approach can be considered as the longest established countermeasure for spoofing in terms of forensic applications, which mainly relies on the visual evaluation of experts. As discussed in Chap. 2, searching for artefacts or noise that appear in the fake fingerprint marks has been in use for decades for detection of forgeries in forensic science.

On the other hand, forensic experts have shown limited ability to detect forgeries especially in the case of fingerprints that are fabricated carefully with well chosen and processed materials. For this reason, biometric research community is bound to come up with fully- or semi- automatic solutions for fingerprint forgery detection, specifically for the cases in which the distinction is almost impossible for human eye whereas it might be much clearer in the proper feature space. In Chap. 3, these discriminant features are found by exploiting fingerprint-specific quality assessment for which properties such as ridge clarity and strength are measured (see Fig. 1.6).

Detecting counterfeit cues in the contextual information is also proposed for face anti-spoofing in Chap. 4. Suspicious appearances such as a hand holding a photo or a display in front of the camera or a background scene moving exactly the same way as the face does can be easily noticed.

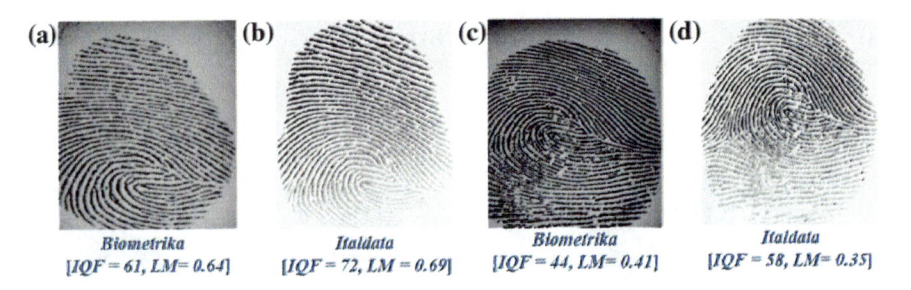

**Fig. 1.6** Quality (IQF) and liveness measure (LM) of (**a–b**) live and (**c–d**) fake fingerprint samples of a subject acquired by two different sensors [16]

## 1.4 Conclusion

Biometrics has become an indispensable instrument in identity management and information security systems today with populations growing fast and becoming more and more mobile. Consistently, security issues and vulnerabilities of biometrics systems develop into a real concern and hence, capture the attention of manufacturers and researchers in this field. Many successful spoofing attempts and possible countermeasures have been published. However, it is safe to say that spoofing is still in its early stages of existence, and it has a huge potential to bear new challenges due to a large number of biometrics traits and a growing range of available sensors.

In this book, spoofing attacks against five biometric modalities are analysed in different chapters, including also multi-modal systems. Additionally in Chaps. 10–13, evaluation methodologies, related standards, legal aspects and ethical issues are discussed. Still, this constitutes just a surface being scratched. Spoofing techniques are fast becoming more sophisticated and anti-spoofing measures have only a limited validity period, indicating that ongoing efforts from both industry and academia is needed.

**Acknowledgments** The authors would like to thank the TABULA RASA (http://www.tabularasa-euproject.org) and BEAT projects (http://www.beat-eu.org) funded under the 7th Framework Programme of the European Union (EU) (grant agreement numbers 257289 and 284989) and the Swiss Center for Biometrics Research and Testing (http://www.biometrics-center.ch) for their support.

## References

1. Lyons M (1994) Napoleon Bonaparte and the legacy of the French Revolution. Macmillan, London
2. UNFPA (2011) State of world population 2011–people and possibilities in a world of 7 billion. UN Report. http://www.unfpa.org/public/home/publications/pid/8726
3. UNWTO (2014) International tourism exceeds expectations with arrivals up by 52 million in 2013. Press Release 14004. http://media.unwto.org/press-release/2014-01-20/international-tourism-exceeds-expectations-arrivals-52-million-2013

4. Paullin CO, Wright JK (1932) Atlas of the historical geography of the united states. Carnegie Institution of Washington, Washington
5. Herley C (2009) So long, and no thanks for the externalities: the rational rejection of security advice by users. In: Workshop on new security paradigms workshop, ACM pp 133–144
6. Information security survey (2003). In: Infosecurity Europe
7. Ratha NK, Connell JH, Bolle RM (2001) An analysis of minutiae matching strength. Audio-and video-based biometric person authentication. Springer, Berlin
8. Jain AK, Ross AA (2011) Security of biometric systems. Introduction to biometrics. Springer, Berlin, pp 259–306
9. Matsumoto T, Matsumoto H, Yamada K, Hoshino S (2002) Impact of artificial gummy fingers on fingerprint systems. In: Electronic imaging 2002, international society for optics and photonics, pp 275–289
10. Duc NM, Minh BQ (2009) Your face is not your password face authentication bypassing lenovo-asus-toshiba. Black Hat Briefings
11. Doctor 'used silicone fingers' to sign in for colleagues. www.bbc.com/news/world-latin-america-21756709. Accessed 09 Apr 2014
12. Yen portraits fool age-verification cameras. http://pinktentacle.com/2008/07/yen-portraits-fool-age-verification-cameras/. Accessed 09 Apr 2014
13. Woman fools japan's airport security fingerprint system. www.smh.com.au/travel/woman-fools-japans-airport-security-fingerprint-system-20090102-78rv.html. Accessed 09 Apr 2014
14. V-series sensors. www.lumidigm.com. Accessed 17 Apr 2014
15. Huang X, Ti C, zhen Hou Q, Tokuta A, Yang R (2013) An experimental study of pupil constriction for liveness detection. In: IEEE workshop on applications of computer vision (WACV), pp 252–258. doi:10.1109/WACV.2013.6475026
16. Rattani A, Poh N, Ross A (2013) A bayesian approach for modeling sensor influence on quality, liveness and match score values in fingerprint verification. In: International workshop on information forensics and security (WIFS), IEEE. pp 37–42

# Chapter 2
# Forgeries of Fingerprints in Forensic Science

**Christophe Champod and Marcela Espinoza**

**Abstract** The objective of this chapter is to provide an account of the considerations made in forensic science regarding issues associated with potential forgeries of fingerprints. We will start with a clarification of terms and define the production of forgeries and the fabrication of evidence based on fingerprints. A short historical account will be given to highlight that the raised issues coincide with the early days of fingerprinting. Various methods of production of forged fingers as published in the forensic literature will then be exposed, distinguishing the techniques requiring the cooperation of the donor and the techniques without the cooperation of the donor. Examples of the various types of forgeries with associated images will be shown. The ability of forensic experts to distinguish between genuine marks and fakes will then be discussed. Although manual inspection techniques, they may also provide a reference to biometrics practitioners in their development of computerised techniques.

## 2.1 Introduction

To introduce this chapter, we felt the need to provide at the outset some clarification on the terms that are used rather loosely in the forensic literature to discuss the issues associated with fingerprint spoofing. It will lead us to reaffirm the need to distinguish forgeries from fabrications and marks from prints. The forensic scenario considered later will be the case of the recovery of forged marks from a donor left intentionally by a third party on objects associated with a crime and whether or not these marks can be distinguished from genuine marks left unintentionally by its legitimate donor. A few documented instances of such cases will be presented.

---

C. Champod (✉) · M. Espinoza
Faculty of Law and Criminal Justice, School of Criminal Justice,
Institute of Forensic Science, University of Lausanne,
Lausanne, Switzerland
e-mail: christophe.champod@unil.ch

M. Espinoza
e-mail: marcela.espinoza@unil.ch

© Springer-Verlag London 2014
S. Marcel et al. (eds.), *Handbook of Biometric Anti-Spoofing*,
Advances in Computer Vision and Pattern Recognition,
DOI: 10.1007/978-1-4471-6524-8_2

The chapter will then elaborate on the techniques used to prepare forged fingers along side with illustrations for most of these techniques. The stigmates used as clues by forensic experts to detect forgeries will then be discussed. These clues are considered by experts in their decision-making process in a rather unstructured and nondocumented way. They form a part of the clues used in an holistic decision process. The final decision regarding the genuineness of a mark remain largely based on the training and experience of the forensic examiner. The reliability of experts to reach conclusions will also be discussed. To conclude this chapter, we will tentatively offer some parallels between the issues raised in forensic science and the search for spoofing detection system in biometric research.

### 2.1.1 Forgeries and Fabrication of Evidence: A Clarification of Terms and Cases

Even though papillary lines (or friction ridge skin—FRS) are found on more areas than the fingertips (they can also be found also on phalanges, palms, and soles), we restrict our presentation to fingers as they are the most targeted area. Friction ridge skin (FRS) refers to the original area of papillary lines that may be subject to forgery, e.g. the finger itself. The term "print" is reserved to the inked (of livescan) impressions taken under controlled conditions from either a genuine area of FRS or from a forgery. When fingers are involved, these prints will be named fingerprints. The term "mark" is used to describe the result of the apposition of impressions from the FRS or its forgery on a surface, generally in the context of a criminal activity. These marks can be left as 3D impressions (e.g. in mastic) or as 2D impressions that are either visible (e.g. in blood) or latent (e.g. left in the form of a natural sweat residue). When left by fingers, we will refer to them as fingermarks. The main distinction between marks and prints is that prints are left under supervised conditions (or under specific deposition instructions or mechanisms), whereas marks are left in an uncontrolled environment and are often latent (not visible to the naked eye). This chapter will concentrate on the risks posed by forgeries used to intentionally leave marks in forensic contexts. Scenarios involving prints, for example as a mean to attack a livescan device, are covered elsewhere in this book.

As pointed out by Bonebreak in 1976 [1], it is important to distinguish between the use of forgeries of fingers and the fabrication of evidence involving a fraudulent use of genuine marks. Both categories received little coverage in the forensic literature, whereas it could be expected (and even more so in the future) that any fingerprint specialist should be familiar and ready to discuss these matters in court [2]. In the literature, the most exhaustive papers are from Wertheim [3, 4] and Geller et al. [5]. Since these contributions, few additional researches (beyond case studies) have been presented in the forensic domain. In the light of the increased possibilities offered by new casting materials, there is merit in revisiting the subject on a regular basis.

Forged fingerprints are generally used by individuals committing a crime who will deposit forged marks of an innocent party in an attempt to implicate a third party or at least to divert the investigative process. To achieve that objective, a forged representation of the target portion of FRS is used as a stamp applied on the objects or surfaces of interest to leave marks. The issue of identity is generally not at stake here; what distinguishes genuine marks from forgeries is the mechanism whereby the marks have been deposited. A genuine mark is the result of the direct contact of an area of FRS on a receiving substrate. This contact generally does not involve any control or willingness of the donor (quite the contrary in criminal cases). The contact will leave a residue that will be visualised or detected using appropriate detection techniques. A forged mark however will be left using a reproduction of FRS that will be applied by a party to mimic the genuine production of a mark. These marks (we chose to name them marks still) will be left intentionally by the forger with the hope for them to be successfully detected by the investigators. This intention will have a bearing on the number, location, and extend of the marks deposited.

Cases involving forged marks have to be distinguished from the cases involving the fabrication of evidence. Cases of fabrication of evidence will take the form of a representation of a genuine mark (with some evidential benefits) that has never existed on the surface from which it purportedly came. Cases of fabrication of evidence are generally associated with police officers who engage into such activities to frame an individual by producing a compelling case with fingerprints. A few cases are worth mentioning (others can be found in [3, 6]):

The 1943 murder of Harry Oakes in the Bahamas is one of the most well-known cases of fabrication. Two corrupt police investigators lifted a fingermark from a drinking glass used by the defendant "Alfred de Marigny" during a police interview. The investigators then testified that the mark came from the dressing screen from Oakes' bed and filed that evidence to incriminate De Marigny. The defence was ultimately able to show the inconsistency between the background of the lift bearing the mark (a lift is an adhesive surface that is used conveniently to take up a mark developed by powdering on a substrate) and the texture of the piece of furniture from the scene from which it allegedly originated [7].

William DePalma was convicted in 1968 based on the fabrication of fingerprint evidence by Sgt. James Bakken who used a forged mark produced from a lift taken from a Xerox copy of a print from DePalma taken in 1957 for a minor offence [8]. Some cases do not necessarily involve deliberate wrongdoing but may simply be the consequence of mislabelling of the fingermark lift. In England, Alan McNamara is claiming that the mark that has been used to associate him with a burglary scene had been lifted from a vase that he touched under completely innocent circumstances and not from a wooden jewellery box (http://news.bbc.co.uk/2/hi/programmes/panorama/1426720.stm). Despite all his efforts to demonstrate the error (with the support of two recognised fingerprint experts), he served 30 months in prison for burglary.

In the case of the murder of Inge Lotz, it is alleged that the police detected marks corresponding to the defendant Mr van der Vyver from a drinking glass and then indicated that that mark was developed with powder from a DVD cover found on the crime scene [9].

A few instances of alleged misconduct have not been settled and are often linked with high profile cases [10].

Another use of fraudulent prints is to avoid identification by producing a friction ridge skin that will not be associated to any known print, either because of being a mirror image of a genuine fingerprint [11], or a synthetic image (no instance of occurrence known at the moment). The cases involving altered fingerprints with a view to avoid detection (in the context of border control, for example) are not covered in this chapter, as they are not considered as forgeries. The same will apply to other anecdotic usage of toeprints instead of fingerprints [12] to hinder the identification or to side-track the investigation.

The intent of the manipulation associated with the production of fake is generally beyond dispute. In the case of fabrication, an intent is difficult to establish as the process can easily be committed either because of chain of custody procedures that are not tight enough or simple inadvertent mix-up of exhibits, without any intent to mislead.

In the range of possibilities to attempt to incriminate someone based on fingerprint evidence, using forged marks is not the most convenient option, compared to the diverted usage of genuine marks or prints, either by placing an object bearing the marks in interest on a crime scene or by placing on the police file marks allegedly connected to the events under consideration.

Actual cases of known fingerprint forgeries are very seldom. Wertheim [6, 13] presented two cases: the Nedelkoff case in the 1940s [14] and the alleged forgeries of Pollock's fingerprints that received recent media attention.[1] Hence, as Wertheim rightly pointed out, most of the disputes are related to case of alleged fabrication of evidence. This is not to say that defendants never make allegations of forgery. A few cases are worth mentioned hereinafter:

> In England, in 1938, a defendant David Pearce demonstrated to his jury the possibilities to transfer a genuine mark from one surface to another using an adhesive surface. Despite his efforts, Pearce was found guilty [15].
>
> The 1980s Mickelberg case (a.k.a. "Perth Mint Swindle") is well known in Australia. Raymond Mickelberg has been charged of fraud for using stolen checks. The prosecution case is based, in part, on a partial fingermark developed with ninhydrin on one of the checks and identified to him. The defendant claimed that the evidence was fabricated by the police using a silicon cast of his hands that he had produced as part of his hobby. The case was portrayed as a miscarriage of justice [16]. After years of controversies, the conviction has been quashed by the Supreme Court of Western Australia (MICKELBERG -v- THE QUEEN [2004] WASCA 145), without however any stance taken of the claim of forgery.

---

[1] "The Mark of a Master", David Grann, The New Yorker, July 12, http://www.newyorker.com/reporting/2010/07/12/100712fa_fact_grann.

The forensic literature on forged finger can be quite confusing because of lack of clear distinction between forgery and fabrication of evidence (see for example [17]). The purpose of this chapter is to focus only on forgeries.

## 2.1.2 A Short Historical Perspective on Fingerprint Forgery

As mentioned previously, documented cases of the use of forged fingerprints by criminals are very seldom. A few anecdotic cases have been reviewed by Wertheim [3] and chronologically in [5]. This is despite the presence of forged fingerprints in fiction and the publicity given throughout the years to the successful production of fake fingers. For example, in 1994, a TV program broadcasted in Holland showed the production of a forged finger of the Minister of Justice used afterwards on a livescan device [18]. We will not attempt here an exhaustive historical account, but will focus on few key papers published in forensic science to argue why the whole issue of forgery did not gain a lot of attention over the years.

The possibility of facing forged fingerprints has been raised immediately at the start of the 20th Century when fingerprint evidence obtained from crime scene marks gained its momentum in various jurisdictions. De Rechter published his early attempts to produce forged fingerprint directly from his own finger using a first mould in plaster followed by counter moulding in latex [19]. However, the risks posed by such productions were quickly considered as limited by the author at the time. Indeed, it was recognised that if a villain decided to produce a forged mark in order to pervert the course of an investigation and focus the attention on a different individual than himself, it would be much more easier to wear gloves in order to avoid leaving any incriminating marks. Goddefroy conceded that marks could be forged but hastily concluded that distinguishing the genuine mark from the fake production was trivial when pores and ridge edges are carefully examined. Indeed, at the time, the moulding materials were not allowing the fine resolution for a faithful reproduction of pores and ridge edges [20].

Carlson in 1920 [21] stressed on the need for an expert to be in a position to exclude the allegation of forgery during his testimony to the identity of a mark and a print. The author highlighted the risks posed by casting materials can be used to produce marks in any matrix of interest (natural secretion or blood).

In 1923, Wehde and Beffel published the first public alert against fingerprint forgeries [22]. They popularised the photo-etching technique for the production of forged fingers without the cooperation of the donor. They claimed that their production was so simple that it will put the whole fingerprint discipline at danger. That claim did not materialise in practice. It is also in the 1920s that the first accounts of the possibility to transfer marks from one surface (a glass plate) to another flat surface were made [23].

The response from the forensic practitioners at that time has been that fingermarks made from forged fingers could easily be detected and such line of inquiry should not be pursued in every cases unless specific circumstances dictate. Clearly the burden of proof regarding the activity associated with the deposition of the mark was shifted from the prosecution side to the defence. Prosecution will then not explore systematically the avenue of forgery unless the defence suggests that possibility. Despite the early invitation by Lee [24] to admit such a possibility and discuss its consequences in court, very few fingerprint examiners were (and still are) prepared to entertain such a debate in court. Cummins stated what is still valid today [25]: only some fingerprint experts having extensive experience in manufacture of counterfeit and their study can make a distinction between a genuine mark and a mark felt by a forged finger based on the characteristics shown by the mark itself.

## 2.2 Production of Fingerprint Forgeries in Forensic Science

The chart in Fig. 2.1 summarises various options available to produce forgeries. These methods are detailed in the next section.

### 2.2.1 Production of a Stamp

#### 2.2.1.1 Production

Based on an image of a target area of FRS or of a mark, rubber (or polymer) stamps can be easily produced through commercial channels using laser engraving for example.

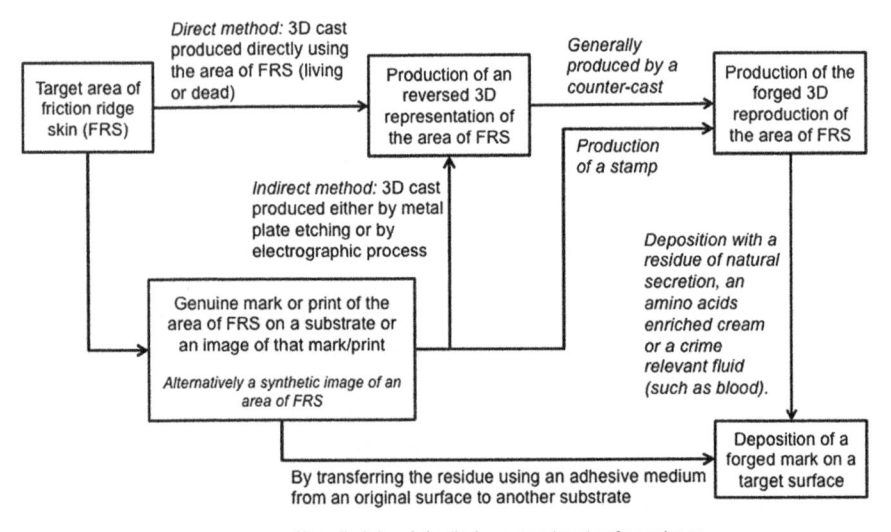

**Fig. 2.1** Various options available to produce forgeries

2   Forgeries of Fingerprints in Forensic Science                                    19

| Genuine mark left by a finger on a glass plate visualized optically using co-axial episcopy | Two forged marks left by the corresponding mould on a glass plate: One visualized optically as a latent residue using co-axial episcopy, the other following the application of aluminium powder. |

**Fig. 2.2** Comparison made by Morisod [26] between a genuine mark left in a glass surface and two forged marks left using sebaceous secretions on the same substrate

It leads to forgeries that lack flexibility but that can be used to leave marks on surfaces. Normally commercial producers of stamps should decline when asked to reproduce fingerprints, but practice has shown that professionals may not follow the line (or rule).

### 2.2.1.2 Example: Production of Fakes Using Stamps

Morisod produced marks left by a rubber stamp commercially produced from an starting black and white image of the target fingerprint [26]. Such a stamp can be used to leave marks composed of a greasy residue (the natural sebaceous secretion from the front head will suffice) left as contaminant on the surface of the forgery (Fig. 2.2).

Morisod also showed that on marks developed with DFO (an amino acid reagent), a clear difference in the amount of residue and its distribution can be seen (Fig. 2.3). This is due to the difficulty on forgeries to reproduce the distribution of the fingerprint eccrine residue along the ridges. Eccrine residue being secreted through the sweat pores of the friction ridge skin, a richer concentration is expected at the location of pores, giving on genuine marks a detection of ridges that appears as a succession of dotted points, especially when visualised in photoluminescence mode.

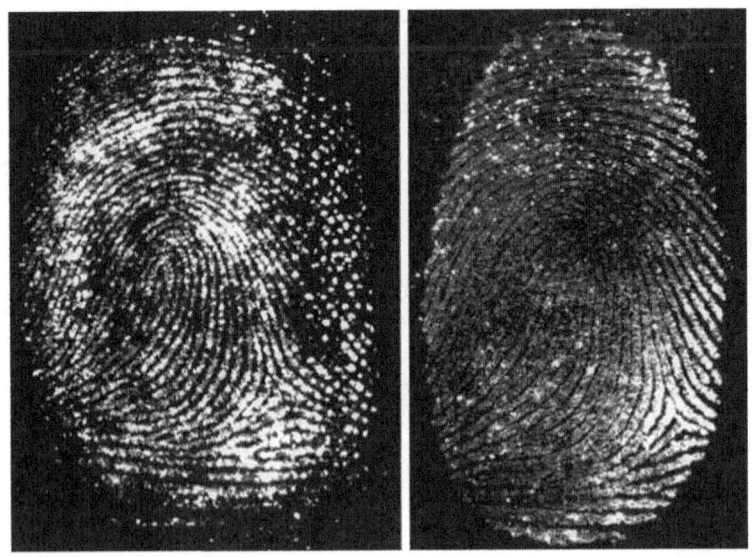

| Genuine mark left on paper detected by DFO and visualized in photoluminescence mode | Forged mark left by the corresponding stamp on paper detected by DFO and visualized in photoluminescence mode |

**Fig. 2.3** Comparison made by Morisod [26] between a genuine mark deposited on paper and detected with DFO and a forged marks also detected with DFO. Note the dotty appearance of the ridges on the genuine mark

## 2.2.2 Casting of a Donor Finger Followed by Counter Casting

### 2.2.2.1 Production

This method ultimately leads to the production of a 3D cast reproduction of the FRS area of the donor. Impressions are then left as marks by the cast simply by greasing it and placing it on the target surface.

The direct casting technique requires some collaboration (or at least the availability of the surface of FRS of interest) of the donor to produce the first mould of the FRS. The material used for this first mould can vary but very good results have been obtained using a thermoplastic material [27]. Other types of material tend to either produce too limited depth of valleys or air bubbles that will then be visible on the counter cast and ultimately on the forged marks. The resolution and the ability to reproduce sweat pores will also depend on the chosen casting material.

Alternatively, and without the cooperation the donor, the initial mould can be obtained indirectly either through the covert capture of a mark that will serve as a blue print for the production of a 3D mould of the ridges. From a 2D image of the target mark, the mould is produced either by a photocopying process (the deposited and fixed toner offering enough relief to allow a subsequent counter-cast), or by metal plate etching.

Once the master cast is obtained, a counter-cast can be produced (simply by pouring another moulding material in the first cast) with various materials: silicon white glue, polyurethanes, latex, or gelatine. One critical aspect to obtain quality forgeries is the care in choosing casting materials that are compatible and limit the production of artefacts or defects.

Very good reproductions can be prepared with gelatine, however they need to be stored in a cool environment and their shelf life is rather limited (less than 5 weeks). A glucose-based formulation allows increasing the shelf life well above 11 weeks [28].

### 2.2.2.2 Example: Casting Techniques with the Cooperation of the Donor

It is important to state that the quality of the forgery will critically depend on the choice of the casting material. The production of artefacts dues to air bubbles depends on the couple of moulding materials used, as shown in Fig. 2.4.

In 2011, Ioan Truta (Boston police department) presented to the forensic community forged marks produced using casting: the first cast of the finger is made in putty, the second mould being produced with AccuTrans® casting medium (polyvinyl siloxane). Marks are then layed down on a smooth surface (white backing cards), developed with black magnetic powder and lifted with transparent adhesive. Figure 2.5 shows a few instances of forged marks compared against genuine marks. When the clarity of the marks is high, some clues of forgeries can be seen (shapes corresponding to air bubbles). However, when the clarity of the marks reduces, these

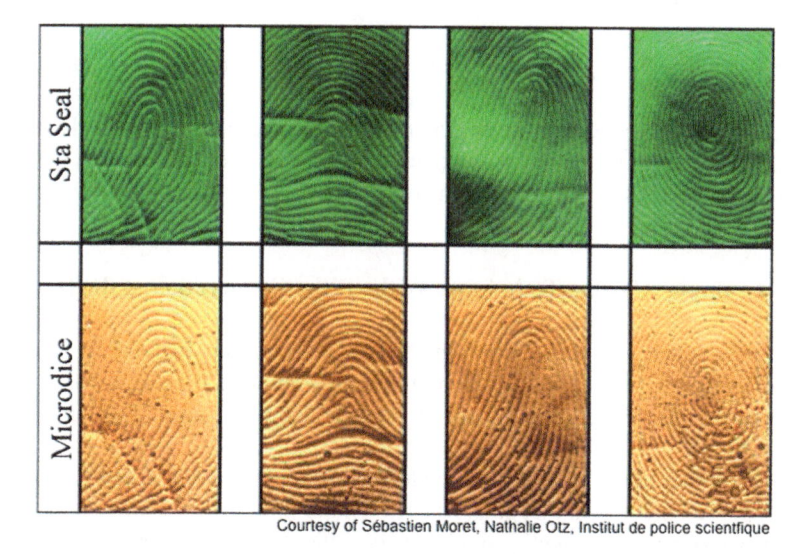

Courtesy of Sébastien Moret, Nathalie Otz, Institut de police scientfique

**Fig. 2.4** Examples of first moulds obtained in our laboratory with four different donors using respectively two casting materials: Sta Seal (a silicone-based moulding material from Detax Dental GmbH & Co, Germany) and Microdice (a dental plaster from Dentsply Odoncia, France)

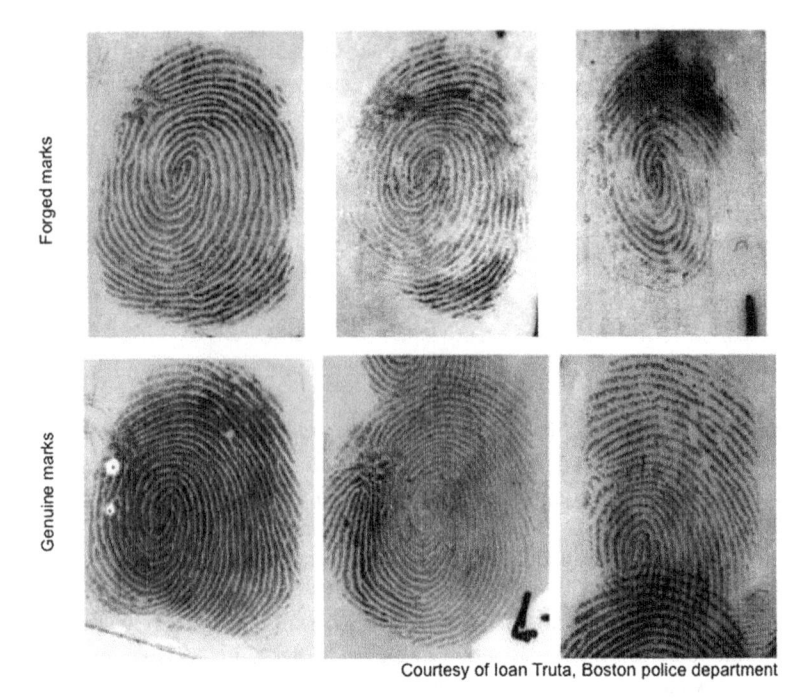

**Fig. 2.5** Genuine and forged marks deposited by Ioan Truta (Boston police department) on *white backing cards* and detected with *black magnetic powder*. The forgery has been prepared using a double casting technique with the cooperation of the donor, the first mould in putty and second mould with AccuTrans

features cannot be distinguished from the usual background issues associated with marks.

The ability to reproduce pores also depends on the choice of materials and to some degree on the donor (who will also impact upon the visibility of pores on genuine marks). Figure 2.6 illustrates a case with very high quality reproduction of the pores.

### 2.2.2.3 Example: Casting Techniques Without the Cooperation of the Donor

Without the cooperation of the donor, the first step consists in obtaining an inversed blueprint of the target FRS. It is done by the acquisition of a genuine mark of high clarity and the preparation of a blueprint using image processing. That process is shown in Fig. 2.7.

Then the blueprint is printed on acetate sheet on a laser printer and a counter-mould is poured using gelatine, glue, or latex. Under pristine deposition conditions, the prints are of very high quality and it is very difficult to observe intrinsic features allowing to distinguishing the genuine from the fake (Fig. 2.8).

When marks are produced, the task of distinguishing genuine from fake is even more difficult even on very high clarity marks, as shown in Fig. 2.9.

Livescan acquisition of a genuine finger

Livescan acquisition of a fake finger

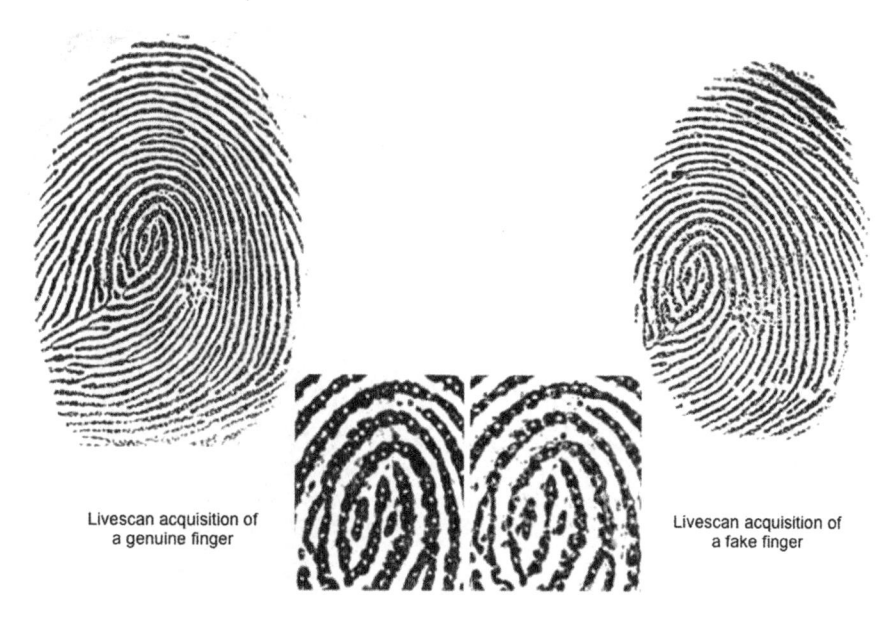

**Fig. 2.6** Comparison between a genuine and a forged finger acquired on an optical livescan device. The forgery has been prepared using a double casting technique with the cooperation of the donor, the first mould is made in a thermoplastic (UtilePlast, Pascal Rosier, France), the second is a silicon molding paste (Siligum, Gédéo, France)

Developed genuine mark obtained from the target finger

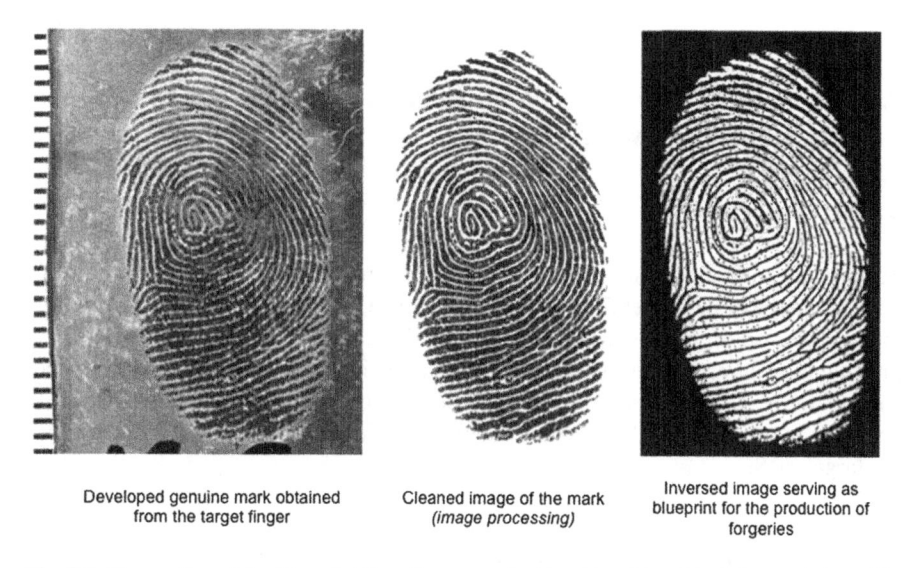

Cleaned image of the mark *(image processing)*

Inversed image serving as blueprint for the production of forgeries

**Fig. 2.7** Preparation of the blueprint (tonally reversed with *white ridges black furrows*) that will serve for the preparation of the forged marks without the cooperation of the donor

Livescan acquisition of
a genuine finger

Livescan acquisition of
a fake finger

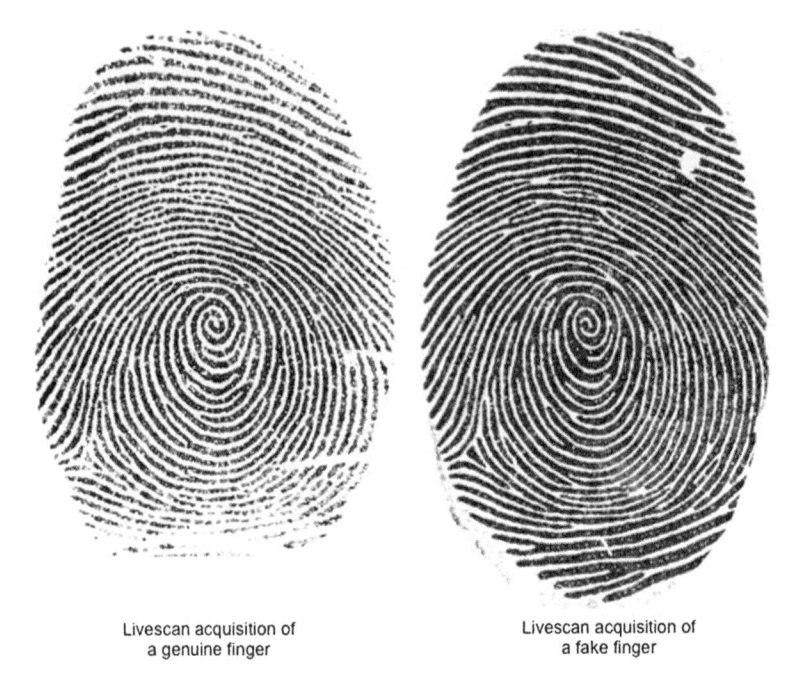

**Fig. 2.8** Comparison between a genuine and a forged finger acquired on an optical livescan device. The forgery has been prepared without the cooperation of the donor starting with a mark detected optically on a glass surface and a latex cast (Gédéo, France)

## 2.2.3 Metal Plate Etching (Photo Engraving) Followed by Counter Casting

### 2.2.3.1 Production

Techniques commonly used to produce printed circuit board (PCB) can be used once an image of the target FRS is available. Hence, this technique does not require the cooperation of the donor. By simply reversing the contrast of the target image, printing it on a transparent media, the valleys (now in black) will protect the copper surface, the rest of the photo sensible layer being exposed to UV light. The chemical acidic etching process will occur on the exposed ridges, producing a 3D mould of the target FRS.

### 2.2.3.2 Example: Metal Plate Etching (Photo Engraving) Followed by Counter Casting, Without Cooperation of the Donor

An example of a mark obtained using a forgery obtained by metal plate etching is given in Fig. 2.10.

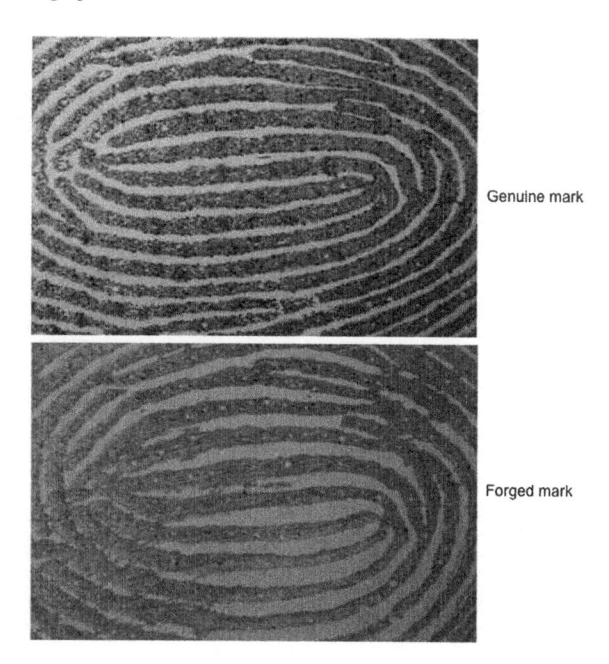

**Fig. 2.9** Comparison between a genuine and a fake mark left on glass and visualised using optical techniques [29]. The forgery has been prepared with the cooperation of the donor. Note the appearance of the somewhat uneven widths of valleys and ridges, but the reproduction of pores on the forgery

## 2.2.4 Transfer of Fingerprint Residue or Powder from One Surface to Another

### 2.2.4.1 Production

In this process, the residue of a genuine mark is lifted by an adhesive material (such as an adhesive tape or a fingerprint lifter) and then transferred to another receiving surface. The technique comes conveniently into play when no collaboration from the donor is required. Technically, it could be said that such a mark is not a forgery, as it will show the transferred attributes of the original mark. However, on the grounds that fraudulent intent is evident, we will consider it as a forgery [30], but the technique has been used in cases of fabrication of evidence. Harper has stressed on the loss of residue during the process but also showed the high quality of the forged mark so produced [30] when examined directly under the microscope (without any detection techniques that would normally muddy the water even more). Harper very rightly stressed upon the importance of considering the context in which the marks were recovered. Identifying forgeries based on the sole intrinsic attributes of the mark is not sufficient to guide reliably on that matter.

**Fig. 2.10** Comparison between a genuine and a fake mark left on glass and visualised using optical techniques [29]. The forgery has been prepared without the cooperation of the donor using a metal plate etching technique. Note forgery the poor reproduction of the edges of the ridges

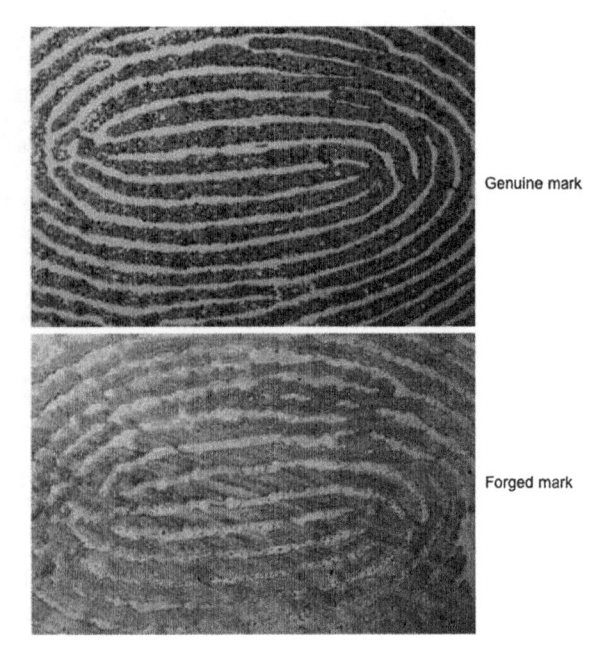

Genuine mark

Forged mark

The operational success rate of such a transfer of residue is low. Some ideal conditions, difficult to meet in practice, are required: an appropriate mark on a smooth surface with enough mark residue to ensure the transfer and a clean smooth receiving surface [31]. An alternative method consists in transferring with adhesive tape a genuine mark developed with dusting powder (such as black or grey magnetic powder) [32].

#### 2.2.4.2 Example: Transfer of Latent Mark from One Surface to Another

Morisod showed (Fig. 2.11) the possibility of such a transfer, successful only when the mark is particularly rich in residue [26]. Artefacts due to the use of the gelatine lift (or any other adhesive) can be observed (edges of the adhesive foil used, air bubbles and deposition of adhesive residue).

### 2.2.5 Direct Impression of a Fingermark to Produce a Forgery

That type of forgery has been suggested very recently [33]. However, to our knowledge, no known forensic cases involving that process has been uncovered in forensic casework. Due to the advances in printing technology, it is conceivable for an image of a fingermark to be printed with an "ink" chosen to simulate the residue of interest (or

**Fig. 2.11** Forged marks developed with aluminium powder by Morisod [32]. The mark originates from a genuine mark of sebaceous residue left on glass and transferred onto another piece of glass using a gelatine lifter (note the marks left by the edges of the lifter and the air bubbles left during the transfer process)

targeted by the detection technique). This method of production of forgeries is directly inspired from a modification of an inkjet printer used to produce artificial deposition amino acids at varying concentrations for quality management purposes [34]. The technique has then been adapted to print images of fingerprints with an inkjet printer replacing the ink with an amino acid colourless solution. It produces forgeries that will be visualised once amino acid reagents are used (such as ninhydrin, DFO, or indanedione/Zn). Kiltz and colleagues documented the differences in image quality observed between forged and genuine marks and suggested the use, on flat surfaces, of a contact-less CWL sensor for an optical acquisition prior any application of a physical or chemical technique [33]. A Hough-Circles algorithm has been used to help with the task of distinguishing genuine from fake [35]. They suggested a shape analysis of the dots constituting the detected marks. It applies to nonporous surfaces (marks were printed on overhead foils) and on images captured with a contact-less CWL sensor. Using horizontal and vertical dot distance measures, they detected a high dot density for genuine fingerprints and a low dot density for forgeries obtained using that printing process. Taking advantage of the high resolution (12,700 dpi) of a CWL sensor, Hildebrandt and coworkers [36] showed that both for marks optically acquired from nonporous surfaces or for marks on paper developed with ninhydrin, an analysis of the texture allowed a successful classification between genuine and fake.

## 2.3 Fingerprint Anti-spoofing in Forensic Science

The detection of forgeries in forensic science relies solely on the visual assessment made by a fingerprint examiner. To our knowledge, there is no systematic measurement techniques that have been proposed to assist the examiner in that task. The approach is holistic and, at present, not fully articulated. We will first review the clues for forgeries upon which the examiners generally rely during their examination and then we will present some data regarding the ability of experts to distinguish between genuine and forged marks.

### 2.3.1 Artefacts (or Clues) Associated for Forged Marks

Artefacts (or clues) of forgeries are described in the specialised literature [3]. It is worth distinguishing the intrinsic features (visible on the mark itself) from the extrinsic features (i.e. the context in which the mark(s) is(are) detected). Needless to say that the intrinsic features are easier to observe using optical techniques rather than following a sequence of detection techniques that may hinder the visibility of fine features such as pores or ridge edges.

The following intrinsic features may be found on forged marks (based on [37] and also on [26, 29]) helping to distinguish them from genuine marks. We will distinguish between the general features observed without any particular magnification and more particular feature that will require appropriate magnification (5x–10x).

General features observed on forgeries:

- Background noise (a type of halo effect) around the mark itself or in areas without ridges. This is due to an interaction on the surface of the mould material bearing no ridge and the substrate.
- An overall shape of the mark that is inconsistent with the natural deposition of a finger.
- Clear and well-defined external contours of the mark, either partially or entirely, as a function of their deposition. Ridges will end abruptly at the boundaries of the forged mark, whereas comparatively, on genuine marks, ridges coming to the border of the mark will tend to fade gently.
- Missing section of ridges, or section of ridges that are of lower clarity compared to highest clarity of the neighbouring (adjacent) ridges.
- Smudged or distorted friction ridges in areas that are not compatible with the dynamics of a natural deposition of a finger on a surface.

- Unexpected appearance of the ridges following the detection technique used. For example, amino-acid reagents tend to develop genuine marks as a series of dots leading to the appearance of papillary lines. Forged marks are laid down with a film of residue that hardly mimics the succession of rich-residue pores.

Particular features observed on forgeries (when the clarity of the mark allows):

- The presence of air bubbles and defects due to the casting material. Note that a careful choice of the casting material can diminish the occurrence of artefacts due to air bubbles.
- The absence of visible sweat pores. Some authors give a lot of weight to the presence of pores attesting the authenticity of a mark (e.g. [31]), but again an adequate choice of the casting materials allows reproducing pores.
- Very narrow valleys compared to the ridges or uneven widths of ridges and valleys.
- The presence of reproducible artefacts on multiple marks from the same area of FRS.

Forged marks may present some specific extrinsic features (very well described as early as 1933 by Lee [38], Harper [30] and reaffirmed in the subsequent forensic literature). They are:

- The detection of the mark from one finger in situations where an associated detection of the marks left by the other fingers or palm would be also expected.
- The detection of multiple apposition of marks representing the same area of friction ridge skin, at times even to the point that they overlap completely and share the same shapes of pores or ridge edges.
- The detection of a mark in an anatomical position that is not consistent with the natural pre-emption of the receiving object.
- The forensic evidence in the case is based only on these fingermarks.

## 2.3.2 Ability of Forensic Expert to Detect Forgeries

Cummins [25] has been the first to test the ability of forensic examiners to distinguish genuine from forged prints (i.e. obtained following an inking process). Eight experts were invited to study four prints. Out of 32 opinions, Cummins counted 20 right answers, 1 doubtful and 11 wrong determinations. Keeping in mind that the forged prints were produced under pristine conditions, it may be expected that the ability to distinguish genuine from fake will diminish when dealing with marks developed using methods that may affect the clarity of marks. Senay submitted forged marks to five examiners who did not show much success in their detection, especially when forgery was not prompted as an issue to consider [31]. It is fair to say that the mere possibility of forged marks is not at the forefront of the consideration of fingerprint experts. For them, the first issue to assess is the question of source. The possibility of a forgery is not explored systematically and it will be waited for the allegation to be made for it to be considered any further. It means that training and experience in this area is rather limited, very ad hoc at best.

Geller et al. [39] reported, following a survey conducted among 152 examiners, that even though a majority (85 %) of professionals were aware of the possibility to forge fingerprints, 57 % only indicated that the threat was credible and 45 % of them indicated that they would not be in a position to distinguish genuine marks from forged marks.

In 2011, Bourquin investigated the risks posed by forgeries and the ability of forensic practitioners to detect them [37]. She elaborated forgeries without the cooperation of the donors. The forgeries were prepared from genuine marks developed with cyanoacrylate fuming, prepared and printed on acetate sheets. The final moulds were obtained with various casting materials. The use of cyanoacrylate fuming as a detection technique allows obtaining in one step an inverse image (white ridges on a dark background). The production of the blueprint is presented in Fig. 2.12.

Forged marks were prepared by apposing the moulds contaminated with an amino acid enriched cream on target surfaces (paper or glass). Marks were detected either with aluminum powder on smooth surfaces or with an amino acids reagent (indanedione/Zn) on porous surfaces. 18 marks (Eight genuine mark and Ten forgeries) had been submitted to 78 fingerprint examiners (from the USA and from Switzerland). Half of the respondents received beforehand a broad guide to help them with the assessment, the other half were just given the task without any guidance. The

Developed mark obtained from the target finger left on a smooth surface, developed with cyanoacrylate fuming

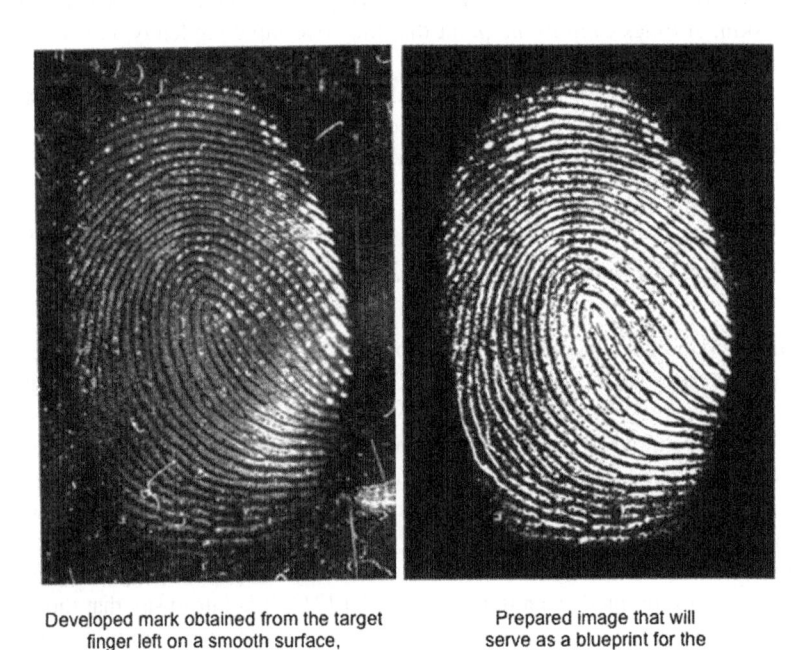

Prepared image that will serve as a blueprint for the production of the final mould

**Fig. 2.12** Preparation of the blueprint that will be used to produce forged moulds for the study by Bourquin [37]

2 Forgeries of Fingerprints in Forensic Science

main lines of the guide were similar to the previous section on the intrinsic features associated with forgeries. The results are given in Table 2.1.

The results confirm how difficult it is to detect forgeries, regardless of the availability of the guidance note. The guide improves slightly the detection power but to the cost of increasing the rate of misclassification of genuine marks as forgeries. The guide put examiners in an "awareness state" that makes them increase their claims of forgeries.

Some examples of the marks (genuine or forged) that led to the most difficulties in terms of classification are given in Fig. 2.13.

**Table 2.1** Results on the test carried out by Bourquin [37] on a population of 78 fingerprint examiners, half of them having some initial guidance, half of them without

| Examiners (78) | With the guide (39) | | Without the guide (39) | |
|---|---|---|---|---|
| | Forged marks (10) | Genuine marks (8) | Forged marks (10) | Genuine marks (8) |
| Declared as genuine (%) | 63 | 55 | 53 | 67 |
| Declared as forgery (%) | 37 | 45 | 47 | 33 |

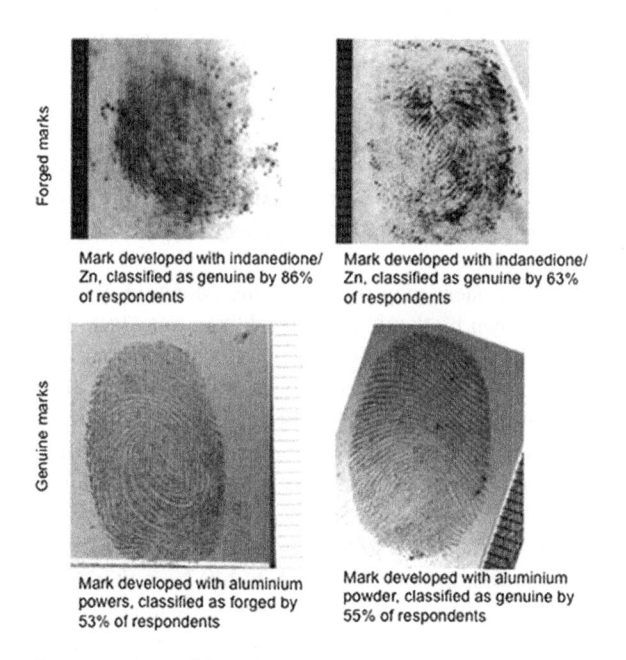

Forged marks:
- Mark developed with indanedione/Zn, classified as genuine by 86% of respondents
- Mark developed with indanedione/Zn, classified as genuine by 63% of respondents

Genuine marks:
- Mark developed with aluminium powders, classified as forged by 53% of respondents
- Mark developed with aluminium powder, classified as genuine by 55% of respondents

**Fig. 2.13** Examples of genuine and forged marks used in the study by Bourquin [37]

## 2.4 Conclusion

In this chapter, we focused mainly on the issue of forgery of friction ridge skin to intentionally leave marks to be detected in association with the investigation of crime. These fake marks will be visible or latent and left intentionally on substrates that will be the focus of the forensic investigation. The aim of such endeavor is to divert the investigation on a noninvolved third party. Although the possibility of such forgeries have been raised sporadically from the early days of fingerprinting, the number of known cases involving such productions is very limited. To the point that the issue of forgery is not considered in every forensic case, the burden of raising the issue is left entirely to the defense.

This is in contrast with the number of cases involving the fabrication of fingerprint evidence (often based on genuine marks). Fabrication of evidence usually does not require forging friction ridge skin, but will involve the claim that a genuine mark recovered under "innocent" circumstances is associated with the crime under investigation. It is more often achieved by tampering with the chain of custody, than by resorting to the use of a forged area of friction ridge skin. Cases of evidence fabrication are often the results of dishonest police practice.

The techniques used produce forgeries have been reviewed and illustrated. In our view, only casting techniques can produced forged marks that will be very difficult to detect, even more so when the donor is cooperative. The appropriate casting techniques are cheap, easy to operate and do not require specialist knowledge.

The attributes of the forged marks have been listed distinguishing between the intrinsic features (obtained directly from the mark(s) itself) from the extrinsic features (associated with the context in which the mark(s) has been discovered). The forensic practitioners should consider both aspects when the issue of forgery has to be evaluated.

Some forensic practitioners may think that the detection of forgeries based on the intrinsic features shown by the detected mark is an easy task. Results from past and more recent tests have shown the complete opposite. When forged marks have been produced using carefully chosen techniques, they cannot be distinguished from genuine marks even when the forgery has been obtained without the cooperation of the donor. That state of affair simply put more weight on the whole crime scene investigation that should provide other extrinsic evidence to help guiding on the genuineness of the collected marks.

The above may offer also some useful parallels to the biometric research community. It is fair to say that as soon as a forgery has been prepared with carefully chosen molding materials, there are, based on intrinsic features, very limited ways to distinguish genuine from fake even when the deposited mark is of very high clarity. Fingerprint experts, despite their expensive exposure to marks (mainly genuine), have shown limited ability to resolve this issue. This state of affair will not improve given the rapid progress made in material technology and printing technology. We suggest that spoof detection research in the context of biometric systems should focus less on intrinsic features but more on extrinsic features. Promising lines in inquiry may be more towards the detection of attributes of the living finger or the spoof material than on the fingerprint features displayed by the acquisition system. Forensic scientists have to rely on the contextual elements surrounding the detection of the marks than on the specific attributes of the acquired images. The same may apply to the biometric world: the prevention or detection of spoofing may benefit more from a careful assessment of the processes underpinning the use of the biometric system than on technological advances.

## References

1. Bonebreak GC (1976) Fabricating fingerprint evidence. Identification News, 3–13 Oct 1976
2. Midkiff C (1994) Forged and fabricated prints: their past and the future? Fingerprint Whorld 19:5–7
3. Wertheim PA (1994) Detection of forged and fabricated latent prints. J Forensic Ident 44(6):652–681
4. Wertheim PA (1998) Integrity assurance: policies and procedures to prevent fabrication of latent print evidence. J Forensic Ident 48(4):431–441
5. Geller B, Almog J, Margot P, Springer E (1999) A chronological review of fingerprint forgery. J Forensic Sci 44(5):963–968
6. Wertheim PA (2008) Latent fingerprint evidence: fabrication, not error. The Champion 16–23 Nov/Dec 2008
7. Wertheim PA (2000) The murder of Sir Harry Oakes. Fingerprint Whorld 26(99):9–28
8. Sherrer H (2011) William DePalma was framed for bank robbery by a policeman faking his fingerprint. http://justicedenied.org/wordpress/archives/1117
9. Altbecker A (2010) Fruit of a poisoned tree: a true story of murder and the miscarriage of justice. Jonathan Ball Publishers, Jeppestown
10. Sherrer H (2003) Defending Mohammad: justice on trial. In: Precht RE (ed) Justice Denied Mag 25:11
11. Johansen GL (2001) Detection of fraudulent fingerprints. Silent Witness 35(1):8–9
12. van der Meulen LJ (1955) False fingerprints: a new aspect. J Crim Law Criminol Police Sci 46(1):122–128
13. Wertheim PA (2008) Case study: fingerprint forgery. Chesapeake Examiner 46(2):12–22
14. Srp LL (1949) Finger print forgeries. Finger Print Ident Mag 30(12):3–4
15. Berry JE (1983) A false impression. Fingerprint Whorld 8(32):107
16. Lovell A (1985) The Mickelberg stitch. Creative Research, Perth
17. Samischenko SS (1995) Forged latent prints. In: International symposium on fingerprint detection and identification, Israel National Police, pp 381–383
18. Groenendal H (1995) Forged latent prints. In: International symposium on fingerprint detection and identification, Israel National Police, pp 373–379
19. De Rechter G (1912) Des fauses empreintes digitales. Archives internationales médecine légale 3(1):215–219
20. Goddefroy E (1913) Peut-on produire de fausses empreintes digitales ? Archives d'anthropologie criminelle de médecine légale et de psychologie normale et pathologique 28(231):207–211
21. Carlson M (1920) Finger-prints can be forged. Va Law Reg 5(10):765–768
22. Wehde A, Beffel JN (1924) Finger-prints can be forged. The Tremonia Publishing Company, Chicago
23. Chapel CE (1941) Fingerprinting: a manual of identification. Coward McCann, New York
24. Lee CD (1934) Finger-prints can be forged. J Crim Law Criminol 25(4):671–674
25. Cummins H (1934) Counterfeit finger-prints. J Crim Law Criminol 25(4):665–671

26. Morisod P (1992) Détection des fausses empreintes digitales. Séminaire de 4ème année, Université de Lausanne/Institut de Police Scientifique et de Criminologie
27. Espinoza M, Champod C, Margot P (2011) Vulnerabilities of fingerprint reader to fake fingerprints attacks. Forensic Sci Int 204(1–3):41–49
28. Mazzi P (2007) Optimisation de la conservation de faux doigts par modification de leur composition. Séminaire de bachelor, Université de Lausanne/Ecole des sciences criminelles/Institut de police scientifique
29. Giroud N (2006) Etude des risques liés à la fabrication de fausses empreintes digitales en gélatine. Séminaire de bachelor, Université de Lausanne/Ecole des sciences criminelles/Institut de police scientifique
30. Harper WW (1937) Fingerprint "forgery" transferred latent fingerprints. J Crim Law Criminol 28(4):573–580
31. Senay P (1990) Empreintes digitales falsifiées [counterfeit fingerprints]. La Gazette de la Gendarmerie Royale du Canada [Royal Canadian Mounted Police Gazette] 52(9):6–7
32. Scott S (2012) Fingerprint forgery and fraud—does fact mirror fiction?/the possibilities of latent print transference abridged version (part 1). Fingerprint Whorld 38(146):4–11
33. Kiltz S, Hildebrandt M, Dittmann J, Vielhauer C, Kraetzer C (2011) Printed fingerprints: a framework and first results towards detection of artificially printed latent fingerprints for forensics. In: Farnand SP, Gaykema F (eds) Image quality and system performance VIII, Proceedings of SPIE-IS&T electronic imaging, SPIE, vol 7867, p 78670U
34. Schwarz L (2009) An amino acid model for latent fingerprints on porous surfaces. J Forensic Sci 54(6):1323–1326
35. Hildebrandt M, Kiltz S, Dittmann J, Vilhauer C (2011) Malicious fingerprint traces: a proposal for an automated analysis of printed amino acid dots using houghcircles. In: Thirteenth ACM multimedia workshop on multimedia and security, pp 33–39
36. Hildebrandt M, Kiltz S, Sturm J, Dittmann J, Vielhauer C (2012) High-resolution printed amino acid traces: a first-feature extraction approach for fingerprint forgery detection. In: Media watermarking, security and forensics, Proceedings SPIE, vol 8303, p 83030J
37. Bourquin AC (2011) Etude des stigmates caractéristiques des fausses traces digitales. Projet de master, Université de Lausanne/Ecole des sciences criminelles/Institut de police scientifique
38. Lee CD (1933) Further discussion of the evidentiary value of fingerprints. Univ PA Law Rev Am Law Reg 8(3):320–323
39. Geller B, Almog J, Margot P (2001) Fingerprint forgery—a survey. J Forensic Sci 46(3):731–733

# Chapter 3
# Fingerprint Anti-spoofing in Biometric Systems

**Javier Galbally, Julian Fierrez, Javier Ortega-Garcia and Raffaele Cappelli**

**Abstract** This chapter is focused on giving a comprehensive description of the state-of-the-art in biometric-based fingerprint anti-spoofing and the big advances that have been reached in this field over the last decade. In addition, after a comprehensive review of the available literature in the field, we explore the potential of quality assessment as a way to enhance the security of the fingerprint-based technology against direct attacks. We believe that, beyond the interest that the described techniques intrinsically have, the case study presented may serve as an example of how to develop and validate fingerprint anti-spoofing techniques based on common and publicly available benchmarks and following a systematic and replicable protocol.

## 3.1 Introduction

"*Fingerprints cannot lie, but liars can make fingerprints.*" Unfortunately, this paraphrase of an old quote attributed to Mark Twain[1] has been proven right in many occasions now.

As the deployment of fingerprint, systems keeps growing year after year in such different environments as airports, laptops, or mobile phones, people are also becoming more familiar to their use in everyday life and, as a result, the security

---

[1] Figures do not lie, but liars do figure.

J. Galbally (✉) · J. Fierrez · J. Ortega-Garcia · R. Cappelli
Biometric Recognition Group—ATVS,
Universidad Autonoma de Madrid, Madrid, Spain
e-mail: javier.galbally@uam.es

J. Fierrez
e-mail: julian.fierrez@uam.es

J. Ortega-Garcia
e-mail: javier.ortega@uam.es

R. Cappelli
Biometric Systems Laboratory (BioLab), Universit'a di Bologna, Bologna Italy
e-mail: raffaele.cappelli@unibo.it

© Springer-Verlag London 2014
S. Marcel et al. (eds.), *Handbook of Biometric Anti-Spoofing*,
Advances in Computer Vision and Pattern Recognition,
DOI: 10.1007/978-1-4471-6524-8_3

weaknesses of fingerprint sensors are becoming better known to the general public. Nowadays, it is not difficult to find web sites or even tutorial videos, which give detailed guidance on how to create fake fingerprints that may be used for spoofing biometric systems.

As a consequence, the fingerprint stands out as one of the biometric traits that has arisen the most attention not only from researchers and vendors, but also from the media and users, regarding its vulnerabilities to spoofing attacks. This increasing interest of the biometric community in the security evaluation of fingerprint recognition systems against spoofing attacks has led to the creation of numerous and very diverse initiatives in this field: the publication of many research works disclosing and evaluating different fingerprint-spoofing approaches [1–3]; the proposal of new anti-spoofing methods [4–6]; related book chapters [7, 8]; PhD and MsC Theses which propose and analyze different fingerprint spoofing and anti-spoofing techniques [9–12]; several patented fingerprint anti-spoofing mechanisms both for touch-based and contactless systems [13–17]; the publication of Supporting Documents and Protection Profiles in the framework of the security evaluation standard Common Criteria for the objective assessment of fingerprint-based commercial systems [18, 19]; the organization of competitions focused on fingerprint-spoofing assessment [20, 21]; the acquisition of specific datasets for the evaluation of fingerprint protection methods against direct attacks [22, 23], the creation of groups and laboratories which have the evaluation of fingerprint security as one of their major tasks [24–26]; or the existence of several European Projects with the fingerprint-spoofing topic as one of their main research interests [27, 28].

The aforementioned initiatives and other analog studies, have shown the importance given by all parties involved in the development of fingerprint-based biometrics to the improvement of the systems security and the necessity to propose and develop specific protection methods against spoofing attacks in order to bring this rapidly emerging technology into practical use. This way, researchers have focused on the design of specific countermeasures that enable fingerprint recognition systems to detect fake samples and reject them, thus improving the robustness of the applications.

In the fingerprint field, besides other anti-spoofing approaches such as the use of multibiometrics or challenge-response methods, special attention has been paid by researchers and industry to the so-called *liveness detection* techniques. These algorithms use different physiological properties to distinguish between real and fake traits. Liveness assessment methods represent a challenging engineering problem as they have to satisfy certain demanding requirements [29]: (i) noninvasive, the technique should in no case be harmful for the individual or require an excessive contact with the user; (ii) user friendly, people should not be reluctant to use it; (iii) fast, results have to be produced in a very short interval as the user cannot be asked to interact with the sensor for a long period of time; (iv) low cost, a wide use cannot be expected if the cost is excessively high; (v) performance, in addition to having a good fake detection rate, the protection scheme should not degrade the recognition performance (i.e., false rejection) of the biometric system.

Liveness detection methods are usually classified into one of two groups: (i) *Hardware-based* techniques, which add some specific device to the sensor in order to detect particular properties of a living trait (e.g., fingerprint sweat, blood pressure, or odor); (ii) *Software-based* techniques, in this case the fake trait is detected once the sample has been acquired with a standard sensor (i.e., features used to distinguish between real and fake traits are extracted from the biometric sample, and not from the trait itself).

The two types of methods present certain advantages and drawbacks over the other and, in general, a combination of both would be the most desirable protection approach to increase the security of biometric systems. As a coarse comparison, hardware-based schemes usually present a higher fake detection rate, while software-based techniques are in general less expensive (as no extra device is needed), and less intrusive since their implementation is transparent to the user. Furthermore, as they operate directly on the acquired sample (and not on the biometric trait itself), software-based techniques may be embedded in the feature extractor module which makes them potentially capable of detecting other types of illegal break-in attempts not necessarily classified as spoofing attacks. For instance, software-based methods can protect the system against the injection of reconstructed or synthetic samples into the communication channel between the sensor and the feature extractor [30–33].

Although, as shown above, a great amount of work has been done in the field of fingerprint spoofing detection and big advances have been reached over the last decade, the attacking methodologies have also evolved and become more and more sophisticated. This way, while many commercial fingerprint readers claim to have some degree of spoof detection embedded, many of them are still vulnerable to spoofing attempts using different artificial fingerprint samples. Therefore, there are still big challenges to be faced in the detection of fingerprint direct attacks.

In the present chapter, after a thorough review of the state-of-the-art in fingerprint anti-spoofing, we analyze and evaluate the potential of quality assessment for liveness detection purposes. In particular, we consider two different sets of features: (i) one based on fingerprint-specific quality measures (FQMs) (i.e., quality measures specifically adapted for fingerprint images); and (ii) a second set based on general image quality measures (IQMs) (i.e., quality measures which may be extracted from any image). Both techniques are tested on publicly available fingerprint spoofing databases where they have reached results fully comparable to those obtained on the same datasets and following the same experimental protocols by top-ranked approaches from the state-of-the-art.

In addition to their very competitive performance, as they are software-based, both methods present the usual advantages of this type of approaches: fast, as they only need one image (i.e., the same sample acquired for verification) to detect whether it is real or fake; nonintrusive; user-friendly (transparent to the user); cheap and easy to embed in already functional systems (as no additional piece of hardware is required).

The rest of the chapter is structured as follows. An exhaustive review of relevant related works in the field of fingerprint anti-spoofing is given is Sect. 3.2. A brief description of large and publicly available fingerprint spoofing databases is presented in Sect. 3.3. A case study based on the use of quality assessment as anti-spoofing tool is introduced in Sect. 3.4 where we give some key concepts about image quality assessment (IQA) and the rationale behind its use for biometric protection. The two fingerprint anti-spoofing approaches studied in the chapter are based on fingerprint-specific and general quality features and are described in Sects. 3.5 and 3.6, respectively. The evaluation of the methods and experimental results are given in Sect. 3.7. Conclusions are finally drawn in Sect. 3.8.

## 3.2 State-of-the-Art in Fingerprint Anti-spoofing

The history of fingerprint forgery in the forensic field is probably almost as old as that of fingerprint development and classification itself. In fact, the question of whether or not fingerprints could be forged was positively answered [34] several years before it was officially posed in a research publication [35].

Regarding modern automatic fingerprint recognition systems, although other types of attacks with dead or altered fingers have been reported [36, 37], almost all the available vulnerability studies regarding spoofing attacks are carried out either by taking advantage of the residual fingerprint left behind on the sensor surface, or by using some type of gummy fingertip (or even complete prosthetic fingers) manufactured with different materials (e.g., silicone, gelatin, plastic, clay, dental molding material, or glycerin). In general, these fake fingerprints may be generated with the cooperation of the user, from a latent fingerprint or even from a fingerprint image reconstructed from the original minutiae template [1–3, 22, 38–42].

These very valuable works and other similar studies, have highlighted the necessity of developing efficient protection methods against spoofing attacks. One of the first efforts in fingerprint anti-spoofing initiated a research line based on the analysis of the skin perspiration pattern, which is very difficult to be faked in an artificial finger [4, 43]. These pioneer studies, which considered the periodicity of sweat and the sweat diffusion pattern, were later extended and improved in two successive works applying a wavelet-based algorithm and adding intensity-based perspiration features [44, 45]. These techniques were finally consolidated and strictly validated on a large database of real, fake, and dead fingerprints acquired under different conditions in [23]. Recently, a novel region-based liveness detection approach also based on perspiration parameters and another technique analyzing the valley noise have been proposed by the same group [46, 47]. Part of these approaches have been implemented in commercial products [48], and have also been combined with other morphological features [49, 50] in order to improve the spoofing detection rates [51].

A second group of fingerprint liveness detection techniques has appeared as an application of the different fingerprint distortion models described in the literature [52–54]. These models have led to the development of a number of liveness detection techniques based on the flexibility properties of the skin [5, 55–57]. In most of these works, the user is required to move his finger while pressing it against the scanner surface, thus deliberately exaggerating the skin distortion. When a real finger moves on a scanner surface, it produces a significant amount of distortion, which can be observed to be quite different from that produced by fake fingers which are usually more rigid than skin. Even if highly elastic materials are used, it seems very difficult to precisely emulate the specific way a real finger is distorted, because the behavior is related to the way the external skin is anchored to the underlying derma and influenced by the position and shape of the finger bone.

Other liveness detection approaches for fake fingerprint detection include: the combination of both perspiration and elasticity-related features in fingerprint image sequences [58]; fingerprint-specific, quality-related features [6, 59]; the combination of the local ridge frequency with other multiresolution texture parameters [49]; techniques which, following the perspiration-related trend, analyze the skin sweat pores visible in high-definition images [60, 61]; the use of electric properties of the skin [62]; using several image processing tools for the analysis of the fingertip surface texture such as wavelets [63], or three very related works using Gabor filters [64], ridgelets [65] and curvelets [66]; and analyzing different characteristics of the Fourier spectrum of real and fake fingerprint images [67–71].

A critical review of some of these solutions for fingerprint liveness detection was presented in [72]. In a subsequent work [73], the same authors gave a comparative analysis of the anti-spoofing methods efficiency. In this last work, we can find an estimation of some of the best performing static (i.e., measured on one image) and dynamic (i.e., measured on a sequence of images) features for liveness detection, that were later used together with some fake finger-specific features in [74] with very good results. Different static features are also combined in [75], significantly improving the results of the individual parameters. Other comparative results of different fingerprint anti-spoofing techniques are available in the results of the 2009 and 2011 Fingerprint Liveness Detection Competitions (LivDet 2009 and LivDet 2011) [20, 21].

In addition, some very interesting hardware-based solutions have been proposed in the literature by applying: multispectral imaging [76, 77], an electrotactile sensor [78], pulse oxiometry [79], detection of the blood flow [13], odor detection using a chemical sensor [80], or a currently very active research trend based on Near Infrared (NIR) illumination and Optical Coherence Tomography (OCT) [81–86].

Very recently, a third type of protection methods which fall out of the traditional two-type classification software- and hardware-based approaches have been started to be analyzed in the field of fingerprint anti-spoofing. These protection techniques focus on the study of biometric systems under direct attacks at the *score level*, in order to propose and build more robust matchers and fusion strategies that increase the resistance of the systems against spoofing attempts [87–92].

Outside the research community, some companies have also proposed different methods for fingerprint liveness detection such as the ones based on ultrasounds [93, 94], light measurements [95], or a patented combination of different unimodal experts [96]. A comparative study of the anti-spoofing capabilities of different commercial fingerprint sensors may be found in [97].

Although the vast majority of the efforts dedicated by the biometric community in the field of fingerprint spoofing and anti-spoofing are focused on touch-based systems, some preliminary works have also been conducted to study the vulnerabilities of contactless fingerprint systems against direct attacks and some protection methods to enhance their security level have been proposed [16, 43, 98].

## 3.3 Fingerprint Spoofing Databases

The availability of public datasets comprising real and fake fingerprint samples and of associated common evaluation protocols is basic for the development and improvement of fingerprint anti-spoofing methods.

However, in spite of the large amount of works addressing the challenging problem of fingerprint protection against direct attacks (as shown in Sect. 3.2), in the great majority of them, experiments are carried out on proprietary databases, which are not made available to the research community.

Currently, the two largest fingerprint spoofing databases publicly available for researchers to test their anti-spoofing algorithms are:

- LivDet DBs (LivDet 2009 DB and LivDet 2011 DB)[2] [20, 21]: These datasets, which share the acquisition protocols and part of the samples, are available at the 2009 and 2011 Fingerprint Liveness Detection Competitions web sites[3, 4] and are divided into the same train and test set used in the official evaluations. They contain over 18,000 real and fake samples coming from more than 100 different fingers acquired with four different flat optical sensors. The gummy fingers were generated, with the cooperation of the users, using six different materials: silicone, gelatine, latex, wood glue, ecoflex and playdoh.
- ATVS-Fake Fingerprint DB (ATVS-FFp DB) [22]: This database is available from the Biometric Recognition Group-ATVS web site.[5] It contains over 3,000 real and fake fingerprint samples coming from 68 different fingers and acquired using a flat optical sensor, a flat capacitive sensor, and a thermal sweeping sensor. The gummy fingers were generated with and without the cooperation of the user, using modeling silicone. Cooperation of the user means that the legitimate user takes part in the generation process (usually placing his finger on a mold in order to produce the negative of the fingerprint), while in the noncooperative process the user inadvertently leaves a latent fingerprint on a surface, which is then recovered by the attacker.

Some samples of real and fake fingerprint images that can be found in the previous databases are shown in Fig. 3.1. For a more detailed description of these fingerprint spoofing databases and more example images, the reader should refer to Appendix A.2 (Fig. 3.2).

---

[2] During the writing of this chapter the 2013 LivDet edition was being held. The DB used in the evaluation will be made public on the web site of the competition once the final results are published.

[3] http://prag.diee.unica.it/LivDet09/.

[4] http://people.clarkson.edu/projects/biosal/fingerprint/index.php.

[5] http://atvs.ii.uam.es/.

3 Fingerprint Anti-spoofing in Biometric Systems

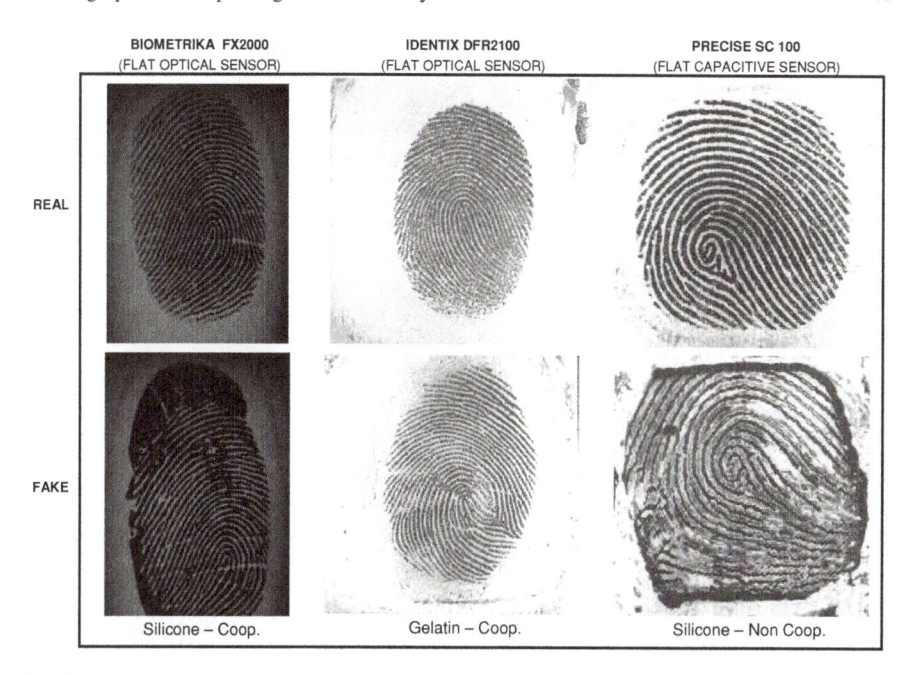

**Fig. 3.1** Typical examples of real and fake fingerprints that may be found in the ATVS-FFp DB and the LivDet 2009 and 2011 DBs described in Sect. 3.3. Fake fingerprints are labeled according to the process (cooperative or noncooperative) and the type of material (silicone, gelatin) used for their generation. For further details on the databases and for more sample images, we refer the reader to Appendix A.2

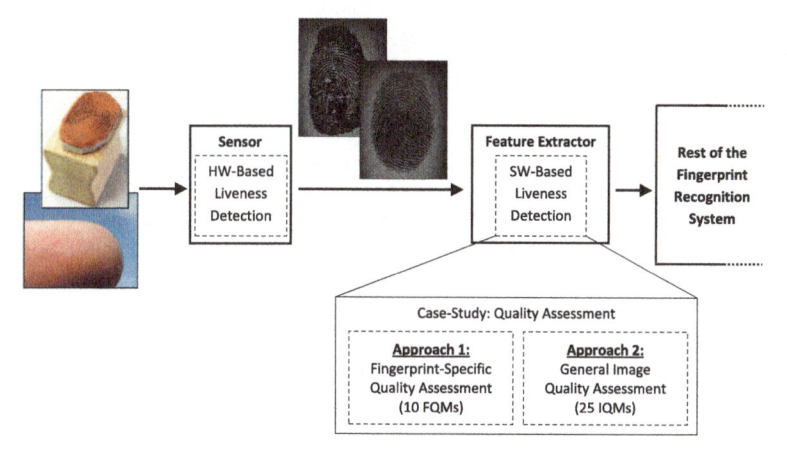

**Fig. 3.2** General diagram of the fingerprint anti-spoofing case study considered in Sect. 3.4. Approach 1 and Approach 2 are described in Sects. 3.5 and 3.6, respectively. Fingerprint-specific Quality Measures stands for Fingerprint Quality Measures, while IQMs stands for Image Quality Measures (IQMs)

## 3.4 Case Study: Quality Assessment Versus Fingerprint Spoofing

The problem of spoof detection can be seen as a two-class classification problem where an input biometric sample has to be assigned to one of two classes: real or fake.

Simple visual inspection of an image of a real fingerprint and a fake sample of the same trait shows that the two images can be very similar and even the human eye may find it difficult to make a distinction between them after a short inspection. Yet, some differences between the real and fake fingerprints may become evident once the images are translated into a proper feature space.

Therefore, the key point of the process is to find a set of discriminant features which permits to build an appropriate classifier which gives the probability of the image "liveness" given the extracted set of features.

In the present chapter, we explore and evaluate the potential of quality assessment for fingerprint liveness detection. In particular, we consider two different sets of features: (i) one based on FQMs (i.e., quality measures specifically adapted for fingerprint images); and (ii) a second set based on general IQMs (i.e., quality measures which may be extracted from any image).

The use of quality assessment for anti-spoofing purposes is motivated by the assumption that: *It is expected that a fake image captured in an attack attempt will have different quality than a real sample acquired in the normal operation scenario for which the sensor was designed.*

Expected quality differences between real and fake samples may include: degree of sharpness, color and luminance levels, local artifacts, amount of information found in both types of images (entropy), structural distortions, or natural appearance. For example, it is not rare that fingerprint images captured from a gummy finger present local acquisition artifacts such as spots and patches, or that they have a lower definition of ridges and valleys due to the lack of moisture.

In the current state-of-the-art, the rationale behind the use of quality assessment features for liveness detection is supported by three factors:

- Image quality has been successfully used in previous works for image manipulation detection [99, 100] and steganalysis [101–103] in the forensic field. To a certain extent, many fingerprint spoofing attacks may be regarded as a type of image manipulation which can be effectively detected, as shown in the present research work, by the use of different quality features.
- Human observers very often refer to the "different appearance" of real and fake samples to distinguish between them. The different metrics and methods implemented here for quality assessment intend to estimate in an objective and reliable way the perceived appearance of fingerprint images.
- Moreover, different quality measures present different sensitivity to image artifacts and distortions. For instance, measures like the mean squared error (MSE) respond more to additive noise, whereas others such as difference measured in the spectral domain are more sensitive to blur; while gradient-related features react to distortions concentrated around edges and textures. Therefore, using a wide

range of quality measures exploiting complementary image quality properties, should permit to detect the aforementioned quality differences between real and fake samples which are expected to be found in many attack attempts.

All these observations lead us to believe that there is sound proof for the "quality-difference" hypothesis and that quality measures have the potential to achieve success in biometric protection tasks.

In the next sections, we describe two particular software-based implementations for fingerprint anti-spoofing. Both methods use only one input image (i.e., the same sample acquired for authentication purposes) to distinguish between real and fake fingerprints. The difference between the two techniques relies on the sets of quality-based features used to solve the classification problem: (i) the first anti-spoofing method uses a set of 10 FQMs (see Sect. 3.5); (ii) the second uses a set of 25 general IQMs (see Sect. 3.6). Later, both techniques are evaluated on two publicly available databases and their results are compared to other well-known techniques from the state-of-the-art (see Sect. 3.7).

## 3.5 Approach 1: Fingerprint-Specific Quality Assessment (FQA)

The fingerprint anti-spoofing approach described in this section was first presented and thoroughly validated in [6]. It is based on a parameterization of ten FQMs taken from a number of approaches for fingerprint image quality computation that have been described in the literature [108].

In general, fingerprint image quality can be assessed by measuring one of the following properties: ridge strength or directionality, ridge continuity, ridge clarity, integrity of the ridge-valley structure, or estimated verification performance when using the image at hand. A number of information sources are used to measure these properties: (i) angle information provided by the direction field, (ii) Gabor filters, which are an alternative option to retrieve the direction information [109], (iii) pixel intensity of the gray-scale image, (iv) power spectrum, and (v) Neural Networks. Fingerprint quality can be assessed either analyzing the image in a holistic manner, or combining the quality from local nonoverlapped blocks of the image.

In the following, we give some details about the 10 FQMs used in this anti-spoofing method. The features implemented have been selected in order to cover the different fingerprint quality-assessment approaches mentioned above so that the maximum degree of complementarity among them may be achieved. This way, the protection method presents a high generality and may be successfully used to detect a wide range of spoofing attacks. A classification of the 10 features and of the information source exploited by each of them is given in Table 3.1.

**Table 3.1** Summary of the 10 Fingerprint-specific Quality Measures (FQMs) implemented in Sect. 3.5 for fingerprint anti-spoofing

| List of 10 FQMs implemented | | | | | |
|---|---|---|---|---|---|
| # | Acronym | Name | Ref. | Property measured | Source |
| 1 | OCL | Orientation certainty level | [104] | Ridge strength | Local angle |
| 2 | PSE | Power spectrum energy | [105] | Ridge strength | Power spectrum |
| 3 | LOQ | Local orientation quality | [106] | Ridge continuity | Local angle |
| 4 | COF | Continuity of the orientation field | [104] | Ridge continuity | Local angle |
| 5 | MGL | Mean gray level | [73] | Ridge clarity | Pixel intensity |
| 6 | SGL | Standard deviation gray level | [73] | Ridge clarity | Pixel intensity |
| 7 | LCS1 | Local clarity score 1 | [106] | Ridge clarity | Pixel intensity |
| 8 | LCS2 | Local clarity score 2 | [106] | Ridge clarity | Pixel intensity |
| 9 | SAMP | Sinusoid amplitude | [107] | Ridge clarity | Pixel intensity |
| 10 | SVAR | Sinusoid variance | [107] | Ridge clarity | Pixel intensity |

All features were either directly taken or adapted from the references given. For each feature, the fingerprint property measured and the information source used for its estimation is given. For a more detailed description of each feature, we refer the reader to Sect. 3.5

As the features used in this approach evaluate fingerprint-specific properties, prior to the feature extraction process, it is necessary to segment the actual fingerprint from the background. For this preprocessing step, the same method proposed in [110] is used.

## 3.5.1 Ridge-Strength Measures

- *Orientation Certainty Level (OCL)* [104], which measures the energy concentration along the dominant direction of ridges using the intensity gradient. It is computed as the ratio between the two eigenvalues of the covariance matrix of the gradient vector. A relative weight is given to each region of the image based on its distance from the centroid, since regions near the centroid are supposed to provide more reliable information [105]. An example of OCL computation for a low- and a high-quality fingerprint is shown in Fig. 3.3.
- *Power Spectrum Energy (PSE)* [105], which is computed using ring-shaped bands of the Fourier Spectrum. For this purpose, a set of band-pass filters is employed to extract the energy in each frequency band. High-quality images will have the energy concentrated in few bands while poor ones will have a more diffused distribution. The energy concentration is measured using the entropy. An example of quality estimation using the global quality index PSE is shown in Fig. 3.4 for a low- and a high-quality fingerprint.

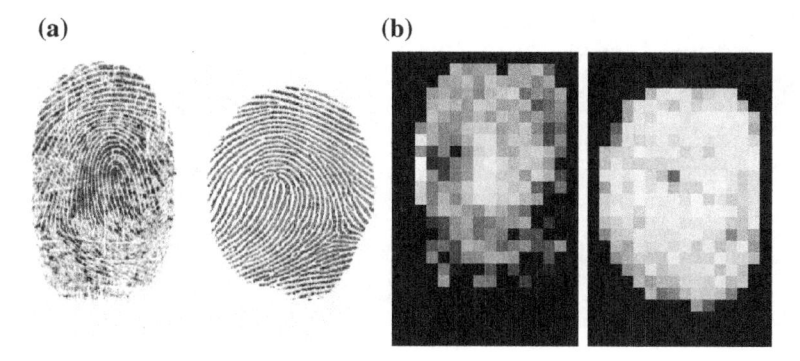

**Fig. 3.3** Computation of the Orientation Certainty Level (OCL) for a low- and a high-quality fingerprint. Panel (**a**) are the input fingerprint images. Panel (**b**) are the blockwise values of the OCL; blocks with brighter color indicate higher quality in the region

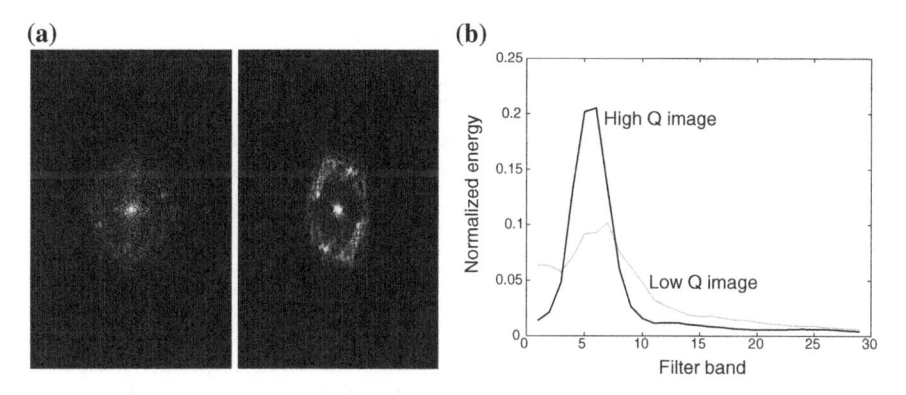

**Fig. 3.4** Computation of the energy concentration in the power spectrum for a low- and a high-quality fingerprint. Panel (**a**) are the power spectra of the images shown in Fig. 3.3. Panel (**b**) shows the energy distributions in the region of interest. The quality values for the low and high-quality image are 0.35 and 0.88 respectively

## 3.5.2 Ridge-Continuity Measures

- *Local Orientation Quality (LOQ)* [106], which is computed as the average absolute difference of the orientation angle with the surrounding image blocks, providing information about how smoothly the direction angle changes from block to block. Quality of the whole image is finally computed by averaging all the LOQ scores of the image. In high-quality images, it is expected that ridge orientation changes smoothly across the whole image, except in singularity regions. An example of LOQ computation is shown in Fig. 3.5 for a low- and a high-quality fingerprint.
- *Continuity of the orientation field (COF)* [104]. This method relies on the fact that, in good quality images, ridges and valleys must flow sharply and smoothly in a locally constant direction. The orientation change along rows and columns of

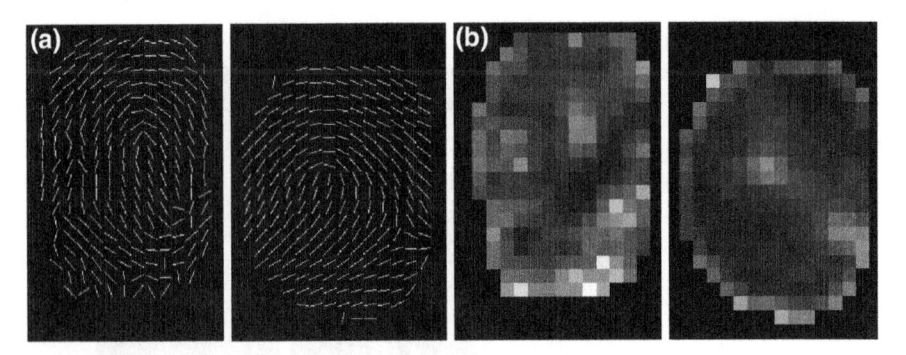

**Fig. 3.5** Computation of the Local Orientation Quality (LOQ) for a low- and a high-quality fingerprint. Panel (**a**) are the direction fields of the images shown in Fig. 3.3a. Panel (**b**) are the blockwise values of the average absolute difference of local orientation with the surrounding blocks; blocks with brighter color indicate higher difference value and thus, lower quality

the image is examined. Abrupt direction changes between consecutive blocks are then accumulated and mapped into a quality score. As we can observe in Fig. 3.5, ridge orientation changes smoothly across the whole image in case of high quality, except in singularity regions.

### 3.5.3 Ridge-Clarity Measures

- *Mean Gray Level (MGL)* and *Standard Deviation Gray Level (SGL)*, computed from the segmented foreground only. These two features had already been considered for liveness detection in [73].
- *Local Clarity Score (LCS1 and LCS2)* [106]. The sinusoidal-shaped wave that models ridges and valleys [107] is used to segment ridge and valley regions (see Fig. 3.6). The clarity is then defined as the overlapping area of the gray level distributions of segmented ridges and valleys. For ridges/valleys with high clarity, both distributions should have a very small overlapping area. An example of quality estimation using the LCS is shown in Fig. 3.7 for two fingerprint blocks coming from a low- and a high-quality fingerprint. It should be noted that sometimes the sinusoidal-shaped wave cannot be extracted reliably, specially in bad quality regions of the image. The quality measure LCS1 discards these regions, therefore being an optimistic measure of quality. This is compensated with LCS2, which does not discard these regions, but they are assigned the lowest quality level.
- *Amplitude and Variance of the Sinusoid that models ridges and valleys (SAMP and SVAR)* [107]. Based on these parameters, blocks are classified as *good* and *bad*. The quality of the fingerprint is then computed as the percentage of foreground blocks marked as *good*.

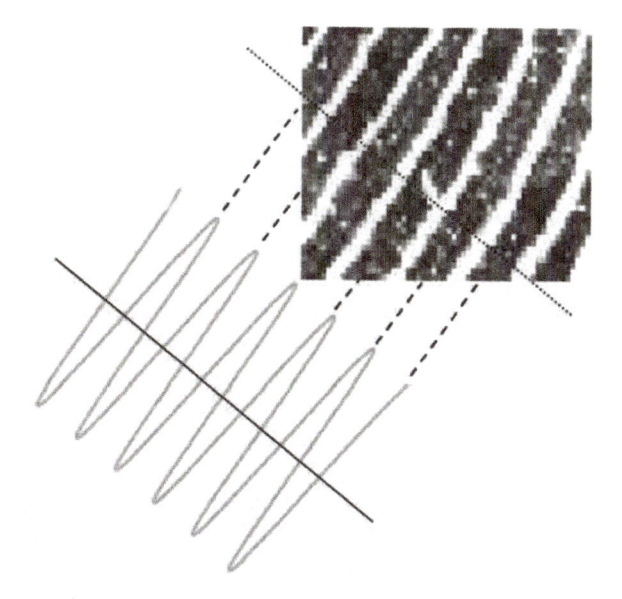

3  Fingerprint Anti-spoofing in Biometric Systems

**Fig. 3.6** Modeling of ridges and valleys as a sinusoid

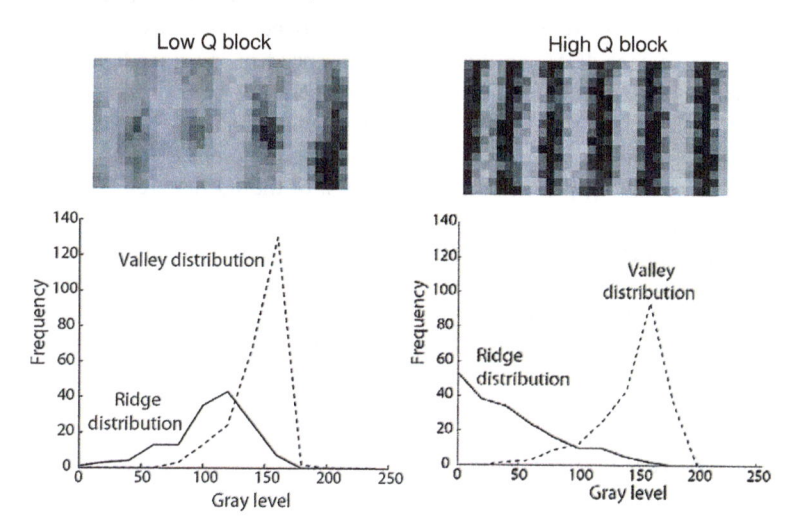

**Fig. 3.7** Computation of the Local Clarity Score (LCS) for two blocks coming from a low- and a high-quality fingerprint. The fingerprint blocks appear on *top*, while below we show the *gray level* distributions of the segmented ridges and valleys. The degree of overlapping for the low- and high-quality blocks is 0.22 and 0.10, respectively

## 3.6 Approach 2: General Image Quality Assessment (IQA)

The goal of an objective image quality measure (IQM) is to provide a quantitative score that describes the degree of fidelity or, conversely, the level of distortion of a given image. Many different approaches for objective IQA have been described in the literature [111]. From a general perspective, IQ metrics can be classified according to the availability of an original (distortion-free) image, with which the distorted image is to be compared. Thus, objective IQA methods can fall in one of two categories: (i) *full-reference* techniques, which include the majority of traditional automatic image quality estimation approaches, and where a complete reference image is assumed to be known (e.g., with a large use in the field of image compression algorithms) [112]; (ii) *no-reference* techniques (also referred as *blind*), which assess the quality of the test image without any reference to the original sample, generally using some pretrained statistical model [113].

The parameterization proposed in this section and applied to fingerprint liveness detection comprises 25 IQMs including both full-reference and blind. In order to generate a system as general as possible in terms of number of attacks detected, we have given priority to IQMs which evaluate complementary properties of the image (e.g., sharpness, entropy, or structure). In addition, to assure a user-friendly nonintrusive system, big importance has been given to the complexity and the feature extraction time of each IQM, so that the overall speed of the final fake detection algorithm allows it to operate in real-time environments.

Furthermore, as the method operates on the whole image without searching for any fingerprint-specific properties, it does not require any preprocessing steps (e.g., fingerprint segmentation) prior to the computation of the IQ features. This characteristic minimizes its computational load.

The final 25 selected IQMs are summarized in Table 3.2. Details about each of these 25 IQMs are given in Sects. 3.6.1 and 3.6.2. For clarity, in Fig. 3.8, we show a diagram with the general IQM classification followed in these sections. Acronyms of the different features are highlighted in bold in the text and in Fig. 3.8.

### 3.6.1 Full-Reference IQ Measures

As described previously, full-reference IQA methods (FR) rely on the availability of a clean undistorted reference image to estimate the quality of the test sample. In the problem of fake detection addressed in this work such a reference image is unknown, as the detection system only has access to the input sample. In order to circumvent this limitation, the same strategy already successfully used for image manipulation detection in [99] and for steganalysis in [101], is implemented here.

The input gray-scale image **I** (of size $N \times M$) is filtered with a low-pass Gaussian kernel ($\sigma = 0.5$ and size $3 \times 3$) in order to generate a distorted version $\hat{\mathbf{I}}$. Then, the quality between both images (**I** and $\hat{\mathbf{I}}$) is computed according to the corresponding

**Table 3.2** List of the 25 Image quality measures (IQMs) implemented in Sect. 3.6 for fingerprint anti-spoofing

List of the 25 IQMs implemented

| # | Type | Acronym | Name | Ref. | Description |
|---|------|---------|------|------|-------------|
| 1 | FR | MSE | Mean squared error | [114] | $MSE(\mathbf{I}, \hat{\mathbf{I}}) = \frac{1}{NM} \sum_{i=1}^{N} \sum_{j=1}^{M} (\mathbf{I}_{i,j} - \hat{\mathbf{I}}_{i,j})^2$ |
| 2 | FR | PSNR | Peak signal to noise ratio | [115] | $PSNR(\mathbf{I}, \hat{\mathbf{I}}) = 10 \log \left( \frac{\max(\mathbf{I}^2)}{MSE(\mathbf{I}, \hat{\mathbf{I}})} \right)$ |
| 3 | FR | SNR | Signal to noise ratio | [116] | $SNR(\mathbf{I}, \hat{\mathbf{I}}) = 10 \log \left( \frac{\sum_{i=1}^{N} \sum_{j=1}^{M} (\mathbf{I}_{i,j})^2}{N \cdot M \cdot MSE(\mathbf{I}, \hat{\mathbf{I}})} \right)$ |
| 4 | FR | SC | Structural content | [117] | $SC(\mathbf{I}, \hat{\mathbf{I}}) = \frac{\sum_{i=1}^{N} \sum_{j=1}^{M} (\mathbf{I}_{i,j})^2}{\sum_{i=1}^{N} \sum_{j=1}^{M} (\hat{\mathbf{I}}_{i,j})^2}$ |
| 5 | FR | MD | Maximum difference | [117] | $MD(\mathbf{I}, \hat{\mathbf{I}}) = \max \| \mathbf{I}_{i,j} - \hat{\mathbf{I}}_{i,j} \|$ |
| 6 | FR | AD | Average difference | [117] | $AD(\mathbf{I}, \hat{\mathbf{I}}) = \frac{1}{NM} \sum_{i=1}^{N} \sum_{j=1}^{M} (\mathbf{I}_{i,j} - \hat{\mathbf{I}}_{i,j})$ |
| 7 | FR | NAE | Normalized absolute error | [117] | $NAE(\mathbf{I}, \hat{\mathbf{I}}) = \frac{\sum_{i=1}^{N} \sum_{j=1}^{M} \|\mathbf{I}_{i,j} - \hat{\mathbf{I}}_{i,j}\|}{\sum_{i=1}^{N} \sum_{j=1}^{M} \|\mathbf{I}_{i,j}\|}$ |
| 8 | FR | RAMD | R-Averaged MD | [114] | $RAMD(\mathbf{I}, \hat{\mathbf{I}}, R) = \frac{1}{R} \sum_{r=1}^{R} \max_{r} \|\mathbf{I}_{i,j} - \hat{\mathbf{I}}_{i,j}\|$ |
| 9 | FR | LMSE | Laplacian MSE | [117] | $LMSE(\mathbf{I}, \hat{\mathbf{I}}) = \frac{\sum_{i=1}^{N-1} \sum_{j=2}^{M-1} (h(\mathbf{I}_{i,j}) - h(\hat{\mathbf{I}}_{i,j}))^2}{\sum_{i=1}^{N-1} \sum_{j=2}^{M} h(\mathbf{I}_{i,j})^2}$ |
| 10 | FR | NXC | Normalized cross-correlation | [117] | $NXC(\mathbf{I}, \hat{\mathbf{I}}) = \frac{\sum_{i=1}^{N} \sum_{j=1}^{M} (\mathbf{I}_{i,j} \cdot \hat{\mathbf{I}}_{i,j})}{\sum_{i=1}^{N} \sum_{j=1}^{M} (\mathbf{I}_{i,j})^2}$ |
| 11 | FR | MAS | Mean angle similarity | [114] | $MAS(\mathbf{I}, \hat{\mathbf{I}}) = 1 - \frac{1}{NM} \sum_{i=1}^{N} \sum_{j=1}^{M} (\alpha_{i,j})$ |
| 12 | FR | MAMS | Mean angle-magnitude similarity | [114] | $MAMS(\mathbf{I}, \hat{\mathbf{I}}) = \frac{1}{NM} \sum_{i=1}^{N} \sum_{j=1}^{M} (1 - [1 - \alpha_{i,j}] \| 1 - \frac{\|\mathbf{I}_{i,j} - \hat{\mathbf{I}}_{i,j}\|}{255} \|)$ |
| 13 | FR | TED | Total edge difference | [118] | $TED(\mathbf{I}, \hat{\mathbf{I}}) = \frac{1}{NM} \sum_{i=1}^{N} \sum_{j=1}^{M} \|\mathbf{I}_{E_{i,j}} - \hat{\mathbf{I}}_{E_{i,j}}\|$ |
| 14 | FR | TCD | Total corner difference | [118] | $TCD(I, \hat{I}) = \frac{\|N_{cr} - \hat{N}_{cr}\|}{\max(N_{cr}, \hat{N}_{cr})}$ |
| 15 | FR | SME | Spectral magnitude error | [119] | $SME(\mathbf{I}, \hat{\mathbf{I}}) = \frac{1}{NM} \sum_{i=1}^{N} \sum_{j=1}^{M} (\|\mathbf{F}_{i,j}\| - \|\hat{\mathbf{F}}_{i,j}\|)^2$ |

**Table 3.2** (Continued)

List of the 25 IQMs implemented

| # | Type | Acronym | Name | Ref. | Description |
|---|------|---------|------|------|-------------|
| 16 | FR | SPE | Spectral phase error | [119] | $SPE(\mathbf{I}, \hat{\mathbf{I}}) = \frac{1}{NM} \sum_{i=1}^{N} \sum_{j=1}^{M} |\arg(\mathbf{F}_{i,j}) - \arg(\hat{\mathbf{F}}_{i,j})|^2$ |
| 17 | FR | GME | Gradient magnitude error | [120] | $SME(\mathbf{I}, \hat{\mathbf{I}}) = \frac{1}{NM} \sum_{i=1}^{N} \sum_{j=1}^{M} (|\mathbf{G}_{i,j}| - |\hat{\mathbf{G}}_{i,j}|)^2$ |
| 18 | FR | GPE | Gradient phase error | [120] | $SPE(\mathbf{I}, \hat{\mathbf{I}}) = \frac{1}{NM} \sum_{i=1}^{N} \sum_{j=1}^{M} |\arg(\mathbf{G}_{i,j}) - \arg(\hat{\mathbf{G}}_{i,j})|^2$ |
| 19 | FR | SSIM | Structural similarity index | [121] | See [121] and practical implementation available in [122] |
| 20 | FR | VIF | Visual information fidelity | [123] | See [123] and practical implementation available in [122] |
| 21 | FR | RRED | Reduced ref. entropic difference | [124] | See [124] and practical implementation available in [122] |
| 22 | NR | JQI | JPEG Quality index | [125] | See [125] and practical implementation available in [122] |
| 23 | NR | HLFI | High-Low frequency index | [126] | $SME(\mathbf{I}) = \frac{\sum_{i=1}^{i_l} \sum_{j=1}^{j_l} |\mathbf{F}_{i,j}| - \sum_{i=i_h+1}^{N} \sum_{j=j_h+1}^{M} |\mathbf{F}_{i,j}|}{\sum_{i=1}^{N} \sum_{j=1}^{M} |\mathbf{F}_{i,j}|}$ |
| 24 | NR | BIQI | Blind image quality index | [127] | See [127] and practical implementation available in [122] |
| 25 | NR | NIQE | Naturalness image quality estimator | [128] | See [128] and practical implementation available in [122] |

All the features were either directly taken or adapted from the references given. In the table: FR denotes Full-Reference and NR No-Reference; $\mathbf{I}$ denotes the reference clean image (of size $N \times M$) and $\hat{\mathbf{I}}$ the smoothed version of the reference image. For other notation specifications and undefined variables or functions, we refer the reader to the description of each particular feature in Sect. 3.6. Also, for those features with no mathematical definition, the exact details about their computation may be found in the given references

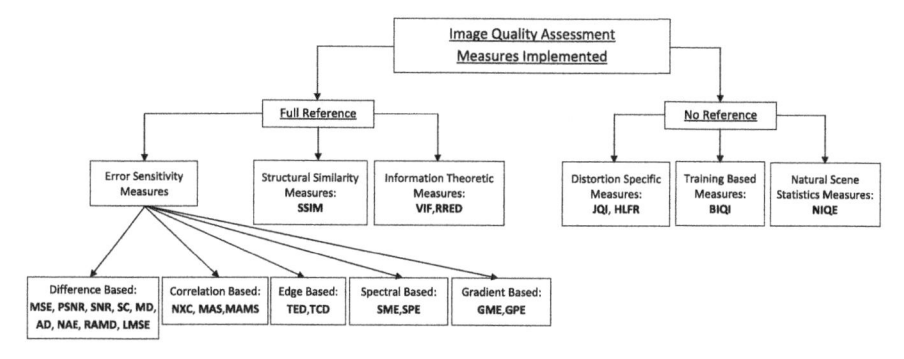

3  Fingerprint Anti-spoofing in Biometric Systems                                51

**Fig. 3.8** Classification of the 25 IQMs implemented in Sect. 3.6. Acronyms (*in bold*) of the different measures are explained in Table 3.2

full-reference IQA metric. This approach assumes that the loss of quality produced by Gaussian filtering differs between real and fake biometric samples. Assumption which is confirmed by the experimental results given in Sect. 3.7.

### 3.6.1.1 FR-IQMs: Error Sensitivity Measures

Traditional perceptual IQA approaches are based on measuring the errors (i.e., signal differences) between the distorted and the reference images, and attempt to quantify these errors in a way that simulates human visual error sensitivity features.

Although their efficiency as signal fidelity measures is somewhat controversial [129], up-to-date, these are probably the most widely used methods for IQA as they conveniently make use of many known psychophysical features of the human visual system [130], they are easy to calculate and usually have very low computational complexity.

Several of these metrics have been included in the 25-feature parameterization proposed in the present work. For clarity, these features have been classified here into five different categories (see Fig. 3.8) according to the image property measured [114]:

- *Pixel Difference measures* [114, 117]. These features compute the distortion between two images on the basis of their pixelwise differences. Here we include: Mean Squared Error (*MSE*), Peak Signal to Noise Ratio (*PSNR*), Signal to Noise Ratio (*SNR*), Structural Content (*SC*), Maximum Difference (*MD*), Average Difference (*AD*), Normalized Absolute Error (*NAE*), R-Averaged Maximum Difference (*RAMD*) and Laplacian Mean Squared Error (*LMSE*). The formal definitions for each of these features are given in Table 3.2.

In the RAMD entry in Table 3.2, $\max_r$ is defined as the $r$-highest pixel difference between two images. For the present implementation, $R = 10$.

In the LMSE entry in Table 3.2, $h(\mathbf{I}_{i,j}) = \mathbf{I}_{i+1,j} + \mathbf{I}_{i-1,j} + \mathbf{I}_{i,j+1} + \mathbf{I}_{i,j-1} - 4\mathbf{I}_{i,j}$.
- *Correlation-based measures* [114, 117]. The similarity between two digital images can also be quantified in terms of the correlation function. A variant of correlation-based measures can be obtained by considering the statistics of the angles between the pixel vectors of the original and distorted images. These features include (also defined in Table 3.2): Normalized Cross-Correlation (*NXC*), Mean Angle Similarity (*MAS*), and Mean Angle-Magnitude Similarity (*MAMS*).

In the MAS and MAMS entries in Table 3.2, $\alpha_{i,j}$ denotes the angle between two vectors, defined as, $\alpha_{i,j} = \frac{2}{\pi} \arccos \frac{\langle \mathbf{I}_{i,j}, \hat{\mathbf{I}}_{i,j} \rangle}{||\mathbf{I}_{i,j}|| \cdot ||\hat{\mathbf{I}}_{i,j}||}$, where $\langle \mathbf{I}_{i,j}, \hat{\mathbf{I}}_{i,j} \rangle$ denotes the scalar product. As we are dealing with positive matrices $\mathbf{I}$ and $\hat{\mathbf{I}}$, we are constrained to the first quadrant of the Cartesian space so that the MD attained will be $\pi/2$, therefore the coefficient $2/\pi$ is included for normalization.
- *Edge-based measures*. Edges and other two-dimensional features such as corners, are some of the most informative parts of an image, which play a key role in the human visual system and in many computer vision algorithms including quality assessment applications [118].

Since the structural distortion of an image is tightly linked with its edge degradation, here we have considered two edge-related quality measures: Total Edge Difference (*TED*) and Total Corner Difference (*TCD*).

In order to implement both features, which are computed according to the corresponding expressions given in Table 3.2, we use: (i) the Sobel operator to build the binary edge maps $\mathbf{I}_E$ and $\hat{\mathbf{I}}_E$; (ii) the Harris corner detector [131] to compute the number of corners $N_{cr}$ and $\hat{N}_{cr}$ found in $\mathbf{I}$ and $\hat{\mathbf{I}}$.
- *Spectral distance measures*. The Fourier transform is another traditional image processing tool which has been applied to the field of IQA [114, 119]. In this work, we will consider as IQ spectral-related features: the Spectral Magnitude Error (*SME*) and the Spectral Phase Error (*SPE*), defined in Table 3.2 (where $\mathbf{F}$ and $\hat{\mathbf{F}}$ are the respective Fourier transforms of $\mathbf{I}$ and $\hat{\mathbf{I}}$), and $\arg(\mathbf{F})$ denotes phase.
- *Gradient-based measures*. Gradients convey important visual information which can be of great use for quality assessment. Many of the distortions that can affect an image are reflected by a change in its gradient. Therefore, using such information, structural and contrast changes can be effectively captured [120].

Two simple gradient-based features are included in the biometric protection system proposed in the present article: Gradient Magnitude Error (*GME*) and Gradient Phase Error (*GPE*), defined in Table 3.2 (where $\mathbf{G}$ and $\hat{\mathbf{G}}$ are the gradient maps of $\mathbf{I}$ and $\hat{\mathbf{I}}$ defined as $\mathbf{G} = \mathbf{G}_x + i\mathbf{G}_y$, where $\mathbf{G}_x$ and $\mathbf{G}_y$ are the gradients in the $x$ and $y$ directions).

### 3.6.1.2 FR-IQMs: Structural Similarity Measures

Although being very convenient and widely used, the aforementioned image quality metrics based on error sensitivity present several problems which are evidenced by their mismatch (in many cases) with subjective human-based quality scoring systems [129]. In this scenario, a recent new paradigm for IQA based on structural similarity was proposed following the hypothesis that the human visual system is highly adapted for extracting structural information from the viewing field [121]. Therefore, distortions in an image that come from variations in lighting, such as contrast or brightness changes (nonstructural distortions), should be treated differently from structural ones.

Among these recent objective perceptual measures, the Structural Similarity Index Measure (*SSIM*), has the simplest formulation and has gained widespread popularity in a broad range of practical applications [121, 132]. In view of its very attractive properties, the SSIM has been included in the 25-feature parameterization.

### 3.6.1.3 FR-IQMs: Information Theoretic Measures

The quality assessment problem may also be understood, from an information theory perspective, as an information-fidelity problem (rather than a signal-fidelity problem). The core idea behind these approaches is that an image source communicates to a receiver through a channel that limits the amount of information that could flow through it, thereby introducing distortions. The goal is to relate the visual quality of the test image to the amount of information shared between the test and the reference signals, or more precisely, the mutual information between them. Under this general framework, IQMs based on information fidelity exploit the (in some cases unprecise) relationship between statistical image information and visual quality [123, 124].

In the present work, we consider two of these information-theoretic features: the Visual Information Fidelity (*VIF*) which measures quality fidelity as the ratio between the total information ideally extracted by the brain from the distorted image and that from the reference sample [123]; and the Reduced Reference Entropic Difference index (*RRED*), which approaches the problem of QA from the perspective of measuring distances between the reference image and the projection of the distorted image onto the space of natural images [124].

## 3.6.2 No-Reference IQ Measures

Unlike the objective reference IQA methods, in general the human visual system does not require of a reference sample to determine the quality level of an image. Following this same principle, automatic no-reference image quality assessment algorithms (NR-IQA) try to handle the very complex and challenging problem of assessing the visual quality of images, in the absence of a reference. Presently,

NR-IQA methods generally estimate the quality of the test image according to some pretrained statistical model. Depending on the images used to train this model and on the *a priori* knowledge required, the methods are coarsely divided into one of three trends [113]:

- *Distortion-specific approaches*. These techniques rely on previously acquired knowledge about the type of visual quality loss caused by a specific distortion. The final quality measure is computed according to a model trained on clean images and on images affected by this particular distortion. Two of these measures have been included in the biometric protection method proposed in the present work.
  The JPEG Quality Index (*JQI*), which evaluates the quality in images affected by the usual block artifacts found in many compression algorithms running at low bit rates such as the JPEG [125].
  The High-Low Frequency Index (*HLFI*), which is formally defined in Table 3.2. It was inspired by previous work which considered local gradients as a blind metric to detect blur and noise [126]. Similarly, the HLFI feature is sensitive to the sharpness of the image by computing the difference between the power in the lower and upper frequencies of the Fourier Spectrum. In the HLFI entry in Table 3.2, $i_l, i_h, j_l, j_h$ are respectively the indices corresponding to the lower and upper frequency thresholds considered by the method. In the current implementation, $i_l = i_h = 0.15N$ and $j_l = j_h = 0.15M$.
- *Training-based approaches*. Similarly to the previous class of NR-IQA methods, in this type of techniques, a model is trained using clean and distorted images. Then, the quality score is computed based on a number of features extracted from the test image and related to the general model [127]. However, unlike the former approaches, these metrics intend to provide a general quality score not related to a specific distortion. To this end, the statistical model is trained with images affected by different types of distortions.
  This is the case of the Blind Image Quality Index (*BIQI*) described in [127], which is part of the 25- feature set used in the present work. The BIQI follows a two-stage framework in which the individual measures of different distortion-specific experts are combined to generate one global quality score.
- *Natural Scene Statistic approaches*. These blind IQA techniques use *a priori* knowledge taken from natural scene distortion-free images to train the initial model (i.e., no distorted images are used). The rationale behind this trend relies on the hypothesis that undistorted images of the natural world present certain *regular* properties which fall within a certain subspace of all possible images. If quantified appropriately, deviations from the regularity of natural statistics ca help to evaluate the perceptual quality of an image [128].
  This approach is followed by the Natural Image Quality Evaluator (*NIQE*) used in the present work [128]. The NIQE is a completely blind image quality analyzer based on the construction of a quality aware collection of statistical features (derived from a corpus of natural undistorted images) related to a multivariate Gaussian natural scene statistical model.

## 3.7 Results

In order to achieve reproducible results, we have only used in the experimental validation the two largest publicly available databases for fingerprint spoofing introduced in Sect. 3.3 and described in detail in Appendix A.2: (i) the LivDet 2009 DB [20] and (ii) the ATVS-FFp DB [22]. This has allowed us to compare, in an objective and fair way, the performance of the proposed system with other existing state-of-the-art liveness detection solutions.

According to their associated protocols, the databases are divided into: train set, used to train the Quadratic Discriminant Analysis classifier (QDA) [133]; and test set, used to evaluate the performance of the protection method. In order to generate unbiased results, there is no overlap between both sets (i.e., samples corresponding to each user are just included in the train or the test set).

The task in *all* the scenarios and experiments described in the next sections is to automatically distinguish between real and fake fingerprints. Therefore, in all cases, results are reported in terms of: the False Genuine Rate (FGR), which accounts for the number of fake samples that were classified as real; and the False Fake Rate (FFR), which gives the probability of an image coming from a genuine sample being considered as fake. The Half Total Error Rate (HTER) is computed as HTER = (FGR + FFR)/2.

### 3.7.1 Results: ATVS-FFp DB

Both the train and the test set of the ATVS-FFp DB contain half of the fingerprint images acquired with and without the cooperation of the user, following a two-fold cross validation protocol. In Table 3.3 we show the detection results of the two systems described in Sects. 3.5 (top row) and 3.6 (bottom row).

The performance of both algorithms is very similar, although in the overall, the method based on general IQA is slightly better in two of the three datasets (Precise and Yubee). In addition, thanks to its simplicity and lack of image preprocessing steps, the IQA-based method is around 30 times faster than the one using fingerprint-specific quality features (tested on the same Windows-based platform). This gives the IQA-based scheme the advantage of being usable in practical real-time applications, without loosing any accuracy.

### 3.7.2 Results: LivDet 2009 DB

The train and test sets selected for the evaluation experiments on this database are the same as the ones used in the LivDet 2009 competition, so that the results obtained by the two described methods based on quality assessment may be directly compared

**Table 3.3** Results obtained in each of the three data subsets comprised in the ATVS-FFp DB by the two biometric protection methods described in Sects. 3.5 and 3.6

|           | Results: ATVS-FFp DB |     |      |         |     |      |       |     |      |
|-----------|----------------------|-----|------|---------|-----|------|-------|-----|------|
|           | Biometrika           |     |      | Precise |     |      | Yubee |     |      |
|           | FFR                  | FGR | HTER | FFR     | FGR | HTER | FFR   | FGR | HTER |
| IQF-based | 4.9                  | 7.6 | 5.8  | 1.8     | 7.0 | 4.4  | 2.2   | 9.7 | 5.9  |
| IQA-based | 9.2                  | 4.0 | 6.6  | 6.8     | 1.5 | 4.2  | 7.9   | 1.9 | 4.9  |

Error rates are given in %. FFR stands for False Fake Rate, FGR for False Genuine Rate (FGR), and HTER for Half Total Error Rate. Biometrika, Precise, and Yubee are the sensors used to acquired each of the subsets (see Sect. 3.3 for further details)

**Table 3.4** Results obtained in each of the three data subsets comprised in the LivDet 2009 DB by: the two biometric protection methods described in Sects. 3.5 and 3.6 (IQF-based and IQA-based, two top rows); each of the best approaches participating in LivDet 2009 [20] (*third row*); the method proposed in [51] which combines perspiration and morphological features (*fourth row*); the method proposed in [63] based on the wavelet analysis of the fingertip texture, according to an implementation from [51] (*fifth row*); the method proposed in [66] based on the curvelet analysis of the fingertip texture, according to an implementation from [51] (*sixth row*); the method proposed in [49] based on the combination of local ridge frequencies and multiresolution texture analysis, according to an implementation from [51] (*bottom row*)

|                                     | Results: LivDet 2009 DB |      |      |            |      |      |         |      |      |
|-------------------------------------|-------------------------|------|------|------------|------|------|---------|------|------|
|                                     | Biometrika              |      |      | CrossMatch |      |      | Identix |      |      |
|                                     | FFR                     | FGR  | HTER | FFR        | FGR  | HTER | FFR     | FGR  | HTER |
| IQF-based                           | 3.1                     | 71.8 | 37.4 | 8.8        | 20.8 | 13.2 | 4.8     | 5.0  | 6.7  |
| IQA-based                           | 14.0                    | 11.6 | 12.8 | 8.6        | 12.8 | 10.7 | 1.1     | 1.4  | 1.2  |
| Best LivDet 2009 [20]               | 15.6                    | 20.7 | 18.2 | 7.4        | 11.4 | 9.4  | 2.7     | 2.8  | 2.8  |
| Marasco et al. [51]                 | 12.2                    | 13.0 | 12.6 | 17.4       | 12.9 | 15.2 | 8.3     | 11.0 | 9.7  |
| Moon et al. [63] reported in [51]   | 20.8                    | 25.0 | 23.0 | 27.4       | 19.6 | 23.5 | 74.7    | 1.6  | 38.2 |
| Nikam et al. [66] reported in [51]  | 14.3                    | 42.3 | 28.3 | 19.0       | 18.4 | 18.7 | 23.7    | 37.0 | 30.3 |
| Abhyankar et al. [49] reported in [51] | 24.2                 | 39.2 | 31.7 | 39.7       | 23.3 | 31.5 | 48.4    | 46.0 | 47.2 |

Error rates are given in %. FFR stands for False Fake Rate, FGR for False Genuine Rate, and HTER for Half Total Error Rate. Biometrika, CrossMatch and Identix are the sensors used to acquire each of the subsets (see Sect. 3.3 for further details)

to the participants of the contest (approximately 30 % of the data in the train set). Results are shown in the first two rows of Table 3.4. For clarity, only the best results achieved in LivDet 2009 for each of the individual datasets is given for comparison (third row).

In [51], a novel fingerprint liveness detection method combining perspiration and morphological features was presented and evaluated on the LivDet 2009 DB following the same protocol (training and test sets) used in the competition. In that work, comparative results were reported with particular implementations of the techniques proposed in: [63], based on the wavelet analysis of the finger tip texture; [66], based on the curvelet analysis of the finger tip texture; and [49] based on the combination of local ridge frequencies and multiresolution texture analysis. In the last four rows of Table 3.4 we also present these results so that they may be compared with the two quality-based methods described in Sects. 3.5 (first row) and 3.6 (second row).

The results given in Table 3.4 show that the method based on general IQA outperforms all the contestants in LivDet 2009 in two of the datasets (Biometrika and Identix), while its classification error is just slightly worse than the best of the participants for the Crossmatch data. Although the results are not as good for the case of the IQF-based method, its performance is still competitive compared to that of the best LivDet 2009 participants.

The classification rates of the two quality-based approaches are also clearly lower than those reported in [51] for the different liveness detection solutions tested.

## 3.8 Conclusions

The study of the vulnerabilities of biometric systems against spoofing attacks has been a very active field of research in recent years [134]. This interest has led to big advances in the field of security-enhancing technologies for fingerprint-based applications. However, in spite of this noticeable improvement, the development of efficient protection methods against known threats (usually based on some type of self-manufactured gummy finger) has proven to be a challenging task.

Simple visual inspection of an image of a real fingerprint and its corresponding fake sample shows that the two images can be very similar and even the human eye may find it difficult to make a distinction between them after a short inspection. Yet, some disparities between the real and fake images may become evident once the images are translated into a proper feature space. These differences come from the fact that fingerprints, as 3-D objects, have their own optical qualities (absorption, reflection, scattering, refraction), which other materials (silicone, gelatin, glycerin) or synthetically produced samples do not possess. Furthermore, fingerprint acquisition devices are designed to provide good quality samples when they interact, in a normal operation environment, with a real 3-D trait. If this scenario is changed, or if the trait presented to the scanner is an unexpected fake artifact, the characteristics of the captured image may significantly vary.

In this context, it is reasonable to assume that the image quality properties of real accesses and fraudulent attacks will be different. Following this "*quality-difference*" hypothesis, in this chapter, after an exhaustive review of the state-of-the-art in fingerprint anti-spoofing methods, we have explored the potential of quality assessment as a protection tool against fingerprint direct attacks.

For this purpose, we have considered two different feature-sets which we have combined with simple classifiers to detect real and fake access attempts: (i) a set of 10 fingerprint-specific quality measures which requires of some preprocessing steps (e.g., fingerprint segmentation); and (ii) a set of 25 complementary general IQMs which may be computed without any image preprocessing.

The two anti-spoofing methods have been evaluated on the two largest publicly available databases following their associated protocols. This way, the results are reproducible and may be fairly compared with other past or future fingerprint anti-spoofing solutions.

Several conclusions may be extracted from the evaluation results presented in the experimental sections of the chapter: (i) The proposed methods, especially the one based on general image quality assessment, are able to generalize well, performing consistently well for different databases, acquisition conditions, and spoofing scenarios; (ii) the error rates achieved by the described protection schemes are in many cases lower than those reported by other state-of-the-art fingerprint anti-spoofing systems which have been tested in the framework of different independent competitions; (iii) in addition to its very competitive performance, the IQA-based approach presents some other very attractive features such as: it is simple, fast, nonintrusive, user-friendly, and cheap, all of them very desirable properties in a practical protection system.

All the previous results validate the "different-quality" hypothesis formulated in Sect. 3.4, and show the great potential of quality assessment as an anti-spoofing tool to secure fingerprint recognition systems.

Overall, this chapter, after a general overview of the progress in the field of fingerprint anti-spoofing has presented an active research line focused on new protection approaches based on quality assessment. The experimental evaluation carried out in the chapter has been performed following a clear and standard methodology based on common protocols, metrics, and benchmarks. We believe that it may serve as a baseline for the validation of future fingerprint anti-spoofing methods.

**Acknowledgments** This work has been partially supported by projects Contexts (S2009/TIC-1485) from CAM, Bio-Shield (TEC2012-34881) from Spanish MECD, TABULA RASA (FP7-ICT-257289) and BEAT (FP7-SEC-284989) from EU, and *Cátedra UAM-Telefónica*.

# References

1. van der Putte T, Keuning J (2000) Biometrical fingerprint recognition: don't get your fingers burned. In: Proceedings of IFIP conference on smart card research and advanced applications, pp 289–303
2. Matsumoto T, Matsumoto H, Yamada K, Hoshino S (2002) Impact of artificial gummy fingers on fingerprint systems. In: Proceedings of SPIE optical security and counterfeit deterrence techniques IV, vol 4677, pp 275–289
3. Thalheim L, Krissler J (2002) Body check: biometric access protection devices and their programs put to the test. c't magazine, pp 114–121
4. Derakhshani R, Schuckers S, Hornak L, O'Gorman L (2003) Determination of vitality from non-invasive biomedical measurement for use in fingerprint scanners. Pattern Recogn 36: 383–396
5. Antonelli A, Capelli R, Maio D, Maltoni D (2006) Fake finger detection by skin distortion analysis. IEEE Trans Inf Forensics Secur 1:360–373
6. Galbally J, Alonso-Fernandez F, Fierrez J, Ortega-Garcia J (2012) A high performance fingerprint liveness detection method based on quality related features. Future Gener Comput Syst 28:311–321
7. Franco A, Maltoni D (2008) Advances in biometrics: sensors, algorithms and systems, chap. fingerprint synthesis and spoof detection. Springer, London, pp 385–406

8. Li SZ (ed) (2009) Encyclopedia of biometrics. Springer, Berlin
9. Coli P (2008) Vitality detection in personal authentication systems using fingerprints. Ph.D. thesis, Universita di Cagliari
10. Sandstrom M (2004) Liveness detection in fingerprint recognition systems. Master's thesis, Linkoping University
11. Lane M, Lordan L (2005) Practical techniques for defeating biometric devices. Master's thesis, Dublin City University
12. Blomme J (2003) Evaluation of biometric security systems against artificial fingers. Master's thesis, Linkoping University
13. Lapsley P, Less J, Pare D, Hoffman N (1998) Anti-fraud biometric sensor that accurately detects blood flow, SmartTouch, LLC, US Patent #5,737,439
14. Setlak DR (1999) Fingerprint sensor having spoof reduction features and related methods, US Patent #5,953,441
15. Kallo I, Kiss A, Podmaniczky JT (2001) Detector for recognizing the living character of a finger in a fingerprint recognizing apparatus, Dermo Corporation, Ltd. U.S. Patent #6,175,64, Jan 16 2001
16. Diaz-Santana E, Parziale G (2006) Liveness detection method. Patent pending. EP06013258, 6
17. Kim J, Choi H, Lee W (2011) Spoof detection method for touchless fingerprint acquisition apparatus, Korea Patent, 0484664
18. Centro Criptologico Nacional (CCN) (2011) Characterizing attacks to fingerprint verification mechanisms CAFVM v3.0. Common Criteria Portal
19. Bundesamt fur Sicherheit in der Informationstechnik (BSI) (2008) Fingerprint spoof detection protection profile FSDPP v1.8. Common Criteria Portal
20. Marcialis GL, Lewicke A, Tan B, Coli P, Grimberg D, Congiu A, Tidu A, Roli F, Schuckers S (2009) First international fingerprint liveness detection competition—livdet 2009. In: Proceedings of IAPR international conference on image analysis and processing (ICIAP), LNCS, vol 5716. pp 12–23
21. Yambay D, Ghiani L, Denti P, Marcialis GL, Roli F, Schuckers S (2012) LivDet2011—fingerprint liveness detection competition 2011. In: 5th International Conference Biometrics (ICB)
22. Galbally J, Fierrez J, Alonso-Fernandez F, Martinez-Diaz M (2011) Evaluation of direct attacks to fingerprint verification systems. J Telecommun Syst, Spec Issue Biometrics Syst Appl 47:243–254
23. Abhyankar A, Schuckers S (2009) Integrating a wavelet based perspiration liveness check with fingerprint recognition. Pattern Recogn 42:452–464
24. Biometrics Institute (2011) Biometric Vulnerability Assessment Expert Group. http://www.biometricsinstitute.org/pages/biometric-vulnerability-assessment-expert-group-bvaeg.html
25. NPL (2010) National Physical Laboratory: biometrics. http://www.npl.co.uk/biometrics
26. CESG (2001) Communications-Electronics Security Group—Biometric Working Group (BWG). https://www.cesg.gov.uk/policyguidance/biometrics/Pages/index.aspx
27. BEAT (2012) BEAT: biometrices evaluation and testing. http://www.beat-eu.org/
28. Tabula Rasa (2010) Trusted biometrics under spoofing attacks (tabula rasa). (http://www.tabularasa-euproject.org/)
29. Maltoni D, Maio D, Jain A, Prabhakar S (2009) Handbook of fingerprint recognition. Springer, London
30. Cappelli R, Maio D, Lumini A, Maltoni D (2007) Fingerprint image reconstruction from standard templates. IEEE Trans Pattern Anal Mach Intell 29:1489–1503
31. Ross A, Shah J, Jain AK (2007) From template to image: reconstructing fingerprints from minutiae points. IEEE Trans Pattern Anal Mach Intell 29:544–560
32. Cappelli R (2009) Handbook of fingerprint recognition, chap. synthetic fingerprint generation. Springer, London, pp 270–302
33. Fen J, Jain A (2011) Fingerprint reconstruction: from minutiae to phase. IEEE Trans Pattern Anal Mach Intell 33:209–223

34. Wehde A, Beffel JN (1924) Fingerprints can be forged. Tremonia Publish Co, Chicago
35. de Water MV (1936) Can fingerprints be forged? Sci News Lett 29:90–92
36. Sengottuvelan P, Wahi A (2007) Analysis of living and dead finger impressions identification for biometric applications. In: Proceedings of international conference on computational intelligence and multimedia applications
37. Yoon S, Feng J, Jain AK (2012) Altered fingerprints: analysis and detection. IEEE Trans Pattern Anal Mach Intell 34:451–464
38. Willis D, Lee M (1998) Biometrics under our thumb. Network computing. Available on line at http://www.networkcomputing.com/
39. Sten A, Kaseva A, Virtanen T (2003) Fooling fingerprint scanners—biometric vulnerabilities of the precise biometrics 100 SC scanner. In: Proceedings of australian information warfare and it security conference
40. Wiehe A, Søndrol T, Olsen OK, Skarderud F (2004) Attacking fingerprint sensors. Gjøvik University College, 200
41. Galbally J, Cappelli R, Lumini A, de Rivera GG, Maltoni D, Fierrez J, Ortega-Garcia J, Maio D (2010) An evaluation of direct and indirect attacks using fake fingers generated from ISO templates. Pattern Recogn Lett 31:725–732 (To appear)
42. Barral C, Tria A (2009) Fake fingers in fingerprint recognition: glycerin supersedes gelatin. Formal to practical security, LNCS, vol 5458. Springer, Berlin, pp 57–69
43. Parthasaradhi S, Derakhshani R, Hornak L, Schuckers S (2005) Time-series detection of perspiration as a liveness test in fingerprint devices. IEEE Trans Syst Man Cybern Part C Appl Rev 35:335–343
44. Schuckers S, Abhyankar A (2004) A wavelet based approach to detecting liveness in fingerprint scanners. In: Proceedings of biometric authentication workshop (BioAW), LNCS, vol 5404. Springer, pp 278–386
45. Tan B, Schuckers S (2006) Comparison of ridge- and intensity-based perspiration liveness detection methods in fingerprint scanners. In: Proceedings of the SPIE biometric technology for human identification III (BTHI III), vol 6202, pp 62020A
46. Tan B, Schuckers S (2008) A new approach for liveness detection in fingerprint scanners based on valley noise analysis. J Electron Imaging 17:011009-1–011009-9
47. DeCann B, Tan B, Schuckers S (2009) A novel region based liveness detection approach for fingerprint scanners. In: Proceedings of IAPR/IEEE international conference on biometrices, LNCS, vol 5558. Springer, pp 627–636
48. NexIDBiometrics (2012). http://nexidbiometrics.com/
49. Abhyankar A, Schuckers S (2006) Fingerprint liveness detection using local ridge frequencies and multiresolution texture analysis techniques. In: Proceedings of IEEE international conference on image processing (ICIP)
50. Marasco E, Sansone C (2010) An anti-spoofing technique using multiple textural features in fingerprint scanners. In: Proceedings of IEEE workshop on biometric measurements and systems for security and medical applications (BIOMS), pp 8–14
51. Marasco E, Sansone C (2012) Combining perspiration- and morphology-based static features for fingerprint liveness detection. Pattern Recogn Lett 33:1148–1156
52. Cappelli R, Maio D, Maltoni D (2001) Modelling plastic distortion in fingerprint images. In: Proceedings of international conference on pattern recognition (ICAPR), LNCS, vol 2013. Springer, pp 369–376
53. Bazen AM, Gerez SH (2003) Fingerprint matching by thin-plate spline modelling of elastic deformations. Pattern Recogn 36:1859–1867
54. Chen Y, Dass S, Ross A, Jain AK (2005) Fingerprint deformation models using minutiae locations and orientations. In: Proceedings of IEEE workshop on applications of computer vision (WACV), pp 150–156
55. Chen Y, Jain AK (2005) Fingerprint deformation for spoof detection. In: Proceedings of IEEE biometric symposium (BSym), pp 19–21
56. Zhang Y, Tian J, Chen X, Yang X, Shi P (2007) Fake finger detection based on thin-plate spline distortion model. In: Proceedings of IAPR international conference on biometrics, LNCS, vol 4642. Springer, pp 742–749

57. Yau WY, Tran HT, Teoh EK, Wang JG (2007) Fake finger detection by finger color change analysis. In: Proceedings of international conference on biometrics (ICB), LNCS, vol 4642. Springer, pp 888–896
58. Jia J, Cai L (2007) Fake finger detection based on time-series fingerprint image analysis. In: Proceedings of IEEE international conference on intelligent computing (ICIC), LNCS, vol 4681. Springer, pp 1140–1150
59. Uchida K (2004) Image-based approach to fingerprint acceptability assessment. In: Proceedings of interenational conference on biometric authentication, LNCS, vol 3072. Springer, pp 194–300
60. Marcialis GL, Roli F, Tidu A (2010) Analysis of fingerprint pores for vitality detection. In: Proceedings of IEEE international conference on pattern recognition (ICPR), pp 1289–1292
61. Memon S, Manivannan N, Balachandran W (2011) Active pore detection for liveness in fingerprint identification system. In: Proceedings of IEEE telecommunications forum (TelFor), pp 619–622
62. Martinsen OG, Clausen S, Nysather JB, Grimmes S (2007) Utilizing characteristic electrical properties of the epidermal skin layers to detect fake fingers in biometric fingerprint systems-a pilot study. IEEE Trans Biomed Eng 54:891–894
63. Moon YS, Chen JS, Chan KC, So K, Woo KC (2005) Wavelet based fingerprint liveness detection. Electron Lett 41(20):1112–1113
64. Nikam SB, Agarwal S (2009) Feature fusion using Gabor filters and cooccrrence probabilities for fingerprint antispoofing. Int J Intell Syst Technol Appl 7:296–315
65. Nikam SB, Argawal S (2009) Ridgelet-based fake fingerprint detection. Neurocomputing 72:2491–2506
66. Nikam S, Argawal S (2010) Curvelet-based fingerprint anti-spoofing. SIViP 4:75–87
67. Coli P, Marcialis GL, Roli F (2007) Power spectrum-based fingerprint vitality detection. In: Proceedings of IEEE workshop on automatic identification advanced technologies (AutoID), pp 169–173
68. Jin C, Kim H, Elliott S (2007) Liveness detection of fingerprint based on band-selective Fourier spectrum. In: Proceedings of international conference on information security and cryptology (ICISC), LNCS, vol 4817. Springer, pp 168–179
69. Jin S, Bae Y, Maeng H, Lee H (2010) Fake fingerprint detection based on image analysis. In: Proceedings of SPIE 7536, sensors, cameras, and systems for industrial/scientific applications XI, pp 75360C
70. Lee H, Maeng H, Bae Y (2009) Fake finger detection using the fractional Fourier transform. In: Proceedings of biometric ID management and multimodal communication (BioID), LNCS, vol 5707. Springer, pp 318–324
71. Marcialis GL, Coli P, Roli F (2012) Fingerprint liveness detection based on fake finger characteristics. Int J Digit Crime Forensics 4(3):1–19
72. Coli P, Marcialis GL, Roli F (2007) Vitality detection from fingerprint images: A critical survey. In: Proceedings of international conference on biometrics (ICB), LNCS, vol 4642. Springer, pp. 722–731
73. Coli P, Marcialis GL (2008) Fingerprint silicon replicas: static and dynamic features for vitality detection using an optical capture device. Int J Image Graph 8(4):495–512
74. Marcialis GL, Coli P, Roli F (2012) Fingerprint liveness detection based on fake finger characteristics. Int J Digit Crime Forensics 4:1–19
75. Choi H, Kang R, Choi K, Jin ATB, Kim J (2009) Fake-fingerprint detection using multiple static features. Opt Eng 48:047202-1–047202-13
76. Nixon KA, Rowe RK (2005) Multispectral fingerprint imaging for spoof detection. In: Proceedings of SPIE 5779, biometric technology for human identification II (BTHI), pp 214–225
77. Rowe RK, Nixon KA, Butler PW (2008) Multispectral fingerprint image acquisition. In: Ratha NK, Govindaraju V (eds) Advances in biometrics: sensors, algorithms and systems, Springer, London, pp 3–23
78. Yau WY, Tran HL, Teoh EK (2008) Fake finger detection using an electrotactile display system. In: Proceedings of international conference on control, automation, robotics and vision (ICARCV), pp 17–20

79. Reddy PV, Kumar A, Rahman SM, Mundra TS (2008) A new antispoofing approach for biometric devices. IEEE Trans Biomed Circuits Syst 2:328–337
80. Baldiserra D, Franco A, Maio D, Maltoni D (2006) Fake fingerprint detection by odor analysis. In: Proceedings of IAPR international conference on biometrics (ICB), LNCS, vol 3832. Springer, pp 265–272
81. Cheng Y, Larin KV (2006) Artificial fingerprint recognition using optical coherence tomography with autocorrelation analysis. Appl Opt 45:9238–9245
82. Manapuram RK, Ghosn M, Larin KV (2006) Identification of artificial fingerprints using optical coherence tomography technique. Asian J Phys 15:15–27
83. Cheng Y, Larin KV (2007) In vivo two- and three-dimensional imaging of artificial and real fingerprints with optical coherence tomography. IEEE Photonics Technol Lett 19:1634–1636
84. Larin KV, Cheng Y (2008) Three-dimensional imaging of artificial fingerprint by optical coherence tomography. In: Proceedings of SPIE biometric technology for human identification (BTHI), vol 6944. pp 69440M
85. Chang S, Larin KV, Mao Y, Almuhtadi W, Flueraru C (2011) Fingerprint Spoof Detection Using Near Infrared Optical Analysis. In: Yang J, Nanni L (eds) State of the art in biometrics. Intechopen, Croatia, pp 57–84
86. Nasiri-Avanaki MR, Meadway A, Bradu A, Khoshki RM, Hojjatoleslami A, Podoleanu AG (2011) Anti-spoof reliable biometry of fingerprints using en-face optical coherence tomography. Opt Photonics J 1:91–96
87. Hariri M, Shokouhi SB (2011) Possibility of spoof attack against robustness of multibiometric authentication systems. SPIE J Opt Eng 50:079001
88. Akhtar Z, Fumera G, Marcialis GL, Roli F (2011) Robustness analysis of likelihood ratio score fusion rule for multi-modal biometric systems under spoof attacks. In: Proceedings of IEEE international carnahan conference on security technology (ICSST), pp 237–244
89. Marasco E, Johnson P, Sansone C, Schuckers S (2011) Increase the security of multibiometric systems by incorporating a spoofing detection algorithm in the fusion mechanism. In: Proceedings of multiple classifier systems (MCS), LNCS, vol 6713. Springer, pp 309–318
90. Marasco E, Ding Y, Ross A (2012) Combining match scores with liveness values in a fingerprint verification system. In: Proceedings of IEEE international conference on biometrics: theory, applications and systems (BTAS), pp 418–425
91. Rattani A, Poh N, Ross A (2012) Analysis of user-specific score characteristics for spoof biometric attacks. In: Proceedings of IEEE computer society workshop on biometrics at the international conference on computer vision and pattern recognition (CVPR), pp 124–129
92. Akhtar Z, Fumera G, Marcialis GL, Roli F (2012) Evaluation of serial and parallel multi-biometric systems under spoofing attacks. In: Proceedings of international conference on biometrics: theory, applications and systems (BTAS), pp 402–407
93. Ultra-Scan (2012). http://www.ultra-scan.com/
94. Optel (2012). http://www.optel.pl/
95. PosID (2012). http://www.posid.co.uk/
96. VirdiTech (2012). http://www.virditech.com/
97. Kang H, Lee B, Kim H, Shin D, Kim J (2003) A study on performance evaluation of the liveness detection for various fingerprint sensor modules. In: Proceedings of international conference on knowledge-based intelligent information and engineering systems (KES), LNAI, vol 2774. Springer, pp 1245–1253
98. Wang L, El-Maksoud RA, Sasian JM, William Kuhn P, Gee K (2009) V.S.V.: A novel contactless aliveness-testing fingerprint sensor. In: Proceedings of SPIE novel optical systems design and optimization XII, vol 7429. p. 742915
99. Bayram S, Avcibas I, Sankur B, Memon N (2006) Image manipulation detection. J Electron Imagingq 15(041):102
100. Stamm MC, Liu KJR (2010) Forensic detection of image manipulation using statistical intrinsic fingerprints. IEEE Trans Inf Forensics Secur 5:492–496
101. Avcibas I, Memon N, Sankur B (2003) Steganalysis using image quality metrics. IEEE Trans Image Process 12:221–229

102. Avcibas I, Kharrazi M, Memon N, Sankur B (2005) Image steganalysis with binary similarity measures. EURASIP J Appl Sig Process 1:2749–2757
103. Lyu S, Farid H (2006) Steganalysis using higher-order image statistics. IEEE Trans Inf Forensics Secur 1:111–119
104. Lim E, Jiang X, Yau W (2002) Fingerprint quality and validity analysis. In: Proceedings of IEEE international conference on image processing (ICIP), vol 1. pp 469–472
105. Chen Y, Dass S, Jain A (2005) Fingerprint quality indices for predicting authentication performance. In: Proceedings of IAPR audio- and video-based biometric person authentication (AVBPA), LNCS, vol 3546. Springer, pp 160–170
106. Chen T, Jiang X, Yau W (2004) Fingerprint image quality analysis. In: Proceedings of IEEE international conference on image processing (ICIP), vol 2. pp 1253–1256
107. Hong L, Wan Y, Jain AK (1998) Fingerprint image enhancement: algorithm and performance evaluation. IEEE Trans Pattern Anal Mach Intell 20(8):777–789
108. Alonso-Fernandez F, Fierrez J, Ortega-Garcia J, Gonzalez-Rodriguez J, Fronthaler H, Kollreider K, Bigun J (2008) A comparative study of fingerprint image quality estimation methods. IEEE Trans Inf Forensics Secur 2(4):734–743
109. Bigun J (2006) Vision with direction. Springer, Berlin
110. Shen L, Kot A, Koo W (2001) Quality measures of fingerprint images. In: Proceedings of IAPR audio- and video-based biometric person authentication (AVBPA), LNCS, vol 2091. Springer, pp 266–271
111. Wong PW, Pappas TN, Safranek RJ, Chen J, Wang Z, Bovik AC, Simoncelli EP, Sheikh HR (2005) Handbook of image and video processing, chap. Section VIII: image and video rendering and Assessment. Academic Press, Amsterdam, pp 925–989
112. Sheikh HRS, Sabir MF, Bovik AC (2006) A statistical evaluation of recent full reference image quality assessment algorithms. IEEE Trans Image Process 15:3440–3451
113. Saad MA, Bovik AC, Charrier C (2012) Blind image quality assessment: A natural scene statatistics approach in the DCT domain. IEEE Trans Image Process 21:3339–3352
114. Avcibas I, Sankur B, Sayood K (2002) Statistical evaluation of image quality measures. J Electron Imaging 11:206–223
115. Huynh-Thu Q, Ghanbari M (2008) Scope of validity of PSNR in image/video quality assessment. Electron Lett 44:800–801
116. Yao S, Lin W, Ong E, Lu Z (2005) Contrast signal-to-noise ratio for image quality assessment. In: Proceedings of international conference on image processing (ICIP), pp 397–400
117. Eskicioglu AM, Fisher PS (1995) Image quality measures and their performance. IEEE Trans Commun 43:2959–2965
118. Martini MG, Hewage CT, Villarini B (2012) Image quality assessment based on edge preservation. Sig Process: Image Commun 27:875–882
119. Nill NB, Bouzas B (1992) Objective image quality measure derived from digital image power spectra. Opt Eng 31:813–825
120. Liu A, Lin W, Narwaria M (2012) Image quality assessment based on gradient similarity. IEEE Trans Image Process 21:1500–1511
121. Wang Z, Bovik AC, Sheikh HR, Simoncelli EP (2004) Image quality assessment: from error visibility to structural similarity. IEEE Trans Image Process 13:600–612
122. LIVE: (2012). http://live.ece.utexas.edu/research/Quality/index.htm
123. Sheikh HR, Bovik AC (2006) Image information and visual quality. IEEE Trans Image Process 15:430–444
124. Soundararajan R, Bovik AC (2012) RRED indices: reduced reference entropic differencing for image quality assessment. IEEE Trans Image Process 21:517–526
125. Wang Z, Sheikh HR, Bovik AC (2002) No-reference perceptual quality assessment of JPEG compressed images. In: Proceedings of IEEE international conference on image processing (ICIP), pp 477–480
126. Zhu X, Milanfar P (2009) A no-reference sharpness metric sensitive to blur and noise. In: Proceedings of international workshop on quality of multimedia experience (QoMEx), pp 64–69

127. Moorthy AK, Bovik AC (2010) A two-step framework for constructing blind image quality indices. IEEE Sig Process Lett 17:513–516
128. Mittal A, Soundararajan R, Bovik AC (2012) Making a completely blind image quality analyzer. IEEE Sig Process Lett. doi:10.1109/LSP.2012.2227726
129. Wang Z, Bovik AC (2009) Mean squared error: love it or leave it? IEEE Sig Process Mag 26:98–117
130. Teo PC, Heeger DJ (1994) Perceptual image distortion. In: Proceedings of international conference on image processing, pp 982–986
131. Harris C, Stephens M (1988) A combined corner and edge detector. In: Proceedings of alvey vision conference (AVC), pp 147–151
132. Brunet D, Vrscay ER, Wang Z (2012) On the mathematical properties of the structural similarity index. IEEE Trans Image Process 21:1488–1499
133. Hastie T, Tibshirani R, Friedman J (2001) The elements of statistical learning. Springer, New York
134. Nixon KA, Aimale V, Rowe RK (2008) Handbook of biometrics, chap. spoof detection schemes. Springer, New York, pp 403–423

# Chapter 4
# Face Anti-spoofing: Visual Approach

**André Anjos, Jukka Komulainen, Sébastien Marcel, Abdenour Hadid and Matti Pietikäinen**

**Abstract** User authentication is an important step to protect information and in this regard face biometrics is advantageous. Face biometrics is natural, easy to use and less human-invasive. Unfortunately, recent work revealed that face biometrics is quite vulnerable to spoofing attacks. This chapter presents the different modalities of attacks to visual spectrum face recognition systems. We introduce public datasets for the evaluation of vulnerability of recognition systems and performance of countermeasures. Finally, we build a comprehensive view of antispoofing techniques for visual spectrum face recognition and provides an outlook of issues that remain unaddressed.

## 4.1 Introduction

Identity theft is a concern that prevents the mainstream adoption of biometrics as *de facto* form of identification in high-security commercial applications [1]. Contrary to password-protected systems, our biometric information is widely available and extremely easy to sample. It suffices a small search on the internet to unveil prelabeled samples from users at specialized websites such as Flickr or Facebook. Images can

---

A. Anjos (✉) · S. Marcel
Idiap Research Institute, rue Marconi 19, 1920 Martigny, Switzerland
e-mail: andre.anjos@idiap.ch

S. Marcel
e-mail: marcel@idiap.ch

J. Komulainen · A. Hadid · M. Pietikäinen
Center for Machine Vision Research (CMV), Department of Computer Science and Engineering (CSE), University of Oulu,
P.O. Box 4500, 90014 Oulu, Finland
e-mail: jukmaatt@ee.oulu.fi

A. Hadid
e-mail: hadid@ee.oulu.fi

M. Pietikäinen
e-mail: mkp@ee.oulu.fi

© Springer-Verlag London 2014
S. Marcel et al. (eds.), *Handbook of Biometric Anti-Spoofing*,
Advances in Computer Vision and Pattern Recognition,
DOI: 10.1007/978-1-4471-6524-8_4

also be easily captured at distance without prior consent. Users may not trust that their biometric samples will not be dishonestly used.

It has been suggested in the past that multimodal biometrics systems can be used to increase authentication performance in higher security environments [2]. However, it has been recently shown [3] that multimodal systems, when naively tuned, can be intrinsically less secure than unimodal ones. This suggests each biometric modality needs to be protected by its own specialized countermeasures. In this chapter, we are particularly concerned with direct or presentation attacks [4] to unimodal 2D (visual spectra) face recognition systems. These so-called *spoofs* [5] are attacks to the input sensors of the biometric system. In this case, attackers are assumed not to have access to the internals of the recognition system and manage to penetrate by only displaying biometric samples of the attacked clients to the input device. This type of attack is, therefore, very easy to reproduce and has great potential to succeed [6].

Face recognition systems, in particular, are known to respond weakly to presentation attacks for a long time [6–8] and are easily spoofed using one of three categories of counterfeits [9]: (1) a photograph; (2) a video or (3) a 3D model of the enrolled person's face. While humans seem quite apt in identifying counterfeits, the same does not seem to hold for face verification systems. Antispoofing for this biometric mode should therefore be treated with priority before face recognition systems can be adopted as replacement for user credentials in unsupervised deployments.

The rest of this chapter is organized as follows: Sect. 4.2 describes face recognition systems and attack types. Section 4.3 introduces available public databases for face antispoofing as well as for assessing robustness of face verification systems. Section 4.4 discusses the state of the art in antispoofing for face recognition. Finally, concluding remarks are drawn in Sect. 4.5.

## 4.2 Attacks to Face Recognition Systems

Attacks to biometric systems can be divided into two types: indirect and direct [10]. Figure 4.1 depicts a flow diagram of a typical biometric recognition system, indicating numbered points where possible attacks can occur. Indirect attacks are performed

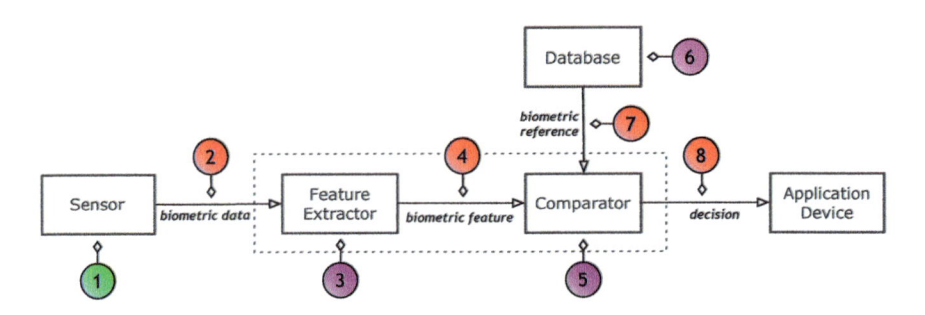

**Fig. 4.1** Possible attack points in a generic biometric system (from [10])

from *within* the recognition system, requiring first that intruders gain access to the internals of such a system. Once inside, indirect attackers can, for example, tamper feature extractors or comparators (types 3 and 5 in Fig. 4.1), manipulate biometric references (type 6) or exploit possible weak points in communication channels (types 2, 4, 7 and 8). Indirect attacks can be dealt with by increasing the security of communication channels and by sealing off the access to the internals of recognition systems so that cyber-criminals cannot leverage from those.

Direct, presentation or *spoofing* attacks [5], are performed at the sensor level (shown as attack type 1 in Fig. 4.1) which is outside the control of the biometric system manufacturer. In such cases, the attacker tries to directly fool the sensor and thus no physical protection mechanisms can be used. In a direct attack, also called *presentation* attack, a person tries to masquerade as another individual by falsifying their biometric characteristic and thereby gaining an illegitimate advantage.

Face recognition systems use conventional image cameras as input sensors. These devices may be used to capture single, multiple photos, or video sequences of users trying to gain access to the protected resources. Figure 4.2 shows an ideal static setup for a face authentication system. In these settings, the camera is embedded into a laptop that is programmed with the face recognition system. Users position themselves such that the camera can capture the face for as long as as the system deems necessary. One important aspect during the recognition process concerns the environmental conditions during data acquisition. It is a well-known fact that poor illumination conditions, pose, and aging among other variations can deteriorate substantially the capacity to recognize individuals [11].

In more modern setups, such as the one represented on Fig. 4.3, users maybe using a mobile phone for accessing protected resources on the phone itself, or as a terminal for other applications. Mobile devices can also be used for identifying other people in applications in forensics or surveillance. In such cases, the environmental acquisition conditions can vary greatly [12]. Presentation attacks further augment

**Fig. 4.2** Example setup of a face recognition system

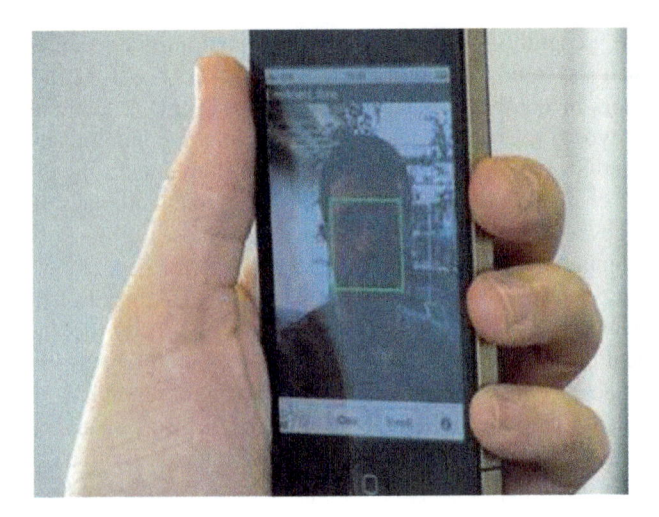

**Fig. 4.3** Using a mobile phone as sensor and system for face recognition

the acquisition variability by introducing at least four more sources of information which we describe next.

## 4.2.1 Attack Inventory

It is possible to spoof face recognition systems by presenting photographs, videos or three-dimensional shaped masks (see Fig. 4.4) of targeted identities [9] to the input camera. While one can also use make-up or even plastic surgery as other means of spoofing, photographs, and videos are probably the most common sources of spoofing attacks because one can easily download or simply capture them without prior user consent. Possibly for this reason, most prior work focuses on these types of attacks.

Four new elements compose the settings of spoofing attempts to face recognition system (Fig. 4.4): (1) the attacker, which is the person trying to impersonate the identity of another client in the system; (2) the sensor used in the acquisition and quality for the client sample being used for the attack; (3) the media used to display the sample; and finally (4) the support used for the attack. An example spoofing attack is shown in Fig. 4.4a. In this example, the attacker uses his own hands to support the fake sample. Figure 4.4b shows another attempt in which the attacker wears a three-dimensional mask of the user being attacked.

### 4.2.1.1 Photo Attacks

A photo-attack consists of displaying a photograph of the attacked identity to the input camera of the face recognition system. Recent work by private security firms

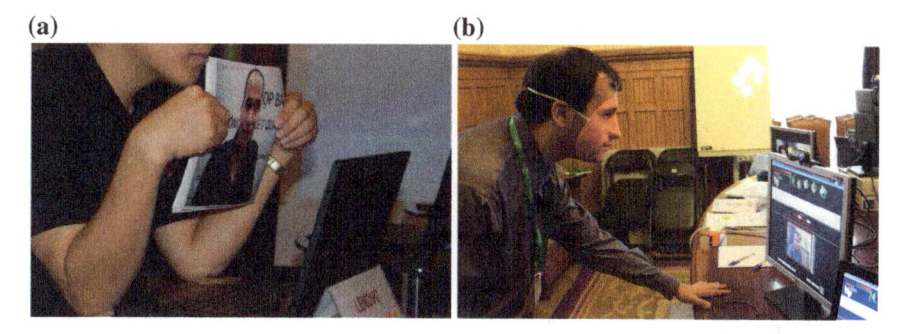

**Fig. 4.4** Example attack scenarios. **a** Hard copy print attack. **b** Mask attack

[6] indicates that many available commercial systems are vulnerable to this kind of attack.

It can be relatively easy to either obtain photos of a valid user through internet searching or by capturing them using a concealed/hidden camera. Once a photo is obtained, one can print it and then present it in front of the camera. An electronic screen (such as a those on modern tablet computers) could also be used to present the photograph to the input camera of the biometric system. Because of the immediate availability and accessibility of all technology required to perform this attack, it should be considered with priority in the context of 2D face recognition systems.

#### 4.2.1.2 Video Attacks

Video attacks represent the second most important threat to 2D face recognition systems simply because they potentialize the probability of success by introducing apparent vitality to the displayed fake biometric. It is intuitive to assume that systems that offer little resistance to photo attacks will present further performance degradation on the presence video attacks. The acquisition of client samples is also becoming increasingly easier with the advent of public video sharing sites and matching reduction of high-quality camera prices. Furthermore, technology commonly deployed on animation software, for modeling fictional characters, could also be subverted into producing realistic looking fake biometric samples, that would still exhibit liveness characteristics.

#### 4.2.1.3 Mask Attacks

Mask attacks require more skills to be well executed and possibly access to extra material as an approximate 3D prototype of the face needs to be constructed. It is the third type of attack conceivable to 2D face recognition systems, but may be more likely to succeed because countermeasures may not be able to explore anymore deformation patterns available on the previously described attacks. Modestly accurate 3D masks can be cheaply manufactured from just two photographs of a person's head: frontal and profile, in websites like http://www.thatsmyface.com/.

Masks that trick 2D face recognition systems may also be manufactured using 2D prints on malleable materials such as cotton tissue available on T-shirts. Once printed, a potential attacker can wear the tissue around its own face, trying to mitigate 2D print effects present on photo and video attacks.

## 4.3 Databases

The first public dataset for studying antispoofing in face recognition appeared in 2010, accompanying the work of Tan and others in [13]. In this work, the authors explore the Lambertian reflectance model to derive differences between the 2D images of the face presented during an attack and a real (3D) face, in real-access attempts. Following the trend of similar past work [14, 15], the authors focus on the binary classification task of face spoofing detection considering pictures of real-accesses and attacks recorded with a conventional webcam. Antispoofing methods that deal with texture analysis (see Sect. 4.4), can use the NUAA Photo Imposter Database to compare results with values published on the original work.

As demonstrated in work by Anjos and others [16, 17], techniques for antispoofing can also exploit motion artifacts present in attacks to discriminate spoofing attempts. In [16], the authors made available a public dataset composed of printed photograph attacks and real-accesses, in which the samples available for the training and evaluating spoofing classifiers are videos. The PRINT-ATTACK database can be used to devise antispoofing methods based on texture or motion or fusion of these techniques [18]. An extension of this database, called the PHOTO-ATTACK database, providing photo attacks using different attack media such as mobile phones and tablets was introduced in [17]. Another extension called REPLAY-ATTACK database, also bringing video attacks using mobile phones and tablets was introduced in [19]. More recently, [20] showed how it is possible to use the later for verifying the resilience of verification systems when exposed to spoofing, as well as how to jointly perform the evaluation of antispoofing and verification systems (see Sect. 9.5) In order to provide such a support, antispoofing databases must implement an authentication protocol with which verification systems can be tested.

Zhang and others in [21] also created a public dataset for face antispoofing containing challenging short sequenced videos of attacks to 50 different identities using printed photographs and videos displayed through a tablet screen. The photo attacks in this database may suffer warping, emulating attackers trying to promote a livenesslook to spoofs. Because this database is also composed of videos, techniques using motion, texture, or fused systems may be trained and evaluated on it.

The first public dataset for 2D face antispoofing to contain 3D mask attacks is that of Erdogmus and Marcel [22]. This database contains data for 17 individuals with both real-access attempts and colored, hard resin composite, eye-pearced mask attacks. Data was collected using both camera modules (depth and visual spectra) of a Kinect for Xbox 360, potentially allowing for a multimodality antispoofing classifier. The 2D visual spectrum face data is composed of short color video sequences of about 10 s.

More detailed information on face antispoofing databases publicly available can be found on Sect. 13.3. Specifically in Appendix A.3, the reader will find details about acquisition, usage protocols as well as a cross-comparison of characteristics between the different sets available.

## 4.4 Methods

Without antispoofing measures most of the state-of-the-art facial biometric systems are basically vulnerable to attacks, since they try to maximize the discrimination between identities, instead of determining whether the presented trait originates from a living legitimate client. Because of the urgent need for enhancing the security and robustness face biometrics, a variety of spoofing detection schemes have been proposed to tackle the problem of presentation attacks. While multimodal analysis [23–25] and multispectral imaging [26–28] provide efficient means for discriminating real faces from fake ones, spoofing detection can be performed also based on the same data that is used for the actual face recognition process.

The following overview of software based spoofing detection schemes concentrates mainly on nonintrusive techniques that can be divided into four categories based on the inspected visual cues: presence of vitality (liveness), motion, facial appearance and context. Also challenge-response approaches are introduced, since random user interaction demand provides an important liveness cue in addition to visual ones.

### 4.4.1 Liveness Detection

Typical countermeasure to spoofing is liveness detection that aims at detecting physiological signs of life, such as eye blinking, facial expression changes and mouth movements. For instance, Pan et al. [9] exploited the observation that humans blink once every 2–4 s and proposed an eye blink-based antispoofing method which uses conditional random field (CRF) framework to model and detect eye blinking. The authors provided also a publicly available data set that contains short video clips of eye blinks and vivid spoofing attacks using photographs. Obviously, such techniques can only be considered with photographs while nowadays videos are ubiquitous and can also be easily used for spoofing attacks.

To provide more evidence of liveness, Eulerian motion magnification [29] has been applied for to enhancing subtle changes in the face region [20, 30] that may not be otherwise observed without a closer inspection. Within the context of the second competition on countermeasures to 2D facial spoofing attacks [18], one team presented a technique for magnifying the small color and motion changes that appear on the face due to the natural human blood flow, thus the algorithm amplifies a set of frequencies within the range of human pulse. The method was able to achieve satisfying performance of 9.13 % in terms of Half-Total Error Rate (HTER) on the competition dataset. Bharadwaj et al. [30] used Eulerian motion magnification as a preprocessing stage for exaggerating macro and micro facial expressions in the input video. Moreover, inspired by the use of optical flow in micro expression detection, histogram of oriented optical flow (HOOF) features [31] were considered for describing observed facial motion patterns. Very impressive results were reported on the Print-Attack and Replay-Attack Databases (0.00 % and 1.25 % in terms of HTER, respectively). However, the algorithm needs to be improved in order to increase its performance in more challenging and adversarial acquisition conditions.

### 4.4.2 Motion Analysis

In addition to facial motion used in liveness detection, also other motion cues can be exploited for face antispoofing. For example, it can be assumed that the movement of planar objects, e.g., video displays and photographs, differs significantly from real human faces which are complex nonrigid 3D objects. Kollreider et al. [32] presented an optical flow-based method to capture and track the subtle relative movements between different facial parts, assuming that facial parts in real faces move differently than on photographs. The method was able to achieve an equal error rate (EER) of 0.5 % on a private data set consisting of real client accesses from XM2VTS database and hard copy attacks from the corresponding live samples. In [33], the same authors propose a method for fusing scores from multiple experts to combine the results of 3D face motion analysis and liveness detection, e.g., eyeblink detection and mouth movement analysis. However, the experiments were conducted on short image sequences which were not made publicly available and no specific error rates were reported.

In another work [34], Bao et al. also used optical flow for motion estimation for detecting attacks produced with planar media such as prints or screens. The movement of planar objects is categorized as translation, rotation, normal, or swing and the eight quantities extracted from the cropped face are used to express the amount of these movements. The eight values are then given to an ad-hoc equation that outputs the probability of a spoofing attack. Experiments on a private database showed a 6 % false-alarm against about 14 % false acceptance.

If a face spoof is not tightly cropped around the targeted face or it has an incorporated background scene, scenic fake face (see Fig. A.10), it should be possible to observe high correlation between the overall motion of the face and the background regions for stationary face recognition systems. Anjos and Marcel [16] proposed a straightforward motion-based antispoofing technique to measure the overall motion correlation between the face and the background regions through simple frame differences. A performance of 9 % in terms of HTER was reported using the publicly available Print-Attack Database [16], thus the motion correlation analysis-based technique is efficient for measuring synchronized shaking of handheld attacks within the scene. However, a drawback is that it can get confused between a fixed support photo-attack and a motionless person while being recognized [16].

### 4.4.3 Facial Reflectance and Texture Properties

The main problem of motion analysis and liveness detection-based antispoofing techniques is that the verification process takes some time or the user needs to be very cooperative. Even though motion is an important visual cue, vitality and nonrigid motion detectors relying only on spontaneous facial movements are powerless under video-replay attacks and the lack of motion may lead to high number of authentication failures if user cooperation demand is not deployed. Another category of antispoofing techniques is based on the analysis of facial appearance properties, such as reflectance and texture, assuming that the disparities between genuine faces and artificial material can be observed in single visual spectra images. Intuitively, the main advantage of single image-based spoofing detection schemes is that they treat video playback attacks as if they were photo attacks, since individual video frames are considered [15].

Li et al. [14] described a method for detecting print-attack face spoofing. The method is based on the analysis of 2D Fourier spectrum, assuming that photographs are usually smaller in size and they would contain fewer high-frequency components compared to real faces. Such an approach may work well for down-sampled photos but is likely to fail for higher-quality images. The database used in the experiments is unfortunately not publicly available.

In a more recent work, Tan et al. [13] considered the Lambertian reflectance to discriminate between the 2D images of face prints and 3D live faces. The method extracts latent reflectance features using either a variational retinex-based method or much simpler difference-of-Gaussians (DoG)-based approach. The features are then fed to different types of classifiers. The idea behind DoG filters is that their bandpass behavior is able to exclude the low frequency information and the very high frequencies (noise), and to keep the "middle" frequency information which is valuable for spoofing detection. The authors reported promising results of area under ROC curve (AUC) from 0.69 to 0.95 on the publicly available NUAA Photograph Imposter Database composed of real-accesses and attacks to 15 subjects using both photo-quality and laser-quality prints of different sizes.

Zhang et al. [21] modified the method of Tan et al. [13] by introducing multiple DoG filters because they suggested that there is no prior knowledge which frequency component is the most discriminative. Thus, they used the concatenated filtered images and an SVM classifier to conduct more experiments on a new publicly available CASIA Face Antispoofing database containing more versatile set of spoofing attacks including cut-photo and video-replay attacks with three different imaging qualities. They noticed that the DoG filter-based method is able to detect well the similar sharp edges in eye regions of cut-photo attacks which make the spoofing attack samples less variational. On the other hand, the performance was very low under video-replay attacks and when high imaging quality was used. Thus, they claim that it may not be always a good idea to pursue high quality in imaging.

Alternatively, it is likely that real faces and fake ones present different texture patterns because of facial texture quality degradation due to recapturing process and disparities in surface and reflectance properties. Bai et al. [15] used microtextures extracted from the specularity component of a recaptured image and a linear SVM classifier to detect printed photo based spoofing attacks. The authors report a 2.2 % false acceptance rate (FAR) against a 13 % false rejection rate (FRR) but also the dataset for this experiment was not made public. The used features try to estimate how smooth the surface of the client face is, i.e., smoother face texture is more likely to come from a printed attacks because the reflection from a natural face tends to be more diffuse. The major drawback of this method is that it requires high resolution input images in order to discriminate the fine microtexture of the used display medium.

Määttä et al. [35] and Chingovska et al. [19] addressed this issue by exploring the structure of facial microtextures using local binary patterns (LBP) [36] on conventional webcam-quality images. Evaluations carried out with three different databases: the NUAA Photograph Impostor Database, Replay Attack Database, and CASIA Face Antispoofing Database showed moderate results with HTER equal to 19.03, 15.16, and 18.17 %, respectively. Furthermore, Kose and Dugelay [37] experimented the performance of the LBP-based countermeasure under mask attacks and satisfactory results were reported of AUC of 0.95 and classification accuracy of 88.1 %.

Recently, Pereira et al. [38] extended the microtexture analysis-based spoofing detection into spatiotemporal domain. In addition to analyzing the structure of facial microtextures, local binary patterns from three orthogonal planes (LBP-TOP) [39] were applied for describing specific dynamic events, e.g., facial motion, shaking, and sudden characteristic reflections of planar display media, which might differentiate real faces from fake ones. Similar visual cue was considered in the work by Pinto et al. [40] as the dynamic artifacts of display devices were exploited for detecting video-replay attacks. More specifically, visual rhythms were computed from the Fourier spectrum of the extracted video noise signatures and the resulting textural information was compressed with gray level co-occurrence matrices (GLCM).

The major drawback of texture analysis-based spoofing detection is that rather high resolution input images are required in order to extract the fine details needed for discriminating genuine faces from spoofing media. While lower imaging quality might be enough for detecting the most crude attack attempts, such as small mobile phone displays and prints with strong artifacts, the grid structure of a display device, or facial pores can be captured only in high-definition close-up images. On the other hand, also high false rejection rate might be an issue if acquisition quality is not good enough. Furthermore, the nature of texture patterns varies a lot due to different acquisition conditions, cameras, and display media as demonstrated in [41]. Thus diverse datasets are needed for training the microtexture-based methods, especially at conventional webcam image quality.

Another interesting approach was introduced in [42] by Gao et al. within single-view recaptured image detection. It is a more general concept of recognizing images of natural scenes and the recaptured natural-scene images, thus could be used for more general object recognition and scene understanding (e.g., in robotics) in addition to spoofing detection. They proposed a general physical model for describing the recapturing process and used a set of physical features and contextual background information from single-view images to discriminate the recaptured images from real scenes. The physics-based features consist of the spatial distribution of specularity that is related to the surface geometry, the image gradient that captures nonlinearity of the recaptured image rendering process, and color, contrast and blurriness properties that describe the quality of the reproduction. The proposed approach outperformed a wavelet-based method described in [43] and a publicly available data set was also released for evaluating methods for recaptured image detection on mobile devices.

### 4.4.4 Contextual Information

Face images captured from face spoofs may visually look very similar to the images captured from live faces, thus face spoofing detection is rather difficult to perform based on only single face image or a relatively short video sequence. Depending on the imaging and fake face quality, even for humans like us it is nearly impossible to tell the difference between a genuine face and a fake one without any scene information or unnatural motion or facial texture patterns. However, we can immediately notice if there is something suspicious going on in the view, e.g., if someone is holding a video display or a photograph in front of the camera. Therefore, scenic cues can be exploited for determining whether display medium is present in the observed scene.

In order to make eyeblink-based liveness detection more robust to video-replay attacks, Pan et al. [44] included scene context matching for checking if the background scene of the stationary face recognition system suddenly changes. Some carefully chosen fiducial points outside the face region are used to describe the expected background scene. The scores of the eye blink and scene context detector components are then fused together and the new setup obtained 0.5 % false acceptance against 0 % false rejection on a new private data set.

Komulainen et al. [45] considered scene information for detecting whether someone is presenting a fake face on a display medium in front of the camera by checking if the boundaries of the spoofing medium, e.g., video screen frame or photograph edges, or the attackers hands are visible in the provided view. Moreover, the authors assumed that a fake face might not be well aligned with the upper half of the torso of the imposter when a natural upper-body profile cannot be observed. Histogram of oriented gradients (HOG) descriptors [46] were used for describing distinctive discontinuities around the detected face and determining whether natural upper-body profile or the boundaries of the spoofing medium is detected in the scene. The experiments the CASIA Face Antispoofing Database and NUAA Photograph Impostor Database showed that contextual information is indeed a very important visual cue for face spoofing detection.

### 4.4.5 Fusion of Countermeasures

Indeed, many visual cues for nonintrusive spoofing detection have been already explored and impressive results have been reported on individual databases. However, the varying nature of spoofing attacks and acquisition conditions makes it impossible to predict how single antispoofing techniques, e.g., facial texture analysis, can generalize the problem in real-world applications. Moreover, we cannot foresee all possible attack scenarios and cover them in databases because the imagination of the human mind always finds out new tricks to fool existing systems. It is reasonable to assume that no single superior technique is able to detect all known, let alone unseen, spoofing attacks. Therefore, the problem of spoofing attacks should be broken down into attack-specific subproblems that are solvable if a proper combination of complementary countermeasures is used. In this manner, a network of attack-specific spoofing detectors could be used to construct a flexible antispoofing framework in which new techniques can be easily integrated to patch the existing vulnerabilities in no time when new countermeasures appear.

Fusion of different antispoofing techniques has not been studied much besides the algorithms [47–49] proposed within the context of the IJCB 2011 competition on countermeasures to 2D facial spoofing attacks [18]. Tronci et al. [48] and Schwartz et al. [47] were able to obtain impressive performance using motion and texture information but at the cost of complexity. In [48], several visual features and support vector machines (SVM) were utilized for detecting print-attacks, whereas in [47] temporal information from videos was accumulated by concatenating descriptions of individual frames which results in very high-dimensional feature vectors. Conversely, Yan et al. [49] wanted to achieve better generalization capabilities and proposed novel liveness clues with clear semantic definitions in order to avoid just extracting specific feature and training a "black box" classifier. However, the algorithm utilized mainly two uncorrelated motion cues, nonrigid motion and face-background consistency analysis, while the only spatial cue, banding analysis, was discarded unless uniform background was observed, since both face and background regions were used for image quality assessment.

In [50], the fusion of simple motion- and texture-based techniques was studied under several types of scenic fake face attacks (see Fig. A.10). The authors provided an intuitive way to explore the fusion potential of different visual cues using mutual error analysis and showed that the moderate performance of the individual methods can be vastly improved by performing fusion at score level. The HTER of the best individual countermeasure was decreased from 11.2 to 5.1 % on the Replay Attack Database. The idea of using complex classification schemes in individual countermeasures was questioned, since the complementarity of the antispoofing techniques was shown to be somewhat independent of the complexity of the classification schemes and nearly same fusion performance was obtained by replacing them with a simple linear one. Thus, suggesting that the use of simple and computationally efficient classifiers should be indeed considered when constructing real-world antispoofing solutions.

## 4.4.6 Challenge-Response Approach

Liveness and motion analysis-based spoofing detection is rather difficult to perform by observing only spontaneous facial motion during short video sequences but the amount of distinctive motion can be increased with user cooperation demand. More importantly, user collaboration itself can be used for revealing spoofing attacks because we humans tend to be interactive whereas a photo or video-replay attack cannot respond to specific (random) action requirements. In particular, a face authentication system prompts a specific action request to the user (challenge), such as a facial expression [25, 51], mouth movement [23, 25] or head rotation [41, 52, 53], and then analyses the user activity in order to check whether the required action was actually performed (response).

While spontaneous nonrigid facial motion is likely to occur during a relatively short authentication process, usually only small head pose changes can be observed. Therefore, challenge-response approach is particularly useful when head pose [52] or 3D structure estimation [41, 53] is utilized for spoofing detection. In [52], photo and video-replay attacks were avoided by giving the user a random head pose as a challenge and tracking the head pose in real time using 3D model and suitable facial feature points. De Marsico et al. [53] reduced the system complexity by measuring the three-dimensionality using projective invariants. Instead of tracking the exact 3D head pose changes, the user can move more freely as long as minimum continuous motion requirement is met, thus the making the authentication process more comfortable. Furthermore, the movement challenge at random intervals and expected response time are assumed to be sufficient to avoid video-replay attacks. Wang et al. [41] presented an approach for measuring three-dimensionality of the face without continuous motion requirement by recovering sparse 3D facial structure from two or more images (or video) captured from different viewpoints. In [51], the user is prompted to perform random sequence of facial expressions. Assuming that the consecutive frames in videos of valid users contain smooth and gradual changes, the presence of tampered or stitched video or image sequences is detected by observing image properties for abrupt changes. More specifically, SIFT flow energy [54] between consecutive frames is computed because the videos with sudden changes typically result in high SIFT flow energy.

The drawback of challenge-response approach is that it requires user cooperation, thus making the authentication process a time-consuming and unpleasant experience. Another advantage of nonintrusive techniques is that from challenge-response based countermeasures it is rather easy to deduce which liveness cues need to be fooled.

For instance, the request for uttering words suggests that analysis of synchronized lip movement and lip reading is utilized, whereas rotating head in a certain direction reveals that the 3D geometry of the head is measured. For nonintrusive approaches, it is usually not known which countermeasures are used, thus the system might be harder to deceive [44].

### 4.4.7 Discussion

The vulnerabilities to spoofing attacks have received more attention and the number of proposed countermeasures is growing steadily. Still, the field of visual face antispoofing is rather immature and there exists no consensus on the best nonintrusive spoofing detection practices. The current publicly available face spoofing databases are beginning to cover a variety of spoofing attacks from high-quality photo attacks to video-replay attacks and impressive results have been reported on individual datasets. However, due to the lack of variation in the collected data, e.g., acquisition conditions and used cameras, it is impossible to determine whether the existing countermeasures can generalize the problem beyond databases.

Since mobile applications represent one of the most probable use cases for face biometrics, device independence is an important property when transferring the developed countermeasures into practice. Currently, challenge-response based methods, especially the ones measuring three-dimensionality of the face [41, 53], seem to be the only imaging device independent approach for detecting photo attacks, whereas for instance facial texture-based algorithms are drastically affected by the varying imaging quality of different cameras [41], let alone the properties of different spoofing media and precaptured targeted face. However, if no specific motion type is requested, the techniques analyzing 3D facial structure are likely to fail under prerecorded video attacks, not to mention animated faces or masks.

On the other hand, the research community has just begun to focus on the problem of presentation attacks and the current publicly available databases have been a very important kick-off for finding out best practices for spoofing detection. The excellent results on simple datasets indicate that more challenging configurations are needed before the visual face antispoofing can reach the next level. In future, more work should be carried out for designing and collecting new databases that contain meaningful number of nonredundant data and a proper evaluation protocol which provides an unbiased comparison between different approaches and their fusion. Databases are a critical component when developing new nonintrusive spoofing detection schemes and evaluating not only their performance but especially their generalization capabilities. The publicly available datasets inevitably affect the antispoofing research trends and might mislead the research focus in wrong direction.

## 4.5 Conclusion

Among tangible threats and vulnerabilities facing current face recognition systems are spoofing (i.e., direct) attacks. One indeed can spoof a face recognition system by presenting to the input camera a photograph, a video or a three-dimensional shaped mask of a targeted identity. An increasing attention has recently been given to this research problem (i.e., face spoofing attacks). This can be attested by the growing number of articles and the various competitions that started to appear in major biometric forums. In this chapter, we revealed the face spoofing threats, presented the evolution of the available databases and protocols for evaluating face spoofing and antispoofing based on visual information, and thoroughly discussed the different approaches which have been proposed in the literature so far. Some open issues and future directions have also been discussed.

Without spoofing countermeasures, most of the state-of-the-art facial biometric systems are vulnerable to attacks, since they try to maximize the discriminability between identities without regards to whether the presented trait originates from a living legitimate client or not. The proposed antispoofing methods in the literature have shown very encouraging results on individual databases but may lack generalization to varying nature of spoofing attacks that can be encountered in real-world applications. This suggests that a network of attack-specific spoofing detectors maybe needed to tackle different spoofing attacks. The existing databases for spoofing and antispoofing analysis have been and are still useful for studying the spoofing problems but one cannot foresee all possible attack scenarios and cover them in databases. As the field evolves, new and more challenging databases can be expected. The imagination of the human mind always finds out new tricks to fool existing biometric systems.

**Acknowledgments** The authors would like to thank the Swiss Innovation Agency (CTI Project Replay) and the TABULA RASA project (http://www.tabularasa-euproject.org) funded under the 7th Framework Programme of the European Union (EU) (grant agreement number 257289) for their financial support.

## References

1. Schuckers SAC (2002) Spoofing and anti-spoofing measures. Information Security Technical Report 7:56–62
2. Sun, T., Li, Q., Qiu, Z.: Advances in Biometric Person Authentication, chap. A Secure Multimodal Biomeric Verification Scheme, pp. 233–240. Springer (2005).
3. Rodrigues, R.N., Ling, L.L., Govindaraju, V.: Robustness of multimodal biometric fusion methods against spoof attacks. Journal of Visual Language and Computing (2009).
4. Galbally J, McCool C, Fierrez J, Marcel S, Ortega-Garcia J (2010) On the vulnerability of face verification systems to hill-climbing attacks. Pattern Recognition 43(3):1027–1038
5. Jain, A.K., Flynn, P., Ross, A.A. (eds.): Handbook of Biometrics. Springer-Verlag (2008).
6. Duc, N.M., Minh, B.Q.: Your face is not your password. In: Black Hat Conference (2009).

7. Thalheim, L., Krissler, J., Ziegler, P.M.: Body check: Biometric access protection devices and their programs put to the test. Heise Online (2002).
8. Toth, B.: Biometric id card debates. Newsletter Biometrie (2005).
9. Pan, G., Wu, Z., Sun, L.: Liveness detection for face recognition. Recent Advances in Face Recognition pp. 109–124 (2008).
10. Ratha, N.K., Connell, J.H., Bolle, R.M.: An analysis of minutiae matching strength. In: Proceedings of the International Conference on Audio- and Video-Based Biometric Person Authentication (AVBPA), pp. 223–228. Springer-Verlag (2001).
11. Li, S.Z., Jain, A.K. (eds.): Handbook of Face Recognition. Springer-Verlag (2011).
12. McCool, C., Marcel, S., Hadid, A., Pietikainen, M., Matejka, P., Cernocky, J., Poh, N., Kittler, J., Larcher, A., Levy, C., Matrouf, D., Bonastre, J.F., Tresadern, P., Cootes, T.: Bi-modal person recognition on a mobile phone: using mobile phone data. In: IEEE ICME Workshop on Hot Topics in Mobile Multimedia (2012).
13. Tan, X., Li, Y., Liu, J., Jiang, L.: Face liveness detection from a single image with sparse low rank bilinear discriminative model. In: Proceedings of the 11th European conference on Computer vision: Part VI, ECCV'10, pp. 504–517 (2010).
14. Li, J., Wang, Y., Tan, T., Jain, A.K.: Live face detection based on the analysis of fourier spectra. In. In Biometric Technology for Human Identification, pp. 296–303 (2004).
15. Bai, J., Ng, T.T., Gao, X., Shi, Y.Q.: Is physics-based liveness detection truly possible with a single image? In: IEEE International Symposium on Circuits and Systems (ISCAS), pp. 3425–3428 (2010).
16. Anjos, A., Marcel, S.: Counter-measures to photo attacks in face recognition: a public database and a baseline. In: Proceedings of IAPR IEEE International Joint Conference on Biometrics (IJCB), Washington DC, USA (2011).
17. Anjos, A., Chakka, M.M., Marcel, S.: Motion-based counter-measures to photo attacks in face recognition (2013).
18. Chakka, M.M., Anjos, A., Marcel, S., Tronci, R., Muntoni, D., Fadda, G., Pili, M., Sirena, N., Murgia, G., Ristori, M., Roli, F., Yan, J., Yi, D., Lei, Z., Zhang, Z., Z.Li, S., Schwartz, W.R., Rocha, A., Pedrini, H., Lorenzo-Navarro, J., Castrillón-Santana, M., Määttä, J., Hadid, A., Pietikäinen, M.: Competition on counter measures to 2-d facial spoofing attacks. In: Proceedings of IAPR IEEE International Joint Conference on Biometrics (IJCB), Washington DC, USA (2011).
19. Chingovska, I., Anjos, A., Marcel, S.: On the effectiveness of local binary patterns in face anti-spoofing. In: IEEE BIOSIG 2012 (2012).
20. Chingovska, I., Anjos, A., Marcel, S.: Anti-spoofing in action: joint operation with a verification system. In: Proceedings of IEEE Conference on Computer Vision and Pattern Recognition, Workshop on Biometrics (2013).
21. Zhang, Z., Yan, J., Liu, S., Lei, Z., Yi, D., Li, S.Z.: A face antispoofing database with diverse attacks. In: ICB (2012).
22. Erdogmus, N., Marcel, S.: Spoofing in 2d face recognition with 3d masks and anti-spoofing with kinect. In: Biometrics: Theory, Applications and Systems Conference (BTAS'13) (2013).
23. Chetty, G., Wagner, M.: Liveness verification in audio-video speaker authentication. In: in Proc. 10th ASSTA conference, pp. 358–363. Macquarie University Press (2004).
24. Frischholz RW, Dieckmann U (2000) Bioid: A multimodal biometric identification system. Computer 33(2):64–68
25. Kollreider K, Fronthaler H, Faraj MI, Bigun J (2007) Real-time face detection and motion analysis with application in liveness assessment. Trans. Info. For. Sec. 2(3):548–558
26. Pavlidis, I., Symosek, P.: The imaging issue in an automatic face/disguise detection system. In: Proceedings of the IEEE Workshop on Computer Vision Beyond the Visible Spectrum: Methods and Applications (CVBVS 2000), pp. 15–24. Washington, DC, USA (2000).
27. Sun L, Huang W, Wu M (2011) Tir/vis correlation for liveness detection in face recognition. Proceedings of the 14th international conference on Computer analysis of images and patterns - Volume Part II., CAIP'11Springer-Verlag, Berlin, Heidelberg, pp 114–121

28. Zhang, Z., Yi, D., Lei, Z., Li, S.Z.: Face liveness detection by learning multispectral reflectance distributions. In: International Conference on Face and Gesture, pp. 436–441 (2011).
29. Wu, H.Y., Rubinstein, M., Shih, E., Guttag, J., Durand, F., Freeman, W.T.: Eulerian video magnification for revealing subtle changes in the world. ACM Trans. Graph. (SIGGRAPH 2012) 31(4) (2012).
30. Bharadwaj, S., Dhamecha, T.I., Vatsa, M., Richa, S.: Computationally efficient face spoofing detection with motion magnification. In: Proceedings of IEEE Conference on Computer Vision and Pattern Recognition, Workshop on Biometrics (2013).
31. Chaudhry, R., Ravich, A., Hager, G., Vidal, R.: Histograms of oriented optical flow and binet-cauchy kernels on nonlinear dynamical systems for the recognition of human actions. In: IEEE Conference on Computer Vision and Pattern Recognition (CVPR (2009).
32. Kollreider K, Fronthaler H, Bigun J (2009) Non-intrusive liveness detection by face images. Image and Vision Computing 27:233–244
33. Kollreider, K., Fronthaler, H., Bigun, J.: Verifying liveness by multiple experts in face biometrics. Computer Vision and Pattern Recognition Workshop pp. 1–6 (2008).
34. Bao, W., Li, H., Li, N., Jiang, W.: A liveness detection method for face recognition based on optical flow field. In: 2009 International Conference on Image Analysis and Signal Processing, pp. 233–236. IEEE (2009).
35. Määttä, J., Hadid, A., Pietikäinen, M.: Face spoofing detection from single images using micro-texture analysis. In: Proceedings of IAPR IEEE International Joint Conference on Biometrics (IJCB), Washington DC, USA (2011).
36. Ojala T, Pietikäinen M, Mäenpää T (2002) Multiresolution gray-scale and rotation invariant texture classification with local binary patterns. IEEE Transactions on Pattern Analysis and Machine Intelligence 24:971–987
37. Kose, N., Dugelay, J.L.: Countermeasure for the protection of face recognition systems against mask attacks. In: FG 2013, IEEE International Conference on Automatic Face and Gesture Recognition, 22–26 April 2013, Shanghai, China. Shanghai, CHINA (2013).
38. Pereira, T.d.F., Komulainen, J., Anjos, A., De Martino, J.M., Hadid, A., Pietikäinen, M., Marcel, S.: Face liveness detection using dynamic texture. EURASIP Journal on Image and Video Processing (2013).
39. Zhao G, Pietikäinen M (2007) Dynamic texture recognition using local binary patterns with an application to facial expressions. IEEE Transactions on Pattern Analysis and Machine Intelligence 29(6):915–928
40. Pinto, A.d.S., Pedrini, H., Schwartz, W.R., Rocha, A.: Video-based face spoofing detection through visual rhythm analysis. In: Conference on Graphics, Patterns and Images (Sibgrapi) (2012).
41. Wang, T., Yang, J., Lei, Z., Liao, S., Li, S.Z.: Face liveness detection using 3d structure recovered from a single camera. In: IAPR International Conference on Biometrics, ICB (2013).
42. Gao, X., Ng, T.T., Qiu, B., Chang, S.F.: Single-view recaptured image detection based on physics-based features. In: IEEE International Conference on Multimedia & Expo (ICME), pp. 1469–1474 (2010).
43. Farid, H., Lyu, S.: Higher-order wavelet statistics and their application to digital forensics. In: in IEEE Workshop on Statistical Analysis in Computer Vision (2003).
44. Pan G, Sun L, Wu Z, Wang Y (2011) Monocular camera-based face liveness detection by combining eyeblink and scene context. Telecommunication Systems 47(3–4):215–225
45. Komulainen, J., Hadid, A., Pietikäinen, M.: Context based face anti-spoofing. In: Proc. the IEEE Sixth International Conference on Biometrics: Theory, Applications and Systems (BTAS 2013), Washington, DC, 2013 (2013).
46. Dalal N, Triggs B (2005) Histograms of oriented gradients for human detection. International Conference on Computer Vision & Pattern Recognition 2:886–893
47. Schwartz, W.R., Rocha, A., Pedrini, H.: Face Spoofing Detection through Partial Least Squares and Low-Level Descriptors. In: Proceedings of IAPR IEEE International Joint Conference on Biometrics (IJCB), Washington DC, USA (2011).

48. Tronci, R., Muntoni, D., Fadda, G., Pili, M., Sirena, N., Murgia, G., Ristori, M., Roli, F.: Fusion of multiple clues for photo-attack detection in face recognition systems. In: Proceedings of IAPR IEEE International Joint Conference on Biometrics (IJCB), Washington DC, USA (2011).
49. Yan, J., Zhang, Z., Lei, Z., Yi, D., Li, S.Z.: Face liveness detection by exploring multiple scenic clues. In: 12th International Conference on Control, Automation, Robotics and Vision, (ICARCV2012) (2012).
50. Komulainen, J., Anjos, A., Hadid, A., Marcel, S., Pietikäinen, M.: Complementary countermeasures for detecting scenic face spoofing attacks. In: IAPR International Conference on Biometrics, ICB (2013).
51. Ng, E.S., Chia, A.Y.S.: Face verification using temporal affective cues. In: International Conference on Pattern Recognition, ICPR, pp. 1249–1252 (2012).
52. Frischholz, R.W., Werner, A.: Avoiding replay-attacks in a face recognition systenm using head-pose estimation. In: Proceedings of the IEEE International Workshop on Analysis and Modeling of Faces and Gestures, AMFG '03. IEEE Computer Society, Washington, DC, USA (2003).
53. De Marsico, M., Nappi, M., Riccio, D., Dugelay, J.L.: Moving face spoofing detection via 3D projective invariants. In: ICB 2012, 5th IAPR International Conference on Biometrics, 29 March-1 April 2012, New Delhi, India. New Delhi, INDIA (2012).
54. Liu C, Yuen J, Torralba A (2011) Sift flow: Dense correspondence across scenes and its applications. IEEE Trans. Pattern Anal. Mach. Intell. 33(5):978–994

# Chapter 5
# Face Anti-spoofing: Multi-spectral Approach

**Dong Yi, Zhen Lei, Zhiwei Zhang and Stan Z. Li**

**Abstract** With the wide applications of face recognition, spoofing attack is becoming a big threat to their security. Conventional face recognition systems usually adopt behavioral challenge-response or texture analysis methods to resist spoofing attacks, however, these methods require high user cooperation and are sensitive to the imaging quality and environments. In this chapter, we present a multi-spectral face recognition system working in VIS (Visible) and NIR (Near Infrared) spectrums, which is robust to various spoofing attacks and user cooperation free. First, we introduce the structure of the system from several aspects including: imaging device, face landmarking, feature extraction, matching, VIS, and NIR sub-systems. Then the performance of the multi-spectral system and each subsystem is evaluated and analyzed. Finally, we describe the multi-spectral image-based anti-spoofing module, and report its performance under photo attacks. Experiments on a spoofing database show the excellent performance of the proposed system both in recognition rate and anti-spoofing ability. Compared with conventional VIS face recognition system, the multi-spectral system has two advantages: (1) By combining the VIS and NIR spectrums, the system can resist VIS photo and NIR photo attacks easily. And users' cooperation is no longer needed, making the system user friendly and fast. (2) Due to the precise key-point localization, Gabor feature extraction and unsupervised learning, the system is robust to pose, illumination and expression variations. Generally, its recognition rate is higher than the VIS subsystem.

D. Yi (✉) · Z. Lei · Z. Zhang · S.Z. Li
Chinese Academy of Sciences, Institute of Automation,
95 Zhongguancun Donglu, Beijing 100190, China
e-mail: dyi@cbsr.ia.ac.cn

Z. Lei
e-mail: zlei@nlpr.ia.ac.cn

Z. Zhang
e-mail: zhiweiscu@gmail.com

S.Z. Li
e-mail: stan.zq.li@gmail.com

## 5.1 Introduction

Although face recognition has achieved great success during the past decades, little effort has been made to assure its security and reliability in real-world applications. It is now increasingly known that existing face recognition systems are susceptible to fake face attacks, through which unauthorized attackers try to access illegal authorities by exhibiting fake faces of an authorized client. Serious consequences may occur if these attacks succeed, yet there still lack effective anti-spoofing techniques.

Attackers can obtain a client's face images by using portable digital cameras or simply downloading from the Internet, and fake faces can be easily produced, for example, printing photos or showing videos on a laptop. Fake faces like photos and video replays are not only easy to implement but also usually quite effective to attack a face recognition system [1], and has become the main concern [1] in the literature as shown in Sect. 5.2. Actually in real-world applications, face recognition systems may encounter various high quality face attacks and low quality real accesses, therefore an excellent anti-spoofing method should distinguish their difference and perform robust in unpredicted situations.

However, as we review the recent development in Sect. 5.2, we find that current researches mainly concentrate on genuine and fake face with little variations. A shortcoming in variation is the quality of attacks: in [2–4], algorithms extract the high frequency information or micro-texture to detect attacks. But as this high frequency information or micro-texture pattern highly depends on the image quality, how will they perform on good quality and bad quality images? Do their algorithms generalize well? We can see that due to the lack of variational data, many questions remain unanswered. Therefore we cannot predict their performance in real-world applications, because practical attacks are probably not limited to one single type as in previous researches.

Therefore, we think "quality robustness" is a big problem in anti-spoofing research. How to classify high quality attacks and low quality real accesses is the key issue to solve this problem. Multi-modal biometrics may be a practical direction, because we have more information available for anti-spoofing. Likewise, multi-spectral face images are naturally stronger than single VIS face image, by fusing which we have more chance to build a quality robust anti-spoofing module. In this chapter, we propose a high performance face recognition system with anti-spoofing module using multi-spectral imaging. We start by introducing the multi-spectral face recognition system, including spectrums selection, hardware, and algorithms. Then we report the performance of the system under licit transaction and spoofing attack. To resist the attacks, we propose an effective multi-spectral countermeasure and test the performance of the system with countermeasures. The experimental results illustrate that the countermeasures resist the attacks perfectly.

---

[1] Mask is also a good choice, but usually it is too expensive to produce client-like masks. So the massive usage of masks rarely appears in the literature.

Compared with existing anti-spoofing approaches, the advantages of our system are obvious. First, our system requires no user cooperation, and therefore is user-friendly and fast. Second, our system, by combining multi-spectral information, is more quality robust and can achieve higher recognition rate than traditional single modal face recognition system.

## 5.2 Related Work

Existing work can be classified as three categories: facial motion detection, facial texture analysis and multi-spectral anti-spoofing methods. The first two are usually applied to VIS face recognition systems. The last one needs extra multi-spectral imaging device to achieve more accurate results.

Facial motion detection techniques expect subjects to exhibit specific facial motion, the detection of which determines the liveness. For methods of this kind, human–computer interaction (HCI) is almost indispensable to detect users' biological motion. The most commonly used motion types include eye blinking [5, 6], head rotation [6, 7], and mouth movement [8], and these motions are mainly detected by adopting optical flow. One main problem of these methods is that users need to be highly cooperative and the duration of liveness detection is relatively long, which will make users feel uncomfortable when using such a system. Another problem is that they cannot deal with some skilled attacks. For example, if the fake face is a photo over a genuine face with eyes and mouth cut out as illustrated in [6], these methods will definitely fail. Therefore, applications of such kind of methods are limited.

Facial texture analysis techniques believe that fake faces probably lack some high frequency information during the reproduction process, and by analyzing and learning the facial texture information, genuine and fake faces can be classified properly. Here the term "texture" represents the high frequency details in face images. In [2] Fourier transform is utilized to extract the high frequency information, and the target face image is judged fake if its energy percentage of high frequency is lower than a certain threshold. In [3] the authors use DoG and LTV algorithms to extract high frequency information from the captured images, and the final model is learned by a complex bilinear sparse low rank logistic regression model. In [4] a more simple but also more powerful LBP+SVM method (named Micro-Texture Analysis, MTA) is proposed, and they achieve very amazing results both on the NUAA [3] and Idiap [9] database. Similarly, [10] also utilize micro-textures and SVM to detect spoofing attacks. However, as noted by [11], most existing spoofing databases did not include enough variations, therefore, the best texture-based methods on the databases may failed in real applications when confronting various imaging environments.

The other class is the multi-spectral methods, which detect the reflectance of object surface under multi-spectrums. To the best of our knowledge, there have been very few papers published in this field, among which two papers are most representative. In [12] Pavlidis and Symosekuses use light at two wavelengths, and a simple threshold method to detect genuine and fake faces. No experiments but only illustrations were reported in their paper. The second one [13] also selects light at two different wavelengths and then LDA is used to make the final decision. However, this paper requires the distance between the user and the system to be exactly 30 cm, and they utilize users' forehead region to measure reflectance. Not only may the forehead be occluded, but also the exact distance is quite demanding and impossible to execute in practice. Furthermore, the wavelengths they select are actually not as optimal as in [12]. Thermal information is another choice, and we refer readers to a common facial thermal imagery database in [14]. But, the high cost also prevents its usage in real practice.

## 5.3 The Multi-spectral Face Recognition System

The multi-spectral face recognition system includes the following modules: multi-spectral image acquisition, face detection, key-point localization, feature extraction, subspace learning, matching, and fusion. To achieve good performance and generalization ability in practical applications, the multi-spectral system uses an EBGM like pipeline to process face image, which is mainly composed of precise key-point localization, Gabor filtering, and PCA. Yi et al. [15] have already shown the high performance of the method on FERET (only in VIS spectrum). For each spectrum, face image is processed separately by its corresponding pipeline, and the similarity scores in multi-spectrums are fused by "sum rule." The details of each module are described as follows.

### 5.3.1 Spectrum Selection and Imaging Device

The use of multiple spectral bands for face biometrics permits to improve the performance and robustness of face recognition in realistic scenarios including uncontrolled illumination conditions. Taking into account the compatibility with normal face recognition system, VIS is selected as the first spectrum for the multi-spectral system. On the other hand, NIR band has become the most used spectral band beyond VIS due to several advantages: radiation which is harmless to health, good-quality images, low-cost cameras, etc. Based on our existing NIR face recognition system [16], we choose the second spectrum as NIR (780 nm). To acquire VIS and NIR images simultaneously, we develop a special imaging device by two CMOS camera modules, which can capture 640 × 480 images in two bands at 15 fps. The synchronization is controlled by the software system.

In the multi-spectral system, two spectrum bands are available and hence can be exploited for recognition in many ways. A common method is to use all spectral bands simultaneously that match VIS to VIS, and NIR to NIR. Currently, we use multi-spectral images in this way, but heterogeneous matching between VIS and NIR may be added into the system in the future. For example, VIS face images are used for enrollment while NIR face images are used for testing.

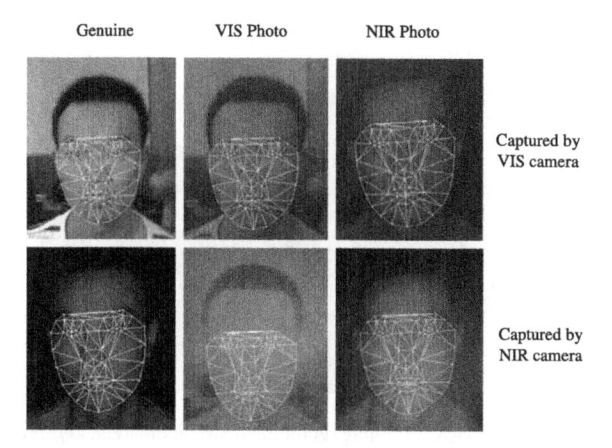

**Fig. 5.1** Some genuine and fake face images in different spectrums and their 76 facial landmarks localized by the ASM landmarker. From *left* to *right*, the *three columns* correspond to genuine face, VIS photo, and NIR photo. Images in the *first row* are captured under visible illumination, and the *second row* are captured under NIR illumination. The fake face images are produced by recapture of the VIS and NIR printed photo by the same system

## 5.3.2 Key-Point Localization

Because face detection is relatively mature than other steps, we skip it. Interested readers can refer to [17] for details. After face detection, we localize the facial landmarks by Active Shape Model (ASM) [18]. ASM is composed of three parts: shape model, local experts, and optimization strategy. In most ASM variants, shape model is usually PCA [19], and we follow this model. For local experts, we use LBP [20] feature and Boosting classifier for each landmark, which is similar to the method in [21]. Based on the output of Boosting classifiers, we can get a confidence map for each landmark. These confidence maps are fed to a Landmark Mean-Shift procedure [22]. Then we can get the final positions of all facial landmarks. For robustness and efficiency, the optimization process is repeated several times on two scales.

The training set of our landmarker is constructed from the MUCT database [23]. Three views (a, d, and e) with small pose variations are used for training. Because the backgrounds of images in the MUCT are almost uniform, we replace them with some random backgrounds and mirror all images to augment the dataset (see Fig. 5.2). The uniform backgrounds of the face images are segmented by GrabCut [24], which is initialized by the results of face detection. Figure 5.1 shows two example images in the FERET database [25] and their 76 facial landmarks localized by the landmarker, from which we can see that the landmarks are robust to small pose variations and have good precision for the next steps.

**Fig. 5.2** Sample images in the MUCT training set for the ASM landmarker. *Left* A color face image in the MUCT database, which has uniform background. *Right* A face image is converted to *gray* scale and the background is replaced by a random image from the Internet

### 5.3.3 Gabor Feature and Subspace Learning

Given an aligned face image and the 76 landmarks, we extract local features on the landmarks by a Gabor wavelet, which is described in [26].

$$\psi_{\mathbf{k},\sigma}(\mathbf{x}) = \frac{k^2}{\sigma^2} e^{-\frac{k^2}{2\sigma^2}x^2} \{e^{i\mathbf{k}\mathbf{x}} - e^{-\frac{\sigma^2}{2}}\} \qquad (5.1)$$

The wavelet is a plane wave with wave vector **k**, restricted by a Gaussian envelope, the size of which relative to the wavelength is parameterized by $\sigma$. The second term in the brace removes the DC component. Following the popular way, we sample the space of wave vectors **k** and scale $\sigma$ in a discrete hierarchy of 5 resolutions (differing by half-octaves) and 8 orientations at each resolution (See Fig. 5.3), thus giving $5 \times 8 = 40$ complex values for each landmark. Because the phase information is sensitive to image shift or misalignment, we drop the phase and use the amplitude as feature for face recognition.

Merging the feature values at all landmarks together, we get a feature vector with $76 \times 40 = 3{,}040$ dimensions. To reduce the dimensionality of feature and remove the redundant information, Principle Component Analysis (PCA) [27] is used to learn a low-dimensional subspace. To remove the large variations caused by extrinsic factors such as illumination and expression, we discard the first several principal components. In the reduced PCA subspace, the similarity of feature vectors are evaluated by Cosine metric.

$$s(\mathbf{x}, \mathbf{y}) = \frac{\mathbf{x}^T \mathbf{y}}{\sqrt{\mathbf{x}^T \mathbf{x} \mathbf{y}^T \mathbf{y}}} \qquad (5.2)$$

5 Face Anti-spoofing: Multi-spectral Approach

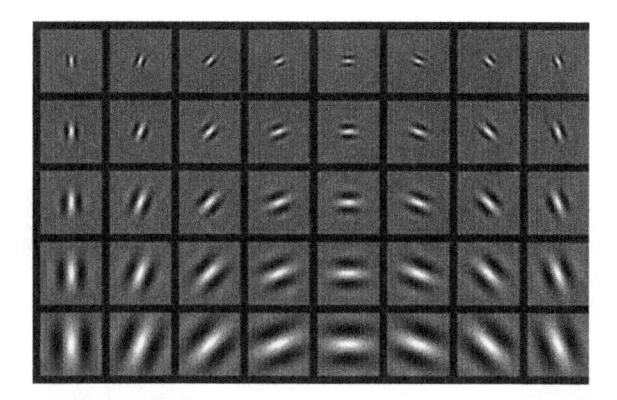

**Fig. 5.3** The real part of the Gabor wavelet in 5 resolutions and 8 orientations

In practice, we usually normalize the feature vector **x** and **y** to unit length as **x**′ and **y**′. Then Eq. (5.2) can be written as

$$s(\mathbf{x}, \mathbf{y}) = s(\mathbf{x}', \mathbf{y}') = \mathbf{x}'^T \mathbf{y}'. \quad (5.3)$$

## 5.4 Performance Under Spoofing Attack

In this section, we build a database to evaluate the performance of the multi-spectral system and analyze the vulnerabilities of the multi-spectral system when confronted to spoofing attacks. Because making 3D mask is expensive, currently we use printed photos (VIS and NIR) to attack the system. In order to obtain comprehensive results, the VIS subsystem and NIR subsystem are also evaluated separately.

### 5.4.1 Database

All face images in the database are acquired by using the self-developed device (5.3), which includes a VIS camera, an NIR camera with some NIR LEDs. VIS and NIR images are synchronized by the system. The imaging device works at a rate of 15 fps for 640 × 480 images. Figure 5.4 shows the scenario of database collection.

The database comprises genuine face images of 100 subjects and their corresponding fake face samples. All subjects are imaged under VIS and NIR illuminations (5 images per subject per spectrum). For the fake faces, photos are printed using both the visible and NIR face image, named as VIS photo and NIR photo respectively. The printed photos are acquired by the same system described above. We use a kind

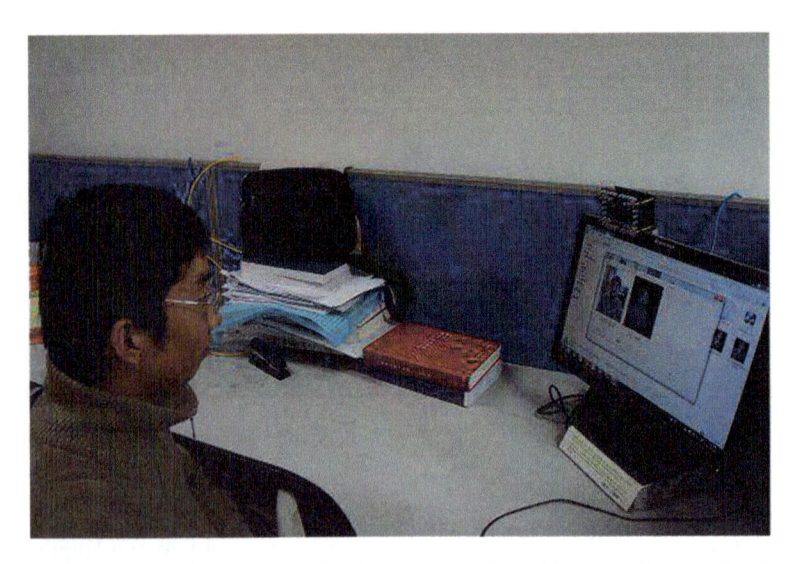

**Fig. 5.4** Setup used for the acquisition of real-accesses for the multi-spectral face spoofing database

of coarse paper as printing material, because its relatively rough surface makes the reflectance weak and the fake face more vivid. Some examples are shown in Fig. 5.5.

In summary, the information about the database is: We denote these kinds of face images as:

- $G_{VIS}$: Genuine subjects captured by VIS camera;
- $G_{NIR}$: Genuine subjects captured by NIR camera;
- $VP_{VIS}$: VIS photo captured by VIS camera;
- $VP_{NIR}$: VIS photo captured by NIR camera;
- $NP_{VIS}$: NIR photo captured by VIS camera;
- $NP_{NIR}$: NIR photo captured by NIR camera.

By observing the face images in Fig. 5.5 we give some conjectures: (1) $VP_{VIS}$ is easy to attack $G_{VIS}$; (2) $NP_{VIS}$ is harder to attack $G_{VIS}$ than $VP_{VIS}$. And by using the color information, we can easily detect the fake samples belonging to $NP_{VIS}$; (3) Due to the strong specular reflectance, $VP_{NIR}$ is hard to attack $G_{NIR}$; (4) $G_{NIR}$ is easily attacked by $NP_{NIR}$. These conjectures will be verified in the following experiments and in the next Sect. 5.5.

## *5.4.2 Protocol for Licit Transactions*

The genuine face images in the database could be used to evaluate the performance of the multi-spectral face recognition system. Here we describe how to use the database to do training, enrollment, and recognition. To illustrate the performance of individual

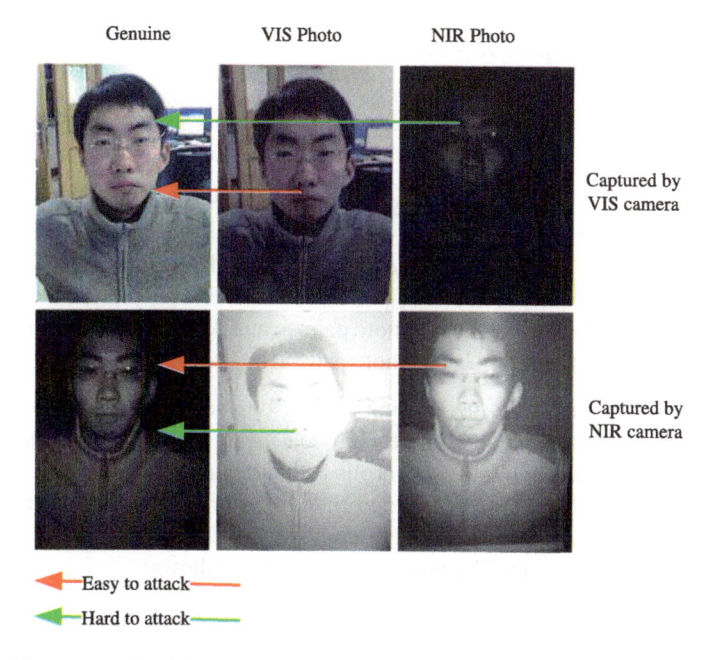

5  Face Anti-spoofing: Multi-spectral Approach    91

**Fig. 5.5** Illustration of multi-spectral face images in the database. From *left* to *right*, the *three columns* correspond to genuine face, VIS photo and NIR photo. Images in the *first row* are captured under visible illumination, and the *second row* are captured under NIR illumination. The fake face images are produced by recapture of the VIS and NIR photo by the same system

modality (VIS and NIR) and the improvement of the multi-spectral fusion, three sub-experiments were conducted:

- VIS vs. VIS;
- NIR vs. NIR;
- VIS + NIR vs. VIS + NIR.

For the three experiments, the database is split into four subsets including:

- Training set: genuine face images of the first 30 subjects, $30 \times 5 = 150$ pairs;
- Development set: genuine face images of the following 30 subjects, $30 \times 5 = 150$ pairs;
- Licit Gallery set: two genuine face images of the other 40 subjects, $40 \times 2 = 80$ pairs;
- Licit Probe set: three genuine face images of the other 40 subjects, $40 \times 3 = 120$ pairs.

The PCA subspace is trained on the training set and the parameters are tuned on the development set. During the testing phase, the parameters of model should remain fixed. The Detection-Error Trade-off (DET) curve is used to illustrate the performance of the system.

## 5.4.3 Protocol for Spoofing Attacks

Similar to the protocols for Licit Transactions, six scenarios are evaluated to illustrate the influence of spoofing attacks to the performance of the system. There are:

- S1.1: using the VIS photos in $VP_{VIS}$ to attack the VIS subsystem;
- S1.2: using the NIR photos in $NP_{VIS}$ to attack the VIS subsystem;
- S2.1: using the VIS photos in $VP_{NIR}$ to attack the NIR subsystem;
- S2.2: using the NIR photos in $NP_{NIR}$ to attack the NIR subsystem;
- S3.1: using the $VP_{VIS}$ and $VP_{NIR}$ photo pairs to attack the multi-spectral system;
- S3.2: using the $NP_{VIS}$ and $NP_{NIR}$ photo pairs to attack the multi-spectral system.

In the attacking scenarios, the training sets, testing sets, and gallery sets are as same as those in licit transaction, and the probe sets are augmented by the printed photos. In these cases the genuine user enrolls with their faces and the attacker tries to access the system with the corresponding printed VIS or NIR photos. A successful attack is accomplished when the system confuses a genuine face image with its corresponding printed photo. The protocol is shown as follows:

- S1.1 Probe set: Licit Probe set described in Sect. 5.4.2 and their corresponding printed photos in $VP_{VIS}$;
- S1.2 Probe set: Licit Probe set described in Sect. 5.4.2 and their corresponding printed photos in $NP_{VIS}$;
- S2.1 Probe set: Licit Probe set described in Sect. 5.4.2 and their corresponding printed photos in $VP_{NIR}$;
- S2.2 Probe set: Licit Probe set described in Sect. 5.4.2 and their corresponding printed photos in $NP_{NIR}$;
- S3.1 Probe set: Licit Probe set described in Sect. 5.4.2 and their corresponding printed photos in $VP_{VIS}$ and $VP_{NIR}$;
- S3.2 Probe set: Licit Probe set described in Sect. 5.4.2 and their corresponding printed photos in $NP_{VIS}$ and $NP_{NIR}$;

The DET curves are also utilized for performance reporting, which describes the relationship between false detection rate and false rejection rate.

## 5.4.4 Results

### 5.4.4.1 Attacking the VIS Subsystem

The experimental results of S1.1 and S1.2 are shown in Figs. 5.6 and 5.7. From the results we can see that the VIS subsystem has good performance when it does not confront spoofing attacks. The FAR@FRR = 3% is about 2%. Furthermore, the score distributions of imposters and true claimants are well separated. These observations indicate that the VIS subsystem performs well on this database. Because the baseline

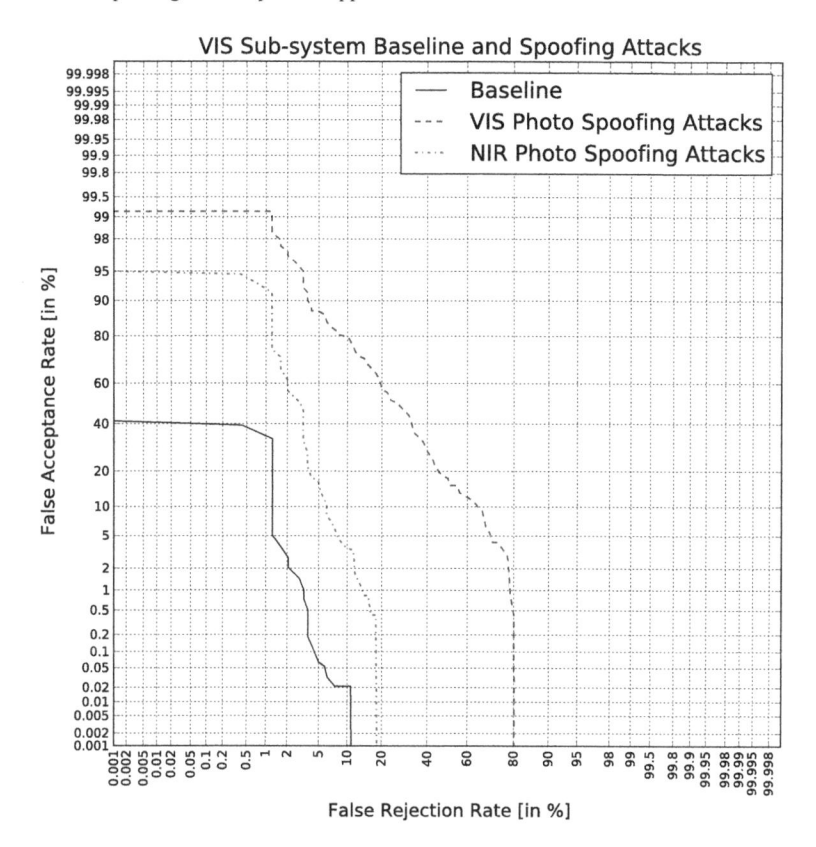

**Fig. 5.6** DET curves for the VIS subsystem baseline and spoofing attacks

is a full unsupervised method, based on local feature + PCA, it is expected to have good generalization ability.

Under the VIS and NIR photo attacks, the performance of the VIS subsystem drops drastically. For example, when FRR = 2% the FAR increases from 3 to 97% and 60% respectively. This indicates that the VIS subsystem is attacked by the VIS and NIR photos, and the VIS photo can attack the system more easily than the NIR photo. Figure 5.7 shows the same phenomenon, the score distribution of the VIS photo is heavily overlapped with the true claimants.

#### 5.4.4.2 Attacking the NIR Subsystem

The experimental results of S2.1 and S2.2 are shown in Figs. 5.8 and 5.9. From the figures we can see similar results as the VIS subsystem. When not confronting spoofing attacks, the NIR subsystem performs well too, and even better than the VIS

**Fig. 5.7** Score distributions for the VIS subsystem baseline and spoofing attacks. **a** Attacked by VIS Photo. **b** Attacked by NIR Photo

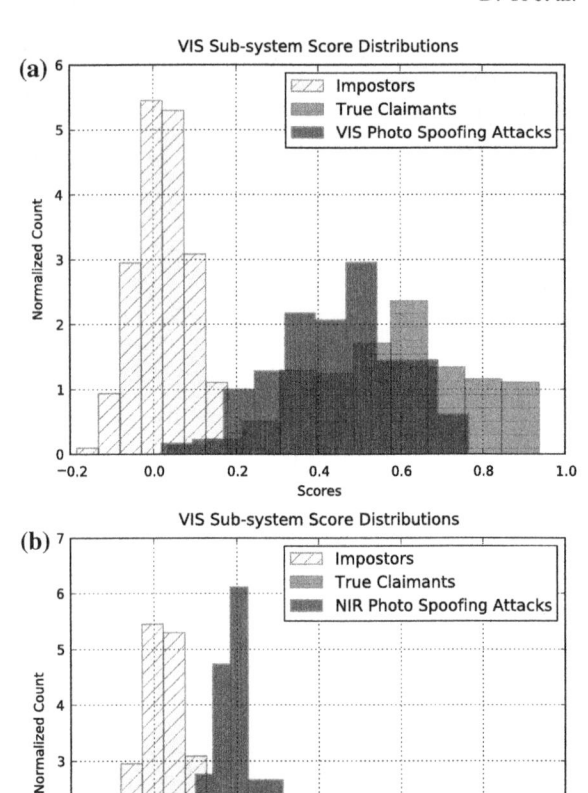

subsystem due to its illumination invariant property. Its EER (equal error rate) is about 2 %, slightly lower than the VIS subsystem.

Under the VIS and NIR photo attacks, the performance of the NIR subsystem drops too, but decline is not as sharp as the VIS subsystem. For example, when FRR = 2 % the FAR increases from 2 to 10 and 78 %, which shows that the NIR face modality is inherently better than the VIS face modality in terms of anti-spoofing. On the contrary with VIS, the NIR subsystem is more easily attacked by the NIR photo, which verifies the conjectures in Sect. 5.4.1.

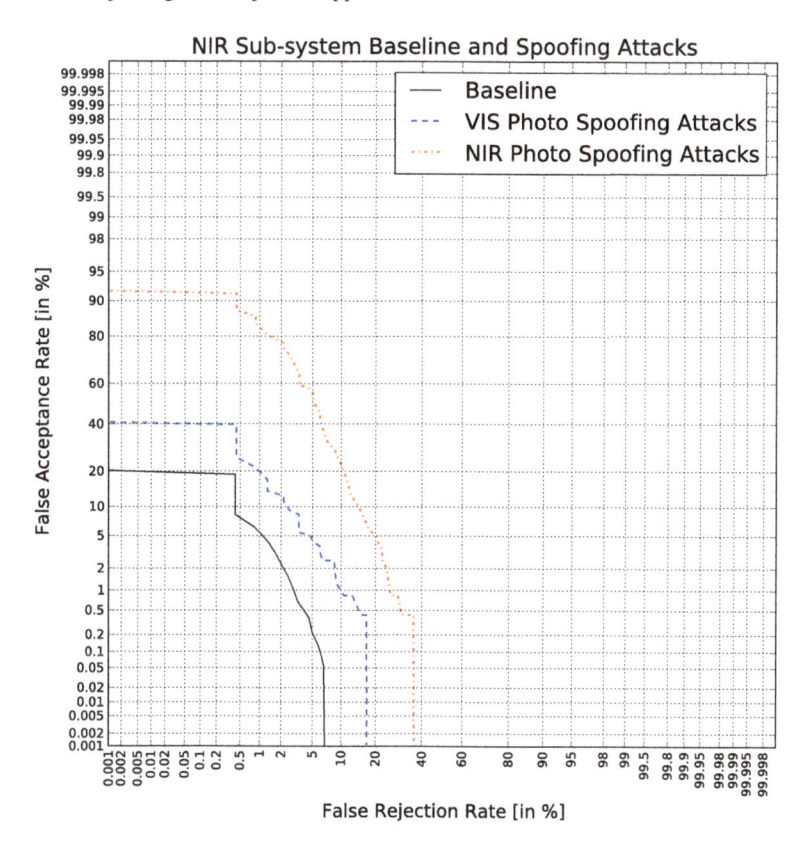

**Fig. 5.8** DET curves for the NIR subsystem baseline and spoofing attacks

### 5.4.4.3 Attacking the Multi-spectral System

By fusing the scores of the VIS and NIR subsystems, we show the experimental results of S3.1 and S3.2 in Figs. 5.10 and 5.11. Compared with the VIS and NIR subsystems, the performance of the multi-spectral system is improved a little, EER from 3 % and 2 to 1.8 %. However, an interesting thing is that the multi-spectral system is vulnerable both to the VIS and NIR photo attack. By the effect of "sum rule," the DET curves and score distributions all achieve a balance between the VIS and NIR subsystems, which result in the multi-spectral system that is weaker than the VIS subsystem to resist the NIR photo attack and is weaker than the NIR subsystem to resist the VIS photo attack.

**Fig. 5.9** Score distributions for the NIR subsystem baseline and spoofing attacks. **a** Attacked by VIS Photo. **b** Attacked by NIR Photo

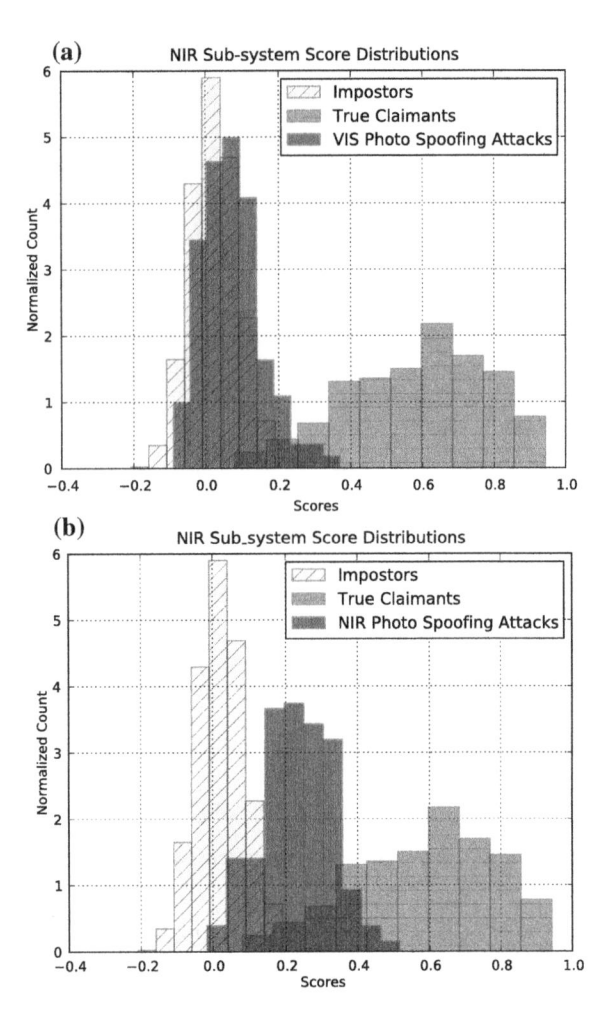

## 5.5 Countermeasure Integration

### 5.5.1 Color and Texture-Based Countermeasure

From the experiments in the previous section, we can see "sum rule" is good to improve the performance of face recognition but not robust to resist the spoofing attacks. Because "sum rule" prefers to get a trade-off between the VIS and NIR subsystems, it makes the multi-spectral system neither robust to VIS photo attack nor to NIR photo attack Table 5.1.

From the results in the previous section, we can see the VIS subsystem is robust to the NIR photo attack, and the NIR subsystem is robust to the VIS photo attack. By

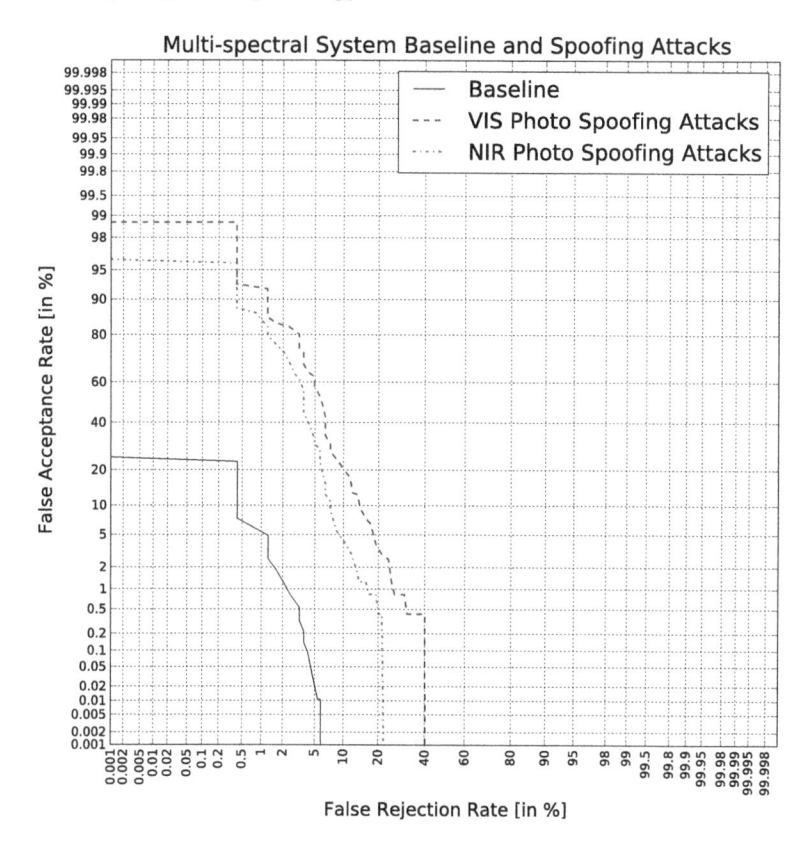

**Fig. 5.10** DET curves for the multi-spectral system baseline and spoofing attacks

**Table 5.1** The information of the multi-spectral face spoofing database

|  | Genuine subjects | VIS photo attack | NIR photo attack |
|---|---|---|---|
| Captured by VIS camera | 100 subjects × 5 | 100 subjects × 5 | 100 subjects × 5 |
| Captured by NIR camera | 100 subjects × 5 | 100 subjects × 5 | 100 subjects × 5 |

combining their advantages, we propose a two-step countermeasure based on color and texture analysis. The color analysis is used to resist the NIR photo attack, because NIR photo captured by the VIS camera has no color. By setting a threshold based on color information, we could easily reject NIR photos. VIS photo usually can pass the color analysis, but it will be rejected by the following texture analysis due to its strong specular reflectance in the NIR spectrum. The process of the countermeasure is shown in Fig. 5.12.

For color analysis, we first crop the face region from image and then use the histogram of chroma (HoC) as feature, where the chroma of each pixel is calculated

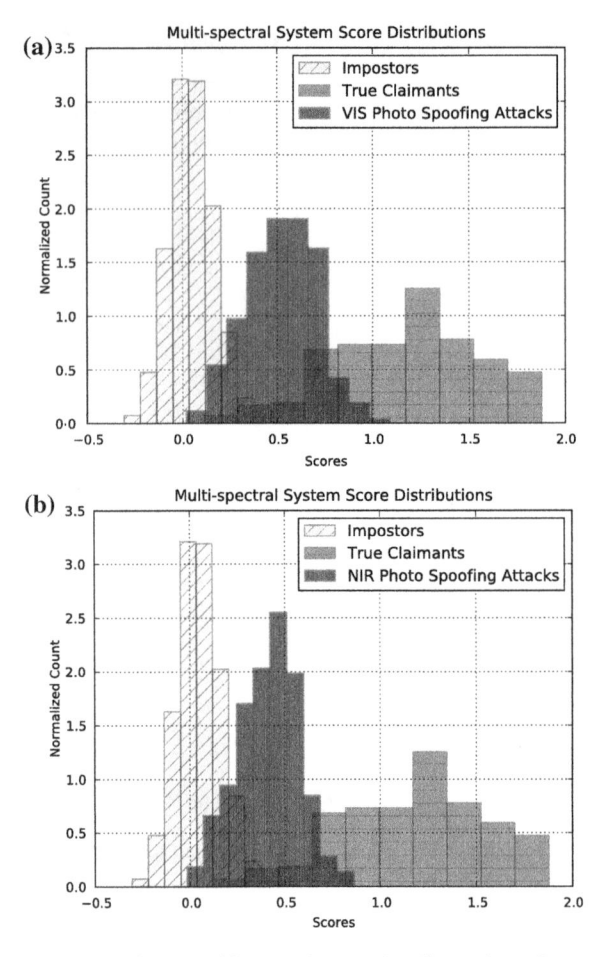

**Fig. 5.11** Score distributions for the multi-spectral system baseline and spoofing attacks. **a** Attacked by VIS Photo. **b** Attacked by NIR Photo

by $\max(R, G, B)-\min(R, G, B)$. For texture analysis, the Gabor features, the same as face recognition (see Sect. 5.3), are used. Finally, the linear SVM is used to train the classifiers based on these two kinds of features respectively.

## 5.5.2 Protocol for Countermeasure

To train the classifiers for our countermeasure and evaluate the performance, we construct three subsets from the database as well:

- Training set: genuine and fake face images of the the first 30 subjects;

# 5 Face Anti-spoofing: Multi-spectral Approach

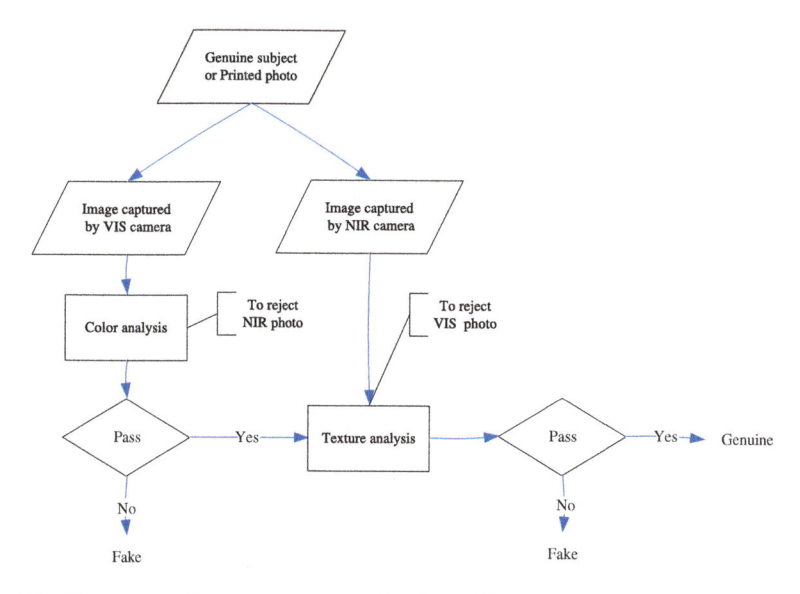

**Fig. 5.12** The process of our countermeasure for the multi-spectral system

- Development set: genuine and fake face images of the following 30 subjects;
- Testing set: genuine and fake face images of the other 40 subjects.

First, we train the color-based classifier using $G_{VIS}$ and $NP_{VIS}$ in the training set. Second, we train the texture-based classifier using $G_{NIR}$ and $VP_{NIR}$. The final countermeasure is constructed according to the structure shown in Fig. 5.12. The performance will be evaluated with respect to two kinds of errors: FLR (False Living Rate) and FFR (False Fake Rate). The lower these two errors, the better the performance of the countermeasure.

To evaluate the influence of the countermeasure to the face recognition system, we usually fix at a evaluation point (e.g., FFR = 1 %). Once fixed, we can incorporate the countermeasure as a pre-processing step into the multi-spectral face recognition system oriented to reject fake samples, and generate the performance of the following three profiles.

- Baseline: The performance of the multi-spectral system;
- Baseline under attacks: The performance under spoofing attacks;
- Baseline + Countermeasure under attacks: The final performance of the multi-spectral system with countermeasure under spoofing attacks.

## 5.5.3 Results

After training the color and texture SVM classifiers, we apply them on the testing set. Because the differences between the genuine and fake samples are obvious, the two

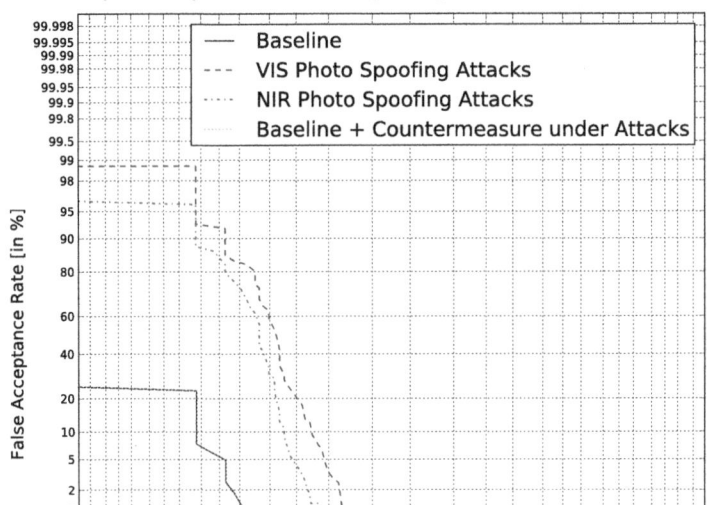

**Multi-spectral System Baseline, Spoofing Attacks and Countermeasure**

**Fig. 5.13** DET curves for the multi-spectral system baseline, spoofing attacks, and countermeasure. Note that the plot of the "baseline + countermeasure under attacks" is invisible because it coincides with the baseline completely (perfect countermeasure)

SVM classifiers are easy to train and both achieve 100 % accuracy on the testing set. The color SVM classifier contains 20 support vectors and the texture SVM classifier contains 52 support vectors.

Due to the high performance of the two SVM classifiers, our countermeasure can reject all fake samples while allowing all genuine samples to pass. Therefore, the countermeasure can fully resist the photo attacks and do not produce any side effects to the multi-spectral system. The DET curve of the final system is shown in Fig. 5.13.

## 5.6 Conclusions

As shown in this chapter, mutli-spectral face recognition has high recognition rate and performs well to anti-spoof printed photo attacks. The success is mainly attributes to the complement of multi-spectral face images, as the VIS subsystem is robust to

NIR photo attack and the NIR subsystem is robust to VIS photo attack. Although the system works perfectly on the database, it is hard to say the anti-spoofing module in the system can appeal to the practical requirements. Limited by the scale and variations of the database, the introduced countermeasure, especially the texture classifier, may be over-fitting to the database. To really apply the anti-spoofing technologies in practice, we must collect more comprehensive spoofing databases, in larger scale, with more variations, such as pose, illumination, expression, etc., as similar as those in traditional face recognition.

**Acknowledgments** This work was supported by the Chinese National Natural Science Foundation Project #61070146, #61105023, #61103156, #61105037, National IoT R&D Project #2150510, European Union FP7 Project #257289 (TABULA RASA http://www.tabularasa-euproject.org), and AuthenMetric R&D Funds.

# References

1. Duc N, Minh B (2009) Your face is not your password. Black Hat Conference
2. Li J, Wang Y, Tan T, Jain AK (2004) Live face detection based on the analysis of fourier spectra. In: Jain AK, Ratha NK (eds) Society of photo-optical instrumentation engineers (SPIE) conference series, vol 5404, pp 296–303
3. Tan X, Li Y, Liu J, Jiang L (2010) Face liveness detection from a single image with sparse low rank bilinear discriminative model. Proceedings of the 11th European conference on computer vision: Part VI., ECCV'10. Springer, Berlin, pp 504–517
4. Maatta J, Hadid A, Pietikainen M (2011) Face spoofing detection from single images using micro-texture analysis. In: Biometrics (IJCB), 2011 international joint conference on, pp 1–7
5. Pan G, Sun L, Wu Z, Lao S (2007) Eyeblink-based anti-spoofing in face recognition from a generic webcamera. In: Computer vision, 2007. ICCV 2007. IEEE 11th international conference on, pp 1–8
6. Kollreider K, Fronthaler H, Bigun J (2008) Verifying liveness by multiple experts in face biometrics. In: Computer vision and pattern recognition workshops, 2008. CVPRW '08. IEEE computer society conference on, pp 1–6
7. Kollreider K, Fronthaler H, Bigun J (2005) Evaluating liveness by face images and the structure tensor. In: Automatic identification advanced technologies, 2005. Fourth IEEE workshop on, pp 75–80
8. Chetty G, Wagner M (2004) Liveness verification in audio-video speaker authentication. In: In proceeding of the 10th ASSTA conference, pp 358–363. Macquarie University Press
9. Anjos A, Marcel S (2011) Counter-measures to photo attacks in face recognition: a public database and a baseline. In: Biometrics (IJCB), 2011 international joint conference on, pp 1–7
10. Bai J, Ng TT, Gao X, Shi YQ (2010) Is physics-based liveness detection truly possible with a single image? In: Circuits and systems (ISCAS), Proceedings of 2010 IEEE international symposium on, pp 3425–3428
11. Zhang Z, Yan J, Liu S, Lei Z, Yi D, Li S (2012) A face antispoofing database with diverse attacks. In: Biometrics (ICB), 2012 5th IAPR international conference on, pp 26–31
12. Pavlidis I, Symosek P (2000) The imaging issue in an automatic face/disguise detection system. In: Computer vision beyond the visible spectrum: methods and applications, 2000. Proceedings of the IEEE workshop on, pp 15–24
13. Kim Y, Na J, Yoon S, Yi J (2009) Masked fake face detection using radiance measurements. J Opt Soc Amer A 26(4)
14. OSU thermal imagery database. http://www.cse.ohiostate.edu/otcbvs-bench/

15. Yi D, Lei Z, Hu Y, Li SZ (2013) Fast matching by 2 lines of code for large scale face recognition systems. CoRR abs/1302.7180
16. Li SZ, Chu R, Liao S, Zhang L (2007) Illumination invariant face recognition using near-infrared images. IEEE Transactions on pattern analysis and machine intelligence 26(Special issue on biometrics: progress and directions)
17. Viola P, Jones M (2011) Robust real time object detection. IEEE ICCV workshop on statistical and computational theories of vision. Vancouver, Canada
18. Cootes TF, Taylor CJ, Cooper DH, Graham J (1995) Active shape models: their training and application. CVGIP: image underst 61:38–59
19. Fukunaga K (1990) Introduction to statistical pattern recognition, 2nd edn. Academic Press, Boston
20. Ahonen T, Hadid A, Pietikainen M (2004) Face recognition with local binary patterns. In: Proceedings of the European conference on computer vision. Prague, Czech, pp 469–481
21. Yi D, Lei Z, Li SZ (2011) A robust eye localization method for low quality face images. In: International joint conference on biometrics (IJCB). Washington, pp 15–21
22. Saragih J, Lucey S, Cohn J (2011) Deformable model fitting by regularized landmark mean-shift. Int J Comput Vis 91:200–215
23. Milborrow S, Morkel J, Nicolls F (2010) The MUCT landmarked face database. Pattern recognition association of South Africa (2010). http://www.milbo.org/
24. Rother C, Kolmogorov V, Blake A (2004) Grabcut: interactive foreground extraction using iterated graph cuts. ACM Trans Graph 23(3):309–314
25. Phillips PJ, Moon H, Rizvi SA, Rauss PJ (2000) The FERET evaluation methodology for face recognition algorithms 22(10):1090–1104
26. Okada K, Steffens J, Maurer T, Hong H, Elagin E, Neven H, von der Malsburg C (1998) The Bochum/USC face recognition system and how it fared in the FERET phase III test
27. Belhumeur P, Hespanha J, Kriegman D (1997) Eigenfaces vs. fisherfaces: recognition using class specific linear projection. IEEE Trans PAMI 19(7):711–720

# Chapter 6
# Iris Anti-spoofing

Zhenan Sun and Tieniu Tan

**Abstract** Iris images contain rich texture information for reliable personal identification. However, forged iris patterns may be used to spoof iris recognition systems. This paper proposes an iris anti-spoofing approach based on the texture discrimination between genuine and fake iris images. Four texture analysis methods include gray level co-occurrence matrix, statistical distribution of iris texture primitives, local binary patterns (LBP) and weighted-LBP are used for iris liveness detection. And a fake iris image database is constructed for performance evaluation of iris liveness detection methods. Fake iris images are captured from artificial eyeballs, textured contact lens and iris patterns printed on a paper, or synthesised from textured contact lens patterns. Experimental results demonstrate the effectiveness of the proposed texture analysis methods for iris liveness detection. And the learned statistical texture features based on weighted-LBP can achieve 99accuracy in classification of genuine and fake iris images.

## 6.1 Introduction

Iris recognition is becoming increasingly popular in security sensitive applications. Like any other information security technology, an iris recognition system has the risk to be attacked by various approaches. Possible attacks to an iris system may be launched at sensor level, data transmission level, image processing level, pattern recognition level, database level, or decision level [1–3]. All these attacks are possible to successfully spoof the iris recognition system by tempering with the identity verification result. Vulnerabilities of iris recognition systems have prevented their deployments in high level security scenarios. Therefore, it is necessary to develop

---

Z. Sun (✉) · T. Tan
Center for Research on Intelligent Perception and Computing,
National Laboratory of Pattern Recognition, Institute of Automation,
Chinese Academy of Sciences, P.O. Box 2728, Beijing 100190, P.R. China
e-mail: znsun@nlpr.ia.ac.cn

T. Tan
e-mail: tnt@nlpr.ia.ac.cn

© Springer-Verlag London 2014
S. Marcel et al. (eds.), *Handbook of Biometric Anti-Spoofing*,
Advances in Computer Vision and Pattern Recognition,
DOI: 10.1007/978-1-4471-6524-8_6

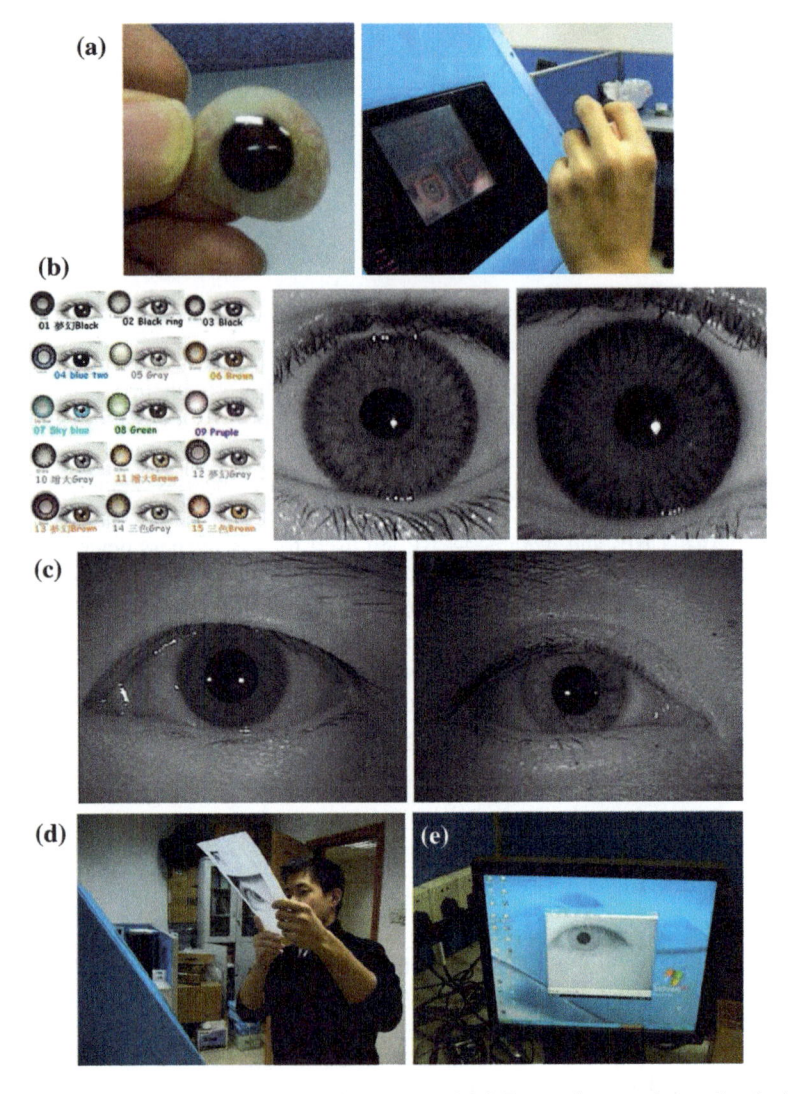

**Fig. 6.1** Example fake iris images. **a** Artificial eye model. **b** Textured contact lens. **c** Synthetic iris images. **d** Iris pattern printed on the paper. **e** Iris image/video displayed on the LCD

intelligent self-protection methods to identify and defend all possible attacks to iris systems.

This chapter mainly addresses the protection methods against the most commonly encountered attacks to an iris recognition system at sensor input level, i.e., iris liveness detection. Presentation of a fake iris pattern to the iris camera is the most popular approach to spoof an iris recognition system Fig. 6.1. Fake iris images may be captured from artificial eyeball (it is usually designed for blind persons with realistic iris-texture pattern) (Fig. 6.1a), textured contact lens (Fig. 6.1b), synthetic iris images Fig. 6.1c, iris pattern printed on the paper (Fig. 6.1d), iris image/video displayed on the LCD (Fig. 6.1e), etc. In 2002, German technology magazine c't conducted a set of well-designed tests to check the security of 11 biometrics systems available on the market, including face, fingerprint, and iris systems [4]. The results are that all tested systems were defeated. The first systematic study on the vulnerability of iris recognition systems to the spoofing attacks was reported by Matsumoto [5]. The printed iris patterns using a high resolution inkjet printer may successfully pass the identity check of all three commercial iris recognition systems with a probability of over 50 % [5]. Therefore, it is greatly important to develop advanced iris liveness detection methods for the security of iris recognition applications.

Iris liveness detection aims to authenticate whether the input iris images are captured from a living subject. Iris liveness detection is an important module in an iris recognition system to reduce the risks of being spoofed by fake iris patterns at the sensor input. Both physiological and optical characteristics of iris biometrics may be used for iris liveness detection. And automatic detection of a fake iris attack may be accomplished at the iris sensor level, at the algorithm level or a combination of both. A brief review of the existing iris liveness detection methods is given as follows.

*Iris liveness detection based on physiological characteristics of human iris.* The eye itself has some physiological characteristics relating to the natural processes performed by living things, which can be exploited for liveness detection. The commonly used physiological characteristics for iris liveness detection include eyeblink, pupillary light reflex, pupillary unrest (hippus), etc.

Eyeblink is a physiological activity of closing and opening the eyelids, which is an informative feature for liveness detection of both face and iris recognition systems. Conditional random fields-based eyeblink detection method was developed to check the liveness of face biometrics [6]. Eyeblink detection is useful to discriminate real iris and static fake iris patterns such as iris photograph because of the visual salience of dynamic features during eyelid movements. However, if the attacker wears cosmetic contact lenses or shows a pre-recorded video, the inherent characteristics of eyeblink is also observable. In addition, the eye blink frequency is variable across different subjects and even the same subject may have variable blink frequency under various conditions, so it is a challenging task to develop a stable eyeblink-based iris liveness detection method in practical applications. The pupil is in the state of rhythmic contraction and dilation called hippus or pupillary unrest under normal conditions [7, 8]. The dynamic change of pupil size will cause the nonlinear deformation of iris texture. So both pupil size variation and iris texture deformation can be used for iris liveness detection. An intuitive solution to detect pupillary unrest (hippus) is to measure the variation of the ratio between pupil and iris diameter in iris image sequences. However, the change of pupil size in normal illumination is not significant. So active illuminators are usually used in iris cameras to cause significant pupil dilation or constriction. Pupil size usually increases in a dark environment (allowing more light in) and decreases in a bright environment (allowing less light in). Such an involuntary biological response of pupil to the intensity (luminance) of light is known as the pupillary light reflex. Huang et al. designed a controllable visible light source in the long range iris image acquisition system to generate four different illumination conditions (simulation from a dim corridor environment to a home interior lighting and bright working areas) that cause pupil constriction [9]. Pupil constriction measurement based on ratio of pupil diameter to iris diameter was demonstrated to have significant difference under different illumination conditions [9]. However, a number of researchers (including Huang et al. [9] and Puhan et al. [10]) have noticed that the pupil size variation-based iris liveness detection methods are only effective in detection of printed iris, photographs, plastic/glass eye opaque contact lens, etc., because such fake iris images do not show the change in pupil's size when illumination changes. If the attackers wear cosmetic contact lens (opaque in outer side and partly transparent in inner side adjacent to pupil [10]) where the pupil boundary is not covered or occluded [9], the fake iris image sequences also show pupillary light reflex. Therefore, both Huang et al. [9] and Puhan et al. [10] suggested to measure the iris texture deformation as an implicit indicator of pupil constriction. Huang et al. proposed to combine pupil size variation and mutual information between cross-frame image patches to better represent the pupil constriction features. And Puhan et al. [10] computed the normalized Hamming distance on binary texture features to quantify textural dissimilarity between localized iris regions for verification of pupillary light reflex. The similarity measure between interframe image regions (e.g., mutual information in [9] and normalized Hamming distance in [10]) is a good approach to detect iris deformation and pupil constriction but it may be sensitive to iris image quality variations in uncontrolled conditions such as defocused, motion blurred, specular reflections, eyelids, and eyelash occluded iris images.

*Iris liveness detection based on optical characteristics of human iris.* Real and fake irises may exhibit significantly different optical characteristics under visible, near-infrared, multispectral, and structured lighting respectively. For example, redeye effect may be a useful evidence of authentic iris but it is an intrusive manner to suddenly generate flash lighting. So it is more natural to use the existing near-infrared illumination in iris imaging for optical liveness evaluation. The main optical characteristics useful for iris liveness detection under near-infrared illumination include frequency distribution, Purkinje images, image quality features, statistical texture features, etc.

Daugman proposed to identify the printed iris pattern based on frequency analysis [11]. The periodic dot printing process will generate focused high frequency in fake iris images so it is possible to utilize the frequency characteristics for iris liveness detection. This method is limited to printed iris detection. In addition, if the fake iris images are captured out of the focusing range, the high frequency components cannot be found in the defocused iris images. So the defocused fake iris images have the risk to be recognized as authentic samples using frequency analysis-based iris liveness detection methods.

Four optical surfaces of human eye (the inner and outer surface of the cornea, anterior and posterior surface of the lens) will generate the corresponding reflection images which are known as Purkinje images. Lee et al. [12] proposed a fake iris detection scheme based on Purkinje images. The Purkinje images-based method is effective for identification of printed iris pattern and glass/plastic eye models but fails to detect contact lens because the pupil is still visible even the attacker wears contact lens.

Galbally et al. proposed to use iris image quality measures for iris liveness detection [13]. A number of iris image quality features including focus features, motion features, occlusion features, global and local contrast, pupil dilation are combined to construct a high-dimensional feature vector for classification of genuine and fake iris images. And then a feature selection method, namely Sequential Floating Feature Selection (SFFS) is used to select the most effective feature set for iris liveness detection. The image quality measures try to provide a comprehensive description of the textural and geometric features of genuine and fake iris images. But it does not design the most effective features specific for iris liveness detection although a variety of popular iris features have been exploited in feature selection.

Genuine and fake iris images have distinctive texture patterns, therefore, well-developed texture analysis and pattern classification methods can be used for iris liveness detection. The texture features useful for iris liveness detection include gray level co-occurrence matrix [14], statistical distribution of iris texture primitives [15], local binary patterns (LBP) [16], and weighted LBP [17]. He et al. proposed a contact lens detection method via statistical texture analysis [14]. Four distinctive features based on gray level co-occurrence matrix (GLCM) are extracted and support vector machine is used for classification of genuine and fake iris images. Wei et al. proposed a texture analysis-based method for contact lens detection [15]. Iris Textons are learned to represent statistical texture features of real and fake iris images. He et al. used Adaboost to learn the most distinctive LBP features for iris spoof detection [16]. Zhang et al. realized high accuracy fake iris detection based on weighted LBP encoding strategy and SVM classifier [17]. Doyle et al. [18] used modified LBP to automatically determine the contact lens type of a person (no contact lens/clear prescription lens/textured cosmetic lens). Texture analysis-based iris liveness detection methods do not need special iris sensors. However, the texture of real and fake iris images is not absolutely distinguishable and the training process of the real/fake iris classification method limits the generality of the iris liveness detection algorithm. Doyle et al. [19] demonstrated that the accuracy of texture analysis-based textured lens detection can drop dramatically in cross-sensor or cross-lens pattern applications.

The multispectral imaging system can illustrate the spectrum-related visual features available in genuine iris images. Lee et al. [20, 21] found the ratio of visual features between iris images captured under 750 and 850 nm illumination is effective for iris liveness detection. The method can distinguish printed fake iris and artificial eyeballs from live iris patterns. Chen et al. [22] combined the multispectral characteristics of conjunctival vessels in eyeball and multispectral characteristics of iris textures from iris images simultaneously captured at near-infrared (860 nm) and blue (480 nm) wavelengths for iris liveness detection. The multispecial visual features are reliable for iris liveness detection but special design of iris sensor is needed.

Connell et al. [23] developed an optical system consisting of a miniature projector and an offset camera to observe the discriminative optical characteristics of genuine

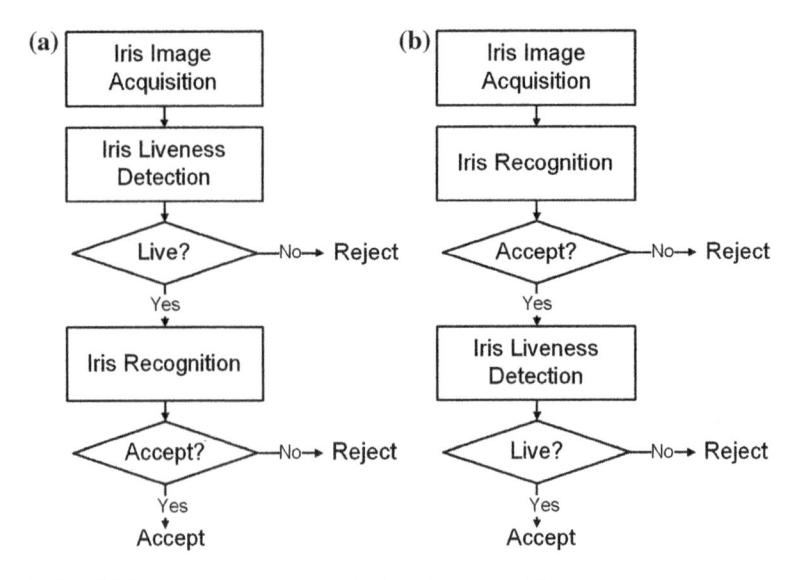

Fig. 6.2 Two iris liveness detection strategies in an iris recognition system

eyeball using structured light projection. A normal eye and one with a patterned contact lens are supposed to generate different deformations of a projected striped pattern [23]. So the light rays projected on the subject's eye can be used to measure their curvature for detection of a patterned contact lens. However, this method has limitation in applications because the structured light projection cannot be always observed in complex environments.

Based on the above analysis, both physiological and optical characteristics have their advantages and disadvantages in iris liveness detection. So it is better to combine all available features together to achieve a more reliable solution to secure iris recognition systems. Iris liveness detection may be performed at different stages in iris recognition. For example, there are two strategies of iris liveness detection (Fig. 6.2). One is to perform iris liveness detection immediately after iris image acquisition (Fig. 6.2a). If the input iris images are identified as fake samples, the current user is rejected immediately and the input iris images are prevented from the following iris recognition process. If the iris liveness detection algorithm is accurate and efficient, it is a good strategy to identify the fake iris images before iris recognition. However, fake iris attack in some applications is a low probability event so false alarms of fake iris images may increase the FRR of iris recognition. So another strategy is only the successfully recognized iris images are checked with liveness detection (Fig. 6.2b). A large portion of fake iris images can be rejected by iris recognition in quality assessment and feature matching steps. So iris recognition is also a good approach for iris liveness detection. This strategy can reduce the risk of false alarm of fake iris images and save time for iris liveness detection since only recognized iris images are checked their liveness characteristics.

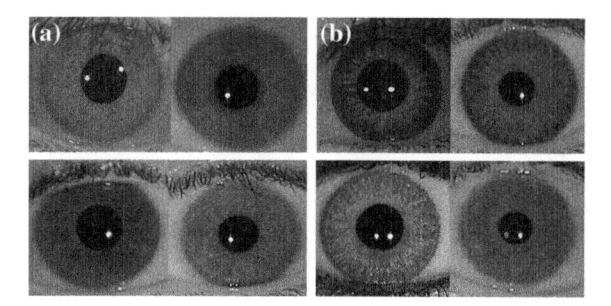

**Fig. 6.3** Comparison of texture features of real and fake iris images. **a** Real iris images. **b** Fake iris images

Although both hardware and software countermeasures may be developed to detect iris liveness, this chapter mainly discusses automatic classification of real and fake iris images at algorithm level. Example real and fake iris images are shown in Fig. 6.3. There are significant differences of texture features between real and fake iris images. The real iris images usually have naturally smooth texture features. In contrast, the fake iris images have coarse texture pattern due to the printed iris texture on contact lens, paper, and other materials. So texture analysis is an effective solution to iris liveness detection. We have proposed four statistical texture analysis methods based on various texture primitives, e.g., gray level co-occurrence matrices (GLCM) [15], iris textons [15], Adaboost selected LBP [16], and weighted LBP [17] for classification of real and fake iris images. And we have also constructed a database including different kinds of fake iris images to test the performance of texture-based iris liveness detection methods. The main contents of this chapter introduce the technical details and testing results of the proposed four texture analysis-based iris liveness detection methods [15–17]. Section 7.13.2 introduces statistical features of gray level co-occurrence matrices for iris liveness detection. Section 7.13.3 presents statistical distribution of iris textons for iris liveness detection. Section 7.9.4 and Sect. 7.9.5 present Adaboost learned and weighted local binary patterns for iris liveness detection respectively. The fake iris image databases and evaluation results of the four iris liveness detection methods are reported in Sect. 7.6.6. Our experiences in iris liveness detection show that statistical texture features are effective to discriminate genuine and fake iris images.

## 6.2 Statistical Features of Gray Level Co-occurrence Matrices for Iris Liveness Detection

Gray level co-occurrence matrices (GLCM) describe the distribution of neighboring pixel pairs with specific pattern of intensity and spatial relations. GLCM is a classic texture analysis method in modeling second order image statistics. The repeated dot patterns of iris texture printed on the cosmetic contact lens (Fig. 6.3b) can be well represented by GLCM.

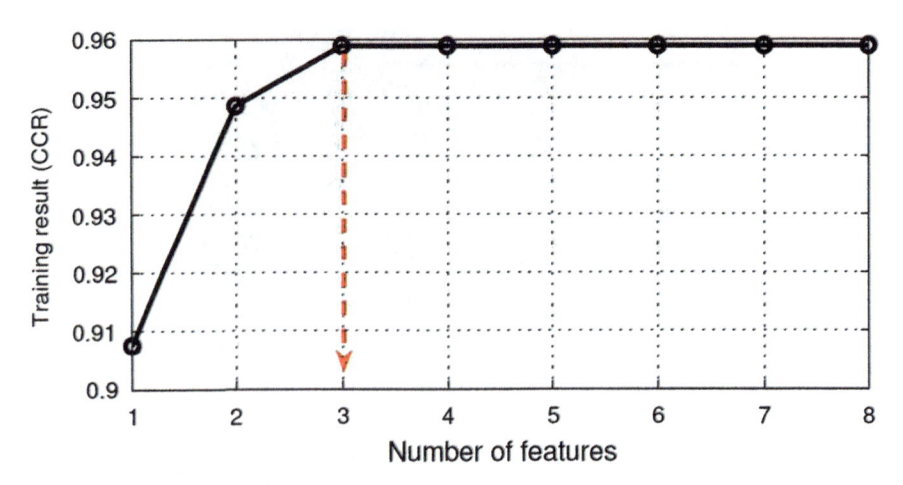

**Fig. 6.4** Feature selection of GLCM-based texture features for iris liveness detection

Haralick et al. defined 14 measures of textural features based on co-occurrence matrix, e.g., homogeneity, contrast, correlation, variance, inverse difference moment, etc. [24]. We adopt these distinctive measures to represent real and fake iris images [15]. These features are orientation dependent so we can obtain four feature values for each measure computed at different orientations ($0°, 45°, 90°, 135°$). The statistics of the four feature values including mean $\overline{X}$ and range ($Max(X) - Min(X)$) are used to represent the texture features of each measure. Therefore, an iris image can be represented by 28 GLCM-based texture features. We found that the feature set shows certain redundancies, indicating only some feature components are necessary for iris liveness detection. Therefore feature selection strategy is employed to find the most effective subset of the GLCM feature set. We tried different combinations of these 28 texture features for classification of real and fake iris images in the training set (Fig. 6.4). The result shows that only three features are enough to achieve high classification rate and more features cannot improve the CCR further. Therefore three GLCM-based texture features are finally selected to characterize iris texture. They are inverse difference moment $f_{idm}$, sum average $f_{sa}$ and sum entropy $f_{se}$ with the following definitions:

$$f_{idm} = \sum_i \sum_j \frac{1}{1+(i-j)^2} p(i,j)$$

$$f_{sa} = \sum_{i=2}^{2N_g} i\, p_{x+y}(i)$$

$$f_{se} = -\sum_{i=2}^{2N_g} p_{x+y}(i) \log(p_{x+y}(i)) \quad (6.1)$$

where $p(i,j)$ is the co-occurrence matrix, $p_{x+y}(k) = \sum_{i=1}^{N_g} \sum_{j=1}^{N_g} p(i,j)$, ($i+j = k, k = 2, 3, \ldots, 2N_g$), and $N_g$ is the number of gray levels.

6 Iris Anti-spoofing

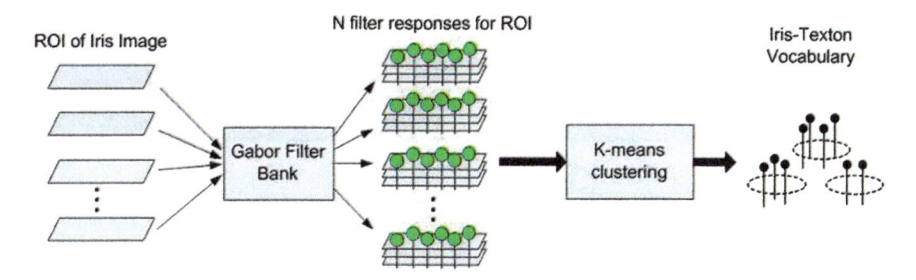

**Fig. 6.5** Flowchart of learning Iris-Texton vocabulary

Euclidean distance is used to measure the dissimilarity between the texture features of two iris images. Finally, SVM is employed to learn a classifier for iris liveness detection.

## 6.3 Statistical Distribution of Iris Textons for Iris Liveness Detection

Iris texture varies from person to person in terms of the number, size, shape, orientation, and location of minute image structures. These minute features are the building blocks (or textons) of iris texture. So it is a good idea to represent iris texture using texton-like concept. However, it is inappropriate to use traditional concept of textons for this purpose due to the irregularity of iris textons. Comparatively, the learning-based texton concepts such as bag-of-word, visual codebook, or visual dictionary in object recognition literature are more suitable for iris texton representation. Local binary patterns are predefined visual dictionary which is universal for statistical texture analysis. LBP cannot precisely describe the freckles, coronas, crypts, furrows, etc., in iris images. So it is desirable to learn a better visual dictionary specific to iris minute features. In addition, it is interesting to find the dominant textons and their distributions in iris images.

Motivated by the popularity of bag-of-words model in object recognition, we propose clustering-based Iris-Texton vocabulary. The flowchart of learning visual iris vocabulary is shown in Fig. 6.5 with the following key steps:

(1) Construct the training dataset. The training set should contain normalized iris images from a large number of subjects so that various representative iris texture patterns can be included.
(2) Filter all iris images in training set with a bank of Gabor filters so that each iris image region is transformed into a feature vector.
(3) Cluster all feature vectors into a compact set of typical iris image patches, i.e., Iris-Texton Vocabulary.

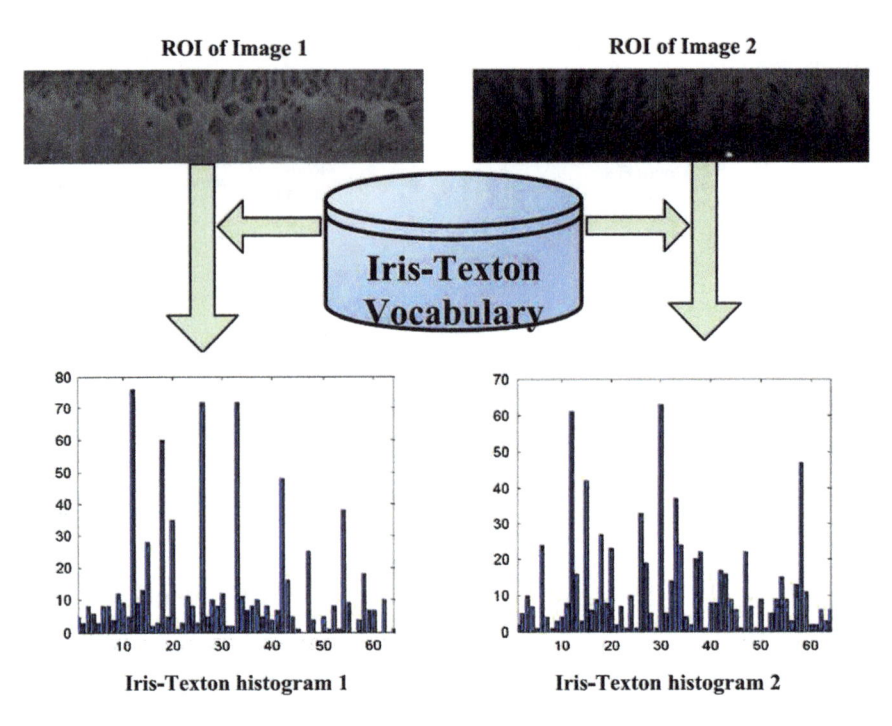

**Fig. 6.6** Distribution of iris textons in real and fake iris images

Iris-Texton vocabulary is well suited to describe the specific texture features of iris images. Therefore statistical distribution of iris textons is adopted for classification of real and fake iris images [15]. The only difference is the training data is replaced with real and fake iris images to learn the specific visual primitives in real/fake iris texture. Finally, the input iris image is represented with the distribution of iris textons (Fig. 6.6). It is expected that real and fake iris images have significantly different constitution of basic texture elements. Chi-square is used to measure the dissimilarity between the statistical texture features of two iris images. Finally, SVM is employed to learn a classifier for classification of real and fake iris images.

## 6.4 Selected Local Binary Patterns for Iris Liveness Detection

Local binary pattern has become a popular method for texture analysis. So it is a straightforward idea to use LBP features to represent the regional texture pattern of fake iris images. However, how to choose appropriate parameters of LBP descriptors is still unknown. In addition, the texture features of fake iris images vary from region to region (Fig. 6.3b). Most discriminating features of fake iris images are distributed on regions close to the iris boundary. So it is necessary to use a machine learning

6 Iris Anti-spoofing

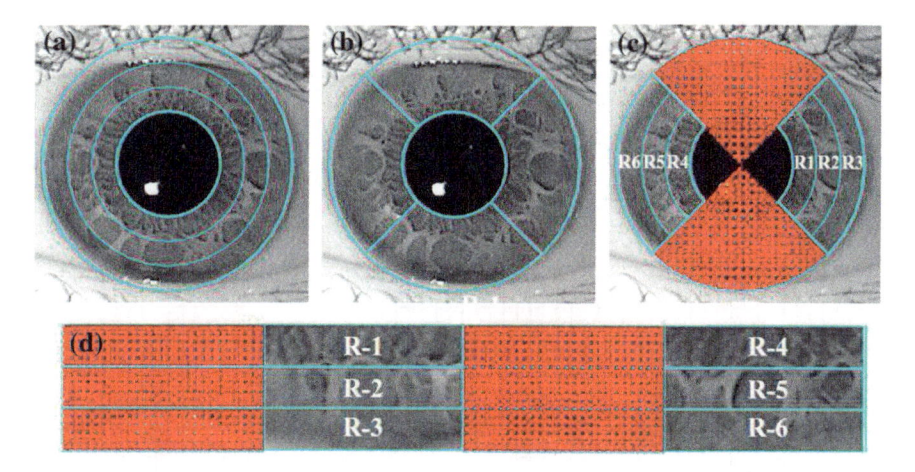

**Fig. 6.7** The ROI of iris images used for iris liveness detection

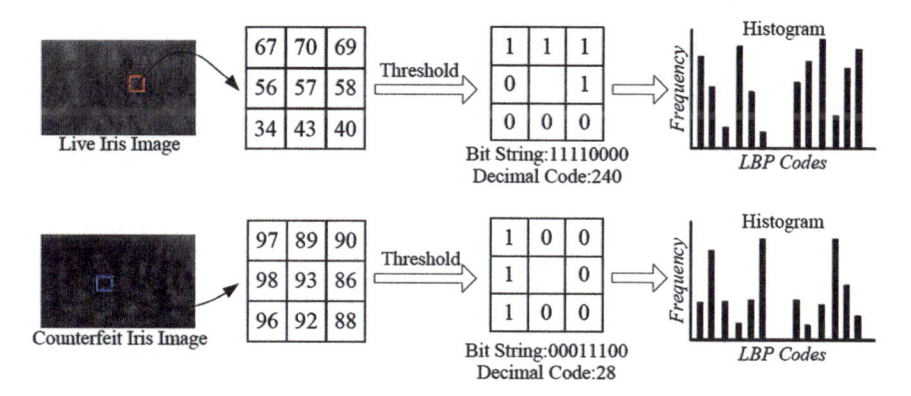

**Fig. 6.8** Illustration of Local binary patterns

method to select the most effective LBP features for iris liveness detection [16]. To avoid eyelids or eyelashes occlusions, the upper and lower regions of iris images are excluded and only the left and right parts are divided into six subregions for LBP feature extraction (Fig. 6.7).

The local binary patterns (LBP) is adopted as texture descriptor. Basically, LBP is defined for each pixel by thresholding its neighborhood pixels with the center pixel value, and considering the result as a binary bit string (Fig. 6.8). We use multiresolution uniform LBPs (including $LBP_{8,1}^{u2}$, $LBP_{8,2}^{u2}$, $LBP_{8,5}^{u2}$, $LBP_{8,7}^{u2}$, $LBP_{12,2}^{u2}$, $LBP_{12,3}^{u2}$, $LBP_{12,5}^{u2}$, $LBP_{16,3}^{u2}$, $LBP_{16,5}^{u2}$, $LBP_{16,7}^{u2}$) for iris texture representation [25]. The numbers of bins of these LBP histograms are 59, 59, 59, 59, 135, 135, 135, 243, 234, and 234 respectively. For six subregions, we totally get 8,220 possible LBP bins. Each bin represents the frequency of one type of micro image structures on a subregion, and is considered as a candidate texture feature. A large pool of regional

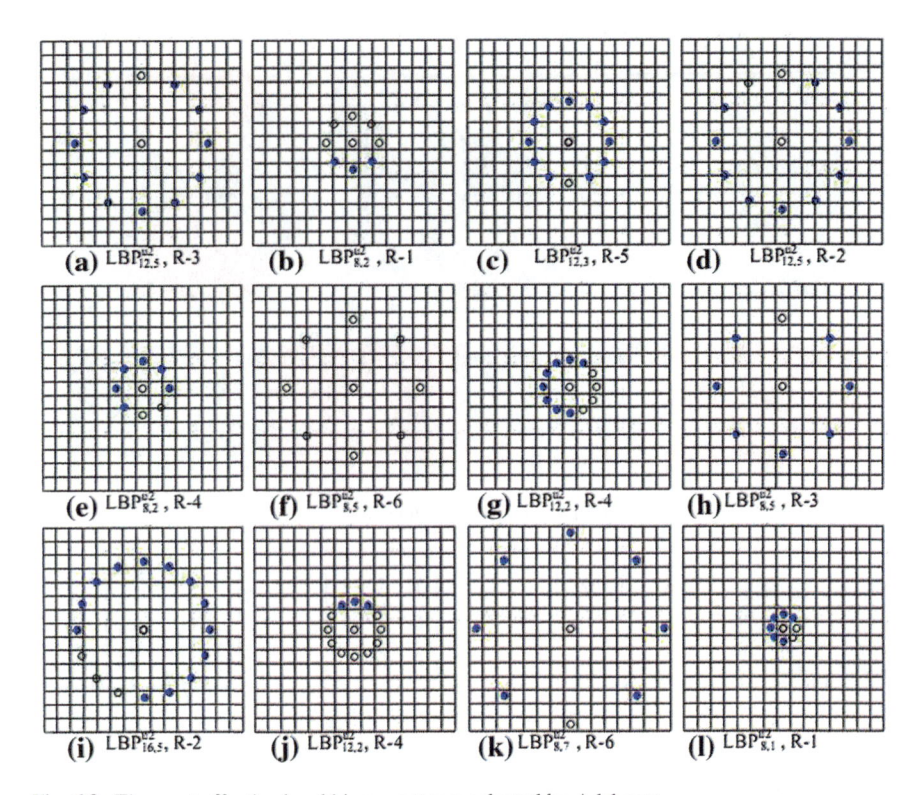

**Fig. 6.9** The most effective local binary patterns selected by Adaboost

LBP features is generated, which contains much redundant information because of the redundancy between different LBP features as well as that between different subregions. The Adaboost algorithm is adopted to learn the most discriminative regional LBP features from the redundant feature pool [26, 27]. Adaboost is particularly efficient for two-class problems, and therefore is suitable for selecting the best LBP features for iris spoof detection. Given a training database, we can learn the most effective local binary patterns based on Adaboost (Fig. 6.9). It should be noted that these LBP features are extracted at different regions of iris images and each texture feature for iris spoof detection is jointly determined by an LBP feature and an image region. Each LBP feature is regarded as weak classifier and an ensemble of the most effective LBP features are combined to construct a strong classifier for iris liveness detection.

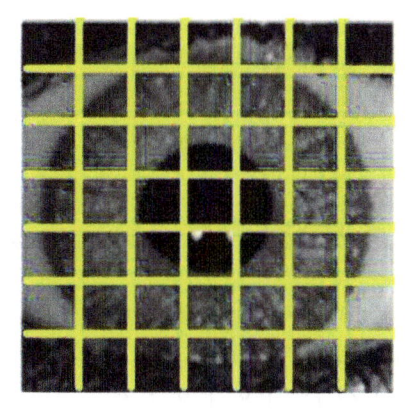

**Fig. 6.10** The ROI of an iris image used for feature extraction

## 6.5 Weighted LBP for Iris Liveness Detection

As introduced above, the LBP feature is capable for iris liveness detection and other coarse classification task. However, the weights of different binary codes are equal in LBP coding, resulting in the sensitiveness of LBP to noise. Therefore, we proposed a weighted LBP (w-LBP) feature which re-ranks the binary digits of LBP according to the gradient direction. The SIFT descriptor is largely invariant to changes of scale, illumination, and local affine distortions, and also in a certain degree of stability to view changes and noise [28]. We use the SIFT descriptor to improve the stability and robustness of LBP.

We extract w-LBP features from iris images. The bounding square block of iris circle is regarded as the ROI for feature extraction (Fig. 6.10). To extract w-LBP features, the first step is to generate the scale space $L(x, y, 3/4)$ from the convolution of a variable-scale Gaussian template $G(x, y, 3/4)$, with an image $I(x, y)$. The second step is to extract a simplified SIFT descriptor for each pixel in its $5 \times 5$ neighborhood, as shown in Fig. 6.11. Arrows denote the magnitude and orientation at each image pixel, and the overlaid circle is weighted Gaussian window. Fig. 6.11b shows the orientation histograms summarizing the visual contents over subregions. In order to achieve orientation invariance, the coordinates of the descriptor and the gradient orientations are rotated relatively to the main orientation, which is determined by all the gradient directions of every scale. The last step is to get a descending rank of the orientation histogram, denoted as $k_{SIFT}(i)$, $\text{Rank}_{SIFT}(i) \in \{0, 1, \ldots, 7\}$, where $i$ is the ID of orientation.

Then, for each pixel, we regard the direction with the larger SIFT histogram entries as the higher bit of binary string. According to the SIFT orientation histogram, we encode w-LBP as

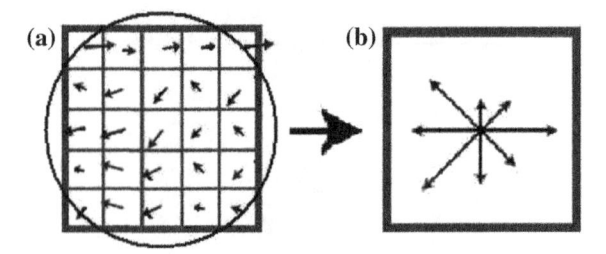

**Fig. 6.11** Simplified SIFT descriptor. **a** Gradients. **b** Descriptor

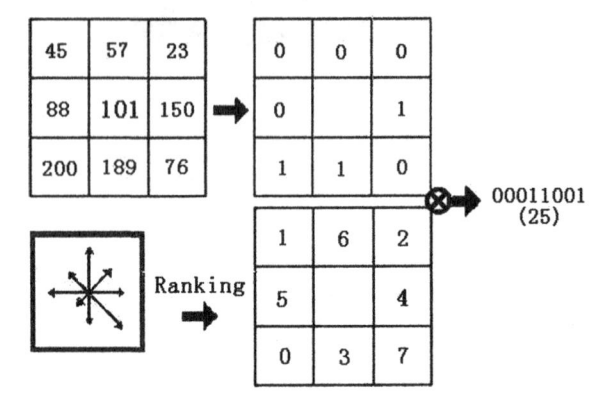

**Fig. 6.12** Diagram of weighted LBP encoding

$$\text{w-LBP}_8 = \sum_{i=0}^{7} \text{sign}\,(g_i - g_c) 2^{\text{Rank}_{\text{SIFT}}(i)}$$

$$\text{sign}\,(g_i - g_c) = \begin{cases} 0, & \text{if } g_i < g_c \\ 1, & \text{if } g_i \geq g_c \end{cases} \quad (6.2)$$

where $g_i$ is gray value of a neighbor pixel, $g_c$ is gray value of the central pixel, and the neighbor pixel ID $i$ corresponds to the ID of orientation histogram. Fig. 6.12 is an illustration of w-LBP encoding.

To achieve gray-scale invariance, w-LBP is extracted at each level of Gaussian scale space, denoted by G1–G6. For G1–G3, we get three w-LBP maps as mentioned above, as shown in Fig. 6.13a. For G4–G6, we extract w-LBP in 24 neighbors shown in Fig. 6.13b. For a specific direction, when at least two of three neighborhood pixels are larger than the center pixel, the value of a binary bit string is set as 1, otherwise 0.

We divide a w-LBP map into $m \times n$ partitions equally, and abandon the first and last rows to avoid the impact of eyelids. In each partition, three statistics of the w-LBP map are exacted, namely, standard deviation of w-LBP histogram, mean, and standard deviation of w-LBP map according to the following formulas.

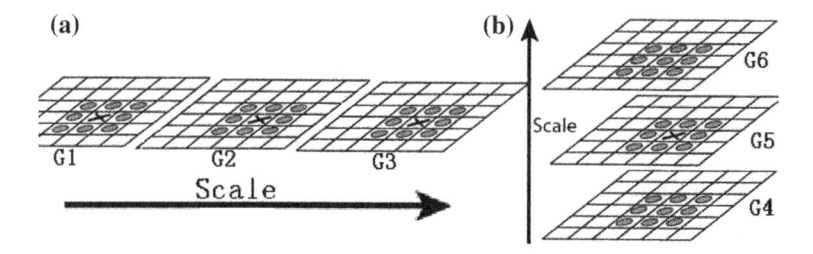

**Fig. 6.13** Diagram of the multiscale weighted LBP features

$$\overline{I_{\text{map}}} = \frac{1}{m \times n} \sum_{i,j} I_{\text{map}}(i, j)$$

$$\sigma_{\text{map}} = \sqrt{\frac{1}{m \times n} \sum_{i,j} (I_{\text{map}}(i, j) - \overline{I_{\text{map}}})^2}$$

$$\sigma_{\text{hist}} = \sqrt{\frac{1}{256} \sum_{i=0}^{255} \left( \text{hist}(i) - \frac{m \times n}{256} \right)^2} \qquad (6.3)$$

where $m$ and $n$ are the size of block, and $I_{\text{map}}$ and $hist$ are map and histogram of w-LBP respectively. The extracted features are used for classification of fake and genuine iris images based on SVM classifier.

## 6.6 Experimental Results

To establish a benchmark for iris liveness detection, we develop a large fake iris image database including various fake iris images captured from printed iris, cosmetic contact lens, and plastic eyeball, and synthesized from cosmetic contact lens patterns.

### 6.6.1 Printed Iris Pattern

High quality iris images can be printed on paper with advanced laser printers. We choose to print color iris images from UPOL database [29] to forge visually realistic iris pattern. The UPOL database contains 384 iris images from left and right eyes of 64 subjects. We randomly select one image of each class for printing. And then an iris camera is used to capture ten iris images from each forged iris pattern. Two examples of the captured fake iris images and the corresponding normalized iris images are shown in Fig. 6.14. The iris texture is clearly preserved on the captured iris images.

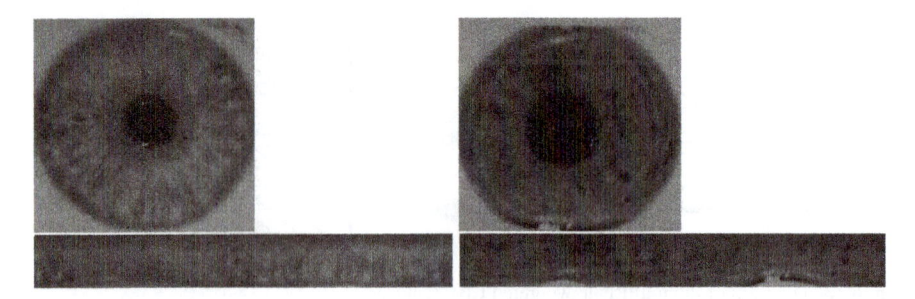

**Fig. 6.14** Two example images captured from the printed iris patterns and the corresponding normalized iris images

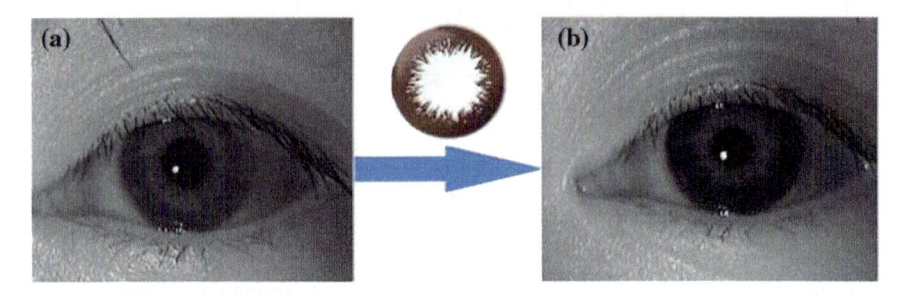

**Fig. 6.15** Example iris image with cosmetic contact lens. **a** Genuine iris image. **b** Fake iris pattern with cosmetic contact lens

## 6.6.2 Textured Contact Lens

Nowadays more and more people wear cosmetic contact lens, which has become the most popular approach to spoof an iris system. There are 74 volunteers wearing 56 kinds of cosmetic contact lens for acquisition of fake iris images (Fig. 6.15).

## 6.6.3 Synthesized Iris Images with Textured Contact Lens

The size of fake iris image database is limited, so we propose to synthesize more samples from the fake iris images with cosmetic contact lens. Firstly the iris image synthesis method based on patch sampling [30] is used to generate artificial iris texture prototypes from the original iris images captured from the subjects wearing cosmetic contact lens. And then intraclass variations such as distortion, defocus, noise, perturbation, and rotation are introduced to generate multiple derivatives for each class. Fig. 6.16 shows an example of image prototype with cosmetic contact lens and its intraclass derivatives.

6 Iris Anti-spoofing

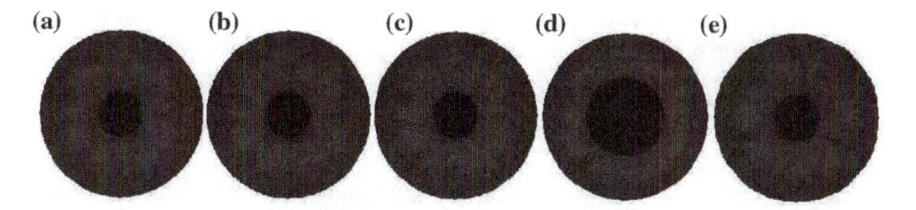

**Fig. 6.16** An iris image prototype of cosmetic contact lens and its intraclass derivatives. **a** Prototype. **b** Defocus sample. **c** Noisy sample. **d** Deformation sample. **e** Rotation sample

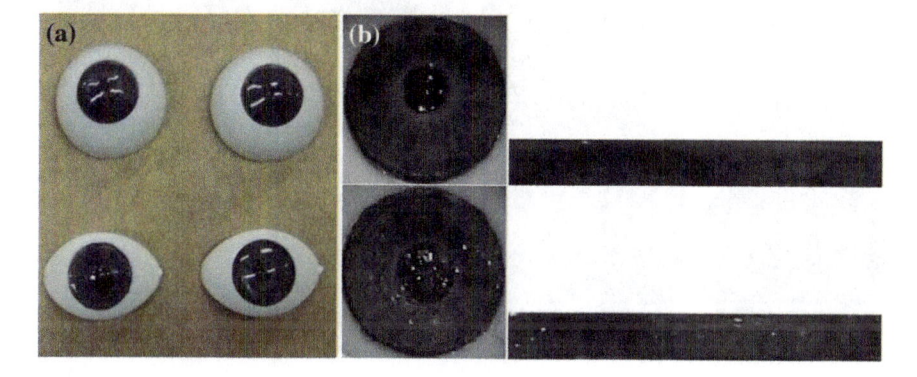

**Fig. 6.17** Forged iris images from plastic eyeball model. **a** Plastic eyeball models. **b** Fake iris images captured from the plastic eyeball model

## 6.6.4 Plastic Eyeball Model

Plastic eyeball with realistic iris texture pattern can be used to spoof iris recognition systems. So we made some plastic eyeball models with iris texture from the UPOL database [29] (Fig. 6.17). And then ten iris images are captured from each plastic eyeball to construct the fake iris image database.

To evaluate the performance of iris liveness detection methods, a fake iris image database DB_All including four datasets, i.e., DB_Print, DB_Contact, DB_Synthesis and DB_Eyeball is constructed (Fig. 6.18). DB_Print contains 640 iris images captured from the printed iris patterns on paper. DB_Contact contains 1,000 iris images captured from the subjects wearing cosmetic contact lens. DB_Synthesis contains 2,400 iris images synthesized from DB_Contact. DB_Eyeball contains 480 iris images captured from the plastic eyeball models.

Four texture analysis-based iris liveness detection methods, i.e., GLCM, Iris-Texton, s-LBP (Adaboost selected local binary pattern) and w-LBP (weighted LBP) are tested on the fake iris image databases. Half of the fake iris images are used for training and the rest for testing. Table 6.1 shows the testing results including CCR (Correct Classification Rate) and EER (Equal Error Rate) of these methods.

A number of conclusions can be drawn from the experimental results.

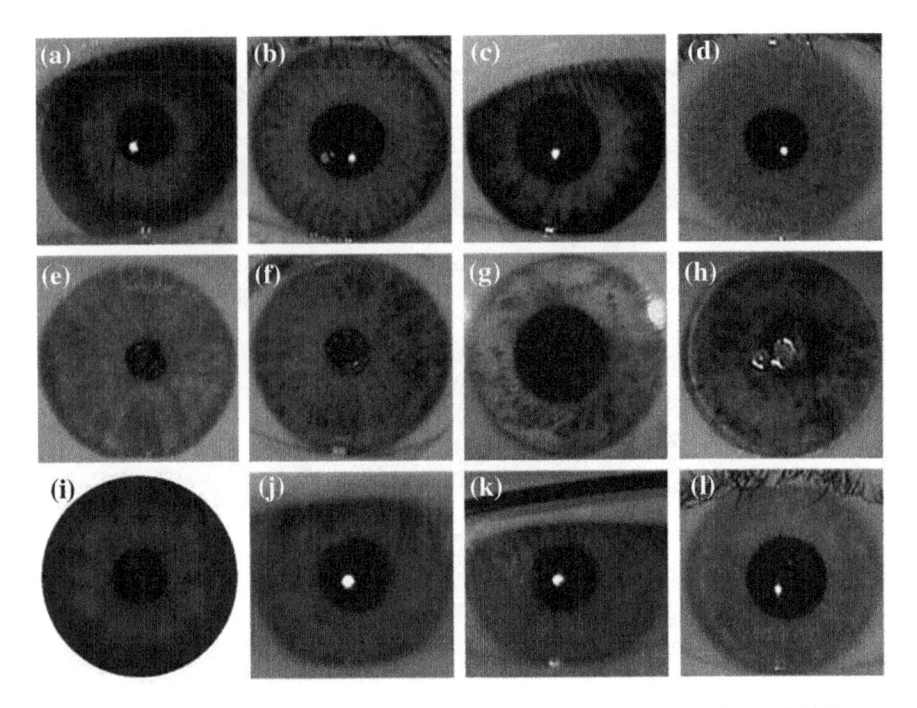

Fig. 6.18 Examples of fake iris images. a–d Iris images with cosmetic contact lens. e, f Iris images captured from the printed iris pattern on paper. g, h Iris images captured from the plastic eyeball models. i Synthesized fake iris image. j–l Genuine iris images

Table 6.1 Testing results of four iris liveness detection methods

| Test database | DB_Print | | DB_Contact & DB_Synthesis | | DB_Eyeball | | DB_All | |
|---|---|---|---|---|---|---|---|---|
| Metrics | CCR(%) | EER(%) | CCR(%) | EER(%) | CCR(%) | EER(%) | CCR(%) | EER(%) |
| Method | | | | | | | | |
| GLCM | 95.78 | 5.33 | 93.72 | 7.23 | 96.13 | 4.72 | 93.85 | 6.56 |
| Iris-Texton | 99.54 | 0.70 | 98.65 | 4.54 | 97.58 | 1.38 | 95.82 | 5.07 |
| s-LBP | 99.67 | 0.54 | 98.36 | 1.82 | 99.80 | 0.47 | 98.22 | 1.07 |
| w-LBP | 99.62 | 0.52 | 99.14 | 0.92 | 99.66 | 0.38 | 99.23 | 0.86 |

1. Texture analysis is an effective method for classification of genuine and fake iris images. Four kinds of fake iris images including printed iris pattern, cosmetic contact lens, synthesized iris pattern, and plastic eyeball model can be successfully identified by these texture-based iris liveness detection methods.
2. There is significant difference between these four statistical texture analysis methods in terms of iris liveness detection performance. So it is important to develop distinctive and robust iris feature representations for classification of genuine and fake iris images.

3. Weighted LBP method achieves the best CCR and EER in iris liveness detection because SIFT descriptor and LBP operator are combined to characterize the robust texture features of fake iris images.
4. It is still difficult to successfully discriminate all genuine and fake iris images since the texture features of some genuine and fake iris images are similar. It is unrealistic to rely on iris liveness detection algorithms to identify all iris spoof attacks. So it is suggested to combine sensor level and algorithm level iris liveness detection approaches to improve the security of iris recognition systems.

## 6.7 Summary

Iris recognition is being deployed in many important applications such as national ID card, banking, social benefit, border control, etc. The risk of security attacks to iris recognition systems increases accordingly driven by the great benefit of fraudulent identity authentication. It is predictable that attackers will pay more efforts to develop advanced methods to spoof iris biometrics. For example, more realistic fake iris patterns may be presented at iris sensor input. So it will become more challenging to develop a reliable security solution to iris recognition with the advancement of iris attack approaches. In this sense, the research of security defense technology for iris recognition will never stop since the attack approaches are dynamically updated. The most challenging problem for secure iris recognition is that the possible attacks to an iris recognition system are unpredictable but the attack patterns in a training database are limited. And the sources of attacks to an iris system are widely distributed at sensor level, iris recognition algorithm level and application level. So it is almost impossible to guarantee a 100 % absolutely secure iris recognition system. But the efforts to protect the security of iris recognition systems are meaningful since the risk can be reduced with intelligent attack detection.

This chapter aims to improve the security level of an iris recognition system against commonly encountered attacks at the iris sensor. Texture analysis methods are proposed to classify the input iris images into genuine and fake samples. Our results show that the learned statistical texture features such as LBP can achieve 99 accuracy in identification of fake iris pattern printed on paper, cosmetic contact lens, and plastic eyeball. The performance of the proposed security enhancement methods for iris biometrics needs more test in practice. It is still unknown whether the texture-based iris liveness detection method can identify more natural fake iris patterns in practice.

## References

1. Ruiz-Albacete V, Tome-Gonzalez P, Alonso-Fernandez F, Galbally J, Fierrez J, Ortega-Garcia J (2008) Direct attacks using fake images in iris verification. In: Schouten B, Juul N, Drygajlo A,

Tistarelli M (eds) Biometrics and identity management, vol 5372., Lecture Notes in Computer ScienceSpringer, Berlin Heidelberg, pp 181–190
2. Schneier B (1999) Inside risks: the uses and abuses of biometrics. Communications of the ACM 42(8):136
3. Schuckers SAC (2002) Spoofing and anti-spoofing measures. Inf Secur Tech Rep 7(4):56–62
4. Thalheim L, Krissler J, Ziegler P (2002) Body check: biometrics defeated'c't magazine. June 3, 2002
5. Matsumoto T (2004) Artificial irises: importance of vulnerability analysis. In: Proceedings of Asian biometrics workshop (AWB), vol. 45
6. Szwoch M, Pieniazek P (2012) Computer Vision and Graphics. Eye blink based detection of liveness in biometric authentication systems using conditional random fields. Springer, Berlin, pp 669–676
7. Adler F (1965) Physiology of the eye: Clinical application the cv mosby company
8. Davision H (1962) The eye. Academic, London
9. Huang X, Ti C, Hou Qz, Tokuta A, Yang R (2013) An experimental study of pupil constriction for liveness detection. In: IEEE Workshop on Applications of Computer Vision (WACV), pp 252–258
10. Puhan N, Sudha N, Suhas Hegde A (2011) A new iris liveness detection method against contact lens spoofing. In: IEEE International Symposium on Consumer Electronics (ISCE), pp 71–74
11. Daugman J (2003) Demodulation by complex-valued wavelets for stochastic pattern recognition. Int J Wavelets Multiresolut Inf Proc 1(01):1–17
12. Lee E, Park K, Kim J (2005) Fake iris detection by using purkinje image. In: Zhang D, Jain A (eds) Advances in biometrics, vol 3832., Lecture Notes in Computer Science.Springer, Berlin Heidelberg, pp 397–403
13. Galbally J, Ortiz-Lopez J, Fierrez J, Ortega-Garcia J (2012) Iris liveness detection based on quality related features. In: IAPR International conference on biometrics (ICB). IEEE pp 271–276
14. He X, An S, Shi P (2007) Statistical texture analysis-based approach for fake iris detection using support vector machines. In: Lee SW, Li S (eds) Advances in biometrics, vol 4642., Lecture Notes in Computer Science.Springer, Berlin, pp 540–546
15. Wei Z, Qiu X, Sun Z, Tan T (2008) Counterfeit iris detection based on texture analysis. In: International conference on pattern recognition (ICPR), pp 1–4
16. He Z, Sun Z, Tan T, Wei Z (2009) Efficient iris spoof detection via boosted local binary patterns. In: Tistarelli M, Nixon M (eds) Advances in biometrics, vol 5558., Lecture Notes in Computer Science.Springer, Berlin, pp 1080–1090
17. Zhang H, Sun Z, Tan T (2010) Contact lens detection based on weighted LBP. In: International conference on pattern recognition (ICPR), pp 4279–4282
18. Doyle JS, Flynn PJ, Bowyer KW (2013) Automated classification of contact lens type in iris images. In: IAPR International conference on biometrics
19. Doyle JS, Bowyer KW, Flynn PJ (2013) Variation in accuracy of textured contact lens detection based on sensor and lens pattern. In: IEEE International conference on biometrics: theory applications and systems (BTAS), pp 1–6
20. Lee SJ, Park KR, Kim J (2006) Robust fake iris detection based on variation of the reflectance ratio between the iris and the sclera. In: Biometrics symposium: special session on research at the biometric consortium conference 2006:1–6
21. Lee SJ, Park KR, Lee YJ, Bae K (2007) Multi-feature based fake iris detection method. Opt Eng 46(12):127–204
22. Chen R, Lin X, Ding T (2012) Liveness detection for iris recognition using multispectral images. Patt Recogn Lett 33(12):1513–1519
23. Connell J, Ratha N, Gentile J, Bolle R (2013) Fake iris detection using structured light. In: IEEE International Conference on Acoustics, Speech and Signal Processing (ICASSP), pp 8692–8696
24. Haralick R, Shanmugam K, Dinstein I (1973) Textural features for image classification. IEEE Trans Sys Man Cybern SMC-3(6) 610–621

25. Ojala T, Pietikainen M, Maenpaa T (2002) Multiresolution gray-scale and rotation invariant texture classification with local binary patterns. IEEE Trans Patt Anal Mach Intell 24(7):971–987
26. He Z, Sun Z, Tan T, Qiu X, Zhong C, Dong W (2008) Boosting ordinal features for accurate and fast iris recognition. In: IEEE conference on computer vision and pattern recognition (CVPR), pp 1–8
27. Schapire R, Singer Y (1999) Improved boosting algorithms using confidence-rated predictions. Mach Learn 37(3):297–336
28. Lowe D (2004) Distinctive image features from scale-invariant keypoints. Int J Comput Vision 60(2):91–110
29. Dobes M, Machala L, Upol iris database. http://www.inf.upol.cz/iris/
30. Wei Z, Tan T, Sun Z (2008) Synthesis of large realistic iris databases using patch-based sampling. In: International conference on pattern recognition (ICPR), pp 1–4

# Chapter 7
# Speaker Recognition Anti-spoofing

Nicholas Evans, Tomi Kinnunen, Junichi Yamagishi, Zhizheng Wu,
Federico Alegre and Phillip De Leon

**Abstract** Progress in the development of spoofing countermeasures for automatic speaker recognition is less advanced than equivalent work related to other biometric modalities. This chapter outlines the potential for even state-of-the-art automatic speaker recognition systems to be spoofed. While the use of a multitude of different datasets, protocols and metrics complicates the meaningful comparison of different

---

N. Evans (✉) · F. Alegre
Department of Multimedia Communications, Campus SophiaTech, EURECOM,
450 Route des Chappes, 06410 Biot, France
e-mail: evans@eurecom.fr

F. Alegre
e-mail: alegre@eurecom.fr

T. Kinnunen
Speech and Image Processing Unit, School of Computing,
University of Eastern Finland (UEF), P.O. Box 111,
FI-80101 Joensuu, Finland
e-mail: tkinnu@cs.uef.fi

J. Yamaghishi
National Institute of Informatics, 2-1-2 Hitotsubashi, Chiyoda-ku, Tokyo 101-8430, Japan

J. Yamaghishi
University of Edinburgh, 10 Crichton Street, Edinburgh EH8 9AB, UK
e-mail: jyamagis@inf.ed.ac.uk

Z. Wu
Emerging Research Lab, School of Computer Engineering,
Nanyang Technological University (NTU), N4-B1a-02 C2I, Nanyang Avenue,
Singapore 639798, Singapore
e-mail: wuzz@ntu.edu.sg

P. De Leon
Department 3-O, Klipsch School of Electrical and Computer Engineering,
New Mexico State University, PO Box 30001 , Las Cruces,
NM88003-8001, USA
e-mail: pdeleon@nmsu.edu

© Springer-Verlag London 2014
S. Marcel et al. (eds.), *Handbook of Biometric Anti-Spoofing*,
Advances in Computer Vision and Pattern Recognition,
DOI: 10.1007/978-1-4471-6524-8_7

vulnerabilities, we review previous work related to impersonation, replay, speech synthesis and voice conversion spoofing attacks. The article also presents an analysis of the early work to develop spoofing countermeasures. The literature shows that there is significant potential for automatic speaker verification systems to be spoofed, that significant further work is required to develop generalised countermeasures, that there is a need for standard datasets, evaluation protocols and metrics and that greater emphasis should be placed on text-dependent scenarios.

## 7.1 Introduction

As one of our primary methods of communication, the speech modality has natural appeal as a biometric in one of two different scenarios: *text-independent* and *text-dependent*. While text-dependent automatic speaker verification (ASV) systems use fixed or randomly prompted utterances with known text content, text-independent recognisers operate on arbitrary utterances, possibly spoken in different languages. Text-independent methods are best suited to surveillance scenarios where speech signals are likely to originate from noncooperative speakers. In authentication scenarios, where cooperation can be readily assumed, text-dependent ASV is generally more appropriate since better performance can then be achieved with shorter utterances. On the other hand, text-independent recognisers are also used for authentication in call-centre applications such as caller verification in telephone banking.[1] On account of its utility in surveillance applications, evaluation sponsorship and dataset availability, text-independent ASV dominates the field.

The potential for ASV to be spoofed is now well recognised [1]. Since speaker recognition is commonly used in telephony or other unattended, distributed scenarios without human supervision, speech is arguably more prone to malicious interference or manipulation than other biometric signals. However, while spoofing is relevant to authentication scenarios and therefore text-dependent ASV, almost all prior work has been performed on text-independent datasets more suited to surveillance. While this observation most likely reflects the absence of viable text-dependent datasets in the recent past, progress in the development of spoofing countermeasures for ASV is lagging behind that in other biometric modalities.[2]

Nonetheless, there is growing interest to assess the vulnerabilities of ASV to spoofing and new initiatives to develop countermeasures [1]. This article reviews the past work which is predominantly text-independent. While the use of different datasets, protocols and metrics hinders such a task, we aim to describe and analyse four different spoofing attacks considered thus far: impersonation, replay, speech synthesis and voice conversion. Countermeasures for all four spoofing attacks are also reviewed and we discuss the directions which must be taken in future work

---

[1] http://www.nuance.com/landing-pages/products/voicebiometrics/freespeech.asp.
[2] http://www.tabularasa-euproject.org/.

to address weaknesses in the current research methodology and to properly protect ASV systems from the spoofing threat.

## 7.2 Automatic Speaker Verification

This section describes state-of-the-art approaches to text-independent automatic speaker verification (ASV) and their potential vulnerabilities to spoofing.

### 7.2.1 Feature Extraction

Since speech signals are nonstationary, features are commonly extracted from short-term segments (frames) of 20–30 ms in duration. Typically, mel-frequency cepstral coefficient (MFCC), linear predictive cepstral coefficient (LPCC), or perceptual linear prediction (PLP) features are used as a descriptor of the short-term power spectrum. These are usually appended with their time-derivative coefficients (deltas and double-deltas) and they undergo various normalisations such as global mean removal or short-term Gaussianization or feature warping [2]. In addition to spectral features, prosodic and high-level features have been studied extensively [3–5], achieving comparable results to state-of-the-art spectral recognisers [6]. For more details regarding popular feature representations used in ASV, readers are referred to [7].

The literature shows that ASV systems based on both spectral and prosodic features are vulnerable to spoofing. As described in Sect. 7.3, state-of-the-art voice conversion and statistical parametric speech synthesisers may also use mel-cepstral and linear prediction representations; spectral recognisers can be particularly vulnerable to synthesis and conversion attacks which use 'matched' parameterisations. Recognisers which utilise prosodic parameterisations are in turn vulnerable to human impersonation.

### 7.2.2 Modelling and Classification

Approaches to ASV generally focus on modelling the long-term distribution of spectral vectors. To this end, the Gaussian mixture model (GMM) [8, 9] has become the *de facto* modelling technique. Early ASV systems used maximum likelihood (ML) [8] and maximum a posteriori (MAP) [9] training. In the latter case, a speaker-dependent GMM is obtained from the adaptation of a previously trained universal background model (UBM). Adapted GMM mean *supervectors* obtained in this way were combined with support vector machine (SVM) classifiers in [10]. This idea lead to the development of many successful speaker model normalisation techniques including nuisance attribute projection (NAP) [11, 12] and within-class covariance normalisation (WCCN) [13]. These techniques aim to compensate for intersession variation, namely differences in supervectors corresponding to the same speaker caused by channel or session mismatch.

Parallel to the development of SVM-based discriminative models, generative factor analysis models were pioneered in [14–16]. In particular, *joint factor analysis* (JFA) [14] can improve ASV performance by incorporating distinct speaker and channel subspace models. These subspace models require the estimation of various hyper-parameters using labelled utterances. Subsequently, JFA evolved into a much-simplified model that is now the state of the art. The so-called *total variability model* or 'i-vector' representation [17] uses latent variable vectors of low-dimension (typically 200–600) to represent an arbitrary utterance. Unlike JFA, the training of an i-vector extractor is essentially an unsupervised process which leads to only one subspace model. Accordingly it can be viewed as a approach to dimensionality reduction, while compensation for session, environment and other nuisance factors are applied in the computationally light back-end classification. To this end, *probabilistic linear discriminant analysis* (PLDA) [18] with length-normalised i-vectors [19] has proven particularly effective.

Being based on the transformation of short-term cepstra, conversion and synthesis techniques also induce a form of 'channel shift'. Since they aim to attenuate channel effects, approaches to intersession compensation may present vulnerabilities to spoofing through the potential to confuse spoofed speech with channel-shifted speech of a target speaker. However, even if there is some evidence to the contrary, i.e., that recognisers employing intersession compensation might be intrinsically more robust to voice conversion attacks [20], all have their roots in the standard GMM and independent spectral observations. Neither utilises time sequence information, a key characteristic of speech which might otherwise afford some protection from spoofing.

## 7.2.3 System Fusion

In addition to the development of increasingly robust models and classifiers, there is a significant emphasis within the ASV community on the study of *classifier fusion*. This is based on the assumption that independently trained recognisers capture different aspects of the speech signal not covered by any individual classifier. Fusion also provides a convenient vehicle for large-scale research collaborations promoting independent classifier development and benchmarking [21]. Different classifiers can involve different features, classifiers, or hyper-parameter training sets [22]. A simple, yet robust approach to fusion involves the weighted summation of the base classifier scores, where the weights are optimised according to a logistic regression cost function. For recent trends in fusion, readers are referred to [23].

While we are unaware of any spoofing or anti-spoofing studies on fused ASV systems, some insight into their likely utility can be gained from related work in fused, multi-modal biometric systems; whether the scores originate from different biometric modalities or sub-classifiers applied to the same biometric trait makes little difference. A common claim is that multi-biometric systems should be inherently resistant to spoofing since an impostor is less likely to succeed in spoofing *all* the different subsystems. We note, however, that [24] suggests it might suffice to spoof only *one* modality under a score fusion setting in the case where the spoofing of a single, significantly weighted sub-system is particularly effective.

## 7.3 Spoofing and Countermeasures

Spoofing attacks are performed on a biometric system at the sensor or acquisition level to bias score distributions toward those of genuine clients, thus provoking increases in the false acceptance rate (FAR). This section reviews past work to evaluate vulnerabilities and to develop spoofing countermeasures. We consider impersonation, replay, speech synthesis and voice conversion.

### *7.3.1 Impersonation*

Impersonation refers to spoofing attacks whereby a speaker attempts to imitate the speech of another speaker and is one of the most obvious forms of spoofing and earliest studied.

#### 7.3.1.1 Spoofing

The work in [25] showed that impersonators can readily adapt their voice to overcome ASV, but only when their natural voice is already similar to that of the target (the *closest* targets were selected from YOHO corpus using an ASV system). Further work in [26] showed that impersonation increased FAR rates from close to 0 % to between 10 and 60 %. Linguistic expertise was not found to be useful, except in cases when the voice of the target speaker was very different to that of the impersonator. However, contradictory findings reported in [27] suggest that even while professional imitators are better impersonators than average people, they are *unable* to spoof an ASV system.

In addition to spoofing studies, impersonation has been a subject in acoustic-phonetic studies [28–30]. These have shown that imitators tend to be effective in mimicking long-term prosodic patterns and the speaking rate, though it is less clear that they are as effective in mimicking formant and other spectral characteristics. For instance, the imitator involved in the studies reported in [28] was not successful in translating his formant frequencies towards the target, whereas the opposite is reported in [31].

Characteristic to all studies involving impersonation is the use of relatively few speakers, different languages and ASV systems. The target speakers involved in such studies are also often public figures or celebrities and it is difficult to collect technically comparable material from both the impersonator and the target. These aspects of the past work makes it difficult to conclude whether or not impersonation poses a genuine threat. Since impersonation is thought to involve mostly the mimicking of prosodic and stylistic cues, it is perhaps considered more effective in fooling human listeners than today's state-of-the-art ASV systems [32].

#### 7.3.1.2 Countermeasures

While the threat of impersonation is not fully understood due to limited studies involving small datasets, it is perhaps not surprising that there is no prior work to investigate countermeasures against impersonation. If the threat is proven to be genuine, then the design of appropriate countermeasures might be challenging. Unlike the spoofing attacks discussed below, all of which can be assumed to leave traces of the physical properties of the recording and playback devices, or signal processing artefacts from synthesis or conversion systems, impersonators are live human beings who produce entirely natural speech.

## 7.3.2 Replay

Replay attacks involve the presentation of previously-recorded speech from a genuine client in the form of continuous speech recordings, or samples resulting from the concatenation of shorter segments. Replay is a relatively low-technology attack within the grasp of any potential attacker even without specialised knowledge in speech processing. The availability of inexpensive, high-quality recording devices and digital audio editing software might suggest that replay is both effective and difficult to detect.

#### 7.3.2.1 Spoofing

In contrast to research involving speech synthesis and voice conversion, spoofing attacks where large datasets are generally used for assessment, e.g. NIST datasets, all the past work to assess vulnerabilities to replay attacks relates to small, often purpose-collected datasets, typically involving no more than 15 speakers. While results generated with such small datasets have low statistical significance, differences between baseline performance and that under spoofing highlight the vulnerability.

The vulnerability of ASV systems to replay attacks was first investigated in a text-dependent scenario [33] where the concatenation of recorded digits was tested against a hidden Markov model (HMM) based ASV system. Results showed an increase in the FAR (EER threshold) from 1 to 89 % for male speakers and from 5 to 100 % for female speakers.

The work in [34] investigated text-independent ASV vulnerabilities through the replaying of far-field recorded speech in a mobile telephony scenario where signals were transmitted by analogue and digital telephone channels. Using a baseline ASV system based on JFA, their work showed an increase in the EER of 1 % to almost 70 % when impostor accesses were replaced by replayed spoof attacks. A physical access scenario was considered in [35]. While the baseline performance of their GMM-UBM ASV system was not reported, experiments showed that replay attacks produced an FAR of 93 %.

#### 7.3.2.2 Countermeasures

A countermeasure for replay attack detection in the case of text-dependent ASV was reported in [36]. The approach is based upon the comparison of new access samples with stored instances of past accesses. New accesses which are deemed too similar to previous access attempts are identified as replay attacks. A large number of different experiments, all relating to a telephony scenario, showed that the countermeasures succeeded in lowering the EER in most of the experiments performed.

While some form of text-dependent or challenge-response countermeasure is usually used to prevent replay attacks, text-independent solutions have also been investigated. The same authors in [34] showed that it is possible to detect replay attacks by measuring the channel differences caused by far-field recording [37]. While they show spoof detection error rates of less than 10 % it is feasible that today's state-of-the-art approaches to channel compensation will render some ASV systems still vulnerable.

Two different replay attack countermeasures are compared in [35]. Both are based on the detection of differences in channel characteristics expected between licit and spoofed access attempts. Replay attacks incur channel noise from both the recording device and the loudspeaker used for replay and thus the detection of channel effects beyond those introduced by the recording device of the ASV system thus serves as an indicator of replay. The performance of a baseline GMM-UBM system with an EER 40 % under spoofing attack falls to 29 % with the first countermeasure and a more respectable EER of 10 % with the second countermeasure.

### 7.3.3 Speech Synthesis

Speech synthesis, commonly referred to as text-to-speech (TTS), is a technique for generating intelligible, natural sounding artificial speech for any arbitrary text. Speech synthesis is used widely in various applications including in-car navigation systems, e-book readers, voice-over functions for the visually impaired and communication aids for the speech impaired. More recent applications include spoken dialogue systems, communicative robots, singing speech synthesisers and speech-to-speech translation systems.

Typical speech synthesis systems have two main components: text analysis and speech waveform generation, which are sometimes referred to as the *front-end* and *back-end*, respectively. In the text analysis component, input text is converted into a linguistic specification consisting of elements such as phonemes. In the speech waveform generation component, speech waveforms are generated from the produced linguistic specification.

There are four major approaches to speech waveform generation. In the early 1970s, the speech waveform generation component used very low-dimensional acoustic parameters for each phoneme, such as formants, corresponding to vocal tract resonances with hand-crafted acoustic rules [38]. In the 1980s, the speech waveform generation component used a small database of phoneme units called 'diphones' (the second half of one phone plus the first half of the following phone) and concatenated them according to the given phoneme sequence by applying signal processing, such as linear predictive (LP) analysis, to the units [39]. In the 1990s, larger speech databases were collected and used to select more appropriate speech units that match both phonemes and other linguistic contexts such as lexical stress and pitch accent in order to generate high-quality natural sounding synthetic speech with appropriate prosody. This approach is generally referred to as 'unit selection', and is used in many speech synthesis systems, including commercial products [40–44]. In the late 1990s another data-driven approach emerged, 'Statistical parametric speech synthesis', and has grown in popularity in recent years [45–48]. In this approach, several acoustic parameters are modelled using a time-series stochastic generative model, typically a hidden Markov model (HMM). HMMs represent not only the phoneme sequences but also various contexts of the linguistic specification in a similar way to the unit selection approach. Acoustic parameters generated from HMMs and selected according to the linguistic specification are used to drive a vocoder (a simplified speech production model with which speech is represented by vocal tract and excitation parameters) in order to generate a speech waveform.

The first three approaches are unlikely to be effective in ASV spoofing since they do not provide for the synthesis of speaker-specific formant characteristics. Furthermore, diphone or unit selection approaches generally require a speaker-specific database that covers all the diphones or relatively large amounts of speaker-specific data with carefully prepared transcripts. In contrast, state-of-the-art HMM-based speech synthesisers [49, 50] can learn individualised speech models from relatively little speaker-specific data by adapting background models derived from other speakers based on the standard model adaptation techniques drawn from speech recognition, i.e. maximum likelihood linear regression (MLLR) [51, 52].

### 7.3.3.1 Spoofing

There is a considerable volume of research in the literature which has demonstrated the vulnerability of ASV to synthetic voices generated with a variety of approaches to speech synthesis. Experiments using formant, diphone and unit selection-based synthetic speech in addition to the simple cut-and-paste of speech waveforms have been reported [33, 34, 53].

ASV vulnerabilities to HMM-based synthetic speech were first demonstrated over a decade ago [54] using an HMM-based, text-prompted ASV system [55] and an HMM-based synthesiser where acoustic models were adapted to specific human speakers [56, 57]. The ASV system scored feature vectors against speaker and background models composed of concatenated phoneme models. When tested with human speech the ASV system achieved an FAR of 0 % and an FRR of 7 %. When subjected to spoofing attacks with synthetic speech, the FAR increased to over 70 %, however this work involved only 20 speakers.

Large-scale experiments using the Wall Street Journal corpus containing 284 speakers and two different ASV systems (GMM-UBM and SVM using Gaussian supervectors) was reported in [58]. Using a state-of-the-art HMM-based speech synthesiser, the FAR was shown to rise to 86 and 81 % for the GMM-UBM and SVM systems, respectively. Spoofing experiments using HMM-based synthetic speech against a forensics speaker verification tool *BATVOX* was also reported in [59] with similar findings. Today's state-of-the-art speech synthesisers thus present a genuine threat to ASV.

### 7.3.3.2 Countermeasures

Only a small number of attempts to discriminate synthetic speech from natural speech have been investigated and there is currently no general solution which is independent from specific speech synthesis methods. Previous work has demonstrated the successful detection of synthetic speech based on prior knowledge of the acoustic differences of specific speech synthesisers, such as the dynamic ranges of spectral parameters at the utterance level [60] and variance of higher order parts of mel-cepstral coefficients [61].

There are some attempts which focus on acoustic differences between vocoders and natural speech. Since the human auditory system is known to be relatively insensitive to phase [62], vocoders are typically based on a minimum-phase vocal tract model. This simplification leads to differences in the phase spectra between human and synthetic speech, differences which can be utilised for discrimination [58, 63].

Based on the difficulty in reliable prosody modelling in both unit selection and statistical parametric speech synthesis, other approaches to synthetic speech detection use F0 statistics [64, 65]. F0 patterns generated for the statistical parametric speech synthesis approach tend to be over-smoothed and the unit selection approach frequently exhibits 'F0 jumps' at concatenation points of speech units.

## 7.3.4 Voice Conversion

Voice conversion is a sub-domain of voice transformation [66] which aims to convert one speaker's voice towards that of another. The field has attracted increasing interest in the context of ASV vulnerabilities for over a decade [67]. Unlike TTS, which requires text input, voice conversion operates directly on speech samples. In particular, the goal is to transform according to a conversion function $\mathscr{F}$ the feature vectors (**x**) corresponding to speech from a source speaker (spoofer) to that they are closer to those of target a speaker (**y**):

$$\mathbf{y} = \mathscr{F}(\mathbf{x}, \boldsymbol{\theta}). \tag{7.1}$$

Most voice conversion approaches adopt a training phase which requires frame-aligned pairs $\{(\mathbf{x}_t, \mathbf{y}_t)\}$ in order to learn the transformation parameters $\boldsymbol{\theta}$. Frame alignment is usually achieved using dynamic time warping (DTW) on *parallel* source-target training utterances with identical text content. The trained conversion function is then applied to new source utterances of arbitrary text content at run-time.

A large number of specific conversion approaches have been reported. One of the earliest and simplest techniques employs vector quantisation (VQ) with codebooks [68] or segmental codebooks [69] of paired source-target frame vectors to represent the conversion function. However, VQ introduces frame-to-frame discontinuity problems. Among the more recent conversion methods, *joint density Gaussian mixture model* (JD-GMM) [70–72] has become a standard baseline method. It achieves smooth feature transformations using a local linear transformation. Despite its popularity, known problems of JD-GMM include over-smoothing [73–75] and over-fitting [76, 77] which has led to the development of alternative linear conversion methods such as partial least square (PLS) regression [76], tensor representation [78], a trajectory hidden Markov model [79], a mixture of factor analysers [80], local linear transformation [73] and a noisy channel model [81]. Non-linear approaches, including artificial neural networks [82, 83], support vector regression [84], kernel partial least square [85] and conditional restricted Boltzmann machines [86], have also been studied. As alternatives to data-driven conversion, frequency warping techniques [87–89] have also attracted attention.

The approaches to voice conversion considered above are usually applied to the transformation of spectral envelope features, though the conversion of prosodic features such as fundamental frequency [90–93] and duration [91, 94] has also been studied. In contrast to parametric methods, unit selection approaches can be applied directly to feature vectors coming from the target speaker to synthesise converted speech [95]. Since they use target speaker data directly, unit selection approaches arguably pose a greater risk to ASV than statistical approaches [96].

In general, only the most straightforward of the spectral conversion methods have been utilised in ASV vulnerability studies. Even when trained using a non-parallel technique and non-ideal telephony data, the baseline JD-GMM approach, which produces over-smooth speech with audible artefacts, is shown to increase significantly the FAR of modern ASV systems [20, 96]; unlike the human ear, current recognisers are essentially 'deaf' to obvious conversion artefacts caused by imperfect signal analysis-synthesis models and poorly trained conversion functions.

#### 7.3.4.1 Spoofing

When applied to spoofing, voice conversion aims to synthesise a new speech signal such that features extracted for ASV are close in some sense to the target speaker. Some of the first work relevant to text-independent ASV spoofing includes that in [32, 97]. The work in [32] showed that a baseline EER increased from 16 to 26% as a result of voice conversion which also converted prosodic aspects not modelled in typical ASV systems. The work in [97] investigated the probabilistic mapping of a speaker's vocal tract information towards that of another, target speaker using a pair of tied speaker models, one of ASV features and another of filtering coefficients. This work targeted the conversion of spectral-slope parameters. The work showed that a baseline EER of 10% increased to over 60% when all impostor test samples were replaced with converted voice. In addition, signals subjected to voice conversion did not exhibit any perceivable artefacts indicative of manipulation.

The work in [20] investigated ASV vulnerabilities using a popular approach to voice conversion [70] based on JD-GMMs, which requires a parallel training corpus for both source and target speakers. Even if converted speech would be easily detectable by human listeners, experiments involving five different ASV systems showed universal susceptibility to spoofing. The FAR of the most robust, JFA system increased from 3% to over 17%.

Other work relevant to voice conversion includes attacks referred to as artificial signals. It was noted in [98] that certain short intervals of converted speech yield extremely high scores or likelihoods. Such intervals are not representative of intelligible speech but they are nonetheless effective in overcoming typical text-independent ASV systems which lack any form of speech quality assessment. The work in [98] showed that artificial signals optimised with a genetic algorithm provoke increases in the EER from 10% to almost 80% for a GMM-UBM system and from 5% to almost 65% for a factor analysis (FA) system.

#### 7.3.4.2 Countermeasures

Some of the first work to detect converted voice draws on related work in synthetic speech detection [100]. While the proposed cosine phase and modified group delay function (MGDF) countermeasures proposed in [63, 99] are effective in detecting spoofed speech (see Fig. 7.1), they are unlikely to detect converted voice with real-speech phase [97].

Two approaches to artificial signal detection are reported in [101]. Experimental work shows that supervector-based SVM classifiers are naturally robust to such attacks whereas all spoofing attacks can be detected using an utterance-level

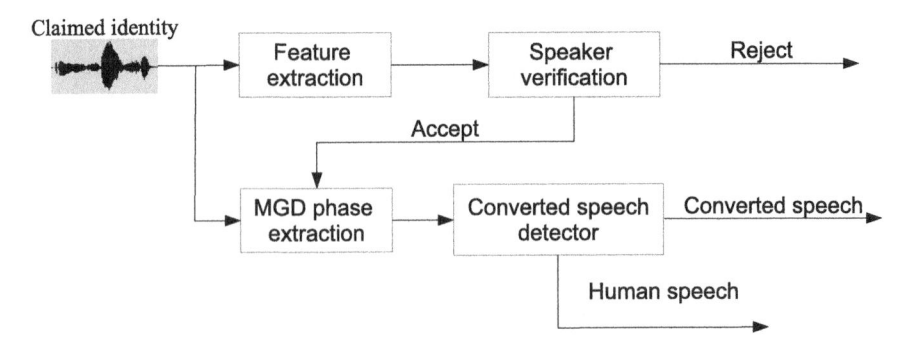

**Fig. 7.1** An example of a spoofed speech detector combined with speaker verification [99]. Based on prior knowledge that many analysis–synthesis modules used in voice conversion and TTS systems discard natural speech phase, phase characteristics parametrised via the modified group delay function (MGDF) can be used for discriminating natural and synthetic speech

variability feature which detects the absence of natural, dynamic variability characteristic of genuine speech. An alternative approach based on voice quality analysis is less dependent on explicit knowledge of the attack but less effective in detecting attacks.

A related approach to detect converted voice is proposed in [102]. Probabilistic mappings between source and target speaker models are shown to yield converted speech with less short-term variability than genuine speech. The thresholded, average pair-wise distance between consecutive feature vectors is used to detect converted voice with an EER of under 3 %.

Due to fact that current analysis–synthesis techniques operate at the short-term frame level, the use of temporal magnitude/phase modulation features, a form of long-term feature, are proposed in [103] to detect both speech synthesis and voice conversion spoofing attacks. Another form of long-term feature is reported in [104]. The approach is based on the local binary pattern (LBP) analysis of sequences of acoustic vectors and is successful in detecting converted voice. Interestingly, the approach is less reliant on prior knowledge and can also detect different spoofing attacks, examples of which were not used for training or optimisation.

## 7.3.5 Summary

As shown above, ASV spoofing and countermeasures have been studied with a multitude of different datasets, evaluation protocols and metrics, with highly diverse experimental designs, different ASV recognisers and with different approaches to spoofing; the lack of any commonality makes the comparison of results, vulnerabilities and countermeasure performance an extremely challenging task. Drawing carefully upon the literature and the authors' own experience with various spoofing

# 7 Speaker Recognition Anti-spoofing

**Table 7.1** A summary of the four approaches to ASV spoofing, their expected accessibility and risk

| Spoofing technique | Description | Accessibility (practicality) | Effectiveness (risk) Text-indep. | Effectiveness (risk) Text-dep. |
|---|---|---|---|---|
| Impersonation [25, 27, 32, 105] | Human voice mimic | Low | Low/unknown | Low/unknown |
| Replay [33, 34] | Replay of pre-recorded utterance | High | High | Low (rand. phrase) to high (fixed phrase) |
| Text-to-speech [54, 55, 58] | Speaker-specific speech generation from text input | Medium (now) to high (future) | High | High |
| Voice conversion [20, 32, 97, 98] | Speaker identity conversion using speech only | Medium (now) to high (future) | High | High |

approaches, we have nevertheless made such an attempt. Table 7.1 aims to summarise the threat of spoofing for the four approaches considered above. *Accessibility (practicality)* reflects whether the threat is available to the masses or limited to the technically knowledgeable. *Effectiveness (risk)*, in turn, reflects the success of each approach in provoking higher false acceptance rates.

Although some studies have shown that impersonation can fool ASV recognisers, in practice, the effectiveness seems to depend both on the skill of the impersonator, the similarity of the attacker's voice to that of the target speaker and on the recogniser itself. Replay attacks are highly effective in the case of text-independent ASV and fixed-phrase text-independent systems. Even if the effectiveness is reduced in the case of randomised, phrase-prompted text-dependent systems, replay attacks are the most accessible approach to spoofing, requiring only a recording and playback device such as a tape recorder or a smart phone.

Speech synthesis and voice conversion attacks pose the greatest risk. While voice conversion systems are not yet commercially available, both free and commercial text-to-speech (TTS) systems with pre-trained voice profiles are widely available, even if commercial off-the-shelf (COTS) systems do not include the functionality for adaptation to specific target voices. While accessibility is therefore medium in the short term, speaker adaptation remains a highly active research topic. It is thus only a matter of time until flexible, speaker-adapted synthesis and conversion systems become readily available. Then, both effectiveness and accessibility should be considered high.

## 7.4 Discussion

In this section, we discuss current approaches to evaluation and some weaknesses in the current evaluation methodology. While much of the following is not necessarily specific to the speech modality, with research in spoofing and countermeasures in ASV lagging behind that related to other biometric modalities, the discussion below is particularly pertinent.

### 7.4.1 Protocols and Metrics

While countermeasures can be integrated into existing ASV systems, they are most often implemented as independent modules which allow for the *explicit detection* of spoofing attacks. The most common approach in this case is to concatenate the two classifiers in series.

The assessment of countermeasure performance on its own is relatively straightforward; results are readily analysed with standard detection error trade-off (DET) profiles [106] and related metrics. It is often of interest, however, that the assessment reflects their impact on ASV performance. Assessment is then non-trivial and calls for the joint optimisation of combined classifiers. Results furthermore reflect the performance of specific ASV systems. As described in Sect. 7.3, there are currently no standard evaluation protocols, metrics or ASV systems which might otherwise be used to conduct evaluations. There is a thus a need to define such standards in the future.

Candidate standards are being drafted within the scope of the EU FP7 TABULA RASA project.[3] Here, independent countermeasures preceding biometric verification are optimised at three different operating points where thresholds are set to obtain FARs (the probability of labelling a genuine access as a spoofing attack) of 1, 5 or 10 %. Samples labelled as genuine accesses are then passed to the verification system.[4] Performance is assessed using four different DET profiles,[5] examples of which are illustrated in Fig. 7.2. The four profiles illustrate performance of the baseline system with zero-effort impostors, the baseline system with active countermeasures, the baseline system where all impostor accesses are replaced with spoofing attacks and, finally, the baseline system with spoofing attacks and active countermeasures.

Consideration of all four profiles is needed to gauge the impact of countermeasure performance on licit transactions (any deterioration in false rejection—difference between first and second profiles) and improved robustness to spoofing (improvements in false acceptance—difference between third and fourth profiles). While the

---

[3] http://www.tabularasa-euproject.org/.

[4] In practice samples labelled as spoofing attacks cannot be fully discarded since so doing would unduly influence false reject and false acceptance rates calculated as a percentage of all accesses.

[5] Produced with the TABULA RASA Score-toolkit: http://publications.idiap.ch/downloads/reports/2012/Anjos_Idiap-Com-02-2012.pdf.

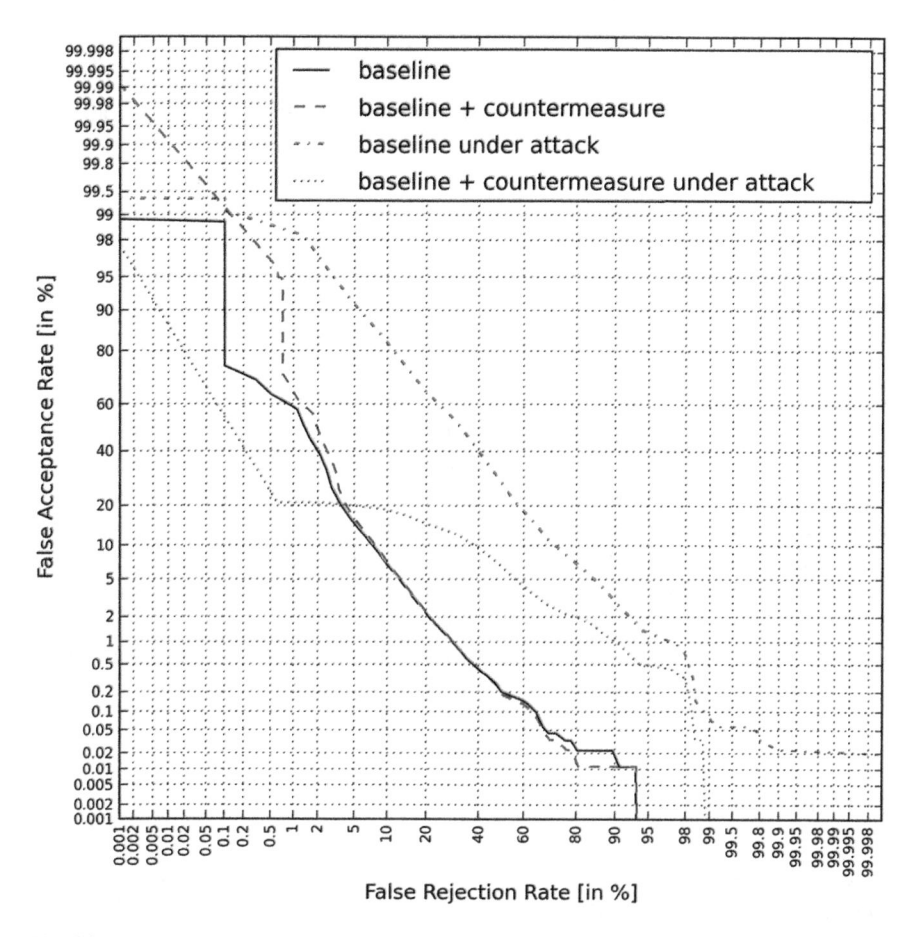

**Fig. 7.2** An example of four DET profiles needed to analyse vulnerabilities to spoofing and countermeasure performance, both on licit and spoofed access attempts. Results correspond to spoofing attacks using synthetic speech and a standard GMM-UBM classifier assessed on the male subset of the NIST'06 SRE dataset

interpretation of such profiles is trivial, different plots are obtained for each countermeasure operating point. Further work is required to design intuitive, universal metrics which represent the performance of spoofing countermeasures when combined with ASV.

## 7.4.2 Datasets

While some works have shown the potential for detecting spoofing without prior knowledge or training data indicative of a specific attack [63, 104, 107], all previous works are based on some implicit prior knowledge, i.e. the nature of the spoofing attack and/or the targeted ASV system is known. While training and evaluation data with known spoofing attacks might be useful to develop and optimise appropriate countermeasures, the precise nature of spoofing attacks can never be known in practice. Estimates of countermeasure performance so obtained should thus be considered at best optimistic. Furthermore, the majority of the past work was also conducted under matched conditions, i.e. data used to learn target models and that used to effect spoofing were collected in the same or similar acoustic environment and over the same or similar channel. The performance of spoofing countermeasures when subjected to realistic session variability is then unknown.

While much of the past work already uses standard datasets, e.g. NIST SRE data, spoofed samples are obtained by treating them with non-standard algorithms. Standard datasets containing both licit transactions and spoofed speech from a multitude of different spoofing algorithms and with realistic session variability are therefore needed to reduce the use of prior knowledge, to improve the comparability of different countermeasures and their performance against varied spoofing attacks. Collaboration with colleagues in other speech and language processing communities, e.g. voice conversion and speech synthesis, will help to assess vulnerabilities to state-of-the art spoofing attacks and also to assess countermeasures when details of the spoofing attacks are unknown. The detection of spoofing will then be considerably more challenging but more reflective of practical use cases.

## 7.5 Conclusions

This contribution reviews previous work to assess the threat from spoofing to automatic speaker verification (ASV). While there are currently no standard datasets, evaluation protocols or metrics, the study of impersonation, replay, speech synthesis and voice conversion spoofing attacks reported in this article indicate genuine vulnerabilities. We nonetheless argue that significant additional research is required before the issue of spoofing in ASV is properly understood and conclusions can be drawn.

In particular, while the situation is slowly changing, the majority of past work involves text-independent ASV, most relevant to surveillance. The spoofing threat is pertinent in authentication scenarios where text-dependent ASV might be preferred. Greater effort is therefore needed to investigate spoofing in text-dependent scenarios with particularly careful consideration being given to design appropriate datasets and protocols.

Second, almost all ASV spoofing countermeasures proposed thus far are dependent on training examples indicative of a specific attack. Given that the nature of spoofing attacks can never be known in practice, and with the variety in spoofing attacks being particularly high in ASV, future work should investigate new countermeasures which generalise well to unforeseen attacks. Formal evaluations with standard datasets, evaluation protocols, metrics and even standard ASV systems are also needed to address weaknesses in the current evaluation methodology.

Finally, some of the vulnerabilities discussed in this paper involve relatively high-cost and high-technology attacks. While the trend of open source software may cause this to change, such attacks are beyond the competence of the unskilled and in such case the level of vulnerability is arguably overestimated. While we have touched on this issue in this article, a more comprehensive risk-based assessment is needed to ensure such evaluations are not overly-alarmist. Indeed, the work discussed above shows that countermeasures, some of them relatively trivial, have the potential to detect spoofing attacks with manageable impacts on system usability.

**Acknowledgments** This work was partially supported by the TABULA RASA project funded under the 7th Framework Programme of the European Union (EU) (grant agreement number 257289), by the Academy of Finland (project no. 253120) and by EPSRC grants EP/I031022/1 (NST) and EP/J002526/1 (CAF).

# References

1. Evans N, Kinnunen T, Yamagishi J (2013) Spoofing and countermeasures for automatic speaker verification. In: Proceedings of interspeech, annual conference of the international speech communication association, Lyon, France
2. Pelecanos J, Sridharan S (2001) Feature warping for robust speaker verification. In: Proceedings of Odyssey 2001: the speaker and language recognition workshop, Crete, Greece, pp 213–218
3. Shriberg E, Ferrer L, Kajarekar S, Venkataraman A, Stolcke A (2005) Modeling prosodic feature sequences for speaker recognition. Speech Commun 46(3–4):455–472
4. Dehak N, Kenny P, Dumouchel P (2007) Modeling prosodic features with joint factor analysis for speaker verification. IEEE Trans Audio Speech Lang Process 15(7):2095–2103
5. Siddiq S, Kinnunen T, Vainio M, Werner S (2012) Intonational speaker verification: a study on parameters and performance under noisy conditions. In: Proceedings of IEEE international conference on acoustics, speech and signal process (ICASSP), Kyoto, Japan, pp 4777–4780
6. Kockmann M, Ferrer L, Burget L, Černocký J (2011) i-vector fusion of prosodic and cepstral features for speaker verification. In: Proceedings of interspeech, annual conference of the international speech communication association, Florence, Italy, pp 265–268
7. Kinnunen T, Li H (2010) An overview of text-independent speaker recognition: from features to supervectors. Speech Commun 52(1):12–40
8. Reynolds D, Rose R (1995) Robust text-independent speaker identification using Gaussian mixture speaker models. IEEE Trans Speech Audio Process 3:72–83
9. Reynolds DA, Quatieri TF, Dunn RB (2000) Speaker verification using adapted Gaussian mixture models. Digital Signal Process 10(1):19–41
10. Campbell WM, Sturim DE, Reynolds DA (2006) Support vector machines using GMM supervectors for speaker verification. IEEE Signal Process Lett 13(5):308–311
11. Solomonoff A, Campbell W, Boardman I (2005) Advances in channel compensation for SVM speaker recognition. In: Proceedings of IEEE international conference on acoustics, speech and signal process (ICASSP), pp 629–632, Philadelphia, USA
12. Burget L, Matějka P, Schwarz P, Glembek O, Černocký J (2007) Analysis of feature extraction and channel compensation in a GMM speaker recognition system. IEEE Trans Audio Speech Lang Process 15(7):1979–1986

13. Hatch AO, Kajarekar S, Stolcke A (2006) Within-class covariance normalization for svm-based speaker recognition. In: Proceedings of IEEE international conference on spoken language process (ICSLP), pp 1471–1474
14. Kenny, P (2006) Joint factor analysis of speaker and session variability: theory and algorithms. technical report CRIM-06/08-14
15. Kenny P, Boulianne G, Ouellet P, Dumouchel P (2007) Speaker and session variability in GMM-based speaker verification. IEEE Trans Audio Speech Lang Process 15(4):1448–1460
16. Kenny P, Ouellet P, Dehak N, Gupta V, Dumouchel P (2008) A study of inter-speaker variability in speaker verification. IEEE Trans Audio Speech Lang Process 16(5):980–988
17. Dehak N, Kenny P, Dehak R, Dumouchel P, Ouellet P (2011) Front-end factor analysis for speaker verification. IEEE Trans Audio Speech Lang Process 19(4):788–798
18. Li P, Fu Y, Mohammed U, Elder JH, Prince SJ (2012) Probabilistic models for inference about identity. IEEE Trans Pattern Anal Mach Intell 34(1):144–157
19. Garcia-Romero D, Espy-Wilson CY (2011) Analysis of i-vector length normalization in speaker recognition systems. In: Proceedings of interspeech, annual conference of the international speech communication association, Florence, Italy, pp 249–252
20. Kinnunen T, Wu ZZ, Lee KA, Sedlak F, Chng ES, Li H (2012) Vulnerability of speaker verification systems against voice conversion spoofing attacks: the case of telephone speech. In: Proceedings of IEEE international conference on acoustics speech and signal process (ICASSP), pp 4401–4404
21. Saeidi R et al (2013) I4U submission to NIST SRE 2012: a large-scale collaborative effort for noise-robust speaker verification. In: Proceedings of interspeech, annual conference of the international speech communication association, Lyon, France
22. Brümmer N, Burget L, Černocký J, Glembek O, Grézl F, Karafiát M, Leeuwen D, Matějka P, Schwartz P, Strasheim A (2007) Fusion of heterogeneous speaker recognition systems in the STBU submission for the NIST speaker recognition evaluation 2006. IEEE Trans Audio Speech Lang Process 15(7):2072–2084
23. Hautamäki V, Kinnunen T, Sedlák F, Lee KA, Ma B, Li H (2013) Sparse classifier fusion for speaker verification. IEEE Trans Audio Speech Lang Process 21(8):1622–1631
24. Akhtar Z, Fumera G, Marcialis GL, Roli F (2012) Evaluation of serial and parallel multibiometric systems under spoong attacks. In: Proceedings of 5th Int. Conference on biometrics (ICB 2012), pp 283–288, New Delhi, India
25. Lau YW, Wagner M, Tran D (2004) Vulnerability of speaker verification to voice mimicking. In: Proceedings of 2004 international symposium on Intelligent multimedia, video and speech processing, 2004. IEEE, pp 145–148
26. Lau Y, Tran D, Wagner M (2005) Testing voice mimicry with the yoho speaker verification corpus. Knowledge-based intelligent information and engineering systems. Springer, Berlin, p 907
27. Mariéthoz J, Bengio S (2005) Can a professional imitator fool a GMM-based speaker verification system? IDIAP Research Report 05–61
28. Eriksson A, Wretling P (1997) How flexible is the human voice?—a case study of mimicry. In: Proceedings of Eurospeech, ESCA European conference on speech communication and technology, pp 1043–1046. http://www.ling.gu.se/anders/papers/a1008.pdf
29. Zetterholm E, Blomberg M, Elenius D (2004) A comparison between human perception and a speaker verification system score of a voice imitation. In: Proceedings of tenth australian international conference on speech science and technology, Macquarie University, Sydney, Australia, pp 393–397
30. Farrús M, Wagner M, Anguita J, Hernando J (2008) How vulnerable are prosodic features to professional imitators? In: The speaker and language recognition workshop (Odyssey 2008), Stellenbosch, South Africa
31. Kitamura T (2008) Acoustic analysis of imitated voice produced by a professional impersonator. In: Proceedings of interspeech, annual conference of the international speech communication association, Brisbane, Australia, pp 813–816

32. Perrot P, Aversano G, Blouet R, Charbit M, Chollet G (2005) Voice forgery using ALISP: indexation in a client memory. In: Proceedings of IEEE international conference on acoustics, speech and signal process (ICASSP), vol 1, pp 17–20
33. Lindberg J, Blomberg M et al (1999) Vulnerability in speaker verification-a study of technical impostor techniques. Proc Eur Conf speech Commun Technol 3:1211–1214
34. Villalba J, Lleida E (2010) Speaker verification performance degradation against spoofing and tampering attacks. In: FALA 10 workshop, pp 131–134
35. Wang ZF, Wei G, He QH (2011) Channel pattern noise based playback attack detection algorithm for speaker recognition. Int Conf Mach Learn Cybern (ICMLC) 4:1708–1713
36. Shang W, Stevenson M (2010) Score normalization in playback attack detection. In: Proceedings of IEEE international conference on acoustics, speech and signal process (ICASSP), pp 1678–1681
37. Villalba J, Lleida E (2011) Preventing replay attacks on speaker verification systems. In: Proceedings of the IEEE international carnahan conference on security technology, (ICCST) 2011, pp 1–8
38. Klatt DH (1980) Software for a cascade/parallel formant synthesizer. J Acoust Soc Am 67:971–995
39. Moulines E, Charpentier F (1990) Pitch-synchronous waveform processing techniques for text-to-speech synthesis using diphones. Speech Commun 9:453–467
40. Hunt A, Black AW (1996) Unit selection in a concatenative speech synthesis system using a large speech database. In: Proceedings of IEEE international conference on acoustics, speech and signal process (ICASSP), pp 373–376
41. Breen A, Jackson P (1998) A phonologically motivated method of selecting nonuniform units. In: Proceedings of IEEE international conference on spoken language process (ICSLP), pp 2735–2738
42. Donovan RE, Eide EM (1998) The IBM trainable speech synthesis system. In: Proceedings of IEEE international conference on spoken language process (ICSLP), pp 1703–1706
43. Beutnagel B, Conkie A, Schroeter J, Stylianou Y, Syrdal A (1999) The AT&T next-gen TTS system. In: Proceedings of joint ASA, EAA and DAEA meeting, pp 15–19
44. Coorman G, Fackrell J, Rutten P, Coile B (2000) Segment selection in the L & H realspeak laboratory TTS system. In: Proceedings of international conference on speech and language processing, pp 395–398
45. Yoshimura T, Tokuda K, Masuko T, Kobayashi T, Kitamura T (1999) Simultaneous modeling of spectrum, pitch and duration in HMM-based speech synthesis. In: Proceedings of Eurospeech, ESCA European conference on speech communication and technology, pp 2347–2350
46. Ling ZH, Wu YJ, Wang YP, Qin L, Wang RH (2006) USTC system for blizzard challenge 2006 an improved HMM-based speech synthesis method. In: Proceedings of the blizzard challenge workshop
47. Black AW (2006) CLUSTERGEN: a statistical parametric synthesizer using trajectory modeling. In: Proceedings of interspeech, annual conference of the international speech communication association, pp 1762–1765
48. Zen H, Toda T, Nakamura M, Tokuda K (2007) Details of the Nitech HMM-based speech synthesis system for the Blizzard Challenge 2005. IEICE Trans Inf Syst E90–D(1):325–333
49. Zen H, Tokuda K, Black AW (2009) Statistical parametric speech synthesis. Speech Communication 51(11):1039–1064. doi:10.1016/j.specom.2009.04.004
50. Yamagishi J, Kobayashi T, Nakano Y, Ogata K, Isogai J (2009) Analysis of speaker adaptation algorithms for HMM-based speech synthesis and a constrained SMAPLR adaptation algorithm. IEEE Trans Speech Audio Lang Process 17(1):66–83
51. Leggetter CJ, Woodland PC (1995) Maximum likelihood linear regression for speaker adaptation of continuous density hidden Markov models. Comput Speech Lang 9:171–185
52. Woodland PC (2001) Speaker adaptation for continuous density HMMs: A review. In: Proceedings of ISCA workshop on adaptation methods for speech recognition, p 119

53. Foomany F, Hirschfield A, Ingleby M (2009) Toward a dynamic framework for security evaluation of voice verification systems. In: IEEE toronto international conference on science and technology for humanity (TIC-STH), pp 22–27. doi:10.1109/TIC-STH.2009.5444499
54. Masuko T, Hitotsumatsu T, Tokuda K, Kobayashi T (1999) On the security of HMM-based speaker verification systems against imposture using synthetic speech. In: Proceedings of Eurospeech, ESCA European conference on speech communication and technology
55. Matsui T, Furui S (1995) Likelihood normalization for speaker verification using a phoneme- and speaker-independent model. Speech Commun 17(1–2):109–116
56. Masuko T, Tokuda K, Kobayashi T, Imai S (1996) Speech synthesis using HMMs with dynamic features. In: Proceedings of IEEE international conference on acoustics, speech and signal process (ICASSP)
57. Masuko T, Tokuda K, Kobayashi T, Imai S (1997) Voice characteristics conversion for HMM-based speech synthesis system. In: Proceedings of IEEE international conference on acoustics, speech and signal process (ICASSP)
58. De Leon PL, Pucher M, Yamagishi J, Hernaez I, Saratxaga I (2012) Evaluation of speaker verification security and detection of HMM-based synthetic speech. IEEE Trans Audio Speech Lang Process 20(8):2280–2290. doi:10.1109/TASL.2012.2201472
59. Galou, G (2011) Synthetic voice forgery in the forensic context: a short tutorial. In: Forensic speech and audio analysis working group (ENFSI-FSAAWG), pp 1–3
60. Satoh T, Masuko T, Kobayashi T, Tokuda K (2001) A robust speaker verification system against imposture using an HMM-based speech synthesis system. In: Proceedings of Eurospeech, ESCA European conference on speech technology
61. Chen LW, Guo W, Dai LR (2010) Speaker verification against synthetic speech. In: Proceedings of 7th international symposium on chinese spoken language processing (ISCSLP), pp 309–312 (29 Nov–3 Dec 2010). doi:10.1109/ISCSLP.2010.5684887
62. Quatieri TF (2002) Discrete-time speech signal processing principles and practice. Prentice-hall, Inc
63. Wu Z, Chng ES, Li H (2012) Detecting converted speech and natural speech for anti-spoofing attack in speaker recognition. In: Proceedings of interspeech, annual conference of the international speech communication association
64. Ogihara A, Unno H, Shiozakai A (2005) Discrimination method of synthetic speech using pitch frequency against synthetic speech falsification. IEICE Trans Fundam Electron Commun Comput Sci 88(1):280–286
65. De Leon PL, Stewart B, Yamagishi J (2012) Synthetic speech discrimination using pitch pattern statistics derived from image analysis. In: Proceedings of interspeech, annual conference of the international speech communication association, Portland, Oregon, USA
66. Stylianou Y (2009) Voice transformation: a survey. In: Proceedings of IEEE international conference on acoustics speech and signal process (ICASSP), pp 3585–3588
67. Pellom BL, Hansen JH (1999) An experimental study of speaker verification sensitivity to computer voice-altered imposters. In: Proceedings of IEEE international conference on acoustics, speech and signal process (ICASSP), vol 2, pp 837–840
68. Abe M, Nakamura S, Shikano K, Kuwabara H (1988) Voice conversion through vector quantization. In: Proceedings of IEEE international conference on acoustics, speech and signal process (ICASSP), pp 655–658
69. Arslan LM (1999) Speaker transformation algorithm using segmental codebooks (STASC). Speech Commun 28(3):211–226
70. Kain A, Macon MW (1998) Spectral voice conversion for text-to-speech synthesis. In: Proceedings of IEEE international conference on acoustics, speech and signal process (ICASSP), vol 1, pp 285–288
71. Stylianou Y, Cappé O, Moulines E (1998) Continuous probabilistic transform for voice conversion. IEEE Trans Speech Audio Process 6(2):131–142
72. Toda T, Black AW, Tokuda K (2007) Voice conversion based on maximum-likelihood estimation of spectral parameter trajectory. IEEE Trans Audio Speech Lang Process 15(8):2222–2235

73. Popa V, Silen H, Nurminen J, Gabbouj M (2012) Local linear transformation for voice conversion. In: Proceedings of IEEE international conference on acoustics, speech and signal process (ICASSP), pp 4517–4520
74. Chen Y, Chu M, Chang E, Liu J, Liu R (2003) Voice conversion with smoothed GMM and MAP adaptation. In: Proceedings of Eurospeech, ESCA European conference on speech communication and technology, pp 2413–2416
75. Hwang HT, Tsao Y, Wang HM, Wang YR, Chen SH (2012) A study of mutual information for GMM-based spectral conversion. In: Proceedings of Interspeech, annual conference of the international speech communication association
76. Helander E, Virtanen T, Nurminen J, Gabbouj M (2010) Voice conversion using partial least squares regression. IEEE Trans Audio Speech Lang Process 18(5):912–921
77. Pilkington NC, Zen H, Gales MJ (2011) Gaussian process experts for voice conversion. In: Twelfth annual conference of the international speech communication association
78. Saito D, Yamamoto K, Minematsu N, Hirose K (2011) One-to-many voice conversion based on tensor representation of speaker space. In: Proceedings of Interspeech, annual conference of the international speech communication association, pp 653–656
79. Zen H, Nankaku Y, Tokuda K (2011) Continuous stochastic feature mapping based on trajectory HMMs. IEEE Trans Audio Speech Lang Process 19(2):417–430
80. Wu Z, Kinnunen T, Chng ES, Li H (2012) Mixture of factor analyzers using priors from non-parallel speech for voice conversion. IEEE Signal Process Lett 19(12):914–917
81. Saito D, Watanabe S, Nakamura A, Minematsu N (2012) Statistical voice conversion based on noisy channel model. IEEE Trans Audio Speech Lang Process 20(6):1784–1794
82. Narendranath M, Murthy HA, Rajendran S, Yegnanarayana B (1995) Transformation of formants for voice conversion using artificial neural networks. Speech commun 16(2):207–216
83. Desai S, Raghavendra EV, Yegnanarayana B, Black AW, Prahallad K (2009) Voice conversion using artificial neural networks. In: Proceedings of IEEE international conference on acoustics, speech and signal process (ICASSP), pp 3893–3896
84. Song P, Bao Y, Zhao L, Zou C (2011) Voice conversion using support vector regression. Electron Lett 47(18):1045–1046
85. Helander E, Silén H, Virtanen T, Gabbouj M (2012) Voice conversion using dynamic kernel partial least squares regression. IEEE Trans Audio Speech Lang Process 20(3):806–817
86. Wu Z, Chng ES, Li H (2013) Conditional restricted boltzmann machine for voice conversion. In: The first IEEE china summit and international conference on signal and information processing (ChinaSIP)
87. Sundermann D, Ney H (2003) VTLN-based voice conversion. In: Proceedings of the 3rd IEEE international symposium on signal processing and information technology, 2003. ISSPIT 2003, pp 556–559
88. Erro D, Moreno A, Bonafonte A (2010) Voice conversion based on weighted frequency warping. IEEE Trans Audio Speech Lang Process 18(5):922–931
89. Erro D, Navas E, Hernaez I (2013) Parametric voice conversion based on bilinear frequency warping plus amplitude scaling. IEEE Trans Audio Speech Lang Process 21(3):556–566
90. Gillet B, King S (2003) Transforming F0 contours. In: Proceedings of Eurospeech, ESCA European conference on speech communication and technology, pp 101–104
91. Wu CH, Hsia CC, Liu TH, Wang JF (2006) Voice conversion using duration-embedded bi-HMMs for expressive speech synthesis. IEEE Trans Audio Speech Lang Process 14(4):1109–1116
92. Helander EE, Nurminen J (2007) A novel method for prosody prediction in voice conversion. In: Proceedings of IEEE international conference on acoustics, speech and signal process (ICASSP), pp IV-509
93. Wu ZZ, Kinnunen T, Chng ES, Li H (2010) Text-independent F0 transformation with non-parallel data for voice conversion. In: Eleventh annual conference of the international speech communication association
94. Lolive D, Barbot N, Boeffard O (2008) Pitch and duration transformation with non-parallel data. Speech prosody 2008:111–114

95. Sundermann D, Hoge H, Bonafonte A, Ney H, Black A, Narayanan S (2006) Text-independent voice conversion based on unit selection. In: Proceedings of IEEE international conference on acoustics, speech and signal process (ICASSP), vol 1, pp I-I
96. Wu Z, Larcher A, Lee KA, Chng ES, Kinnunen T, Li H (2013) Vulnerability evaluation of speaker verication under voice conversion spoong: the effect of text constraints. In: Proceedings of interspeech, annual conference of the international speech communication association, Lyon, France
97. Matrouf D, Bonastre JF, Fredouille C (2006) Effect of speech transformation on impostor acceptance. In: Proceedings of IEEE international conference on acoustics, speech and signal process (ICASSP), vol 1, pp I-I
98. Alegre F, Vipperla R, Evans N, Fauve B (2012) On the vulnerability of automatic speaker recognition to spoofing attacks with artificial signals. In: Proceedings of EURASIP Euro signal processing conference (EUSIPCO)
99. Wu Z, Kinnunen T, Chng ES, Li H, Ambikairajah E (2012) A study on spoofing attack in state-of-the-art speaker verification: the telephone speech case. In: Signal and information processing association annual summit and conference (APSIPA ASC), 2012 Asia-Pacific, pp 1–5
100. De Leon PL, Hernaez I, Saratxaga I, Pucher M, Yamagishi J (2011) Detection of synthetic speech for the problem of imposture. In: Proceedings of IEEE international conference on acoustic, speech and signal process (ICASSP), pp 4844–4847, Dallas, USA
101. Alegre F, Vipperla R, Evans N, et al (2012) Spoofing countermeasures for the protection of automatic speaker recognition systems against attacks with artificial signals. In: Proceedings of interspeech, annual conference of the international speech communication association
102. Alegre F, Amehraye A, Evans N (2013) Spoofing countermeasures to protect automatic speaker verification from voice conversion. In: Proceedings of IEEE international conference on acoustic, speech and signal process (ICASSP)
103. Wu Z, Xiao X, Chng ES, Li H (2013) Synthetic speech detection using temporal modulation feature. In: Proceedings of IEEE international conference on acoustic, speech and signal process (ICASSP)
104. Alegre F, Vipperla R, Amehraye A, Evans N (2013) A new speaker verification spoofing countermeasure based on local binary patterns. In: Proceedings of interspeech, annual conference of the international speech communication association, Lyon, France
105. Hautamki RG, Kinnunen T, Hautamki V, Leino T, Laukkanen AM (2013) I-vectors meet imitators: on vulnerability of speaker verification systems against voice mimicry. In: Proceedings of interspeech, annual conference of the international speech communication association
106. Martin A, Doddington G, Kamm T, Ordowski M, Przybocki M (1997) The DET curve in assessment of detection task performance. In: Proceedings of Eurospeech, ESCA European conference on speech communication and technology, pp 1895–1898
107. Alegre F, Amehraye A, Evans N (2013) A one-class classification approach to generalised speaker verification spoofing countermeasures using local binary patterns. In: Proceedings of international conference on biometrics: theory, applications and systems (BTAS), Washington DC, USA

# Chapter 8
# Gait Anti-spoofing

John D. Bustard, Mohammad Ghahramani, John N. Carter,
Abdenour Hadid and Mark S. Nixon

**Abstract** Gait recognition is a relatively new biometric and as a result relatively little effort has yet been devoted to studying spoofing attacks against it. This chapter examines the effects of two different spoofing attacks against two different state-of-the-art gait recognition systems. The first attack uses *clothing impersonation* where an attacker replicates the clothing of a legitimately enrolled individual. The second attack is a *targeted attack* where an imposter deliberately selects the legitimately enrolled subject whose gait signature is closest to the attacker. The analysis presented here reveals that both systems are vulnerable to both attacks. In particular, if both attacks are combined and the systems have acceptance thresholds set at the EER of their baseline performance, the attacks cause the FAR to rise from 5 % to between 60 and 95 %. The chapter describes two countermeasures that can be applied to minimise the effects of the spoofing attacks. Using the same acceptance thresholds the countermeasure to clothing attacks reduces the FAR performance under clothing impersonation from 40 to 15 %. Likewise, the targeting countermeasure reduces the FAR for targeted attacks from 20 to 2.5 % sufficient to even improve on the baseline performance.

---

J.D. Bustard (✉) · J.N. Carter · M.S. Nixon
University of Southampton, University Rd, Southampton SO17 1BJ, UK
e-mail: jdb@ecs.soton.ac.uk

J.N. Carter
e-mail: jnc@ecs.soton.ac.uk

M.S. Nixon
e-mail: msn@ecs.soton.ac.uk

M. Ghahramani · A. Hadid
Pentti Kaiteran katu 1, 90570 Oulu, Finland
e-mail: mghahram@ee.oulu.fi

A. Hadid
e-mail: hadid@ee.oulu.fi

© Springer-Verlag London 2014
S. Marcel et al. (eds.), *Handbook of Biometric Anti-Spoofing*,
Advances in Computer Vision and Pattern Recognition,
DOI: 10.1007/978-1-4471-6524-8_8

## 8.1 Introduction

Gait biometrics aim to recognise people from their walking style. It is a relatively new biometric modality and has a valuable advantage over other features, such as iris and fingerprint, in that it can be easily captured from a distance. This makes it an attractive option in video surveillance applications.

The current state-of-the-art gait recognition systems use body silhouette or model based approaches [1]. Of these techniques relatively more approaches use the human silhouette as the basis of recognition, and of these approaches, those which use the averaged silhouette have proved most popular [2]. The earliest techniques achieved recognition rates exceeding 90 % and this is matched by the most recent approaches on databases extending to 300 subjects. Much of the earlier work was conducted on data acquired using controlled conditions but later recognition was demonstrated on outdoor derived data, though with slightly lower performance.

In terms of spoofing there has been relatively little investigation into attacks. As with other vision-based biometrics, gait recognition may be vulnerable to replay attacks of recordings of valid subjects played back on displays placed in front of cameras. However, this may be less of a concern for three-dimensional systems as replay attacks require precise synchronised replay attacks simultaneously performed against multiple cameras, which is a significant technical barrier for most attackers. Likewise, as gait recognition is a behavioural biometric, synthetic artefact attacks cannot impersonate a gait signature.

Four existing spoofing investigations have been performed. Three of these are very similar. They use worn accelerometer sensors to provide signatures of gait movement. The gait sensor approach is less practical than the more traditional, vision-based gait recognition systems as many potential gait recognition applications focus on flexible general access control where having to attach sensors prior to access would diminish its convenience advantages. Despite this limitation, the studies provide valuable analysis of the challenges of gait spoofing.

The first investigation had a small number of subjects (22) and made no attempt to select subjects with similar build. However, the subjects could walk while viewing the spoofing target's gait, in fact they walked behind the target to be spoofed copying their movements. Using this system the active spoofing attempts could be identified as there were relatively few spoofing attempts that had a lower matching score than the worst genuine match scores. This study is too small to draw strong conclusions, however, it indicates that the dynamics of gait movement may be difficult to impersonate.

The second study had an even smaller number of subjects (13). To enable spoofing the response of an accelerometer sensor attached to the leg was projected onto a wall. The subjects could view this response and see how their own appeared as they walked. Using this visualisation they could adjust their movement to match the response of the target. The signature was used as the basis for recognition. Using this technique they found that it was possible to alter a gait signature to achieve a match percentage of over 60 % against a target's gait signature. The authors described this as evidence that gait was vulnerable to spoofing, however this result is contradicted by a third study which questions the significance of the risk that a 60% match represents.

The third study had the smallest number of attackers (6) although it used a much larger group of 50 subjects to establish validation thresholds. Like the other studies it used an accelerometer approach and focused on whether imposters could improve their spoofing performance through practice. To measure this effect there were two sequences of attacking attempts. The first used six attackers making 60 attempts. The second used a longer sequence of 160 mimicking attempts by a single attacker. Of the six attackers studied only one came close to matching the signature, however, the match was not close enough to fall within a 95% confidence interval, four of the six actually had worse performance when trying to replicate gait. The studies conclusions were that practice often decreased performance and that physiology placed real limits on a subject's ability to replicate another person's gait.

Only one recent piece of research has yet demonstrated whether the, more common, machine vision-based gait recognition techniques are vulnerable to spoofing attacks [3]. Vision-based systems often use a subject's body silhouette shape as part of a subject's biometric signature. This provides improved recognition performance. However, this also offers another basis for attacks. The fourth study uses this route, demonstrating how impersonating a target's clothing can effectively spoof two different gait recognition systems. Clothing impersonation is one of the most straightforward and unobtrusive methods for performing gait attacks. It is an important vulnerability to address as such an attack is relatively straightforward. It is likely that such an approach will already be used by an attacker to unobtrusively enter a secure area where uniforms or formalised styles of dress are common. This attack can be viewed as a similar approach to that of wearing a 3D mask in order to spoof a facial recognition system. The same paper also identifies another, more general, *targeted* attack. This attack assumes that the attacker has freedom to select which subject the attacker is going to impersonate. It simply involves selecting a target with a similar gait signature. The paper reveals that such an approach can result in successful impersonation attacks and when combined with a clothing impersonation can significantly increase the chances that an attacker is falsely accepted by a system. The *targeted* attacks performed in the paper require the attacker to have access to the gait system and the legitimate subject enrollment data. This makes the attack impractically challenging for many attackers. Simpler, more heuristic, target selection approaches, such as personal judgement, are likely to be less effective, but as with clothing impersonation, a likely attack approach for those attempting unobtrusive access.

Two example gait recognition systems have been used to investigate the effectiveness of clothing and targeted spoofing attacks:

The first system produced by the University of Oulu is a 2D gait system [4, 5] (UOULU). It uses 2D dynamic texture descriptors, namely Local Binary Patterns from Three Orthogonal Planes (LBP-TOP), to describe human gait in a spatio-temporal way. A video sequence of a person's walking is thought as spatio-temporal volume. The LBP-TOP description is formed by calculating the LBP features from XY, XT and YT planes of volumes and concatenating the histograms to catch the transition information in spatio-temporal domain. Gentle AdaBoost is used to perform feature selection and to build a strong classifier.

The second system, produced by the University of Southampton uses a 3D average silhouette-based gait recognition system (USOU). The system uses shape from silhouette third reconstruction to synthesise a profile silhouette sequence from which an average silhouette is constructed. 3D volumetric data is used to synthesise silhouettes from a fixed viewpoint relative to the subject. The resulting silhouettes are then passed to a standard 2D gait analysis technique; in this case the average silhouette. The advantage of using three-dimensional data is that silhouettes from any arbitrary viewpoint can be synthesised, even if the viewpoint is not directly seen by a camera. Silhouettes are taken from a side-on orthogonal viewpoint. This view is not seen by any camera and so must be synthesised. The use of a side-on viewpoint facilitates comparison with previous results. To generate the average silhouette images the centre of mass is found for each frame. The average silhouette is then found by summing the centre of mass aligned silhouettes. The average silhouette is treated as the feature vector and used for leave-one-out recognition, using nearest-neighbour classification and the euclidean distance as the distance metric between samples.

### 8.1.1 Baseline Dataset

The Southampton gait database [6] has been used for the experimental evaluation. It contains multiple views and detailed camera calibration information. The database consists of recordings of 227 subjects walking through the Southampton Gait Tunnel [6] at least nine times. Each recording consists of eight synchronised video sequences of approximately 140 frames. One hundred and thirteen subjects were randomly selected for computing the baseline performance of the systems, i.e. the performance when the systems are not confronted to spoofing attacks. Nine recordings of each of the 113 subjects were used, one for enrolment and eight for testing. This results in one enrolment video for each user and $8 * 113$ test client (positive sample) videos for each user. When producing impostor scores all the other clients are used, yielding $8 * 112 * 113$ zero effort impostor attacks.

The enrollment and test sequences were obtained on the same day, when the subject was wearing the same clothing. Significantly, lower performance could be expected if subjects were to change their clothing between enrollment and validation [7]. Similarly no subjects were carrying any objects in the recorded data which could also degrade the systems recognition capability.

### 8.1.2 Baseline Systems

This section provides a brief overview of how both example systems work. Further information is available in publications [4, 5, 8] which describe the systems in more detail.

### 8.1.2.1 USOU Gait Recognition System

The first stage of processing the recorded data was to convert the captured images into colour from their original raw Bayer format, using nearest-neighbour interpolation. Background estimation and segmentation was then performed to find the subjects silhouette; modelling each background pixel with a single Gaussian distribution per colour channel. The distribution for each pixel was found using previously captured video footage, where no subject was present. The background segmentation was performed by calculating the distance between a pixel and its corresponding background distribution, where a pixel would be marked as background if its distance was less than a global threshold; linked to the standard-deviation found by the background estimation. Shadow labelling and removal was performed to reduce the number of pixels incorrectly marked as foreground. Binary morphological post-processing was then performed to reduce noise levels and smooth the silhouettes shape. Finally, all regions except that with the greatest area were removed and any holes in the remaining region were filled. Radial distortion caused by the camera optics was removed by the use of a nonlinear transformation. The reconstructed volumetric data was smoothed using binary erosion and dilation morphological operators to reduce the level of noise and reconstruction artefacts. Gait cycles were detected by finding the instances where the length of the bounding box encompassing a subject is minimal in the direction of travel. This was found by fitting local polynomials to the length variation and locating potential maxima values. The time for a gait cycle was determined by finding the first maxima in the cross correlation of the length variation. This corresponds to the first half gait cycle. The first set of length peaks that were separated by the half gait cycle were identified. The first and third peaks were selected to identify a complete gait cycle. Sagittal silhouettes for each frame within this cycle were calculated. The centre of mass of each of the voxels was used to align each frame on top of one another and the sagittal silhouettes were then averaged to produce a signature for each recording. Each signature was then compared to determine the average pixel difference between them. Detection error trade-off (DET) curves were then calculated to identify how false accept and false reject validation rates change with respect to one another, as a result of different validation thresholds.

### 8.1.2.2 UOULU Gait Recognition System

The silhouette extraction process is the same as that used with the USOU Gait recognition system. Gait cycles were estimated using the width of the bottom part (feet) of the silhouette. The sagittal silhouette images were stacked to a space time volume and LBP-TOP features were calculated using a grid defined by the centroid of the silhouette in each frame. Histogram of the LBP-TOP features was used to represent each gait sample. A boosted classifier was trained on the training set to get a matching function between two histograms. Based on the matching scores of all samples in the test data, DET curve was calculated to identify the validation performance on different thresholds.

In more details, the UOULU gait recognition system works as follows. First, a video sequence of a person's walking can be thought as spatio-temporal volume. The volume is partitioned into subvolumes. Using the sub-volume representation, motion and shape are encoded on three different levels: pixel-level (single bins in the histogram), region-level (sub-volume histogram) and global-level (concatenated sub-volume histograms). Second, LBP-TOP description is formed by calculating the LBP features from XY, XT and YT planes of volumes and concatenating the histograms to catch the transition information in spatio-temporal domain. The LBP-TOP features from each sub-volume are extracted and concatenated to encode motion and shape characteristics. Third, to use the multi-resolution information, original uniform patterns are improved with ordering sampling points according to the sampling angle, by which they will also produce codes that satisfy the bit transition condition and any number of sampling points can be used on different LBP kernels. Fourth, the length of the LBP-TOP histogram representation can be quite large depending on the number of sampling points and number of sub-volumes that are used. A better and more compact representation can be obtained by using feature selection methods. Gentle AdaBoost was used to perform feature selection and to build a strong classifier. Instead of building a classifier that gives the identity of the person from one sample, a two-class classifier was trained, which classifies whether two samples come from the same person or not.

## 8.1.3 Baseline Evaluation

### 8.1.3.1 USOU Gait Evaluation

As can be seen in Fig. 8.1 using the 3D baseline approach, the equal error rate (EER) is around 6%. This is an encouraging result, reflecting a high correct classification rate (CCR) in recognition based on this data (91%). Provided subjects are recorded and validated wearing the same clothing and not carrying objects, the 3D gait recognition approach is comparable to other widely used biometrics such as 2D-face, provided such face images are recorded in a similarly unconstrained lighting setup as the gait tunnel. From a manual examination of each of the recordings that were incorrectly classified, there are two main causes of failure: shape from silhouette distortion, and variation in arm swing. The distortion is caused by inaccurate camera calibration, which produces different body shapes at different points in the tunnel. Arm swing magnitude appears less constrained than leg dynamics. Weighting to the silhouette could be used to address this issue.

### 8.1.3.2 UOULU Gait Evaluation

Figure 8.1 also shows that the UOULU system has an EER of about 4.5%. This result is indeed encouraging. This performance can be explained by the use of

**Gait DET**

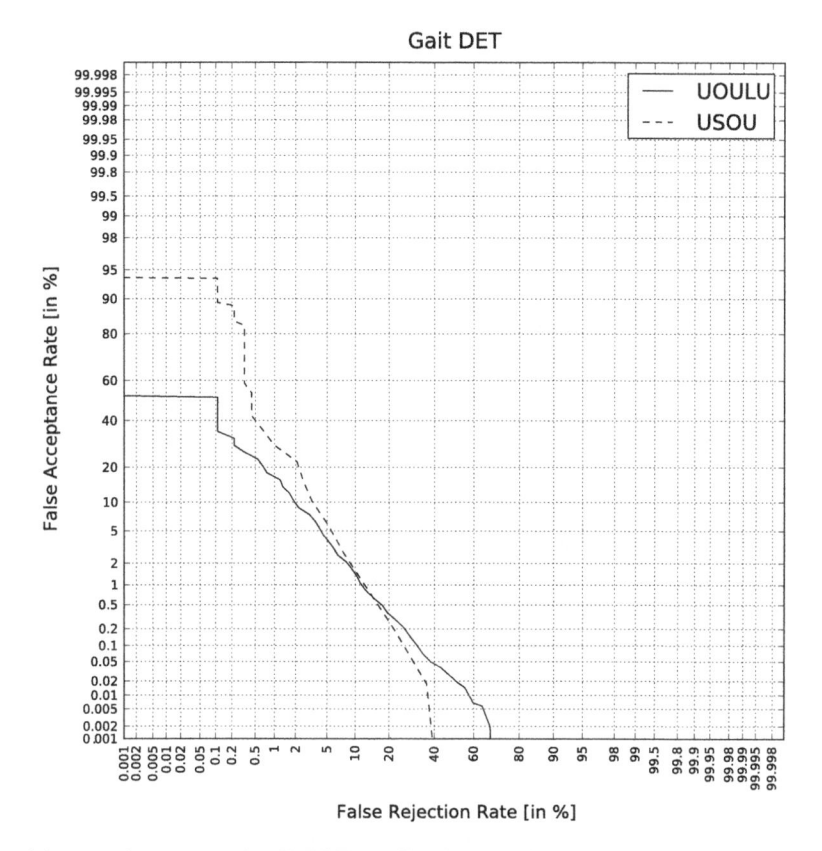

**Fig. 8.1** Detection error trade-off (DET) profiles for the UOULU and USOU gait recognition systems on the baseline USOU gait database

spatio-temporal analysis that combines both motion and shape cues. However, the result is obtained with data that is recorded while the subjects are wearing the same clothing in all samples. We believe the performance may decrease when more covariate conditions and spoofing attacks are included, as has been observed in many studies on other databases such as the USF gait database.

## 8.2 Attacks

This section describes experiments which analyse the effect of the clothing and targeted attacks on the two example gait recognition systems. Attacks are performed with the same equipment and experimental procedure as that of the baseline gait recognition results. A successful attack is performed when the difference between the signature of an attacker and their target are below the systems verification threshold.

This section describes different spoofing scenarios including (i) clothing impersonation, (ii) deliberate selection of a target that has a similar build to the attacker and (iii) combination of clothing and target selection. This yielded in four protocols for studying gait under spoofing attacks:

- **Baseline performance:** The original Southampton gait database without spoofing attacks is considered for computing client and impostor scores. This provides the performance under normal settings.
- **Clothing attacks:** The attacks are calculated by comparing each of the uniform recordings of each subject against the uniform recordings of all of the other subjects. This provides insights into how clothing impersonation affects the performance.
- **Targeted attacks:** The attacks are measured by comparing each of the normal clothes recordings of each subject against each of the normal clothes recordings of the subject with most similar build. This provides insights into how selection of the target affects the performance.
- **Targeted clothing attacks:** The attacks are the same as targeted attacks except that instead of using the normal clothing recordings the uniform clothing recordings are used. This is equivalent to each subject selecting the person with the most similar build and impersonating their clothing.

## 8.2.1 Gait Spoofing Dataset

To analyse the performance under spoofing attacks, new data (referred to as the USOU Gait Spoofing Database) has recently been recorded at the University of Southampton [9]. This consists of 22 subjects (14 male and 8 female), between 20 and 55 years old. The subjects were recorded walking through the same tunnel in both their normal clothes and whilst wearing a common uniform. The uniform consists of white overalls. By having every subject wear the same clothes, the degree to which one subject could impersonate another by mimicking their clothes can be investigated. The uniform clothing appearance was achieved by having subjects wear white overalls over their normal clothes. Each recording of normal or uniform clothing was repeated between 10 and 35 times depending on subject availability.

For the purpose of this analysis there is an assumption that the attacker may have complete knowledge of the system they are targeting. We have therefore based the selection of a target on the similarity of the gait silhouette. The expectation is that such a signature could be obtained through covert surveillance, for example by recording the target walking down the street. This represents an upper bound on the effectiveness of target selection for a target pool of 22 subjects.

8 Gait Anti-spoofing

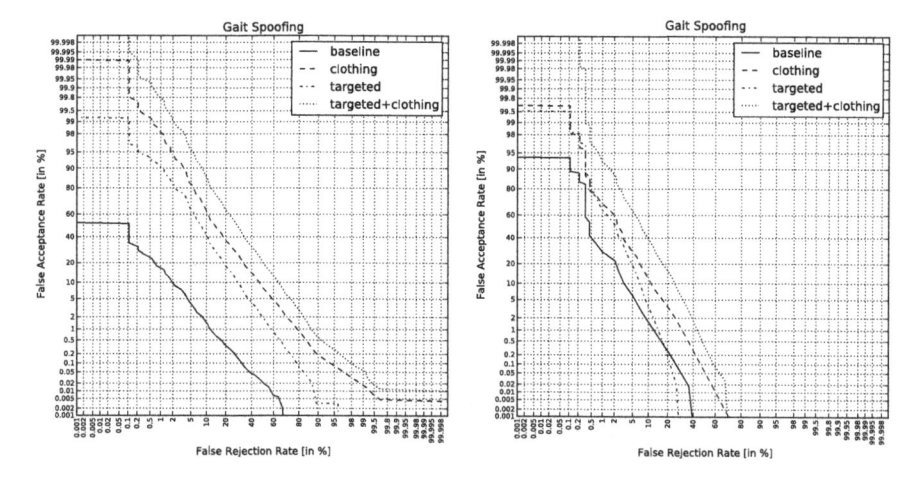

**Fig. 8.2** Gait biometric performance under different kinds of spoofing attacks (false acceptance rates superimposed for spoofing performance comparison). The *left graph* is for UOULU 2D system and the *right graph* shows the performance of the 3D USOU system

## 8.2.2 Spoofing Results

The results of our experiments are shown in Fig. 8.2 in the form of DET profiles which illustrate the dynamic behaviour of the two gait verification systems (UOULU and USOU) as the decision thresholds are changed. The DET curves show how the false acceptance rate varies relative to the false rejection rate. The percentage of successful attacks is equivalent to the false accept rate of the systems when attacked. The lowest profiles (curves labelled baseline in Fig. 8.2) are that of the baseline performance when the systems are not confronted to attacks. They are important to gain insight into the effect of the spoofing as our focus is on the degradation in performance caused by spoofing attacks relative to these baselines. The curves labelled clothing show the average false accept rate when attackers replicate the clothing of their target but are unable to select which person they are attacking. This curve shows that clothing impersonation does convey a small advantage, increasing the EER of the 3D gait system from 6 to 12 % and increasing the 2D gait system from 4 to 28 %. The curves labelled targeted show how effective spoofing attempts are when an attacker selects a target that is most similar to them without also impersonating their clothing. In terms of EER these kinds of attacks seem to be less effective than clothing impersonation. The curves that combine target selection and clothing impersonation show a significant raise in the EERs compared to the baseline performance, indicating serious vulnerabilities from such combined attacks. This can also be seen in the score distributions in Figs. 8.3 and 8.4 showing a clear overlap between the distributions of the true claimants and the attackers of the 2D gait system. The curves in Fig. 8.6 indicate that the state-of-the-art systems used for gait recognition are quite sensitive to spoofing attacks and this is the case not only at FRR of 2 % but for any chosen FRR value.

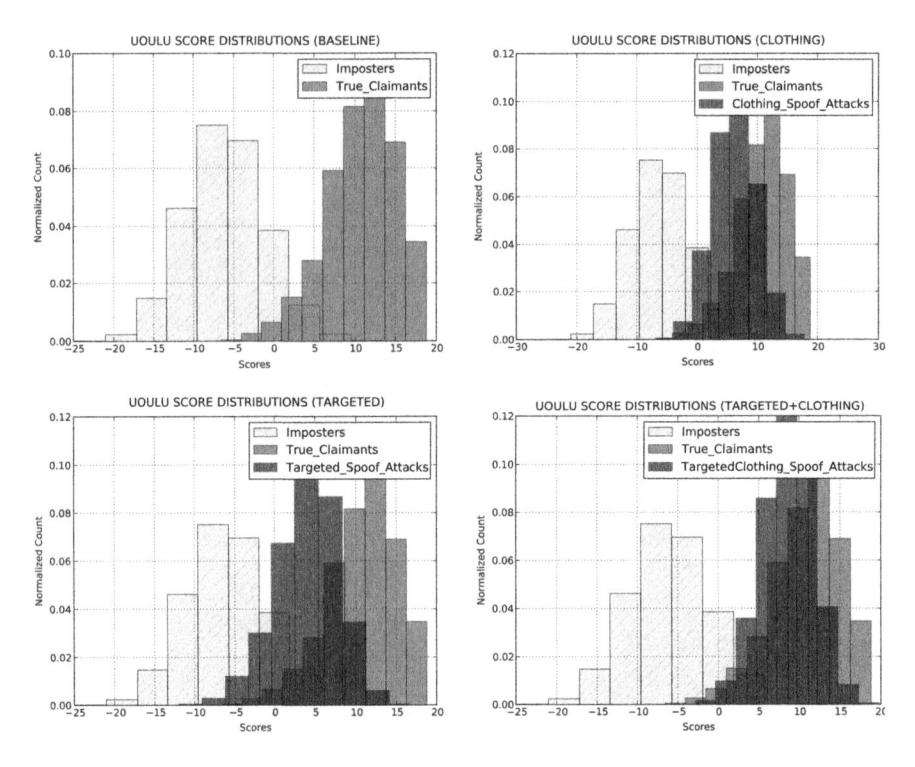

**Fig. 8.3** Score distributions showing the overlap between the true claimants and the attacks

## 8.3 Countermeasures

Unlike the majority of biometric spoofing, such as gummy fingerprint or facial photo attacks, both clothing impersonation and targeting have no artificial traits that can be detected. They therefore require an adaptation of the gait recognition algorithm to make it intrinsicly robust to such attacks.

### 8.3.1 Clothing Impersonation Countermeasures

This section examines methods for increasing the robustness of the 2D UOULU gait recognition system to clothing impersonation attacks. The following observations have been used to develop countermeasures:

1. The overall human body has various types of information to be extracted and selected for gait recognition. Body shape (built), overall body movement and body limbs movement patterns could greatly contribute to gait recognition. In case of spoofing attacks, these types of information may be altered to attack the system. Hence, the baseline system is vulnerable to altered information as

8 Gait Anti-spoofing

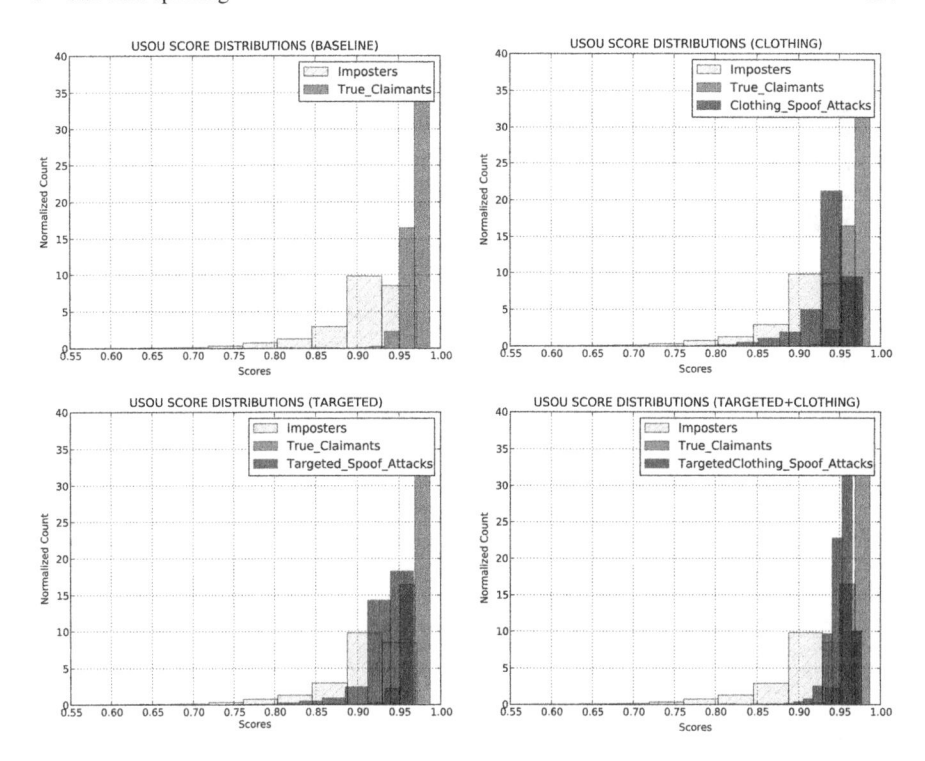

**Fig. 8.4** Score distributions showing the overlap between the true claimants and the attacks

boosting did not learn from attacks and could potentially over-fit the training data.
2. The baseline 2D gait system analyses the body in four divided regions. Based on the type of spoofing attacks (target or clothing), the information extracted from body portions could be altered. The overall histogram considers the overall portion and combines the altered information of body portions that are more vulnerable to spoofing attacks to those carrying movement information than body built and shape information.

The ideas used to solve the shortcomings of the baseline system to better cope with spoofing attacks are:

- Prevent over-training by employing a histogram distance as the classifier.
- Divide the body into multiple horizontal portions, as shown in see Fig. 8.5.

The gait recognition database does not contain camera and viewpoint changes. Hence, we can divide the body into multiple regions to prevent altered information from body parts that are vulnerable to spoofing attacks to combine with the overall information. We extract LBP-TOP features from each body part and concatenate the overall histogram to separate information extracted from body regions.

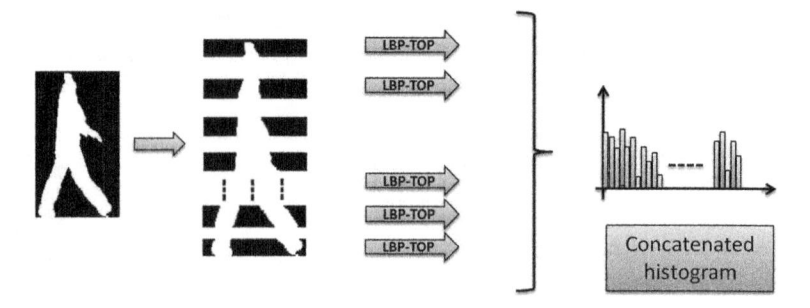

**Fig. 8.5** Block diagram of our proposed initial gait anti-spoofing solution (part-based 2D gait recognition)

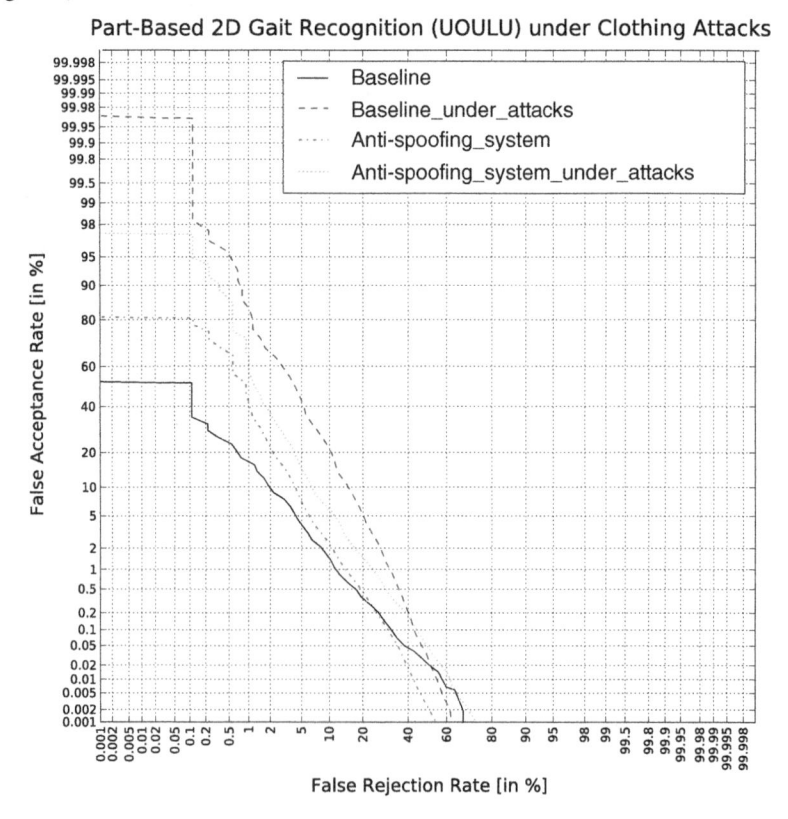

**Fig. 8.6** The DET Curves of the initial anti-spoofing system (part-based 2D gait recognition system) for 'Clothing targeted attacks' and comparison with baseline results

#### 8.3.1.1 Experimental Setup

A successful attack is performed when the difference between the signature of an attacker and their target are below the system's verification threshold. In the clothing impersonation scenario, the attacks are calculated by comparing each of the uniform recordings of each subject against the uniform recordings of all of the other subjects while the targeted clothing attacks are equivalent to each subject selecting the person with the most similar build and impersonating their clothing.

A revised evaluation protocol has been used in order to training the countermeasures using spoofing data. Some subjects were excluded from testing and used only for training. Both the 'normal clothes' and 'uniform' recordings of excluded subjects can be used to learn the type of attacks, and thus improve the robustness to attacks. The data is required to comprise reasonably high number of non-excluded subjects to ensure that the targeting would have a realistic effect. On the other hand, there is a need for enough excluded subjects to ensure that effective training is performed.

The dataset has been split in half with 11 subjects being used as training subjects and 11 for testing. We considered to have 6-fold cross validation on 50/50 splits of the dataset to prevent any distinctive characters dominating the results. We addressed this by creating six different subsets, repeating the training and testing on each set and then combining the scores.

#### 8.3.1.2 Results

The results of the experiments are presented as the DET curve in Fig. 8.6 for 'Clothing attacks'. The body is divided into 10 equal horizontal regions and LBP-TOP features are extracted and concatenated to obtain 10 sets of histograms as the resulting feature vector. The figure shows four plots comparing the baseline system 'baseline', baseline system under attacks, anti-spoofing system performance using the baseline database and anti-spoofing system performance on the spoofing database. As expected, the figure clearly shows performance improvement against spoofing attacks but at the cost of slight performance degradation of the baseline dataset. A similar conclusion can also be made on the results of the experiments, shown in Fig. 8.7 for 'Clothing targeted attacks'. Due to more challenging spoofing attacks, the performance improvement is less significant than in the 'clothing attack' scenario.

The experimental results showed that this gait anti-spoofing system significantly increases the robustness of the baseline system against spoofing attacks but, as expected, at the cost of some performance degradation on baseline tests not including spoofing attacks. Using our anti-spoofing initial solution under 'clothing attacks' at FRR of 5 %, the FAR performance gain was in the order of 25 % (as the FAR of the baseline system which was 40 % dropped till 15 % using the countermeasure).

### 8.3.2 Targeted Attacks

This section describes an approach to countering targeted attacks. It is challenging to counteract the effects of targeted attacks as such attacks increase the likelihood that the most similar impersonations are selected and there is nothing artificial in a targeted attack that makes it identifiable. Countermeasures rely on obtaining a more

**Part-Based 2D Gait Recognition (UOULU) under Clothing-Targetted Attacks**

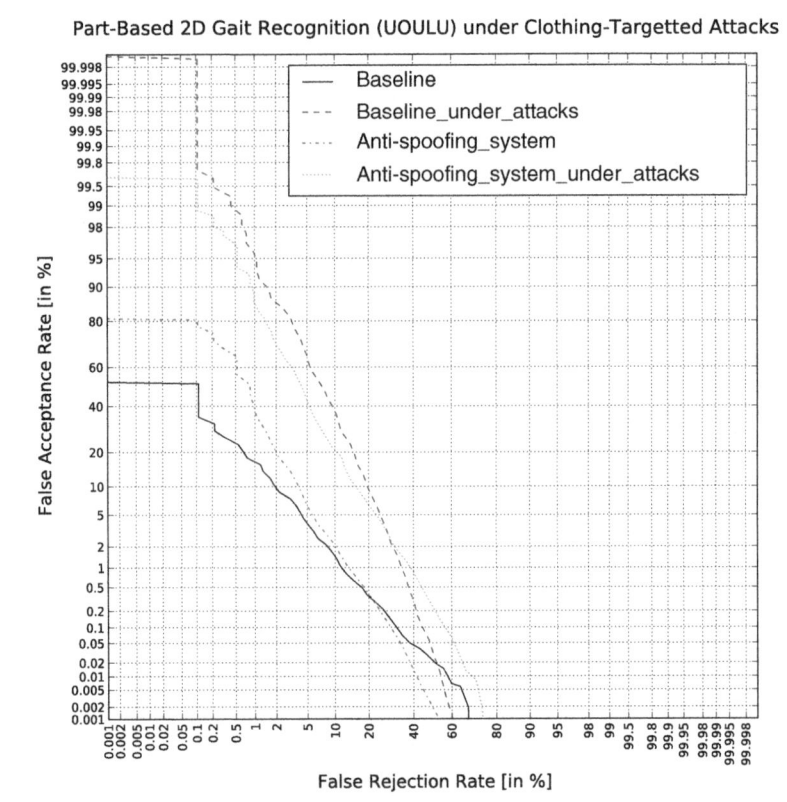

**Fig. 8.7** The DET Curves of the initial anti-spoofing system (part-based 2D gait recognition system) for 'Clothing attacks' and comparison with baseline results

distinctive signature that is harder for an attacker to obtain or providing more accurate estimates of subject's variation in gait signatures so more precise verifications can be performed. Targeted attacks highlight the importance of securing both the recognition system and enrollment databases to make it harder for attackers to identify the best targets. In addition, targeted attacks demonstrate the advantage of using biometric features that are harder for attackers to obtain. Unfortunately, in many cases this is at odds with the main advantages of non contact biometrics, such as gait, where the biometric signature is visible at a distance. However, as the 3D gait recognition system has a full 3D reconstruction of the walking subject there is additional information above a traditional 2D gait silhouette. The described countermeasure constructs two additional gait signatures using the front and top silhouettes as shown in Fig. 8.8. These silhouettes are highly correlated with each other and a simple concatenation of these signatures does not produce any significant defense against targeted attacks. However, by using a MAX fusion rule where the largest match score of the three silhouettes is selected, significant improvements in performance can be made.

8  Gait Anti-spoofing

**Fig. 8.8** Example of the 3 different average silhouettes that capture the appearance and shape of the walking subject from the side front and top. Used to provide a countermeasure against targeted attacks

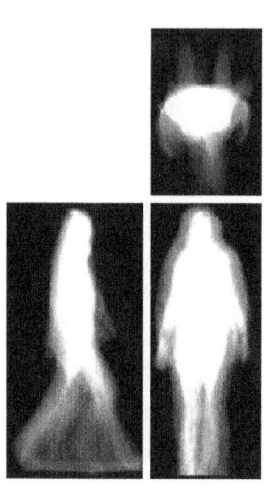

#### 8.3.2.1 Experimental Setup

The countermeasures to targeted spoofing attacks are evaluated with the same equipment and experimental procedure as that used to evaluate the effects of spoofing. A successful attack is performed when the difference between the signature of an attacker and their target are bellow the system's verification threshold.

#### 8.3.2.2 Results

The results of the experiments are shown in Fig. 8.9. The figure shows the affect on false acceptance rates as a result of using the three fused gait signatures side, front and top. The curve labelled 'Baseline' shows the performance of the gait recognition system using only the side average silhouette. The curve labelled 'Baseline_under_attacks' shows the performance when targeted attacks are performed on the system. The third curve labelled 'Anti-spoofing_system_under_attacks' shows the performance of the attacked system when the countermeasure is applied. The final curve labelled 'Anti-spoofing_system' shows the effects on the baseline system without attacks when the countermeasure system is in place.

As the multi-signature approach increases the quantity of biometric features available the countermeasure has the potential to improve both the baseline and the attack performance. For verification systems tuned to performance levels near the equal error rate, both baseline and attack performance is improved and in some cases the attacks provide negligible increase in false acceptance rates. However, for verification systems tuned to very low or very high false rejection rates the false acceptance rate is increased. In the case of the very low false rejection rate the false acceptance rater reaches 100 % indicating that at least one of the signatures of one of the subjects can be replicated by an attacking target more reliably than the subject themselves.

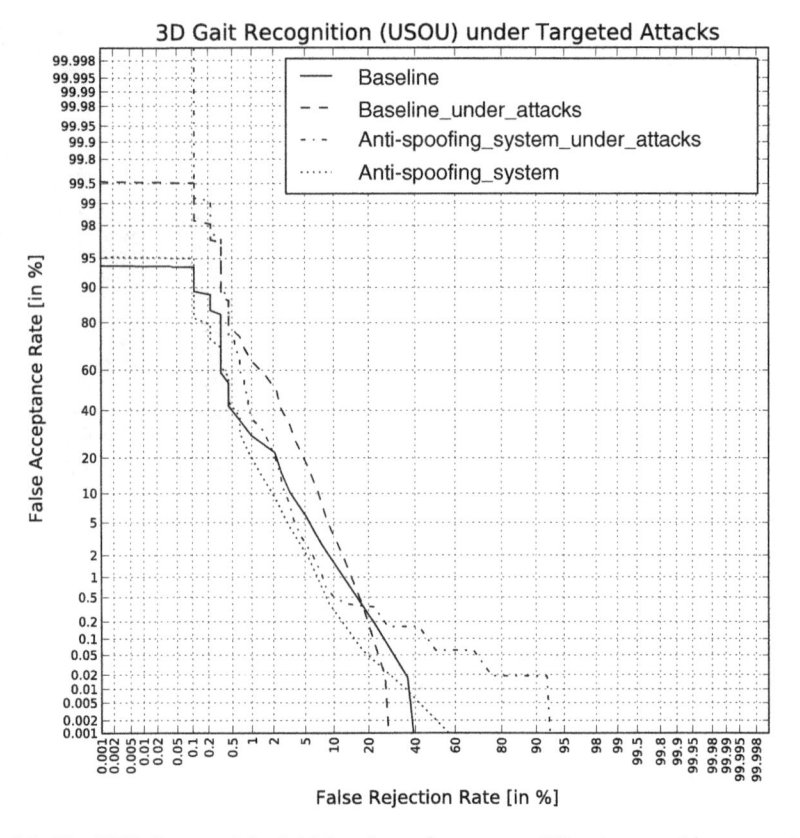

**Fig. 8.9** The DET Curves of the initial anti-spoofing system (3D gait recognition system) for 'Targeted attacks' and comparison with baseline results

However, such levels of false rejection are impractical for current gait recognition systems.

Using the multi-signature countermeasure, at a false rejection rate of 5%, the baseline false acceptance rate falls from approximately 5 to 2%. Likewise at a false rejection rate of 5% the attacked performance drops from 20 to 2.5%.

## 8.4 Further Work

Study of clothing is an important factor to both the study of gait as a biometric and to the study of spoofing. In order to further this analysis investigation of the effects of other covariates would be valuable, such as the effect of wearing different shoes. The future study of targeting will encompass theoretical modelling of the underlying distribution of gait signatures to better understand how increasing the number of targets increases the effectiveness of targeted attacks. There is also value in exploring additional gait features beyond those outlined in this chapter. Such features may improve the baseline performance and could help to limit the increase in FAR caused by targeted attacks. Additional work also remains in examining the effects of targeted attacks on other biometrics.

## 8.5 Conclusions

This chapter has shown how two example of gait recognition systems can be spoofed using clothing impersonation and targeted attacks. These attacks are particularly challenging as they have no artificial traits that can be detected. They are therefore applicable even under attentive human supervision. Countermeasures to both attacks were presented, both countermeasures provide a significant defense against these attacks, however, in the case of clothing attacks they do so at a slight reduction in baseline performance.

**Acknowledgments** The authors would like to thank the Academy of Finland and the TABULA RASA project (http://www.tabularasa-euproject.org) funded under the 7th Framework Programme of the European Union (EU) (grant agreement number 25728) for their financial support.

## References

1. Nixon M, Carter J (2006) Automatic recognition by Gait. Proc IEEE 94(11):2013–2024
2. Nixon MS, Tan TN, Chellappa R (2005) Human identification based on Gait. International series on biometrics. Springer, New York
3. Hadid A, Ghahramani M, Kellokumpu V, Pietikainen M, Bustard J, Nixon M (2012) Can gait biometrics be spoofed? In: 21st International Conference on Pattern Recognition (ICPR ), pp 3280–3283 2012
4. Kellokumpu V, Zhao G, Li SZ, Pietikainen M (2009) Dynamic texture based gait recognition. 3rd IAPR/IEEE International conference on biometrics, pp 1000–1009 2009
5. Kellokumpu V, Zhao G, Pietikäinen M (2010) Dynamic textures for human movement recognition. ACM International conference on image and video retrieval, CIVR '10, 470–476 2010
6. Seely RD, Samangooei S, Middleton L, Carter J, Nixon M (2008) The University of Southampton multi-biometric tunnel and introducing a novel 3d gait dataset. In: Biometrics: theory, applications and systems. IEEE, 2008
7. Sarkar S, Phillips PJ, Liu Z, Vega IR, Grother P, Bowyer KW (2005) The humanid gait challenge problem: data sets, performance, and analysis. IEEE Trans Pattern Anal Mach Intell 27:162–177
8. Seely RD (2010) On a three-dimensional gait recognition system. Ph.D. thesis, University of Southampton
9. Matovski D, Nixon M, Mahmoodi S, Carter J (2011) The effect of time on gait recognition performance. IEEE Trans Inf Forensics Secur 7(2):543–552

## Chapter 9
# Multimodal Anti-spoofing in Biometric Recognition Systems

Giorgio Fumera, Gian Luca Marcialis, Battista Biggio, Fabio Roli
and Stephanie Caswell Schuckers

**Abstract** While multimodal biometric systems were commonly believed to be intrinsically more robust to spoof attacks than unimodal systems, recent results provided clear evidence that they can be evaded by spoofing a single biometric trait. This pointed out that also multimodal systems require specific anti-spoofing measures. In this chapter, we introduce the issue of multimodal anti-spoofing, and give an overview of state-of-the-art anti-spoofing measures. Such measures mainly consist of developing ad hoc score fusion rules that are based on assumptions about the match score distribution produced by fake biometric traits. We discuss the pros and cons of existing measures, and point out the current challenges in multimodal anti-spoofing.

## 9.1 Introduction

Other chapters of this book addressed the issue of "anti-spoofing" in unimodal biometric systems. In this kind of system, anti-spoofing consists of an additional module, also called "liveness detector," that is used as a countermeasure to spoof attacks. This countermeasure is able to detect if the biometric signal acquired by

---

G. Fumera (✉) · G. L. Marcialis · B. Biggio · F. Roli
Department of Electrical and Electronic Engineering, University of Cagliari,
Piazza d'Armi, 09123 Cagliari, Italy
e-mail: fumera@diee.unica.it

G. L. Marcialis
e-mail: marcialis@diee.unica.it

B. Biggio
e-mail: battista.biggio@diee.unica.it

F. Roli
e-mail: roli@diee.unica.it

S. C. Schuckers
Department of Electrical and Computer Engineering, Clarkson University,
PO Box 5720, Potsdam, NY 13699, USA
e-mail: sschucke@clarkson.edu

© Springer-Verlag London 2014
S. Marcel et al. (eds.), *Handbook of Biometric Anti-Spoofing*,
Advances in Computer Vision and Pattern Recognition,
DOI: 10.1007/978-1-4471-6524-8_9

some sensors belongs to a "live" person or is an artificial replica: for example, a fake finger, or a 2d photo of a face.

Anti-spoofing in multimodal biometric systems, or, for the sake of brevity, "multimodal anti-spoofing," is not a clear concept as in the unimodal case. On the basis of what has been discussed in other chapters, we can define multimodal anti-spoofing as follows:

1. Fusion of multiple liveness detectors for a single biometric. This can be motivated by the fact that different approaches to liveness detection can be "complementary," thus they can be combined at different levels to improve the liveness detection performance (for example, fingerprint liveness detectors which combine fake-based and live-based features according to [1]). This definition comes from the fact that liveness detection is substantially a two-class classification problem where an individual liveness detector can be seen as a classifier. Approaches aimed at fusing multiple liveness detectors appeared in [1–4]. Therefore, in this case, "multimodal anti-spoofing" refers to the combination of "modalities" defined by each individual liveness detector.
2. Fusion of liveness detector and matcher. In this case, the different "modalities" are given by the two heterogeneous classifiers, namely, the uni-biometric verification system and the liveness detector. This very recent topic has been considered in [5–7].
3. Multibiometric systems where no liveness detection is performed [8]. In this case, each "modality" consists of a different kind of biometric trait (e.g., fingerprint and face), which is processed by a different biometric verification module. The proposed anti-spoofing measures for this kind of system consist of ad hoc score fusion rules, capable to exploit the information coming from a match score generated when comparing a spoofed biometric against the related genuine template(s) [9–12].

Definitions 1 and 2 refer to unimodal biometric systems. Therefore, for sake of clarity and with respect to the scope of this book, we will focus on definition 3 only, where "multimodal anti-spoofing" means protecting multimodal biometric systems against spoof attacks by using robust score-level fusion rules. This topic is very recent, since the first papers were published in 2009.

The rest of this chapter is organized as follows. Section 9.2 states the problem. Section 9.3 presents the current state of the art on multimodal spoofing, with an introduction aimed at pointing out how this problem was perceived in the biometric community before 2009. Section 9.4 reports experimental evidences on the effectiveness on anti-spoofing measures described in Sect. 9.3. Finally, Sect. 9.5 is devoted to a discussion on current challenges in multimodal anti-spoofing, and to a summary of recent achievements in the "TABULA RASA" research project.

## 9.2 Problem Statement

In this chapter, we will refer to multimodal biometric *verification* systems, whose aim is to verify a claimed identity on the basis of different biometric traits submitted by the user. In multimodal biometric verification, a person submits $N$ different biometrics, and claims a certain identity. A feature set $x_i$ is extracted from the $i$th biometric, and compared by a matching algorithm with the template of the claimed identity. The output is a match score $s_i$ for the $i$th biometric system. Match scores $\{s_1, \ldots, s_N\}$ coming from such matchers are processed by a "fusion rule" module, which produces a "combined" match score that is finally used to accept of reject the claimed identity. This can be done according to two basic approaches:

1. The distribution of genuine and impostor match scores of individual matchers are used for estimating the joint likelihoods, and the Likelihood Ratio (LR) rule is used [9].
2. The distribution of genuine and impostor match scores are derived from the fused scores, and the final decision is made by setting an appropriate acceptance threshold.

Let $\{s_1, \ldots, s_N\}$ be the set of match scores coming from the $N$ matchers, and let $I \in \{0, 1\}$ be the Boolean random variable denoting whether the verification attempt comes from an impostor ($I = 1$) or a genuine user ($I = 0$). The approach 1 above requires that the joint probability likelihood ratio is evaluated:

$$\text{LR}(s_1, \ldots, s_N) = \frac{P(s_1, \ldots, s_N | I = 0)}{P(s_1, \ldots, s_N | I = 1)} = \frac{P(s_1 | I = 0) \cdot \ldots \cdot P(s_N | I = 0)}{P(s_1 | I = 1) \cdot \ldots \cdot P(s_N | I = 1)}, \tag{9.1}$$

where $P(s_i | I = 0)$ and $P(s_i | I = 1)$ are the match score distributions of genuine users and of impostors, respectively, for the $i$th matcher. Joint distributions $P(s_1, \ldots, s_N | I = 0)$ and $P(s_1, \ldots, s_N | I = 1)$ can be derived by factorizing individual likelihoods under the hypothesis that match scores are independent given $I$. This hypothesis is commonly accepted in multimodal biometric verification, since it is reasonable that match scores derived from the comparison of different kinds of biometrics are independent on each other. A threshold $\lambda$ is then set, and, if $LR(s_1, \ldots, s_N) > \lambda$, the user is accepted as genuine; otherwise, it is rejected as an impostor.

In the approach 2 above, a fusion rule $f(s_1, \ldots, s_N)$ is applied to the set of match scores, to derive a novel match score:

$$s = f(s_1, \ldots, s_N; \Theta), \tag{9.2}$$

where $\Theta$ is a set of parameters which can be estimated from an additional validation set. If $\Theta = \emptyset$ no parameters are necessary and the rule is referred to as a "fixed" one, otherwise it is referred to as a "trained" rule. For example, well-known fixed rules are the maximum score, or the sum or product of the $N$ scores. Examples of trained rules are the weighted sum and the weighted product of the $N$ scores.[1] The final score $s$ is compared to an acceptance threshold $s^*$, as usually done for uni-biometric systems. If $s > s^*$, the user is accepted as genuine; otherwise, it is rejected as an impostor. In this chapter, we will consider both approaches above.

When a spoof attack is performed, one or more of the $N$ required biometrics are counterfeited with an artificial replica. In this case, we could expect that:

1. $M < N$ biometrics have been counterfeited, so that they should be similar to the corresponding biometrics of the claimed identity.
2. The remaining $N - M$ biometrics are noncounterfeited, so that they belong to one or more impostors.

Thus, the problem is to reject users that attempt a spoof attack, as well as users that do not attempt a spoof attack, but claim a different identity, by classifying them as impostors ($I = 1$), and to classify the other users as genuine ($I = 0$). This implies that detecting the liveness of submitted biometric is not the focus of such systems.

In absence of spoof attacks, biometric systems are evaluated on the basis of two kinds of errors:

- the fraction of impostors accepted as genuine users, called False Acceptance Rate (FAR);
- the fraction of genuine users rejected as impostors, called False Rejection Rate (FRR); Genuine Acceptance Rate (GAR = 1 − FRR) can be used as well.

By varying the acceptance threshold one obtains different pairs of FAR and GAR values. Plotting FAR (GAR) as a function of FAR leads to the well-known DET (ROC) curve.

In presence of spoof attacks, the evaluation of a third kind of error has been proposed in [12], and is also adopted in this chapter, namely, the rate of accepted spoof attacks, called Spoof-False Acceptance Rate (SFAR). A spoof false accept is defined as the case where the fusion rule falsely accepts an attacker when one or more of the modalities in a multimodal system have been successfully spoofed. We will call SROC (Spoof-ROC) the curve obtained by plotting GAR as a function of SFAR, to distinguish it from the standard ROC curve.

It is important to note that, at a specific operating point (i.e., for a given acceptance threshold), the FRR does not change under a spoof attack. Therefore, reporting the ROC and SROC curves related to the same system allows one to easily evaluate the performance when the system is under standard operation conditions or under spoof attacks, respectively. More precisely, for a given operating point whose FRR value is denoted as FRR*, the effect of a spoof attack is represented by the SFAR that is obtained by the intersection of the SROC curve with the horizontal line given by FRR = FRR*.

---

[1] Also the LR rule and similar ones can be referred to as trained rules, as they require the estimation of likelihoods.

## 9.3 State of the Art on Multimodal Biometric Spoofing

In this section, we review recent works that pointed out the vulnerability of multimodal systems to spoof attacks against a single biometric trait. We then describe the anti-spoofing measures proposed so far against such a vulnerability.

### 9.3.1 Are Multimodal Systems More Secure than Unimodal Ones?

About a decade ago, the use of multimodal systems to implement anti-spoofing measures was proposed [13–15]:

> [...] multibiometric systems provide anti-spoofing measures by making it difficult for an intruder to simultaneously spoof the multiple biometric traits of a legitimate user. By asking the user to present a random subset of biometric traits, the system ensures a live user is indeed present at the point of data acquisition [13].

The rationale is that, even if an intruder is able to fabricate a perfect replica of a given trait (e.g., a fingerprint), he/she is not guaranteed to be wrongly recognized as a genuine user, since the system may not require the submission of that trait. This would force intruders to spoof more than one trait, making multimodal systems a deterrent against such attacks.

Subsequently, a stronger belief spread in the biometric community, about the security of multimodal systems against spoof attacks, i.e., evading them always requires an intruder to spoof *all* the involved traits (or at least more than one), *regardless* of the adoption of any anti-spoofing measure like the one above, and, most important, of the considered score fusion rule. This would imply that multimodal systems are *intrinsically* more secure than unimodal ones against spoof attacks, in the sense that their evasion requires a higher effort by the intruder. Although this is far from evident, until a few years ago no work questioned or attempted to verify such a belief. This issue has been addressed first in [9, 10, 12]. These works studied the performance of multimodal biometric systems that use parallel score fusion rules, where only a subset of the modalities used in the system, or even a *single* one, are spoofed, and the attacker merely presents his/her own biometric traits for the remaining biometric(s). They even argued that this would make such systems *more vulnerable* than unimodal ones:

> Intuitively, a multimodal system is intrinsically more secure than unimodal systems since it is more difficult to spoof two or more biometric traits than a single one. However, is it really necessary to spoof all the fused biometric traits to crack a multimodal system? This question is especially important when a very secure biometric (e.g., retina scan) is combined with another that is easily spoofed (e.g., face). In this scenario, the benefits of adding the face information may be negated by reduction in overall security [9].

> If an intruder can break the multimodal system by attacking only one mode, then the multimodal system is not more secure than the least secure mode (i.e., the "weakest link"). In this case, we can even argue that the multimodal system is less secure than its unimodal

systems alone since the use of several modes leads to a bigger number of vulnerability points, increasing the possibility of an intruder to take advantage of at least one of these vulnerabilities. For example, consider a multimodal system combining signature and fingerprint traits under a spoof attack. In this scenario, a forger can choose which trait to spoof according to his skills, what may increase his chances of being successful [10].

In fact, empirical evidences provided in [9, 10, 12], and subsequently in [7] showed that parallel multimodal systems that combine two to four different modalities, and use several state-of-the-art score fusion rules, can be evaded by spoofing a single trait. Moreover, the probability of accepting spoof impostors as genuine users (i.e., the SFAR) was shown to be significantly affected by the choice of the score fusion rule. Despite this interesting result, designing score fusion rules that are robust to spoof attacks without degrading significantly the performance in the absence of spoofing is still an open issue, as well as thoroughly assessing the security of standard score fusion rules to understand whether and under what circumstances some fusion rules may be intrinsically more secure than others. Accordingly, another open issue remains that of deriving clear guidelines to help system designers to select the most appropriate score fusion rule for the task at hand (e.g., depending on the level of *security* and performance in the absence of spoofing required by their system).

It is worth pointing out also that the aforementioned result was obtained by *simulating* spoof attacks, under the assumption that, in a successful spoof attack, the match score distribution of fake traits equals that of live, genuine traits. This corresponds to a scenario in which the attacker is able to produce a replica which is (statistically) indistinguishable by the matcher from the original, live trait. Accordingly, to simulate a successful spoofing attempt, a randomly drawn genuine score was used for the spoofed modality, while the impostor scores were used for the other modalities (i.e., assuming the attacker supplied his/her own biometric).

In [9] a biometric system combining face and fingerprint modalities was considered, and the LR and Weighted sum were used as score fusion rules. For instance, when the operational point was set to FAR = 0.1 %, under a simulated face spoofing attack a SFAR of about 40 % was measured. In other words, the probability that an impostor is wrongly accepted as a genuine user by submitting a replica of the face of the targeted client is 400 times higher than for standard impostors. An even more disruptive effect was observed for fingerprint spoofing, for which the SFAR became almost 100 %. This means that the considered multimodal system can be evaded almost with certainty by providing a "good" fingerprint replica.

Similar results were reported in [10] for face spoofing. Contrary to [9], fingerprint spoofing was investigated using a data sets of scores coming from real spoof attacks, obtained from the Fingerprint Liveness Detection Competition 2009 [16]. In this case, setting the operational point to FAR = 0.1 %, the SFAR was about 8 %, i.e., about an order of magnitude lower than in the case of simulated attacks, but still much higher than the desired value of 0.1 %.

In [12] a multimodal database consisting of face, iris, and fingerprint match scores from genuine and imposter pairs was used. This database was created by West Virginia University and is available on the CITeR website [17]. Besides two modality systems, the investigation was extended to a three modality system, where one or two modalities are spoofed. The sum fusion rule was considered. A spoof attempt was simulated using a genuine match score in place of an impostor match score, as in [9]. Even using three modalities, spoofing only one trait was found to significantly increase the probability that an attacker is accepted as a genuine user. For instance, the point at which FRR equals FAR (which is known as the equal error rate, EER) was chosen as the operating point of the system by setting the corresponding threshold level, and the corresponding SFAR was analyzed based on the same threshold. Reported results show an EER (FRR/FAR) of 0.05%. For this operating point, when one of three modalities is spoofed, the average SFAR is 4.9%, with an associated FRR of 0.05%. When two of three modalities are spoofed the SFAR jumps up to an average of 97.4%, that is, over 97% of the time, a person will be able to spoof the system by spoofing two of three modalities.

Finally, in [7] four different modalities were considered, one face and three fingerprints. The LR and sum fusion rules were used. Spoof attacks were simulated again as in [9]. As an example, setting the operational point to EER = 0.32%, when the sum rule was used, it was observed that spoofing a *single* fingerprint lead to a SFAR of 9–56% (depending on which of the three fingers is spoofed). Using the LR rule, the ERR was much lower, about 0.004%. However, the SFAR was 57–91%. This means that spoofing a single trait can allow an attacker to evade even a multimodal system that combines four different modalities. Moreover, we point out that the LR fusion rule was found to be more vulnerable than the simplest sum rule, although it is known to be optimal in the Neyman-Pearson sense (provided that a reliable estimate of the genuine and impostor score distributions is available). Indeed, while its EER is much lower than the one of the sum rule, its SFAR was significantly higher.

In our subsequent work, we extended this investigation to *real* spoof attacks, focusing on biometric systems involving two modalities, face and fingerprint [11, 18–21]. To this aim, we collected in our Lab several face and fingerprint data sets, fabricated fake traits using several techniques, and evaluated several multimodal systems using different sensors, matchers, and score fusion rules (see Sect. 9.4). All our results clearly confirmed that spoofing a single trait can drastically increase the probability that an impostor is wrongly accepted as a genuine user by a multimodal system. For instance, in [11] we observed that, using the sum, LR and LDA score fusion rules, and setting the operational point to FAR = 0.1%, the SFAR that can be attained by face and fingerprint spoofing was respectively beyond 20 and 50% (depending on the score fusion rule and on the spoofing technique used). In [20] we found that also multimodal systems using *serial* score fusion rules exhibit the same vulnerability.

To sum up, empirical evidence collected so far clearly shows that sole use of multiple modalities does not guarantee that a biometric system can not be evaded by spoofing a single biometric trait. In the next section we overview anti-spoofing measures proposed so far for multimodal systems that use parallel score fusion rules, and always require the user to submit all the considered traits.

**Table 9.1** Results obtained in [12] that show the benefits of selecting the EER operating point according to a trade-off between FRR and SFAR (EERspoof)

| Operating point | FAR (%) | FRR (%) | SFAR (one modality) (%) | SFAR (two modalities) (%) |
|---|---|---|---|---|
| EER | 0.05 | 0.05 | 4.9 | 97.4 |
| EERspoof | $\ll 0.001$ | 2.89 | 0.31 | 2.89 |

The first row reports FAR, FRR, and SFAR when one or two modalities are spoofed attained when the EER operating point (FAR = FRR) is chosen. The second row reports the same performance measures when the EERspoof operating point is considered (FAR = SFAR when two modalities are spoofed)

## 9.3.2 Countermeasures to Spoof Attacks in Multimodal Systems

In [9, 10, 12] different anti-spoofing measures have been proposed, aimed at reducing the probability (SFAR) that an intruder, by spoofing a single trait, can break multimodal systems that require users to submit *all* the considered traits, and use parallel score fusion rules. All the proposed countermeasures act on the score fusion rule. The simplest one consists of modifying the criterion for choosing the threshold on the fused score [12]; another one involves some modification of existing fusion rules [9, 10]; another one consists of a novel, ad hoc fusion rule [9]. They are summarized in the following, and their pros and cons are discussed.

While the decision threshold on the fused score is usually set according to a desired trade-off between FRR and FAR, the anti-spoofing measure proposed in [12] consists of setting it according to a trade-off between FRR and SFAR. For instance, if the operational point is set at the ERR, where FRR = FAR, it is suggested in this paper that in order to improve security of the fusion algorithm, a new threshold is considered where SFAR equals FRR. This is called the Spoof EER (EERspoof). Other operating points could also be selected, depending on the application requirements for FRR, FAR, and SFAR.

For instance, in the experiments summarized in Sect. 9.3.1, setting the threshold at the EER operating point led to a FAR (and FRR) equal to 0.05 %, while the average SFAR was 4.9 % for a single spoofed trait, and 97.4 % for two spoofed traits. As also reported in Table 9.1, setting the operating point at EERspoof, a better trade-off between FRR and SFAR can be achieved at 2.89 % EERspoof for the case where two modalities are spoofed. If the operating point of 2.89 % EERspoof is chosen, the corresponding FRR is 2.89 % and FAR turned out to be $\ll 0.001$ %. In other words, the new operating point decreases SFAR from 97.4 to 2.89 % when two modalities are spoofed. Similarly, the average SFAR attained under spoofing of one modality decreases from 4.9 to 0.31 %. However, this comes at a sacrifice to FRR which increases from 0.05 to 2.89 %. The trade-off in these adjusted error rates may be preferred given the threat of a spoof attack. In summary, adjusting the operating point according to a system assessment based on SFAR can ensure for a more secure system. The main advantage of this anti-spoofing measure is that it can be applied to any score fusion rule, and is very simple to implement. One drawback is that a higher security comes at a cost of increased FRR. Another drawback is that the match score distribution produced by spoof attacks, and consequently the corresponding SFAR as a function of the decision threshold, are very difficult to estimate. This issue was addressed in [12] by assuming that such a distribution equals the one of the corresponding genuine traits, which is the approach proposed in [9] (see Sect. 9.3.1, and below). Note that, under this assumption, SFAR = GAR for any value of the decision threshold. This can be a pessimistic assumption. Moreover, it does not allow the proposed anti-spoofing measure to be applied, when the original criterion is the so-called zeroFAR, i.e., setting the decision threshold to the lowest value at which the estimated FAR equals 0. In this case, under the above assumption the threshold should be set so that SFAR = 0. This however implies GAR = 0, which is clearly not acceptable.

More complex anti-spoofing measures involve the modification of existing score fusion rules. In [9] the well-known LR rule was considered [see Eq. (9.1)] [9] proposes to estimate $P(s_i|I = 1)$ by taking int account also auxiliary information about the "security degree" of each matcher against spoof attacks, and about the probability that an attack against any subset of matchers occur. Denoting with $T_i \in \{0, 1\}$ and $F_i \in \{0, 1\}$ the Boolean random variables that indicate respectively whether a spoof attack has been attempted against the $i$th matcher, and whether it was "successful", $P(s_i|I)$ can be estimated by marginalizing the distribution $P(s_i, T_i, F_i|I)$[2]:

$$P(s_i|I) = \sum_{T_1,\ldots,T_N,F_1,\ldots,F_N} P(T_1,\ldots,T_N|I) \times \prod_{i=1}^{M} P(F_i|T_i)P(s_i|F_i, I). \quad (9.3)$$

In this model, the security of the $i$th matcher is defined as the probability that a spoof attack against it is successful, $P(F_i = 1|T_i = 1)$. As pointed out in [9], this value should be manually set according to general knowledge. Obviously, $P(F_i = 1|T_i = 0) = 0$. The other two distributions in the right-hand side of Eq. (9.3) were modeled in [9] according to the following assumptions: (i) spoof attacks against any of the $2^N - 1$ subsets of one or more matchers are equiprobable, i.e., $P(T_1,\ldots,T_N|I = 1) = 1-\alpha$, if $T_1 = \cdots = T_N = 0$, and $P(T_1,\ldots,T_N|I = 1) = \frac{\alpha}{2^N-1}$ otherwise, where $\alpha$ is the probability that some spoof attack has been attempted; (ii) genuine users will never provide a fake trait, i.e., $P(T_1,\ldots,T_N|I = 0) = 0$ for $T_1 = \cdots = T_N = 1$, and thus $P(s_i|F_i = 1, I = 0)$ need not to be modeled; (iii) the match score distributions in absence of successful spoof attacks, $P(s_i|F_i = 0, I = 0)$ and $P(s_i|F_i = 0, I = 1)$, equal respectively to the standard genuine and impostor distributions, and can thus be modeled from training data; (iv) the match score distribution of a successful attack equals the corresponding genuine distribution: $P(s_i|F_i = 1, I = 1) = P(s_i|F_i = 0, I = 0)$. It follows that $P(s_i|I)$ is a mixture of the score distributions of genuine users and impostors distributions.

---

[2] In [9] quality measures of the biometric samples in each modality were also considered. For the sake of simplicity we do not include them in our description.

The above anti-spoofing strategy allows one a finer tuning of the score fusion rule, with respect to the one of Johnson et al. [12]. On the other hand, it is tailored to the LR rule only, and is based on the same pessimistic assumption about the score distribution of successful spoof attacks (which was originally proposed in that work). Moreover, it trades a higher flexibility for the necessity of defining the probability $\alpha$ of a spoof attack, and the security of each matcher, $P(F_i = 1|T_i = 1)$, which are difficult to estimate in practice. Finally, also this countermeasure has the drawback of increasing the FRR, since the mass of the distribution $P(s_i|I = 1)$ is shifted towards the genuine distribution.

A simplification of the ExtLR rule was proposed in [10], to avoid an ad hoc choice of the parameters $\alpha$ and $P(F_i = 1|T_i = 1)$. The former was set to $\alpha = 0.5$, based on the rationale that no a priori information about the occurrence of spoof attack is usually available. The latter was set to 1 according to the worst-case assumption that each spoof attack will be successful.

A similar approach was also proposed in [22], although not specifically tailored to biometric applications. In particular, the underlying idea of this approach was to learn *secure* classifiers in adversarial settings, including spam filtering, intrusion detection, and biometrics, by modeling the distribution of carefully crafted attacks which may be not present in the training data.

Finally, a novel, ad hoc score fusion rule was proposed in [9]. The rationale is to explicitly defining, by high-level linguistic expressions, the decision criteria to fuse the information consisting of the match scores, the quality measures of the acquired traits (if available), and the prior information about the security of each matcher. To this aim, a fuzzy score fusion rule was devised. The input data and the output score were associated respectively to the linguistic expressions "high score/quality/security," and "high output" (using the convention that the higher the output value, the higher the probability that the user is genuine), which were modeled as fuzzy variables. In particular, the output was associated to the three linguistic values "low," "medium" and "high." The proposed fuzzy rules were defined for a biometric system involving two modalities, according to the criterion that "low security biometric system cannot faithfully perform the recognition task alone; and similarity scores with low quality should have low weights in the final output" [9]. For instance, two of these rules can be phrased as: "if the two match scores are "high", then the output is "high" (independently on the quality measures and security levels)"; "if one of the matchers has a 'low' security and produces a 'high' score, while the other produces a "low" match score (independently on its security level), then the output is 'high' ,"

The main advantage of this anti-spoofing strategy lies in the possibility to explicitly defining high-level rules to fuse the input information. On the other hand, the drawback is that the number of fuzzy rules grows exponentially with the number of matchers, which makes it difficult to define them for biometric systems involving three or more modalities. Moreover, empirical evidence provided in [9] shows that also this anti-spoofing measure is likely to increase the FRR.

To sum up, specific anti-spoofing measures proposed so far for multimodal systems are based on more or less complex manipulations of the score fusion rule, and sometimes require the knowledge of information difficult to estimate. Moreover, an inherent feature of these measures is that they trade a higher security against spoof attacks for a higher FRR. In the next section, we give an overview of the performance of some of these anti-spoofing measures, on publicly available datasets including real spoof attacks.

## 9.4 Experimental Evidences and Discussion

In this section, we present some experimental results from our previous works, with the aim of pointing out the vulnerability of multimodal systems to spoof attacks against a single biometric trait, and to show how such a vulnerability can be mitigated by one of the anti-spoofing measures described in Sect. 9.3.2. We chose the Extended LR to this aim, since it is tailored to improve the robustness of the well-known LR score fusion rule. We describe the datasets used in our experiments in Sect. 9.4.1, and the experimental protocol in Sect. 9.4.2. The results are presented and discussed in Sect. 9.4.3.

### 9.4.1 Datasets of Spoofed Samples

*Fingerprint spoofing* We used the LivDet 2011 data set, created for the Second Fingerprint Liveness detection competition [23]. It includes 80 clients (distinct fingers). Different impressions of live and fake fingers were acquired in two different sessions, separated by about two weeks. All the ten fingers were considered. Fake fingerprints were created by the consensual method [24]. Gelatine, silicone, alginate, and latex, were used as the casting materials, while plasticine- and silicon-like materials were used for molds. Fingerprint images were acquired using the well-known Biometrika FX2000 and Italdata ET10 optical sensors, which have respectively a resolution of 569 dpi and 500 dpi, and a sensing area of $13.2 \times 25$ mm and approximately $30.5 \times 30.5$ mm. Images of latex fake fingerprints turn out to be very similar to the images of the corresponding live fingerprints, while fakes obtained using other materials exhibit some artifacts. The fake fingerprints LivDet 2011 dataset represents the state of the art in fingerprint spoofing, and thus provides a reasonable set of realistic scenarios.

*Face spoofing* We used three publicly available datasets: the *Photo Attack* and Personal Photo Attack [18], and the *Print Attack* dataset [25, 26]. In the Photo Attack and Personal Photo Attack datasets, two different kinds of face spoof attacks were considered. The live face images of each client were collected in two sessions, with a time interval of about 2 weeks between them, under different lighting conditions and facial expressions. Spoofed face images for the Photo Attack dataset were constructed using the following "photo attack" method, also used in [26, 27]. It consists of displaying a photo of the targeted client on a laptop screen (or printing it on paper), and

**Table 9.2** Characteristics of the fake fingerprint and fake face datasets used in our experiments

| Data set | Number of clients | Number of spoofed images per client | Number of live images per client |
| --- | --- | --- | --- |
| LivDet11-Alginate | 80 | 3 | 5 |
| LivDet11-Gelatin | 80 | 3 | 5 |
| LivDet11-Silicone | 80 | 3 | 5 |
| LivDet11-Latex | 80 | 3 | 5 |
| Photo attack | 40 | 60 | 60 |
| Personal photo attack | 25 | 3 (avg.) | 60 |
| Print attack | 50 | 12 | 16 |

of showing it to the camera. To this end, the testing "live" face images of the clients were used. This simulates a pessimistic scenario in which the attacker can obtain photos of the targeted client under a setting similar to the one of the verification phase. The Personal Photo Attack dataset has been built using personal photos voluntarily provided by 25 of the 50 clients (on average, 3 photos for each client), that were acquired in different times and under different environmental conditions than those of the live training and testing images. This simulates a more realistic scenario where the attacker is able to collect a photo of the targeted client, e.g., from the Web. According to the above observations, we expect that the fake score distribution of our Photo Attack dataset, provided by a given matching algorithm, will be very similar to that of the genuine users. This may not be true for the Personal Photo Attack, instead, whose effectiveness strongly depends on the ability of the attacker to obtain images similar to the templates used by the system.

The Print Attack dataset was constructed during the Competition on Countermeasures to 2D Facial spoof attacks, in 2011. It consists of 200 video clips of printed-photo attack attempts to 50 clients, under different lighting conditions, and of 200 genuine access attempts from the same clients. We extracted the "live" and spoofed face images from the corresponding videos. In particular, for each client, we extracted 12 "live" face images and 16 spoofed face images from each video clip.

Table 9.2 reports the size of all the datasets described above.

### 9.4.2 Experimental Protocol

We used a similar experimental protocol as in [9, 12]:

- We built $5 \times 3 = 15$ *chimerical* datasets, by randomly associating face and fingerprint images of pairs of clients of the available five fingerprint and three face datasets. Building chimerical datasets is a widely used approach in experimental investigations on multimodal biometrics [8].

- Each chimerical dataset was randomly subdivided into five pairs of training and testing sets. Forty percentage of the "virtual" clients was included into the training set,[3] and the remaining 60% for the testing set. All the above procedure was repeated five times, for different random associations of face and fingerprint images of pairs of clients (namely, creating different "virtual" clients). In each run, the parameters of the trained fusion rules have been estimated on the training set. The results reported below refer to the average testing set performance, over the resulting 25 runs.
- The fake match scores were computed by comparing each fake image of a given client with the corresponding template image.
- We normalized all match scores in [0, 1] using the min-max technique [8]. The normalization parameters were estimated on the training set.
- The performance was assessed by computing the DET curves (FRR vs FAR). Note that, in the evaluation of spoof attacks, the DET curve reports FRR vs SFAR [12]. In both cases, the performance increases as the curve gets closer to the origin.

We used the NIST Bozorth3[4] and the VeryFinger[5] matching algorithms, for fingerprint verification. They are both based on matching the fingerprint minute details, called "minutiae." As they exhibited very similar behaviors, we will only report the results for Bozorth3. The Elastic Bunch Graph Matching (EBGM) algorithm was used for face verification.[6] It is based on representing a face with a graph, whose nodes are the so-called face "landmarks" (centered on the nose, eyes, and other points detected on the face). These nodes are labeled by a feature vector, and are connected by edges representing geometrical relationships among them. We also carried out some preliminary experiments using the Principal Component Analysis (PCA) and the Linear Discriminant Analysis (LDA), which yield again very similar results to that of the EBGM algorithm, and are thus omitted for sake of clarity.

We investigated three attack scenarios using the fake traits of our datasets: (a) only fingerprints are spoofed, (b) only faces are spoofed, (c) both fingerprints and faces are spoofed (bi-modal or double spoofing). For the scenarios (a) and (b), we also evaluated simulated spoof attacks under the pessimistic scenario defined in [9, 10, 12]: fictitious fake scores were generated by randomly drawing a set of genuine match scores from the testing set.

The fusion rules we considered are: sum, product, weighted sum (LDA), LR, and Extended LR. Since the bi-modal system considered in these experiments is the same as in [9], we used for the Extended LR rule the same values of the parameters as in [9] (i.e., the probability that a spoofing attack against either matcher is successful, and the prior probability of a spoof attack: see Sect. 9.3.2).

---

[3] The clients of a chimerical dataset are usually referred to as "virtual" clients, since they do not correspond to a real person or identity. They are indeed created by randomly associating the biometric traits of different "real" clients.

[4] http://www.nist.gov/itl/iad/ig/nbis.cfm

[5] http://www.neurotechnology.com/verifinger.html

[6] http://www.cs.colostate.edu/evalfacerec/algorithms5.php

## 9.4.3 Results and Discussion

We report in the following a representative set of results, related to the following pairs of spoof attacks:

1. LivDet11-Latex and Photo Attack;
2. LivDet11-Gelatin and Print Attack;
3. LivDet11-Alginate and Personal Photo Attack.

We do not report here any result related to fake fingerprints fabricated with silicone (LivDet11-Silicone), since they attained very similar results to that fabricated with latex (LivDet11-Latex), as also reported in [11]. Tables 9.3, 9.4 and 9.5 report the average performance and the standard deviation attained on each data set by all fusion rules, for three operating points: EER (when FAR = FRR), FAR = 1%, and FAR = 0.1%. This allows us to directly compare the performance of the different fusion rules under standard operating conditions (in terms of FAR and FRR), and their robustness to spoof attacks (in terms of SFAR). Each operating point was fixed on the DET curve obtained without spoof attacks, namely, by considering genuine users and impostors (non-spoof attacks). The FRR at each selected operating point is reported in the first column (labeled as *no spoof*) of Tables 9.3, 9.4 and 9.5. The SFAR attained by the different spoof attacks at the same operating point is reported in the remaining columns. This allows us to understand to which extent a fusion rule is robust: once the operating point is fixed, the effect of spoofing is only to increase the FAR (actually, the SFAR) as it only affects impostor match scores, while the FRR remains unchanged.

When no spoofing attack is performed, all fusion rules exhibited almost the same performance, except for the Sum rule (see the *no spoof* column in Tables 9.3, 9.4 and 9.5). The Sum rule performed much worse, because of the strong performance imbalance between the fingerprint and the face matcher: the genuine users and impostors score distributions of the face matcher exhibited indeed a much higher overlapping.

Spoofing a single biometric trait always led to a SFAR higher than the corresponding FAR in the considered multimodal systems, for all the adopted fusion rules (see the *fing.*, *s-fing.*, *face* and *s-face* columns in Tables 9.3, 9.4 and 9.5). This provides evidence that multimodal systems are not intrinsically robust to spoof attacks against a single biometric trait. In particular, fingerprint spoofing was almost always much more harmful than face spoofing. Also this behavior is due to the performance imbalance between the fingerprint and the face matcher, which caused all fusion rules, except for Sum, to give a higher weight to the former. Therefore, the Sum rule exhibited the worse performance in the absence of attacks, and the highest vulnerability to face spoof attacks, while it turned out to be the least vulnerable to fingerprint spoofing. Spoofing both traits led to an even higher SFAR (see the *both* column in Tables 9.3, 9.4 and 9.5). No that the SFAR values reported in Tables 9.3, 9.4 and 9.5 under the *fing.* columns show that latex-based fingerprint spoofing appears more effective than using gelatin-based fake fingerprints; in turn, the latter appears more effective than using alginate-based fake fingerprints.

**Table 9.3** EER, FRR at FAR = 1 %, and FRR at FAR = 0.1 % for the considered fusion rules on the Livdet11-Latex and Photo Attack datasets (*no spoof*)

| Rule | no spoof | face | s-face | fing. | s-fing. | both |
|---|---|---|---|---|---|---|
| | EER % | SFAR % | SFAR % | SFAR % | SFAR % | SFAR % |
| Sum | 9.98 ± 2.1 | 33.25 ± 3.9 | 37.82 ± 3.8 | 44.07 ± 4.8 | 79.85 ± 3.8 | 60.89 ± 2.9 |
| Product | 3.49 ± 1.4 | 5.72 ± 2.1 | 6.43 ± 2.2 | 70.06 ± 5.4 | 96.11 ± 1.8 | 73.10 ± 4.9 |
| LDA | 3.32 ± 1.5 | 8.39 ± 4.3 | 9.87 ± 4.8 | 70.79 ± 5.6 | 96.36 ± 2.2 | 74.09 ± 5.4 |
| LR | 3.60 ± 1.4 | 5.58 ± 2.8 | 6.36 ± 3.2 | 71.41 ± 5.1 | 96.46 ± 2.2 | 73.47 ± 5.1 |
| Ext. LR | 3.61 ± 1.4 | 5.64 ± 2.7 | 6.40 ± 3.1 | 71.49 ± 5.0 | 96.38 ± 2.2 | 73.57 ± 5.1 |
| | FRR % at FAR = 1% | SFAR % | SFAR % | SFAR % | SFAR % | SFAR % |
| Sum | 17.41 ± 3.2 | 15.58 ± 1.6 | 20.46 ± 1.9 | 28.38 ± 5.2 | 69.00 ± 6.1 | 46.00 ± 3.8 |
| Product | 5.15 ± 2.7 | 1.93 ± 0.4 | 2.28 ± 0.5 | 63.22 ± 4.7 | 94.37 ± 3.1 | 66.57 ± 4.4 |
| LDA | 5.05 ± 2.6 | 2.17 ± 0.5 | 2.73 ± 0.7 | 64.91 ± 4.7 | 95.12 ± 3.1 | 67.83 ± 4.6 |
| LR | 5.46 ± 2.6 | 1.22 ± 0.4 | 1.43 ± 0.5 | 64.94 ± 4.7 | 95.22 ± 3.1 | 66.38 ± 4.7 |
| Ext. LR | 5.63 ± 2.8 | 1.17 ± 0.4 | 1.38 ± 0.5 | 64.68 ± 4.8 | 94.94 ± 3.3 | 66.03 ± 4.8 |
| | FRR % at FAR = 0.1% | SFAR % | SFAR % | SFAR % | SFAR % | SFAR % |
| Sum | 22.76 ± 3.5 | 8.84 ± 1.1 | 12.68 ± 1.5 | 21.65 ± 4.9 | 62.68 ± 6.7 | 37.30 ± 3.9 |
| Product | 8.59 ± 4.1 | 0.30 ± 0.1 | 0.36 ± 0.1 | 53.41 ± 5.5 | 90.62 ± 4.1 | 56.79 ± 4.9 |
| LDA | 7.99 ± 3.7 | 0.26 ± 0.1 | 0.32 ± 0.2 | 56.32 ± 5.3 | 92.45 ± 3.8 | 58.66 ± 5.2 |
| LR | 8.91 ± 4.1 | 0.14 ± 0.1 | 0.17 ± 0.1 | 56.23 ± 6.0 | 92.39 ± 3.9 | 57.48 ± 6.0 |
| Ext. LR | 9.46 ± 5.2 | 0.16 ± 0.1 | 0.19 ± 0.1 | 56.13 ± 5.7 | 90.97 ± 5.5 | 57.27 ± 6.0 |

The SFAR corresponding to the same operating points is reported for real spoof attacks against fingerprint (*fing.*), face (*face*), and both traits (*both*), and for the simulated spoof attacks against fingerprints (*s-fing.*), and face (*s-face*). Results are averaged over 25 runs, and are reported as mean and standard deviation

Let us now focus on the Extended LR rule, which was specifically designed to counteract spoof attacks. At the considered operating points, it performed similarly to the LR rule, independently on the kind of attack, although it was expected to improve the robustness of the LR rule. Moreover, it exhibited a SFAR higher than that of the LR rule, at operating points characterized by FAR values lower than the ones considered in Tables 9.3, 9.4 and 9.5 (these results are not reported here, due to lack of space). This suggests that the assumption about the score distribution of fake traits on which the Extended LR rule is based is too pessimistic. This can also be argued by the fact that the SFAR of the simulated spoof attacks always overestimates the corresponding SFAR under a real spoof attack.

With regard to this behavior, Tables 9.3, 9.4 and 9.5 show that the difference between the SFAR of simulated face spoofing and of real face spoofing (*face* and *s-face* columns) is much lower than in the case of fingerprint spoofing (*fing.* and *s-fing.* columns), for all the considered fusion rules. In particular, for face spoofing this difference is often very small. This means that the assumption underlying the

**Table 9.4** Results attained on the Livdet11-Gelatin and Print Attack data set

| Rule | no spoof | face | s-face | fing. | s-fing. | both |
|---|---|---|---|---|---|---|
| | EER % | SFAR % | SFAR % | SFAR % | SFAR % | SFAR % |
| Sum | 14.35 ± 2.2 | 46.31 ± 3.0 | 47.26 ± 2.6 | 29.98 ± 3.0 | 76.38 ± 5.1 | 58.97 ± 3.9 |
| Product | 5.25 ± 1.6 | 16.31 ± 4.4 | 21.20 ± 5.5 | 53.54 ± 8.6 | 92.94 ± 3.0 | 68.01 ± 7.9 |
| LDA | 4.32 ± 1.8 | 29.54 ± 9.9 | 38.27 ± 8.5 | 53.28 ± 10.3 | 94.02 ± 3.4 | 69.51 ± 10.1 |
| LR | 4.16 ± 1.6 | 17.68 ± 8.7 | 28.65 ± 12.3 | 56.31 ± 9.5 | 94.88 ± 2.7 | 66.64 ± 10.8 |
| Ext. LR | 4.18 ± 1.6 | 16.52 ± 7.9 | 27.68 ± 12.3 | 56.02 ± 9.6 | 94.84 ± 2.8 | 66.16 ± 10.9 |
| | FRR % at FAR = 1% | SFAR % | SFAR % | SFAR % | SFAR % | SFAR % |
| Sum | 28.04 ± 5.1 | 32.84 ± 2.3 | 39.50 ± 1.0 | 8.42 ± 2.8 | 56.24 ± 8.9 | 40.90 ± 3.5 |
| Product | 8.87 ± 3.2 | 4.87 ± 0.9 | 7.50 ± 1.5 | 38.40 ± 7.7 | 88.61 ± 4.9 | 52.89 ± 6.7 |
| LDA | 6.43 ± 2.9 | 10.42 ± 4.1 | 23.48 ± 7.8 | 41.88 ± 7.7 | 91.61 ± 4.7 | 56.57 ± 6.5 |
| LR | 6.58 ± 3.0 | 3.34 ± 1.4 | 8.18 ± 5.9 | 45.46 ± 7.9 | 92.98 ± 4.1 | 52.52 ± 8.2 |
| Ext. LR | 6.64 ± 3.0 | 3.15 ± 1.3 | 7.03 ± 4.8 | 45.39 ± 7.8 | 92.95 ± 4.2 | 52.22 ± 8.0 |
| | FRR % at FAR = 0.1% | SFAR % | SFAR % | SFAR % | SFAR % | SFAR % |
| Sum | 34.52 ± 5.7 | 22.08 ± 4.5 | 36.08 ± 1.4 | 3.86 ± 1.9 | 46.04 ± 9.8 | 31.93 ± 4.6 |
| Product | 13.82 ± 4.2 | 1.05 ± 0.3 | 1.90 ± 0.4 | 26.08 ± 7.2 | 82.45 ± 6.5 | 38.21 ± 7.2 |
| LDA | 9.98 ± 3.7 | 1.39 ± 0.6 | 4.61 ± 2.9 | 31.64 ± 7.8 | 88.62 ± 5.6 | 41.27 ± 7.0 |
| LR | 10.73 ± 4.3 | 0.37 ± 0.2 | 0.81 ± 0.5 | 33.78 ± 8.2 | 89.53 ± 5.3 | 38.04 ± 8.4 |
| Ext. LR | 10.61 ± 4.4 | 0.40 ± 0.2 | 0.81 ± 0.4 | 34.15 ± 7.9 | 89.67 ± 5.4 | 38.59 ± 7.9 |

See the caption of Table 9.3 for the details

simulation of spoof attacks made in [9] is too pessimistic, especially for fingerprint spoofing. Note that results of Tables 9.3 and 9.4 refer to face spoof attacks obtained by using face images taken from the testing set, that are thus similar to the template of the targeted users. Thus, the corresponding fake score distribution is likely to be similar to that of the genuine users, but this is a pessimistic attack scenario.

The above results suggest that the assumption that the fake score distribution equals the one of genuine users can be often violated by real spoof attacks, and that a more realistic modeling of the fake score distribution should be adopted for designing robust score fusion rules.

## 9.5 Current Challenges in Multimodal Anti-spoofing

In this chapter, we reviewed the main achievements in the field of multimodal anti-spoofing. We summarized empirical evidence showing that multimodal biometric systems are not intrinsically robust to spoof attacks against one biometric trait, and that the probability of accepting spoof impostors as genuine users especially

## 9 Multimodal Anti-spoofing in Biometric Recognition Systems

**Table 9.5** Results attained on the Livdet11-Alginate and Personal Photo Attack dataset

| Rule | no spoof | face | s-face | fing. | s-fing. | both |
|---|---|---|---|---|---|---|
|  | EER % | SFAR % | SFAR % | SFAR % | SFAR % | SFAR % |
| Sum | 10.57 ± 1.5 | 10.75 ± 3.5 | 37.97 ± 4.1 | 14.80 ± 1.6 | 78.32 ± 3.2 | 16.63 ± 4.0 |
| Product | 4.08 ± 1.1 | 6.12 ± 1.8 | 8.05 ± 2.0 | 25.09 ± 6.0 | 95.62 ± 1.6 | 30.36 ± 9.0 |
| LDA | 3.89 ± 1.3 | 6.48 ± 2.4 | 11.63 ± 3.7 | 25.16 ± 5.6 | 95.81 ± 1.8 | 28.75 ± 7.5 |
| LR | 4.14 ± 1.1 | 5.03 ± 1.9 | 7.89 ± 2.4 | 25.43 ± 6.0 | 95.97 ± 1.7 | 28.52 ± 6.9 |
| Ext. LR | 4.14 ± 1.1 | 5.17 ± 1.7 | 8.31 ± 2.8 | 25.88 ± 5.5 | 96.03 ± 1.7 | 28.78 ± 7.1 |
|  | FRR % at FAR = 1 % | SFAR % | SFAR % | SFAR % | SFAR % | SFAR % |
| Sum | 18.80 ± 3.0 | 1.40 ± 1.0 | 20.37 ± 2.3 | 2.83 ± 0.8 | 66.84 ± 4.8 | 2.94 ± 1.6 |
| Product | 6.38 ± 2.2 | 1.47 ± 0.6 | 2.33 ± 0.3 | 13.61 ± 4.4 | 93.18 ± 2.8 | 15.36 ± 6.1 |
| LDA | 6.21 ± 2.4 | 1.47 ± 0.7 | 2.84 ± 0.8 | 14.53 ± 4.4 | 94.09 ± 2.8 | 15.48 ± 6.2 |
| LR | 6.64 ± 2.5 | 1.15 ± 0.5 | 1.71 ± 0.4 | 15.01 ± 4.7 | 94.41 ± 2.8 | 14.81 ± 5.9 |
| Ext. LR | 6.63 ± 2.5 | 1.13 ± 0.5 | 1.64 ± 0.3 | 14.86 ± 4.6 | 94.29 ± 2.9 | 14.64 ± 5.8 |
|  | FRR % at FAR = 0.1 % | SFAR % | SFAR % | SFAR % | SFAR % | SFAR % |
| Sum | 24.59 ± 3.3 | 0.17 ± 0.2 | 12.53 ± 1.4 | 0.82 ± 0.5 | 60.14 ± 5.0 | 0.66 ± 0.7 |
| Product | 9.81 ± 3.1 | 0.17 ± 0.1 | 0.38 ± 0.1 | 6.27 ± 3.1 | 89.14 ± 3.6 | 6.05 ± 3.9 |
| LDA | 9.21 ± 3.1 | 0.17 ± 0.1 | 0.36 ± 0.2 | 7.23 ± 3.2 | 91.26 ± 3.5 | 6.40 ± 3.9 |
| LR | 10.55 ± 4.6 | 0.15 ± 0.1 | 0.15 ± 0.1 | 6.82 ± 3.8 | 90.86 ± 3.9 | 5.52 ± 3.8 |
| Ext. LR | 10.85 ± 6.5 | 0.15 ± 0.1 | 0.18 ± 0.1 | 7.33 ± 3.8 | 88.69 ± 10.8 | 6.24 ± 3.7 |

See the caption of Table 9.3 for the details

depends on the chosen score fusion rule. In particular, multimodal systems that use well-known *trained* score fusion rules, like the LR, turned out to be potentially more vulnerable than systems that use simpler, *fixed*, rules (e.g., the product rule), even though the LR is optimal according to the Neyman-Pearson criterion, provided that the genuine and impostor distributions are reliably estimated. Despite the reported results, no specific guidelines on how to determine the most suitable fusion rule for the task at hand have been given yet. It is still an open issue to understand whether and to what extent score-level fusion rules are vulnerable to spoof attacks, and under what circumstances some rules may be intrinsically more secure than others. Nevertheless, the reported empirical evidences suggest us that ad hoc anti-spoofing measures should be adopted also in multimodal systems (like the one originally proposed in [13]).

We then considered recently proposed anti-spoofing measures that consist of modifying existing score fusion rules, and of developing novel ones, by exploiting additional information about spoof attacks, in terms of specific assumptions on the corresponding match score distribution. We focused in particular on the approach proposed in [9], and subsequently used in [7, 10, 12], for evaluating the vulnerability of multimodal systems against spoof attacks, and for designing robust score fusion rules. It is based on the assumption that the match score distribution produced by successful spoof attacks equals that of genuine users. While this approach does not require one to fabricate spoof attacks in order to estimate the corresponding match score distribution, the above assumption is often violated in practice, and turns out to be too pessimistic. This can lead one to overestimate the vulnerability of multimodal systems. Moreover, when the above assumption is used in the design of robust score fusion rules like the Extended LR [9], it can even make the resulting multimodal system *less* robust to real spoof attacks.

Accordingly, a suitable assumption for the match score distribution produced by spoof attacks is crucial in the design of robust score fusion rules, if no information from liveness detection modules is exploited. In principle, this requires one to fabricate a large variety of spoof attacks to analyze the corresponding match score distribution. However, this would affect the scalability of a multimodal biometric system, since the fake score distribution should be re-estimated as novel genuine users are added. It would also affect the acceptability of the system, since genuine users would have to provide replicas of their own biometrics.

A possible solution is to develop realistic models of the fake score distribution that are *representative* of different kinds of spoof attacks, and can be used by the designers of multimodal systems without the need of actually fabricating any spoof attack. A preliminary attempt towards this direction was made by the authors in [21, 28]. The model proposed in that work consists of simulating a family of fake score distributions that exhibit an *intermediate* behavior between the impostor and the genuine distribution, parametrized by a measure of the relative distance to the latter. However, such a model was based on a limited empirical evidence, and, thus, it may not properly account for the wide variability of spoof attack distributions induced, e.g., by different spoof fabrication techniques and materials. Extending this preliminary model and collecting larger empirical evidence on spoof attack distributions to overcome such limitations is indeed part of the authors' ongoing work. Further, we advocate that security of multimodal biometric systems to spoof attacks should be evaluated and improved based on a *proactive* what-if analysis, i.e., by anticipating potential (and novel) spoof attacks that may be incurred during system operation, as also suggested in our recent work on the security of pattern recognition systems [29]. To this end, relying on a well-suited *simulation* model of the spoof distribution has the main advantage of allowing system designers to thoroughly assess the security of multimodal systems against a large number of spoof attack scenarios, instead of considering a limited number of cases corresponding to spoof attacks fabricated in a laboratory setting. This approach may also shed some light on the open issue mentioned at the beginning of this section, i.e., it may help understanding the security properties of standard score-level fusion rules in a more systematic manner.

Another approach for improving the robustness of multimodal systems is to integrate the match score with the score provided by liveness detectors, through suitable fusion rules. Although building a liveness detector requires one to collect samples of spoof attacks, it is not required that such samples are taken from the genuine users of the multimodal biometric system under design. This approach is under investigation in the "TABULA RASA" research project,[7] and preliminary results are reported in [7]. Note that this approach does not fall within the definition of "multimodal anti-spoofing" considered in Sect. 9.1, since state-of-the-art liveness detection is related to the integration of liveness and match scores in *unimodal* biometric systems [6]. We also argue that the aforementioned spoof simulation model may be also exploited to the same end, i.e., to train fusion rules that combine matching algorithms and liveness detectors without submitting any fake trait to the matching algorithm to estimate the corresponding score distribution.

To sum up, the issue of multibiometric anti-spoofing has been raised only recently in the biometric community, and it has quickly become one of the most relevant open problems in this field. Further and more systematic theoretical and experimental investigations of this issue are therefore needed, taking into account the large variety of biometrics and of possible score-level fusion rules.

**Acknowledgments** This work has been partly supported by the TABULA RASA project, 7th Framework Research Programme of the European Union (EU), grant agreement number: 257289; by the project CRP-18293 funded by Regione Autonoma della Sardegna (RAS), L.R. 7/2007, Bando 2009; and by a grant awarded to B. Biggio by RAS, PO Sardegna FSE 2007-2013, L.R. 7/2007 "Promotion of the scientific research and technological innovation in Sardinia."

# References

1. Marcialis GL, Coli P, Roli F (2012) Fingerprint liveness detection based on fake finger characteristics. Int J Digital Crime Forensics (IJDCF) 4(3):1–19
2. Ghiani L, Marcialis GL, Roli F (2012) Fingerprint liveness detection by local phase quantization. In: International conference pattern record (ICPR), IEEE pp 537–540.
3. Ghiani L, Marcialis GL, Roli F (2012) Experimental results on the feature-level fusion of multiple fingerprint liveness detection algorithms. Proceedings of 14th ACM workshop on multimedia and security (MMSec). ACM, Coventry, UK, pp 157–164
4. Marasco E, Sansone C (2012) Combining perspiration- and morphology-based static features for fingerprint liveness detection. Pattern Recogn Lett 33(9):1148–1156
5. Abhyankar A, Schuckers SAC (2009) Integrating a wavelet based perspiration liveness check with fingerprint recognition. Pattern Recogn 42(3):452–464
6. Marasco E, Ding Y, Ross A (2012) Combining match scores with liveness values in a fingerprint verification system. In: Proceedings of IEEE 5th International conference biometrics: theory, applications and systems (BTAS), Washington DC (USA).
7. Marasco E, Johnson PA, Sansone C, Schuckers SAC (2011) Increase the security of multibiometric systems by incorporating a spoofing detection algorithm in the fusion mechanism. In: Sansone C, Kittler J, Roli F (eds) Proceedings of the 10th International workshop multiple classifier systems (MCS), LNCS, vol 6713, pp 309–318. Springer, Naples, Italy
8. Ross AA, Nandakumar K, Jain AK (2006) Handbook of multibiometrics. Springer Publishers, New York
9. Rodrigues RN, Ling LL, Govindaraju V (2009) Robustness of multimodal biometric fusion methods against spoof attacks. J Vis Lang Comput 20(3):169–179
10. Rodrigues RN, Kamat N, Govindaraju V (2010) Evaluation of biometric spoofing in a multimodal system. In: International conference biometrics: theory applications and systems (BTAS), pp 1–5.

---

[7] http://www.tabularasa-euproject.org/

11. Biggio B, Akhtar Z, Fumera G, Marcialis G, Roli F (2012) Security evaluation of biometric authentication systems under real spoofing attacks. IET Biometrics 1:11–24
12. Johnson P, Tan B, Schuckers S (2010) Multimodal fusion vulnerability to non-zero effort (spoof) imposters. In: IEEE International workshop on information forensics and security (WIFS), pp 1–5.
13. Jain AK, Ross A (2004) Multibiometric systems. Commun ACM 47(1):34–40
14. Jain AK, Ross A, Pankanti S, Member S (2006) Biometrics: A tool for information security. IEEE Trans Inf Forensics Secur 1:125–143
15. Ross A (2007) An introduction to multibiometrics. Proceedings of 15th european signal processing conference (EUSIPCO 2007). Poznan, Poland, pp 20–24
16. Marcialis GL, Lewicke A, Tan B, Coli P, Grimberg D, Congiu A, Tidu A, Roli F, Schuckers SAC (2009) 1st International fingerprint liveness detection competition—LivDet (2009) In: Foggia P, Sansone C, Vento M (eds) Proceedings of 15th International conference image analysis and processing (ICIAP), LNCS, vol 5716, pp 12–23. Springer, Vietri sul Mare, Italy
17. Adler A, Schuckers SAC (2009) Security and liveness, overview. In: Li SZ, Jain AK (eds) Encycl Biometrics. Springer, US, pp 1146–1152
18. Biggio B, Akhtar Z, Fumera G, Marcialis GL, Roli F (2011) Robustness of multi-modal biometric verification systems under realistic spoofing attacks. In: Ross A, Prabhakar S, Kim J (eds) Jain AK. International joint conference on biometrics (IJCB), IEEE, pp 1–6
19. Akhtar Z, Biggio B, Fumera G, Marcialis G (2011) Robustness of multi-modal biometric systems under realistic spoof attacks against all traits. Proceedings of IEEE workshop on biometric measurements and systems for security and medical applications (BioMS 2011). Milan, Italy, pp 5–10
20. Akhtar Z, Fumera G, Marcialis G, Roli F (2012) Evaluation of serial and parallel multibiometric systems under spoofing attacks. In: Proceedings of IEEE 5th International conference biometrics: theory, applications and systems (BTAS), Washington DC, USA, pp 283–288.
21. Akhtar Z, Fumera G, Marcialis G, Roli F (2011) Evaluation of multimodal biometric score fusion rules under spoof attacks. Proceedings of 5th IEEE/IAPR International conference biometrics (ICB). New Delhi, India, pp 402–407
22. Biggio B, Fumera G, Roli F (2011) Design of robust classifiers for adversarial environments. In: IEEE International conference on systems, Man, and Cybernetics (SMC), pp 977–982.
23. Yambay D, Ghiani L, Denti P, Marcialis GL, Roli F, Schuckers S (2012) LivDet2011 - Fingerprint liveness detection competition 2011. In: 5th International conference biometrics (ICB).
24. Coli P, Marcialis GL, Roli F (2007) Vitality detection from fingerprint images: a critical survey. In: Lee SW, Li SZ (eds) Proceedings of international conference biometrics (ICB), LNCS, vol 4642., SpringerSeoul, Korea, pp 722–731
25. Anjos A, Marcel S (2011) Counter-measures to photo attacks in face recognition: a public database and a baseline. In: International joint conference on biometrics (IJCB).
26. Chakka MM, Anjos A, Marcel S, Tronci R, Muntoni D, Fadda G, Pili M, Sirena N, Murgia G, Ristori M, Roli F, Yan J, Yi D, Lei Z, Zhang Z, Li ZS, Schwartz WR, Rocha A, Pedrini H, Lorenzo-Navarro J, Castrillón-Santana M, Maatta J, Hadid A, Pietikainen M (2011) Competition on counter measures to 2-D facial spoofing attacks. In: Proceedings of IAPR IEEE International joint conference on biometrics (IJCB). Washington DC, USA.
27. Zhang Z, Yi D, Lei Z, Li SZ (2011) Face liveness detection by learning multispectral reflectance distributions. In: International conference automatic face and gesture recognition, pp 436–441.
28. Akhtar Z, Fumera G, Marcialis G, Roli F (2011) Robustness evaluation of biometric systems under spoof attacks. In: Maino G, Foresti G (eds) International Conference on Image Analysis and Processing (ICIAP), LNCS, vol 6978, pp 159–168. Springer, Berlin
29. Biggio, B., Fumera, G., Roli, F.: Security evaluation of pattern classifiers under attack. IEEE Transactions on Knowledge and Data Engineering 99(PrePrints), 1 (2013).

# Chapter 10
# Evaluation Methodologies

**Ivana Chingovska, André Anjos and Sébastien Marcel**

**Abstract** Anti-spoofing systems, regardless of the technique, biometric mode or degree of independence of external equipment, are most commonly treated as binary classification systems. The two classes that they differentiate are genuine accesses and spoofing attacks. From this perspective, their evaluation is equivalent to the established evaluation standards for the binary classification systems. However, the anti-spoofing systems are designed to operate in conjunction with recognition systems and as such can affect their performance. From the point of view of a recognition system, the spoofing attacks are a separate class that they need to detect and reject. As the problem of spoofing attacks detection grows to this pseudo-ternary status, the evaluation methodologies for the recognition systems need to be revised and updated. Consequentially, the database requirements for spoofing databases become more specific. The focus of this chapter is the task of biometric verification and its scope is threefold: first, it gives the definition of the spoofing detection problem from the two perspectives. Second, it states the database requirements for a fair and unbiased evaluation. Finally, it gives an overview of the existing evaluation techniques for anti-spoofing systems and verification systems under spoofing attacks.

## 10.1 Introduction

The problem of spoofing and anti-spoofing can be seen from two different perspectives. As implied directly by the definition of the task of anti-spoofing systems to discriminate between two classes: genuine accesses and spoofing attacks, the problem is most often designed as binary classification problem. On the other hand,

---

I. Chingovska (✉) · A. Anjos · S. Marcel
Idiap Research Institute, rue Marconi 19, 1920 Martigny, Switzerland
e-mail: ivana.chingovska@idiap.ch

A. Anjos
e-mail: andre.anjos@idiap.ch

S. Marcel
e-mail: marcel@idiap.ch

spoofing attacks are directed toward deceiving recognition systems, regardless of whether there is an anti-spoofing algorithm to prevent them to do so, or not. From that perspective, the problem of spoofing and anti-spoofing is not limited only to binary classification systems, as the isolated anti-spoofing systems are. It is of equal importance to transfer the problem understanding to the domain of biometric recognition systems (in particular, in this chapter, biometric verification systems).

This concept shift may influence the biometric verification systems at several levels. First of all, spoofing attacks represent another class of input samples for the verification systems, which may cause changes in their internal algorithms to gain greater spoofing resilience. Two most prominent attempts for such changes are multimodal fusion [1–5] and fusion of a verification system with an anti-spoofing system [6–9]. Second, the problem restatement needs to modify the evaluation standards for verification systems. Finally, it may play a key role in the process of their parameterization.

While the first aspect of the spoofing and anti-spoofing problem under the umbrella of a verification system is out of scope of this chapter, we will thoroughly inspect all the modifications that the evaluation standards need to undergo to accustom to the new setting. The main reason is that once the danger of spoofing attacks is acknowledged, the verification performance of the biometric systems is not the only measurement of their quality. Important property to assess is their robustness to spoofing attacks. Only in that case, one can say that the overall performance of the system is being estimated. In this context, by verification system we could consider any type of system that can produce verification scores given a biometric sample as an input. No assumption on the mechanism the system employs for protection against spoofing attacks, if any, is needed. The system may be solely any baseline biometric verification algorithm which disregards the hazard of spoofing attacks, or a multimodal system or a fusion with an anti-spoofing algorithm. In any case, the system can be regarded as a black box, and the full evaluation can be done based on the verification scores it outputs for the input samples.

Mutual comparison of verification systems is the second matter of their evaluation with regards to spoofing. For example, it is of great importance to observe the performance change of a verification system before and after an integration with a anti-spoofing system. Blending in a spoofing countermeasure into an existing verification system can increase its robustness to spoofing, but at the same time it can affect its verification performance. The evaluation methodology which is going to be deployed should be able to assess the trade-off between these two effects.

Issues regarding the aspect of parameterization and tuning of the verification systems when spoofing attacks have a non-negligible prior will be also touched upon in this chapter.

With the previous observations in mind, stating the problem of spoofing and anti-spoofing from the perspective of an anti-spoofing system, as well as from the perspective of a verification system is the primary objective of this chapter (Sect. 10.2). Thorough review of the evaluation strategies for isolated anti-spoofing systems, as well as for verification systems commonly used in the literature will follow in Sect. 10.4. As a prerequisite, the concepts we are going to evaluate entail certain database structure that will be covered in Sect. 10.3.

## 10.2 Problem Statement

When treating spoofing as a binary classification problem, designers are interested in determining the capacity of a given system to discriminate between genuine accesses (positives) and attacks (negatives).[1] These systems, which do not have any capacity to perform biometric verification, are only exposed to elements of these two classes. Figure 10.1 represents these settings in a block diagram. In order to evaluate a given system, one feeds data from each of the two classes involved on the assessment. Scores collected from the evaluated system are fed into an evaluation framework which can compute error rates or draw performance figures. This workflow, typical for evaluation of binary classification systems, is widely deployed by countermeasure developers as well [6, 10–15]. The database design and the evaluation of anti-spoofing systems comprise to the standards of general binary classification systems and will be revisited in Sects. 10.3.1 and 10.4.2, respectively.

A less considered perspective is how biometric verification systems treat spoofing attacks. The classical approach puts biometric verification systems into the set of binary classifiers. Normally, such systems are designed to decide between two categories of verification attempts: genuine users (positives) and the so-called zero-effort impostors (negatives) [16]. Spoofing attacks represent a new type of samples that can be presented at the input of this system. Considering that both spoofing attacks and impostors need to be rejected, it is still possible to regard the problem as a binary classification task where the genuine users are the positives, while the union

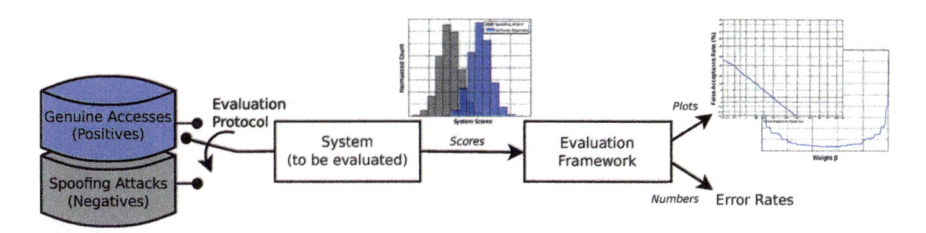

**Fig. 10.1** Evaluation of a (unknown) system with regards to its capacity to discriminate spoofing attacks from genuine accesses

---

[1] In this chapter, we shall treat as *positive class* or simply as *positives*, examples in a (discriminative) binary classification system one wishes to keep and, as *negative class* or *negatives*, examples that should be discarded.

of spoofing attacks and impostors are the negatives. Nevertheless, tuning of different properties of the verification system to make it more robust to spoofing attacks may require a clearly separated class of spoofing attacks. Furthermore, the correct ratio of spoofing attacks and impostors in the negative class union is, at most times, unknown at design time. Applications in highly surveilled environments may consider that the probability of a spoofing attack is small, while applications in unsurveilled spaces may consider it very high. Spoofing attacks, therefore, should be considered as a third separate category of samples that the verification systems need to handle.

From such a viewpoint, biometric verification can be cast into a pseudo-ternary classification problem. While as binary classifiers, verification systems comply to standard evaluation methods; in this new perspective their concept and evaluation need to be changed accordingly. Figure 10.2 depicts these new settings. Instead of inputting a single set of negative examples, this new evaluation method requires two subclasses of negative samples: samples coming from zero-effort impostors and the ones coming from spoofing attacks.

Researchers generally simplify the pseudo-ternary classification problem so that it suits the binary nature of the verification systems. A common approach is to reduce it to two binary classification problems, each of which is responsible for one of the two classes of negatives. According to this, the verification system can be operating in two scenarios or operation modes: (1) when it receives genuine accesses as positives and only zero-effort impostors as negatives, and (2) when it receives only genuine accesses as positives and spoofing attacks as negatives. Sometimes the first scenario is called a *normal operation mode* [17–19]. As it is going to be discussed in Sect. 10.4.3, it is beneficial to simplification that the positives (genuine accesses) that are evaluated completely match in both scenarios.

The workflow of the verification system confronted with spoofing attacks, from the input to the evaluation stage, is represented in Fig. 10.2. The score histogram displays three distinctive groups of data: the positive class and the two negative ones. If the mixing factor between the negative classes is known at design time, system evaluation can be carried using known binary classification analysis tools. Since that is usually not the case, the evaluation tools for the verification systems need to be adapted to the new settings.

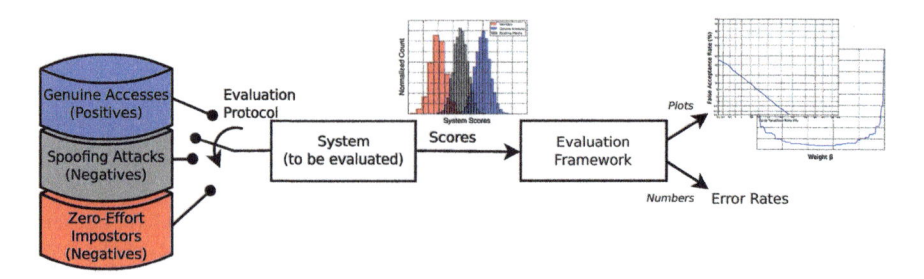

**Fig. 10.2** Evaluation of a (unknown) system with regards to its capacity to discriminate genuine accesses from zero-effort impostors *and* spoofing attacks

The new concept for verification systems explained above requires a database design and evaluation methodologies adapted to the enhanced negative class, regardless of the system's robustness to spoofing and how it is achieved. An overview of the research efforts in this domain will be given in Sects. 10.3.2 and 10.4.3, respectively.

## 10.3 Database Requirements

The use of databases and associated evaluation protocols allow for objective and comparative performance evaluation of different systems. As discussed on Sect. 10.2, the *spoofability* of a system can be evaluated on isolated anti-spoofing systems, but also on fully functional verification systems. The simple evaluation of anti-spoofing systems requires only that database and evaluation protocols consider two data types: genuine accesses and spoofing attacks. The evaluation of verification systems, merged with spoofing counter-measures or not, requires the traceability of identities contained in each presented sample, so that tabs are kept for probe-to-model matching and non-matching scenarios. The particular requirements for each of the two cases are given in Sects. 10.3.1 and 10.3.2. Databases for each of these two settings exist in the literature. An exhaustive listing of databases that allow for the evaluation of spoofing resilience in isolated anti-spoofing or biometric verification systems is given in Sect. 10.3.3.

### *10.3.1 Databases for Evaluation of Anti-spoofing Systems*

The primary task of a database for evaluation of anti-spoofing systems is to provide samples of spoofing attacks along with samples of genuine accesses. The identity information of clients in each sample need not to be present and can be discarded in case it is. The two sets of samples, which will represent the negative and the positive class for the binary classification problem, are just by themselves sufficient to train and evaluate an anti-spoofing system. It is a common practice that a database for binary classification provides a usage protocol which breaks the available data into three datasets [20]:

- *Training set* $\mathscr{D}_{\text{train}}$, used to train an anti-spoofing model;
- *Development set* $\mathscr{D}_{\text{dev}}$, also known as validation set, used to optimize the decisions in terms of model parameters estimation or model selection;
- *Test set* $\mathscr{D}_{\text{test}}$, also known as evaluation set, on which the performance is finally measured.

In the case of spoofing databases, it is recommended that the 3 datasets do not contain overlapping client data in order to avoid biasing related to client specific traits and to improve generalization [21]. A database with this setup completely satisfies the requirements of a two-class classification problem, as the isolated spoofing detection is.

The process of generating spoofing attacks requires genuine access samples that will serve as a basis to create the fake copies of the biometric trait. These may or may not be the same samples as the genuine access samples of the database. In any case, if they are provided alongside the database, it can be enhanced with new types of spoofing attacks in future.

## 10.3.2 Databases for Evaluation of Verification Systems

If a database is to serve for evaluation of a verification system, it needs to possess similar properties of a biometric database. Training and testing through biometric databases require (preferably) disjoint sets of data used for enrollment and verification of different identities. In practice, many databases also present a separation of the data in three sets as described above. Data from the training set can be used to create background models. The development data should contain enrollment (gallery) samples to create the user-specific models, as well as probe samples to match against the models. Similar specifications apply for the test set. The matching of the development probe samples against the user models should be employed to tune algorithms' parameters. Evaluation is carried out by matching probe samples of the test set against models created using the enrollment samples. The identity of the model being tested and the gallery samples are annotated to each of the scores produced so that the problem can be analyzed as a binary classification one: if model identity and probe identity match, the score belongs to the positive class (genuine client), otherwise, the score belongs to the negative class (zero-effort impostors). Usually, all identities in the three datasets are kept disjoint for the same reasons indicated in Sect. 10.3.1. Following this reasoning, a first requirement for a spoofing database aspiring to be equally adapted to the needs of anti-spoofing and verification systems, is provision of separate enrollment samples, besides the genuine access and spoofing samples.

The pseudo-ternary problem of spoofing as explained in Sect. 10.2 imposes scenario for matching genuine accesses, zero-effort impostors, and spoofing attacks against the models. In order to conform to this second requirement, the simplification of the pseudo-ternary problem introduced in Sect. 10.2 is of great help. In the case of the first scenario, or the normal operation mode, matching entries equivalent to the entries for genuine users and zero-effort impostors for a classical biometric verification database are needed. In the case of the second scenario, the provided entries should match the spoofing samples to a corresponding model or enrollment sample.

To unify the terminology, we formalize the two scenarios of operation of the verification system as below:

- *Licit* scenario: A scenario consisting of genuine users (positives) and zero-effort impostors (negatives). The positives of this scenario are created by matching the genuine access samples of each client to the model or enrollment samples of the same client. The negatives can be created by matching the genuine access samples of each client to the model or enrollment samples of other clients. This scenario is suitable to evaluate a verification system in a normal operation mode. Evidently, no spoofing attacks are present in this scenario;

- *Spoof* scenario: A scenario consisting of genuine users (positives) and spoofing attacks (negatives). The positives of this scenario are created by matching genuine access samples of each client to the models or enrollment samples of the same client. The negatives are created by matching the spoofing attacks of each client to the model or enrollment samples of the same client. No zero-effort impostors are involved in this scenario.

The licit scenario is necessary for evaluation of the verification performance of the system. The spoof scenario is necessary for evaluation of the system's robustness to spoofing. If we follow a convention to match *all* the genuine access samples to the model or enrollment samples of the same client in both scenarios, we will end up having the same set of positives for the two scenarios. This agreement, as will be shown in Sect. 10.4.3, plays an important role in some approaches for evaluation of the verification systems.

To better illustrate how to create the scenarios out of the samples present in any spoofing database, let us assume a simple hypothetical spoofing database containing one genuine access and one spoofing attack of two clients with identities A and B. Let us assume that the database also contains enrollment samples for A and B allowing computation of models for them. The matching of the samples with the models in order to create the positives and the negatives of the two scenarios is given in Table 10.1. To exemplify an entry in the table, L+ in the first row means that entries that match genuine accesses of client A to the model of client A belong to the subset of positives of the licit scenario. The same applies for L+ in the third row, this time for client B. Similarly, S- in the second row means that entries that match spoofing attacks of client A to the model of client A belong to the subset of negatives in the spoof scenario.

Instead of creating a spoofing database and then creating the licit and spoof scenario from its samples, an alternative way to start with is to use an existing biometric database which already has enrollment samples as well as data for the licit scenario.

**Table 10.1** Creating licit and spoof scenarios out of the samples in a spoofing database

| Probe | Model for | A | B |
|---|---|---|---|
| A | Genuine access | L+, S+ | L− |
|   | Spoofing attack | S− | No match done |
| B | Genuine access | L− | L+, S+ |
|   | Spoofing attack | No match done | S− |

+ stands for positives, − for negatives. L is for licit and S for spoof scenario. Note that the positives are the same for both L and S scenarios

All that is needed is creating the desirable spoofing attacks out of the existing samples. One should note, however, that the *complete* system used for the acquisition of samples, including the sensor, should be kept constant through all the recordings as differentiation may introduce biases. For example, consider a situation in which a speaker verification system is evaluated with data collected with a low-noise microphone, but in which attack samples are collected using noisier equipment. Even if attacks do pass the verification threshold, it is possible that potential counter-measures may rely on the additional noise produced by the new microphone to identify attacks. If that is the case, then such a study may be producing a less effective anti-spoofing system.

### 10.3.3 Overview of Available Databases for Spoofing

Table 10.2 contains an overview of the existing anti-spoofing databases that are publicly available. The columns, that refer to properties discussed throughout this section, refer to:

- *Database*: the database name;
- *Trait*: the biometric trait on the database;
- *# Subsets*: the number of subsets in the database referring to existing separate set for training, developing, and testing systems;
- *Overlap*: if there is client overlap between the different database subsets (training, development, and testing);
- *Recognition*: if the database can be used to evaluate a verification system resilience to spoofing (i.e., contains enrollment samples);
- *Existing DB*: if the database is a spin-off of an existing biometric database not originally created for spoofing evaluation;
- *Sensor*: If the sensors used to acquire the spoofing samples are the same as those used to acquire the genuine accesses.

**Table 10.2** Catalog of evaluation features available on spoofing databases available

| Database | Trait | # Subsets | Overlap | Recognition | Existing DB | Sensor |
|---|---|---|---|---|---|---|
| ATVS-FFp [19] | Fingerprint | 2 | No | No | No | Yes |
| LivDet 2009 [22] | Fingerprint | 2 | ? | No | No | Yes |
| LivDet 2011 [15] | Fingerprint | 2 | ? | No | No | Yes |
| LivDet 2013 [23] | Fingerprint | 2 | ? | No | No | Yes |
| NUAA PI [13] | Face | 2 | No | No | No | Yes |
| CASIA FAS [24] | Face | 2 | No | No | No | Yes |
| Replay Attack [25] | Face | 3 | No | Yes | No | Yes |
| Yale Recaptured [26] | Face | 1 | Yes | No | Yes | No |

All databases are fully described on the book appendix. For detailed column description, please see text

## 10.4 Evaluation Techniques

Several important concepts about evaluation of binary classification systems have been established and followed by the biometric community. Primarily, they are used to evaluate verification systems, which have a binary nature. They are also applicable in the problem of anti-spoofing as a binary classification problem.

In Sect. 10.4.1 we revisit the basic notation and statistics for evaluation of any binary classification system. After that recapitulation, we give an overview of how the error rates and methodologies are adapted particularly for anti-spoofing systems in Sect. 10.4.2 and verification systems under spoofing attacks in Sect. 10.4.3.

### 10.4.1 Evaluation of Binary Classification Systems

The metrics for evaluation of binary classification systems are associated to the types of errors and how to measure them, as well as to the threshold and evaluation criterion [27]. A binary classification system is subjected to two types of errors: False Positive (FP) and False Negative (FN). Typically, the error rates that are reported are False Positive Rate (FPR), which corresponds to the ratio between FP and the total number of negative samples and False Negative Rate (FNR), which corresponds to the ratio between FN and the total number of positive samples.

Alternatively, many algorithms for binary classification report different error rates, but still equivalent to FPR and FNR. For example, True Positive Rate (TPR) refers to the ratio of correctly classified positives and can be computed as 1—FNR. True Negative Rate (TNR) gives the ratio of correctly detected negatives, and can be computed as 1—FPR.

To compute the error rates, the system needs to compute a decision threshold $\tau$ which will serve as a boundary between the output scores of the genuine accesses and spoofing attacks. By changing this threshold one can balance between FPR and FNR: increasing FPR reduces FNR and vice-versa. However, it is often desired that an optimal threshold $\tau^*$ is chosen according to some criterion. Two well-established criteria are Minimum Weighted Error Rate (WER) and Equal Error Rate (EER) [27]. In the first case, the threshold $\tau^*_{\text{WER}}$ is chosen so that it minimizes the weighted total error rate as in Eq. 10.1 where $\beta \in [0, 1]$ is a predefined parameter which balances between the importance (cost) of FPR and FNR. Very often, they have the same cost of $\beta = 0.5$, leading to Minimum Half Total Error Rate (HTER) criteria. In the second case, the threshold $\tau^*_{\text{EER}}$ ensures that the difference between FPR and FNR is as small as possible (Eq. 10.2). The optimal threshold, also referred to as *operating point* should be determined using the data in the development set, denoted in the equations below as $\mathscr{D}_{\text{dev}}$.

$$\tau^*_{\text{WER}} = \arg \min_{\tau} \beta \cdot \text{FPR}(\tau, \mathscr{D}_{\text{dev}}) + (1 - \beta) \cdot \text{FNR}(\tau, \mathscr{D}_{\text{dev}}) \qquad (10.1)$$

$$\tau^*_{\text{EER}} = \arg \min_{\tau} |\text{FPR}(\tau, \mathscr{D}_{\text{dev}}) - \text{FNR}(\tau, \mathscr{D}_{\text{dev}})| \qquad (10.2)$$

Regarding the evaluation criteria, once the threshold $\tau^*$ is determined, the systems usually report the WER (Eq. 10.3) or its special case for $\beta = 0.5$, HTER (Eq. 10.4). Since in a real world scenario the final system will be used for data which have not been seen before, the performance measure should be reported on the test set $\mathscr{D}_{stest}$.

$$\text{WER}(\tau, \mathscr{D}_{test}) = \beta \cdot \text{FPR}(\tau, \mathscr{D}_{test}) + (1 - \beta) \cdot \text{FNR}(\tau, \mathscr{D}_{test}) \quad (10.3)$$

$$\text{HTER}(\tau, \mathscr{D}_{test}) = \frac{\text{FPR}(\tau, \mathscr{D}_{test}) + \text{FNR}(\tau, \mathscr{D}_{test})}{2} \quad [\%] \quad (10.4)$$

#### 10.4.1.1 Graphical Analysis

Important tools in evaluation of classification systems are the different graphical representations of the classification results. For example, an intuition about how good the discriminating power of a binary classification system is, one can get by plotting its output score distributions for the positive and the negative class, as in Fig. 10.3a. Better separability between the two classes means better results in terms of error rates.

To summarize the performance of a system and to present the trade-off between FPR and FNR depending on the threshold, the performance of the binary classification systems are often visualized using Receiver Operating Characteristic (ROC) and Detection-Error Tradeoff (DET) [28] curves. They plot the FPR versus the FNR (or some of the equivalent error rates) for different values of the threshold. Sometimes, when one number is needed to represent the performance of the system in order to compare several systems, Area Under ROC curve (AUC) values are reported. Usually it is computed for ROC curves plotting FPR and TPR and, in this case, the higher the AUC the better the system. Figure 10.3b illustrates the DET curve for a hypothetical binary classification system.

Unfortunately, curves like ROC and DET can only display *a posteriori* performance. When reading values directly form the plotted curves, we implicitly choose a threshold on a dataset and the error rates are reported on the same dataset. Although ROC and DET give a clear idea about the performance of a single system, as explained in [29], comparing two systems with these curves can lead to biased conclusions. To solve this issue, [29] proposes the so-called Expected Performance Curve (EPC). It

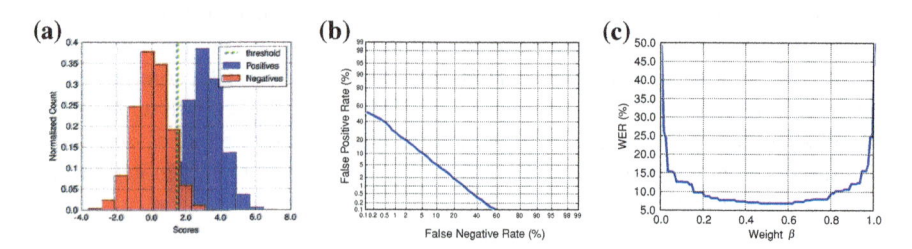

**Fig. 10.3** Evaluation plots for hypothetical anti-spoofing system. **a** Score distributions. **b** DET curve. **c** EPC curve

fills in for two main disadvantages of the DET and ROC curves: 1. it plots the error rate on the test set depending on a threshold selected a-priori on the development set; and 2. it accounts for varying relative cost $\beta \in [0; 1]$ of FPR and FNR when calculating the threshold.

Hence, in the EPC framework, an optimal threshold $\tau^*$ is computed using Eq. 10.1 for different values of $\beta$, which is the variable parameter plotted on the abscissa. Performance for the calculated values of $\tau^*$ is then computed on the test set. WER, HTER, or any other measure of importance can be plotted on the ordinate axis. EPC curve is illustrated in Fig. 10.3c for a hypothetical classification system.

## 10.4.2 Evaluation of Anti-spoofing Systems

In the domain of anti-spoofing, the number of errors known as FP and FN refer to the number of spoofing attacks which are incorrectly classified as genuine accesses and the number of genuine accesses incorrectly classified as spoofing attacks, respectively. Thus, the error rate FPR is associated with the ratio between FP and the total number of spoofing attacks, and FNR with the ratio between FN and the total number of genuine accesses.

Since the positives and the negatives are associated with the action of *acceptance* and *rejection* by the anti-spoofing system, a common practice is to replace FPR and FNR with their synonyms False Accept Rate (FAR) and False Reject Rate (FRR), respectively. Some publications deviate from this convention and utilize other synonyms, which are listed in Table 10.3.

For a more general framework, where the system is specialized to detect any kind of suspicious or subversive presentation of samples, be it a spoofing attack, altered sample or artifact, [32] has assembled a different set of notations for error measurements. Such a system reports False Suspicious Presentation Detection (FSPD) in the place of FNR and False Non-Suspicious Presentation Detection (FNSPD) in the place of FPR. To summarize the error rates into one value, some authors use accuracy [12, 26, 33], which is the ratio of the overall errors that the system made

**Table 10.3** Typically used error rates in anti-spoofing and their synonyms

| Error rate | Acronym | Synonyms |
|---|---|---|
| False Positive Rate | FPR | False Accept Rate (FAR), False Spoof Accept Rate [8], False Living Rate (FLR) [14] |
| False Negative Rate | FNR | False Reject Rate (FRR), False Alarm Rate [10], False Live Rejection Rate [8], False Fake Rate (FFR) [14] |
| True Positive Rate | TPR | True Accept Rate |
| True Negative Rate | TNR | True Reject Rate, detection rate [10, 11, 30], detection accuracy [31] |
| Half Total Error Rate | HTER | Average Classification Error (ACE) [14] |

and the total number of samples. Finally, to graphically represent the performance of the anti-spoofing systems, score distribution plots [34], ROC, DET, and EPC curves are often used.

### 10.4.3 Evaluation of Verification Systems Under Spoofing Attacks

The classical approach regards a biometric verification system as a binary classification system. In the scope of biometric verification systems, False Match Rate (FMR) and False Non-Match Rate (FNMR) are the most commonly used terms for the error rates FPR and FNR. FMR stands for the ratio of incorrectly accepted zero-effort impostors and FNMR for the ratio of incorrectly rejected genuine users. These and the equivalent error rates are often substituted with other synonyms which are different by different authors. The most common of them are listed in Table 10.4. Although not always equivalent [16], we adopt the convention in [35], where FMR and FNMR are substituted with FAR and FPR, respectively.

Simplifying the ternary classification into two binary classification problems, as explained in Sect. 10.2, is the key step that sets the standards for the evaluation of verification systems. The systems are usually evaluated separately in the two modes of operation associated with the two scenarios stated in Sect. 10.3.2. This section focuses on the error rates and plots typical for this evaluation.

While the verification performance metrics is well established and widely used, the metrics for spoofing evaluation is not unified and is ambiguous in different publications. In fact, even the nomenclature regarding the spoofing attacks themselves is not coordinated. For example, several authors do not make a clear distinction between a spoofing attack and a zero-effort impostor and refer to both types of samples as impostors. The nature of the sample can be concluded by the scenario that is being used: licit or spoof. The error rate associated with spoofing attacks in these systems is again FAR. The ambiguous character of FAR in this case can often lead to confusion.

**Table 10.4** Typically used error rates in biometric verification and their synonyms

| Scenario | Error rate | Synonyms |
|---|---|---|
| Licit | False Negative Rate | False Reject Rate (FRR), False Non-Match Rate [8, 37], Pmiss [6]) |
| Spoof | False Positive Rate | False Accept Rate (FAR) [17], Spoof False Acceptance Rate [2, 5], Liveness False Acceptance Rate [36], Success Rate [18, 19], Attack Success Rate [37] |
| Both | False Positive Rate | False Accept Rate (FAR), False Match Rate [8, 37], Pfa [6] |
| Both | True Positive Rate | True Accept Rate, Genuine Acceptance Rate [32, 38] |
| Union | False Positive Rate | System False Acceptance Rate (SFAR) [36], Global False Acceptance Rate (GFAR) [8] |
| | False Negative Rate | Global False Rejection Rate (GFRR) |

## 10 Evaluation Methodologies

The importance of a clear distinction between the terminology for the error rates reporting on the misclassified zero-effort impostors and spoofing attacks was outlined in [36]. Besides Liveness False Acceptance Rate (LFAR) as a ratio of spoofing attacks that are incorrectly accepted by the system, [36] defines error rates connected to the total number of accepted negatives, regardless of whether they come from zero-effort impostors or spoofing attacks. For example, the union of FAR in licit scenario and LFAR in spoof scenario is called System False Acceptance Rate (SFAR). A detailed overview of all the metrics utilized by various authors is given in Table 10.4. The table contains two metrics of error rates for negatives: for the licit and spoof scenario. It also reports the overall error rates that occur when both scenarios are considered as a union.

The adopted terminology in the remainder of this text is as follows:

- FRR—ratio of incorrectly rejected genuine users (both licit and spoof scenario)
- FAR—ratio of incorrectly accepted zero-effort impostors (in the licit scenario)
- SFAR—ratio of incorrectly accepted spoofing attacks [2] (in the spoof scenario)
- GFAR—ratio of incorrectly accepted zero-effort impostors and spoofing attacks.

Researchers generally follow three main methodologies for determining the effect of spoofing attacks over the verification systems and obtaining the error rates. The differences between the three evaluation methodologies are in the way of computation of the decision threshold.

### 10.4.3.1 Evaluation Methodology 1

Two decision threshold calculations are performed separately for the two scenarios, resulting into two separate values of the error rate (HTER or EER) [2, 17, 39–41]. FRR, FAR and SFAR are reported depending on the decision threshold obtained for the scenario they are derived from. One weak point of this type of evaluation is that it neglects that there is only one verification system at disposal and it should have only one operating point corresponding to one decision threshold. Furthermore, the decision threshold and the reported error rates of the spoof scenario are irrelevant in a real-world scenario. The problem arises because the spoof scenario assumes that all the possible misuses of the system come from spoofing attacks. It is not likely that any system needs to be tuned to operate in such a scenario. Therefore, the error rates depending on the threshold obtained under the spoof scenario are not a relevant estimate of the system's performance under spoofing attacks. Furthermore, the error rates for the licit and spoof scenarios cannot be compared, because they rely on different thresholds.

### 10.4.3.2 Evaluation Methodology 2

This methodology adapts for more realistic performance evaluation. It takes advantage of the assumption that the licit and spoof scenarios share the same positive samples: a requirement mentioned to be beneficial in Sect. 10.3.2. In this case, the system will obtain the same FRR for the both scenarios regardless of the threshold. Once the threshold of the system is chosen, FAR and SFAR can be reported and compared. The threshold can be chosen using various criteria, but almost always using the licit scenario. Most of the publications report error rates for the two scenarios using a threshold chosen to achieve a particular desired value of FRR [1, 3–7, 18, 19, 37, 38, 42].

The issue that the evaluation methodology 2 oversees is that a system whose decision threshold is optimized for one type of negatives (for example, the zero-effort impostors), cannot be evaluated in a fair manner for another type of negatives (the spoofing attacks). If the system is expected to be exposed to two types of negatives in the test or deployment stage, it is fair that the two types of negatives play a role in the decision of the threshold in the development stage.

### 10.4.3.3 Evaluation Methodology 3

This methodology aims at filling in the gaps of the evaluation methodology 2 and establishes a criteria for determining a decision threshold which considers the two types of negatives. To this end, a new error measurement $FAR_\omega$ is introduced as a weighted error rate for the two negative classes. It is calculated as in Eq. 10.5.

$$FAR_\omega = (1 - \omega) \cdot FAR + \omega \cdot SFAR \tag{10.5}$$

The weight factor $\omega$ can be interpreted as the relative importance or cost of SFAR with regards of FAR. In the cases, when the prior of impostors and spoofing attacks for a given system can be estimated, $\omega$ can be interpreted as the ratio of spoofing attacks among all the misuses of the system.

Then, the optimal classification threshold is chosen using one of two criteria. The first one corresponds to the EER criteria from Eq. 10.2 and it minimizes the difference between $FAR_\omega$ and FRR on the development set. The new decision threshold determination is given in Eq. 10.6. The second one corresponds to the Minimum HTER criteria and selects a threshold that minimizes $HTER_\omega$ as in Eq. 10.7.

$$\tau^*_{EER_\omega} = \arg \min_\tau |FAR_\omega(\tau, \mathscr{D}_{dev}) - FRR(\tau, \mathscr{D}_{dev})| \tag{10.6}$$

$$\tau^*_{HTER_\omega} = \arg \min_\tau \frac{FAR_\omega(\tau, \mathscr{D}_{dev}) + FRR(\tau, \mathscr{D}_{dev})}{2} \tag{10.7}$$

Finally, using the determined threshold, different error rates can be computed and reported on the test set. Among them, $HTER_\omega$, an error rate analogous to HTER is suggested and calculated as in Eq. 10.8.

$$HTER_\omega(\tau, \mathscr{D}) = \frac{FAR_\omega(\tau, \mathscr{D}) + FRR(\tau, \mathscr{D})}{2} \quad [\%] \tag{10.8}$$

### 10.4.3.4 Graphical Analysis

Following the typical convention for binary classification system, biometric verification systems use score distributions, ROC or DET curves to graphically present their performance. The plots for a traditional biometric verification system regard the genuine users as a positive and the zero-effort impostors as a negative class. The details about these types of plots are given in Sect. 10.4.2.

When using graphical representation of the results, the researchers usually follow the evaluation methodology 2. This means that all the tuning of the algorithms, in particular in computation of the decision thresholds, is performed using the licit scenario, while the plots may represent the results for one of the scenarios or for both of them.

When only the licit scenario is of interest, the score distribution plot contains the distributions only for the genuine users and the zero-effort impostors. If evaluation with regards to the vulnerability to spoofing is desired, the score distribution plot gets an additional distribution corresponding to the scores that the system outputs for the spoofing samples in the spoof scenario. As a result, the score distribution plot presents three score distributions, which, illustratively for a hypothetical verification system, are given in Fig. 10.4a.

An information about the dependence of SFAR on the chosen threshold can be obtained directly from the score distribution plot. An example is shown in Fig. 10.4b, where the full green line represents how SFAR varies with shifting the threshold, while the vertical dashed green line represents the threshold at a chosen operating point.

Typically, ROC and DET curves visualize the trade-off between FAR and FRR for a biometric system with no danger of spoofing attacks anticipated. The closest analogy to the ROC and DET curves when evaluating a system exposed to spoofing attacks can be found using the evaluation methodology 2. First, the curve using the licit scenario is plotted. Then, it can be overlaid with a curve for the spoof scenario. For the licit scenario, the vertical axis represents FAR, while for the spoof scenario it represents SFAR. However, meaningful comparison of the two curves is possible only if the number of genuine access samples in both licit and spoof scenario is the same. In such a case, a certain selected threshold will result in the same value of FRR for both the scenarios. By drawing a vertical line at the point of the obtained FRR, one can examine the points where it cuts the curves for the licit and spoof scenario, and can compare FAR and SFAR for the given system. Illustration of this analysis is given in Fig. 10.4c.

The drawback of the DET curve coming from its a-posteriori evaluation feature explained in [29] and obstructing fair comparison of two systems, is not a concern here. The plot does not compare different systems, but the same system with a single operating point under different set of negative samples.

As an alternative figure delivering similar information as DET, [1, 38] suggest to plot FAR versus SFAR. Thresholds are fixed in order to obtain all the possible values of FAR for the licit scenario and SFAR is evaluated on the spoof scenario and plotted on the ordinate axis. By plotting the curves for different verification systems, the plot enables to compare which of them is less prone to spoofing given a

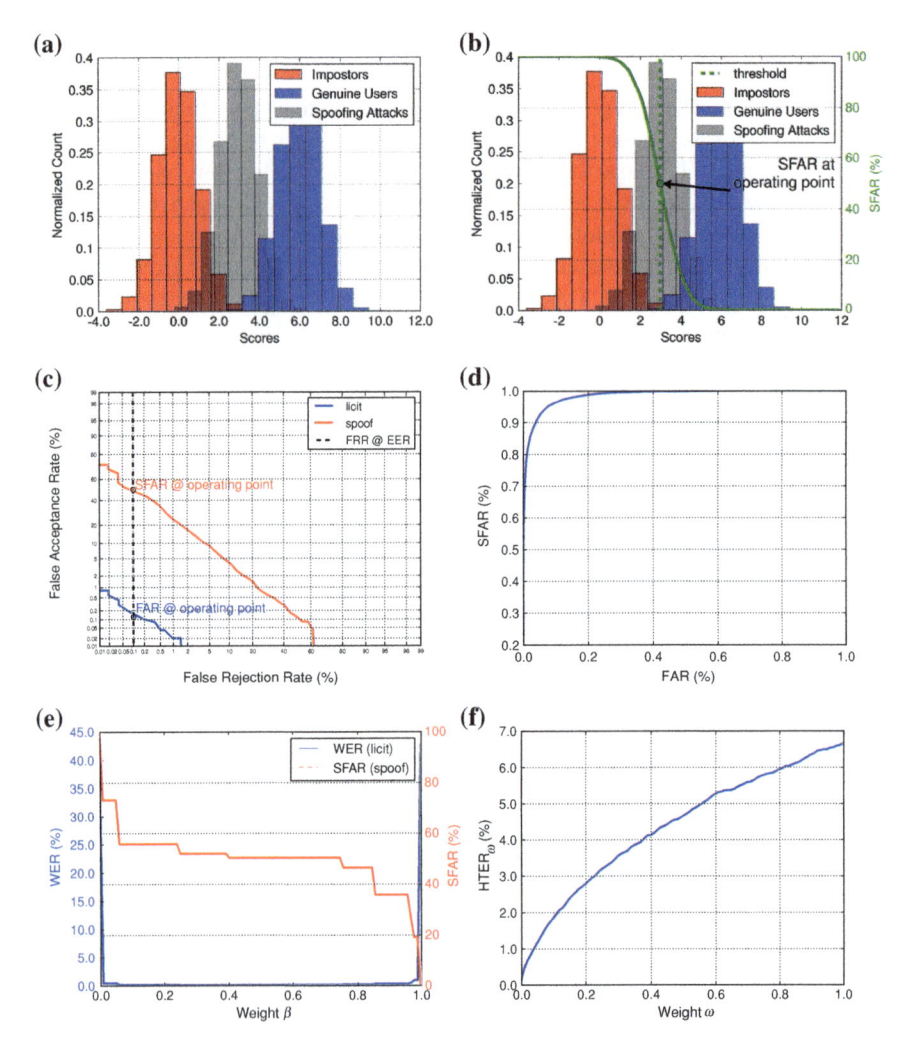

**Fig. 10.4** Performance and spoofing vulnerability evaluation plots for hypothetical verification system. **a** Score distributions. **b** Score distributions with SFAR line. **c** DET curve. **d** FAR versus SFAR curve. **e** EPC curve. **f** EPSC curve

particular verification performance. However, this comparison suffers from the same drawback as the DET: a-posteriori evaluation. As such, its fairness is limited. This plot is illustrated in Fig. 10.4d.

The logic for plotting the EPC curve is similar if one wants to follow the evaluation methodology 2. One has to vary the cost parameter $\beta$ which balances between FAR and FRR of the licit scenario and choose the threshold accordingly. Using the selected threshold, one can plot WER on the licit scenario. Afterwards, to see the method's resilience to spoofing depending on $\beta$, the WER curve can be overlaid with SFAR curve using the spoof scenario, as shown in Fig. 10.4e for a hypothetical system.

A graphical evaluation for the evaluation methodology 3 cannot be easily derived from the existing ROC or DET curves. The hyperparameter of this evaluation scheme is the cost parameter $\omega$, and the graphical evaluation should focus on plotting how the error rates vary with regards to its change. A plot of that kind will enable comparison of systems for a range of values of $\omega$. A plot similar to EPC, where the plotted error rates depend on $\omega$ may be useful. This plot, called Expected Performance and Spoofability Curve (EPSC) iterates over a range of values for $\omega$ and calculates the decision threshold like in Eq 10.6. Unlike for EPC, in the decision threshold calculation for EPSC both the licit and spoof scenario take place, because both FAR and SFAR contribute with a certain weight. The threshold should be calculated using the development set. Then, a relevant error rate on the test set, like $HTER_\omega$ is plotted on the ordinate axis. The EPSC curve for a hypothetical verification system showing $HTER_\omega$ is given in Fig. 10.4f. The threshold is obtained on the development set using the criteria in Eq. 10.6.

The convenience of EPSC for evaluation of verification systems under spoofing attacks is covered by several properties. First, since it follows the evaluation methodology 3, it provides that both types of negatives participate in threshold decision process. Second, it presents a-priori results: the thresholds are calculated on the development set, while the error rates are reported on the test set. This ensures unbiased comparison between algorithms. Furthermore, this comparison is enabled for a range of values for the cost parameter $\omega$. This is of interest for any application for which the prior of zero-effort impostors and spoofing attacks among the fraudulent usages of the system can vary or is not known in advance.

Besides $HTER_\omega$, other error rates of interest may be plotted on the EPSC plot, like SFAR or $FAR_\omega$.

## 10.5 Conclusions

Anti-spoofing systems in biometrics can rarely be imagined working as stand-alone. Their task is to perform an additional check on the decision of a biometric verification systems in order to detect a fraudulent user who possesses a copy of a biometric trait of a genuine user. Unless they have perfect detection rate, they inevitably affect the performance of the verification system they protect.

Traditionally, the anti-spoofing systems have been evaluated as binary classification systems, and in reason: by nature they need to distinguish between two classes—genuine accesses and spoofing attacks. However, the above observation throws a light on the critical issue of establishing a methodology for evaluation of verification systems with regards to spoofing attacks. This equally applies for verification systems with or without any mechanism for handling spoofing attacks.

This task requires reformulation of the problem of biometric verification. They, as well, are, by definition, binary classification systems distinguishing between genuine accesses and zero-effort impostors. With the spoofing attacks in play, the problem scales to pseudo-ternary classification problem, with two types of negatives: zero-effort impostors and spoofing attacks.

As a result of the above observations, this chapter covers the problem of spoofing evaluation from two perspectives: evaluation of anti-spoofing systems alone and evaluation of verification systems with respect to spoofing attacks. The evaluation in the first case means straightforward application of well-established evaluation methodologies for binary classification systems, in error rates (FAR, FRR, HTER etc.), decisions on operating point (Minimum WER, EER etc.) and graphical representation of results (ROC, DET, and EPC curves). The second perspective requires a simplification of the pseudo-ternary problem, in, for example, two binary classification problems. This, on the other hand, imposes certain database requirements, and spoofing databases which do not satisfy them cannot be used for the evaluation of biometric verification systems under spoofing attacks. Depending on the steps undertaken to simplify the pseudo-ternary problem, the evaluation paradigm for the system differs. In particular, in this chapter, we discussed three evaluation methodologies, together with the error rates and the plots associated with them.

As the interest for spoofing and anti-spoofing in almost all biometric modes is growing both in research, but even more in industrial environment, a common fair criteria for evaluation of anti-spoofing systems and of verification systems under spoofing attacks is becoming of essential importance. For the time being, there is a lot of inconsistency in the error rates conventions, as well as the evaluation strategies used in different publications.

**Acknowledgments** The authors would like to thank the projects BEAT (http://www.beat-eu.org) and TABULA RASA (http://www.tabularasa-euproject.org) both funded under the 7th Framework Programme of the European Union (EU) (grant agreement number 284989 and 257289) respectively.

# References

1. Rodrigues RN, Ling LL, Govindaraju V (2009) Robustness of multimodal biometric fusion methods against spoofing attacks. J Vis Lang Computing 20(3):169–179
2. Johnson PA, Tan B, Schuckers S (2010) Multimodal fusion vulnerability to non-zero (spoof) imposters. In: IEEE international workshop information forensics and security
3. Akhtar Z, Fumera G, Marcialis GL, Roli F (2011) Robustness evaluation of biometric systems under spoof attacks. In: 16th International conference on image analysis and processing, pp 159–168
4. Akhtar Z, Fumera G, Marcialis GL, Roli F (2011) Robustness analysis of likelihood ration score fusion rule for multi-modal biometric systems under spoof attacks. In: 45th IEEE international carnahan conference on security technology, pp 237–244
5. Akhtar Z, Fumera G, Marcialis GL, Roli F (2012) Evaluation of serial and parallel multibiometric systems under spoofing attacks. In: 5th IEEE international conference on biometrics: theory, applications and systems
6. Villalba J, Lleida E (2011) Preventing replay attacks on speaker verification systems. In: 2011 IEEE international carnahan conference on security technology (ICCST), pp 1–8
7. Marasco E, Johnson P, Sansone C, Schuckers, S (2011) Increase the security of multibiometric systems by incorporating a spoofing detection algorithm in the fusion mechanism. In: Proceedings of the 10th international conference on multiple classifier systems, pp 309–318

8. Marasco E, Ding Y, Ross A (2012) Combining match scores with liveness values in a fingerprint verification system. In: 5th IEEE international conference on biometrics: theory, applications and systems
9. Chingovska I, Anjos A, Marcel S (2013) Anti-spoofing in action: joint operation with a verification system. In: Proceedings of IEEE conference on computer vision and pattern recognition, workshop on biometrics
10. Pan G, Sun L, Wu Z, Lao S (2007) Eyeblink-based anti-spoofing in face recognition from a generic webcamera. In: IEEE 11th international conference on computer vision, 2007. ICCV 2007, pp 1–8
11. Bao W, Li H, Li N, Jiang W (2009) A liveness detection method for face recognition based on optical flow field. In: International conference on Image analysis and signal processing, 2009. IASP 2009, pp 233–236
12. yan J, Zhang Z, Lei Z, Yi D, Li SZ (2012) Face liveness detection by exploring multiple scenic clues. In: 12th International conference on control, automation, robotics and vision (ICARCV 2012), China
13. Tan X, Li Y, Liu J, Jiang L (2010) Face liveness detection from a single image with sparse low rank bilinear discriminative model. In: Proceedings of European conference on computer vision (ECCV), LNCS, vol 6316. Springer, pp 504–517
14. Galbally J, Alonso-Fernandez F, Fierrez J, Ortega-Garcia J (2012) A high performance fingerprint liveness detection method based on quality related features. Future Gener Comput Syst 28(1):311–321
15. Yambay D, Ghiani L, Denti P, Marcialis G, Roli F, Schuckers S (2012) LivDet 2011—fingerprint liveness detection competition 2011. In: 2012 5th IAPR international conference on biometrics (ICB), pp 208–215
16. Mansfield AJ, Wayman JL, Dr Rayner D, Wayman JL (2002) Best practices in testing and reporting performance. NPL Report CMSC
17. Galbally-Herrero J, Fierrez-Aguilar J, Rodriguez-Gonzalez JD, Alonso-Fernandez F, Ortega-Garcia J, Tapiador M (2006) On the vulnerability of fingerprint verification systems to fake fingerprints attacks. In: IEEE international carnahan conference on security technology, pp 169–179
18. Ruiz-Albacete V, Tome-Gonzalez P, Alonso-Fernandez F, Galbally J, Fierrez J, Ortega-Garcia J (2008) Direct attacks using fake images in iris verification. In: Proceedings of COST 2101 workshop on biometrics and identity management, BIOID, Springer, pp 181–190
19. Galbally J, Fierrez J, Alonso-Fernandez F, Martinez-Diaz M (2011) Evaluation of direct attacks to fingerprint verification systems. Telecommunication systems, special issue on biometrics 47(3):243–254
20. Hastie T, Tibshirani R, Friedman JH (2001) The elements of statistical learning: data mining, inference, and prediction: with 200 full-color illustrations. Springer, New York
21. Lui YM, Bolme D, Phillips P, Beveridge J, Draper B (2012) Preliminary studies on the good, the bad, and the ugly face recognition challenge problem. In: 2012 IEEE computer society conference on computer vision and pattern recognition workshops (CVPRW), pp 9–16
22. Marcialis GL, Lewicke A, Tan B, Coli P, Grimberg D, Congiu A, Tidu A, Roli F, Schuckers S (2009) First international fingerprint liveness detection competition - livdet 2009. In: Proceeding of IAPR international conference on image analysis and processing (ICIAP), LNCS, vol 5716. pp 12–23
23. Ghiani L, Yambay D, Mura V, Tocco S, Marcialis G, Roli F, Schuckers S (2013) Livdet 2013—fingerprint liveness detection competition. In: IEEE International conference on biometrics (ICB)
24. Zhiwei Z, Yan J, Liu S, Lei Z, Yi D, Li SZ (2012) A face antispoofing database with diverse attacks. In: Proceedings of IAPR international conference on biometrics (ICB), pp 26–31
25. Chingovska I, Anjos A, Marcel S (2012) On the effectiveness of local binary patterns in face anti-spoofing. In: Proceedings of IEEE international conference of the biometrics special interest group (BIOSIG), pp 1–7

26. Peixoto B, Michelassi C, Rocha A (2011) Face liveness detection under bad illumination conditions. In: 2011 18th IEEE International conference on image processing (ICIP), pp 3557–3560
27. Poh N, Bengio S (2006) Database, protocols and tools for evaluating score-level fusion algorithms in biometric authentication. Pattern Recognit J 39(2):223–233
28. Martin A, Doddington G, Kamm T, Ordowski M (1997) The det curve in assessment of detection task performance. In: Proceedings of eurospeech, pp 1895–1898
29. Bengio S, Keller M, Mariéthoz J (2003) The expected performance curve. Technical report IDIAP-RR-85-2003, IDIAP
30. Wang L, Ding X, Fang C (2009) Face live detection method based on physiological motion analysis. Tsinghua Sci Technol 14(6):685–690
31. Zhang Z, Yi D, Lei Z, Li S (2011) Face liveness detection by learning multispectral reflectance distributions. In: 2011 IEEE international conference on automatic face gesture recognition and workshops (FG 2011), pp 436–441
32. Johnson P, Lazarick R, Marasco E, Newton E, Ross A, Schuckers S (2012) Biometric liveness detection: framework and metrics. In: International biometric performance conference
33. Gao X, Tsong Ng T, Qiu B, Chang SF (2010) Single-view recaptured image detection based on physics-based features. In: IEEE international conference on multimedia and expo (ICME), Singapore
34. Tronci R, Muntoni D, Fadda G, Pili M, Sirena N, Murgia G, Ristori M, Ricerche S, Roli F (2011) Fusion of multiple clues for photo-attack detection in face recognition systems. In: Proceedings of the 2011 international joint conference on biometrics, IJCB '11, IEEE Computer Society, pp 1–6
35. Jain AK, Flynn P, Ross AA (eds) (2008) Handbook of biometrics. Springer, New York
36. Adler A, Schuckers S (2009) Security and liveness, overview. In: Jain AK, Li SZ (eds) Encyclopedia of biometrics. Springer, New York
37. Galbally J, Cappelli R, Lumini A, de Rivera GG, Maltoni D, Fiérrez J, Ortega-Garcia J, Maio D (2010) An evaluation of direct attacks using fake fingers generated from iso templates. Pattern Recogn Lett 31(8):725–732
38. Rodrigues R, Kamat N, Govindaraju V (2010) Evaluation of biometric spoofing in a multimodal system. In: 2010 Fourth IEEE international conference on biometrics: theory applications and systems (BTAS)
39. Matsumoto T, Matsumoto H, Yamada K, Hoshino S (2002) Impact of artifical "gummy" fingers on fingerprint systems. In: SPIE Proceedings: optical security and counterfeit deterrence techniques, vol. 4677
40. Patrick P, Aversano G, Blouet R, Charbit M, Chollet G (2005) Voice forgery using alisp: indexation in a client memory. In: Proceedings. (ICASSP '05). IEEE international conference on acoustics, speech, and signal processing, 2005, vol 1, pp 17–20
41. Alegre F, Vipperla R, Evans N, Fauve B (2012) On the vulnerability of automatic speaker recognition to spoofing attacks with artificial signals. In: Signal processing conference (EUSIPCO), 2012 proceedings of the 20th European, pp 36–40
42. Bonastre JF, Matrouf D, Fredouille C (2007) Artificial impostor voice transformation effects on false acceptance rates. In: INTERSPEECH, pp 2053–2056

# Chapter 11
# Related Standards

**Christoph Busch**

**Abstract** This chapter reports about the relevant international standardization activities in the field of biometrics and describes a harmonized taxonomy for terms in the field of liveness detection. The scope and progress of the presentation attack detection standard ISO/IEC 30107 is discussed.

## 11.1 Introduction

Biometric systems are characterized by two essential properties. On one hand, functional components or subsystems are usually dislocated. While the enrollment may take place as a part of an employment procedure with the personal department or as a part of an ePassport application in the municipality administration, the biometric verification takes place likely at a different location, when the data subject (e.g., the staff member) is approaching a certain enterprise-gate (or any other physical border gate) or when the citizen is traveling with his new passport. On the other hand, while the biometric enrollment is likely to be a supervised capture process and often linked with training on sensor interaction such supervision does not exist for the verification process. To the contrary, the verification is often conducted based on a probe sample that was generated in a unsupervised capture process. In consequence for the verification not only usability of the sensor and ease of human–machine interaction is essential but moreover a measure of confidence that the probe sample was in deed collected from the subject that was initially enrolled and not from an biometric artifact that pretends the presence of the enrollee.

In most cases, the comparison of probe a biometric sample with the stored biometric reference will be dislocated from the place of enrollment. Some applications store the reference in a centralized or de-centralized database. More prominent are token-based concepts like the ICAO ePassports [1, 2] as they allow the subject to keep control of his/her personal biometric data as the traveling individuals decide themselves whether and when they provide the token to the controlling instance.

C. Busch (✉)
Fraunhofer IGD, Fraunhoferstr 5, 64283 Darmstadt, Germany
e-mail: christoph.busch@igd.fraunhofer.de

The recognition task is likely to fail, if the biometric reference is not readable according to a standardized format. Any open system concept does require the use of an open standard in order to allow that for the recognition task a component from any different suppliers can be used. The prime purpose of a biometric reference is to represent a biometric characteristic. This representation must, on the one hand, allow a good biometric performance but at the same time the encoding format must fully support the interoperability requirements. Thus, encoding of a biometric sample (i.e., fingerprint image or face image) according to the ISO/IEC Biometric data interchange format [3] became a prominent format structure for many applications. The image itself is stored with high compression ratio for which JPEG2000 [4] and Wavelet Scalar Quantization (WSQ) [5] turned out to be quite efficient encoding schemes.

For all data interchange formats, it is essential to store along with the representation of the biometric characteristic essential information (meta data) on the capture process and the generation of the sample. Metadata that is stored along with the biometric data includes information such as size and resolution of the image but also relevant data that impacted the data capturing process: Examples for such metadata are the Capture Device Type ID, that identifies uniquely the device that was used for the acquisition of the biometric sample and also the Certification block data that reports the Certification authority, which had tested the capture device and the corresponding Certification scheme that was used for this purpose. These data fields are contained in standardized interchange records [3, 6, 7].

An essential information that was furthermore considered helpful for the verification capture process is some measure to describe the reliability of the capture device against spoofing attacks. This is more pressing, if capture device and decision systems are dislocated. Thus, ISO/IEC has started in 2011 to work on a standard that is covering this issue and will be introduced in this chapter. We will outline the strategy behind this standardization process, cover the taxonomy that was established so far, and discuss the constraints to be considered in the respective standardization project.

## 11.2 International Standards Developed in ISO/IEC SC37

International standardization in the field of information technology is driven by a Joint Technical Committee (JTC1) formed by the International Organization for Standardization (ISO) and the International Electrotechnical Commission (IEC). An important part of the JTC1 is the Sub-Committee 37 (SC37) that was established in 2002. First standards developed in SC37 became available in 2005 and have found wide deployment in the meantime. More than 700 million implementations according to SC37 standards are estimated to be in the field at the time of this writing. Essential topics that are covered by SC37 include the definition of a *Harmonized Biometric Vocabulary* (ISO/IEC 2382-37) that removes contradictions in the biometric terminology [8, 9], a harmonized definition of a (ISO/IEC SC37 SD11) that describes the distributed subsystems, which are contained in deployed systems [10], a common programming interface *BioAPI* (ISO/IEC 19784-1) that

11 Related Standards

supports ease of integration of sensors and SDKs [11] and also the definition of SC37 has over its first 10 years of work concentrated on the development of the ISO/IEC 19794 family, which includes currently the following 13 parts:

- Part 1: Framework (IS)
- Part 2: Finger minutiae data (IS)
- Part 3: Finger pattern spectral data (IS)
- Part 4: Finger image data (IS)
- Part 5: Face image data (IS)
- Part 6: Iris image data (IS)
- Part 7: Signature/Sign time series data (IS)
- Part 8: Finger pattern skeletal data (IS)
- Part 9: Vascular image data (IS)
- Part 10: Hand geometry silhouette data (IS)
- Part 11: Signature/Sign processed dynamic data (IS)
- Part 12: – void –
- Part 13: Voice data (WD)
- Part 14: DNA data (IS).

The first part includes relevant information that is common to all subsequent modality specific parts such as an introduction of the layered set of SC37 standards and an illustration of a general biometric system with a description of its functional subsystems namely the capture device, signal processing subsystem, data storage subsystem, comparison subsystem, and decision subsystem [3]. Furthermore, this framework part illustrates the functions of a biometric system such as enrolment, verification, and identification and explains the application context of biometric data interchange formats. Part 2 to Part 14 then detail the specification and provide modality related data interchange formats for both image interchange and template interchange on feature level. The 19794-family gained relevance, as the International Civic Aviation Organization (ICAO) adopted image based representations for finger, face, and iris for storage of biometric references in Electronic Passports. Thus, the corresponding ICAO standard 9303 [2] includes a normative reference to ISO/IEC 19794. ICAO estimated in February 2013 that there were over 480 million Electronic Passports issued by 101 member states of ICAO.

## 11.3 The Development of Presentation Attack Detection Standard ISO/IEC 30107

For more than a decade along with the enthusiasm for biometric technologies the insight into potential risks in biometrics systems was developed and is documented in the literature [12–14]. Within the context of this chapter, the risks of subversive attacks on the biometric capture device became a major concern in unsupervised applications. Over the years, academic and industry research developed countermeasures in order to detect biometric presentation attacks that constitute a subversive activity. From a general perspective, a subversion attack can be conducted from an outsider that interacts with a biometric capture device but could as well be undertaken from an experienced insider. However, the need to develop a harmonized perspective for presentation attacks that are conducted by biometric capture subjects became obvious. Thus, the motivation to develop a standard that is related to liveness detection and spoofing was supported from stakeholders of all three communities that are active in SC37 namely from industry (essentially representatives from vendors working fingerprint-, vein-, face-, and iris-modality), from academia and research projects (e.g., European projects on liveness detection) as well as from governmental agencies (e.g., responsible for testing laboratories). The latter took the lead and have started the development of a standard with a new work item proposal that was successfully balloted in 2011. Since then, experts from the biometric community as well as the security community have intensively contributed to the working draft of a new standard that is entitled "ISO/IEC Information Technology—Biometrics—Presentation attack detection" [15]. The intention of this standard is to provide a harmonized definition of terms and a taxonomy of attack techniques, a set of testing methods and data formats that can transport measured robustness against said attacks.

The objectives of a standardization project are best understood by analyzing the scope clause. For the Presentation Attack Detection (PAD) standard, the scope indicates that it aims at establishing beyond the taxonomy and terms and definitions a specification and characterization of presentation attack detection methods. A second objective is to develop a common data format devoted to presentation attack assessments and a third objective is to standardize principles and methods for performance assessment of PAD-algorithms. This field of standardization work becomes sharpened, when topics that are outside the scope are considered: Outside this current standardization project are definition of specific PAD detection method as well as detailed information about countermeasures that both are commonly valuable IPR of the industrial stakeholders. In addition, a vulnerability assessment of PAD is out of scope at this point in time. We will discuss the latter briefly in Sect. 11.6.

## 11.4 Taxonomy for Presentation Attack Detection

Literature and science specifically in a multidisciplinary community as in biometrics tends to struggle with a clear and noncontradictonary use and understanding of its terms. Thus, ISO/IEC has undertaken significant efforts to develop a Harmonized Biometric Vocabulary (HBV) [9] that contains terms and definitions useful also in the context of discussions about presentation attacks. Without going into detail of the terminology definition process it is important to note that biometric *concepts* are always discussed in context (e.g., of one or multiple biometric subsystems) before a *term* and its *def inition* for said concept can be developed. Thus terms are defined in groups and overlap of groups ("concept clusters") and the interdependencies of its group members necessarily lead to revision of previously found definitions. The result

# 11 Related Standards

of this work was recently published as ISO/IEC 2382-37 [8] and is also available online [9]. It is of interest to consider here definitions in the HBV, as they are relevant for the taxonomy and terminology that is under development in ISO/IEC 30107 [15]. The following list contains definitions of interest:

- *Biometric characteristic*: biological and behavioral characteristic of an individual from which distinguishing, repeatable biometric features can be extracted for the purpose of biometric recognition (37.01.02).
- *Biometric feature*: numbers or labels extracted from biometric samples and used for comparison (37.03.11).
- *Biometric capture subject*: individual who is the subject of a biometric capture process (37.07.03).
- *Biometric capture process*: icollecting or attempting to collect a signal(s) from a biometric characteristic, or a representation(s) of a biometric characteristic(s,) and converting the signal(s) to a captured biometric sample set (37.05.02).
- *Impostor*: subversive biometric capture subject who attempts to being matched to someone else's biometric reference (37.07.13).
- *Identity concealer*: subversive biometric capture subject who attempts to avoid being matched to their own biometric reference (37.07.12).
- *Subversive biometric capture subject*: biometric capture subject who attempts to subvert the correct and intended policy of the biometric capture subsystem (37.07.17).
- *Subversive user*: user of a biometric system who attempts to subvert the correct and intended system policy (37.07.18).
- *Uncooperative biometric capture subject*: biometric capture subject motivated to not achieve a successful completion of the biometric acquisition process (37.07.19).
- *Uncooperative presentation*: presentation by a uncooperative biometric capture subject (37.06.19).

In order to formulate a common understanding of attacks on biometric systems, the list of above terms was expanded with the following concepts that provided in the 5th Working Draft of ISO/IEC 30107 [15]. Note that these terms are still subject to discussion in the subcommittee and might be changed in the final version of the standard.

- *Artefact*: artificial object or representation presenting a copy of biometric characteristics or synthetic biometric patterns.
- *Artefact species*: artefacts based on sources whose biometric characteristics differ but which are otherwise identical (e.g., based on a common medium and production method but with different biometric characteristic sources).
- *Artefact type*: artefacts based on a common medium and production method and a single biometric characteristic source.
- *Presentation attack*: presentation of an artefact or human characteristic to the biometric capture subsystem in a fashion that could interfere with the intended policy of the biometric system.

- *Presentation attack detection (PAD)*: automated determination of a presentation attack.
- *Liveness*: the quality or state of being alive, made evident by anatomical characteristics (e.g., skin or blood absorption of illumination), involuntary reactions or physiological functions (e.g., iris reaction to light, heart activity, pulse), or voluntary reactions or subject behaviors (e.g., squeezing together fingers in hand geometry or a biometric presentation in response to a directive cue).

Note that the use of the above terms is recommended and similar terms such as *fake* should be deprecated despite their intense previous use in the literature. In the development of ISO/IEC 30107, a framework was defined to understand presentation attack characteristics and also detection methods. Figure 11.1 illustrates the potential targets in a generic biometric system [10] that could be attacked. In the following, we concentrate only on attack presentations that occur at the capture device.

The framework defined in [15] considers two types of attacks. On the one hand, the *Active Imposter Presentation Attack* is considered, which attempts to subvert the correct and intended policy of the biometric capture subsystem and in which the attacker aims to be recognized as a specific data subject known to the system (e.g., an impersonation attack). On the other hand, the framework considers an *Identity Concealer Presentation Attack* as attempt of the attacker to avoid being matched to its own biometric reference in the system.

An attacker be it an active imposter or an identity concealer will use an object for attack that is interacting with the capture device. Moreover, the potential of his attack will depend on his knowledge, the window of opportunity and other factors that we will discuss in Sect. 11.6. However for the object that is employed the standard widens the scope from *gummy fingers* and considers various categories of objects that could be used in a presentation attack. Figure 11.2 illustrate that aside of

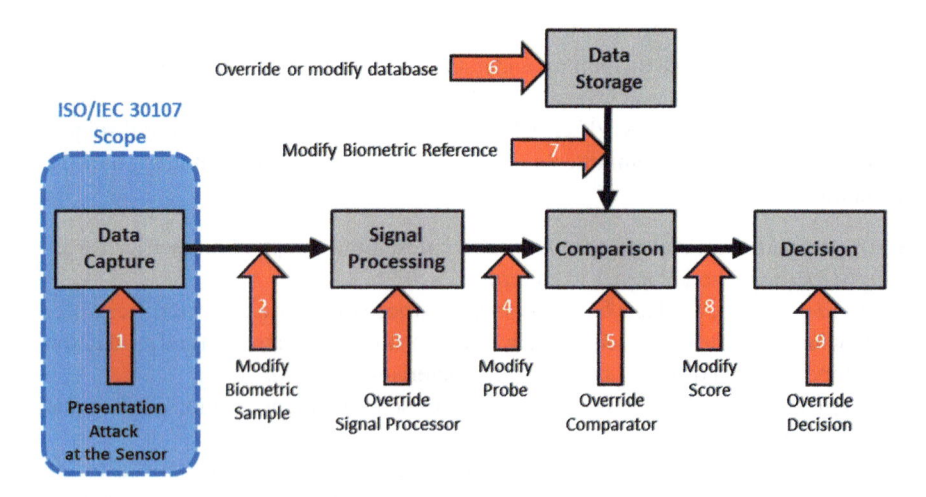

**Fig. 11.1** Examples for points of attacks (from [15])

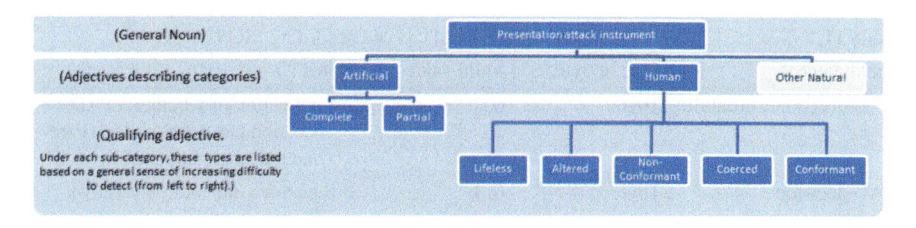

**Fig. 11.2** Categories of objects used in presentation attacks (from [15])

artificial objects (i.e., $artefacts$) natural material could be used. When the expected biometric characteristic from an enrollee is absent and replaced by an *attack presentation characteristic* (i.e., the attack presentation object) this could be a human tissue from a deceased person (i.e., a cadaver part) or it could be an altered fingerprint [16], which is targeting on distortion or mutilation of a fingerprint—likely from an *Identity Concealer*. Moreover, an attacker might present his genuine characteristic but identification is avoided with non-conformant behavior with respect to the data capture regulations, e.g., by extreme facial expression or by placing the with tip or the side of the finger. But attack objects can also include other natural material such as onions or potatoes.

Detailed information about countermeasures (i.e., anto-spoofing techniques) to defend the biometric system against presentation attacks are out of scope of the standard in order to avoid conflicts of interests for industrial stakeholders. However, the standard does discuss a general classification in terms of detection on the level of a biometric subsystem (e.g., artefact detection, liveness detection, alteration detection, nonconformance detection) and through detection of noncompliant interaction in violation with system security policies (e.g., geographic or temporal exception).

## 11.5 Data Formats

One of the objectives of the ISO/IEC 30107 standard is to transport information about the presentation attack detection results from the capture device to subsequent signal processing or decision subsystems. The container to transmit such information is the open data interchange format (DIF) according to the ISO/IEC 19794 series [3]. This subsection outlines the conceptual data fields that are considered for a PAD record. A selection of fields is illustrated in Table 11.1. It should be noted that this table is neither complete nor finalized in the discussion of the standardization group. However, it indicates that the result of the PAD functionality should be encoded as a scalar value in the range of 0–100 in analogy to the encoding of the sample quality assessment that is potentially also conducted by the capture device and stored as a quality score according to ISO/IEC 29794-1 [17].

In the absence of standardized assessment methods, a PAD score would be encoded on a range of 0 (i.e., indicative of an attack) to 100 (i.e., indicative of a

**Table 11.1** Selected data fields considered for a PAD record according ISO/IEC 30107

| Field name | Size in bytes | Valid values | Notes |
|---|---|---|---|
| PAD decision availability | 1 byte | 0, 1 | An indication of whether a PAD decision has been made, where one indicates a decision |
| PAD decision | 1 byte | 0, 1 | If the above indicator is positive, the nature of the decision, where one indicates possible attack attempt |
| PAD result | 1 byte | 0–100 | PAD score between 0 and 100 provided by the attack detection mechanism, with lower scores being indicative of attack presentation objects and higher scores indicative of genuine capture attempts |
| PAD parameters | | text string | Any external parameters (e.g., threshold) directly related to the technique employed to make the PAD decision |
| Risk level | 1 byte | 0–254 | Current risk level; a value of 0 indicating no risk and 254 indicating every transaction certainly an attack attempt |
| Level of supervision | 1 byte | 1–5 | Level of supervision/surveillance during the capture process |

Note that entries in the table are working draft elements and subject to further discussions in ISO/IEC SC37

genuine capture attempt) the reliability that the transmitted biometric sample can be trusted. Any decision based on this information is at the discretion of the receiver. The described PAD data record is likely to become an integral part of the representation header in ISO/IEC 19794-x. Remaining challenges are to allow optional encoding as a capture device may or may not encode such additional information and further to achieve backwards compatibility with already deployed system that need to parse DIFs according to 19794-1:2006 or 19794-1:2011.

## 11.6 Metrics Under Development

In order to evaluate the reliability of PAD record that is transmitted in an interchange record two evaluations are foreseen. The first relevant information is to transport for the capture device that was encoding the interchange record the performance testing results that were elaborated by an independent testing laboratory. Test procedures as such are well known since the biometric performance testing standards ISO/IEC

19795-1 was established in 2006 [18]. This framework for Biometric Performance Testing and Reporting was developed on the basis of established concepts such as the *Best Practices in Testing and Reporting Performance of Biometric Devices* [19] and it defines in which way algorithm errors such as false-match-rate (FMR) and false-non-match-rate (FNMR) as well as system errors such as false-accept-rate (FAR) and false-reject-rates (FRR) must be reported. For testing of presentation attack detection unfortunately such established concepts do not exist. Thus, various national approaches have been proposed are now discussed as the standard ISO/IEC 30107 is under development. However, some metrics appear familiar to a testing expert and are indeed derived from biometric performance testing metrics.

A starting point for such metrics is given by the presentation-attack-detection-rate (PADR), which is defined as the proportion of presentation attacks with a defined level of difficulty detected by a system. The PADR could be defined for multiple presentation attack samples of one *artefact type*, or for multiple presentation attack samples of multiple *artefact types* or in the best case for multiple *artefact species*. A challenge in this definition is that unlike for biometric performance testing aka *technology testing* a large corpus of testing samples can not be assumed to be available. Top national laboratories are in possession of no more than 60 artefact species for a fingerprint recognition system. In this case, it becomes essential that the proportion is computed not to a potentially large number samples all of one singe artefact type, that are all of similar material properties and stemming from the same biometric source. At least the denominator should be defined by the number of *artefact species* as outlined in Sect. 11.4. Note that one single artefact species would correspond to the set of fingerprint artefacts all made with the same *recipe* and the same materials but with different friction ridge patterns from different fingerprint instances. A complementary measure to the PADR is the presentation attack non-detection rate (PA-NDR), which constitute the proportion of presentation attacks with a defined level of difficulty not detected by a system.

An essential difference of PAD testing is that obviously there is beyond the mere statistical observations as expressed by PADR and PA-NDR metrics the need to categorize the attack potential itself. Such methodology is well established in the scope of Common Criteria testing that developed the Common Methodology for Information Technology Security Evaluation [20]. It might be desirable to replace the indication of an *defined level of difficulty* according to the PADR definition by an attack potential attribute of a biometric presentation attack expressing the effort expended in the preparation and execution of the attack in terms of elapsed time, expertise, knowledge about the capture device being attacked, window of opportunity and equipment, graded as *no rating*, *minimal*, *basic*, *enhanced-basic*, *moderate* or *high*. Such gradings are established in Common Criteria testing and would allow a straightforward understanding of a PAD result for security purposes.

## 11.7 Conclusion and Future Work

This chapter introduces the standardization work that began recently in the area of presentation attack detection. While metrics are not yet well established the current working draft already contains a mature taxonomy of presentation attack detection terms and also a sound categorization of attack objects. The discussions on encoding details of the PAD interchange record are ongoing and the reader might want to contribute to this process via his national standardization body. By separation of work tasks in ISO/IEC JTC1 discussion of security related topics is not in scope of ISO/IEC 30107. However the Common Criteria concept of attack potential should be seen as both a good categorization for the criticality of an attack and the precondition to conduct later a security evaluation based on the results of a ISO/IEC 30107 metric. However, this link needs to be established and thus there is space for many activities as future work.

**Acknowledgments** The author would like to thank Elaine Newton for all the hard work of being editor of ISO/IEC 30107 and also all SC37 WG3 experts for their valuable contributions to this standard.

## References

1. International Civil Aviation Organization (2004) TAG 15 MRTD/NTWG: biometrics deployment of machine readable travel documents. Version 2.0
2. International Civil Aviation Organization (2011) NTWG: supplement to Doc9303-version 11. http://www2.icao.int/en/MRTD/Downloads/Supplements
3. ISO/IEC (2011) JTC1 SC37 biometrics: ISO/IEC 19794–1:2011 information technology—biometric data interchange formats—part 1: framework. International Organization for Standardization
4. ISO/IEC (2004) TC JTC1 SC 29 coding of audio, picture, multimedia and hypermedia information: ISO/IEC 15444–1:2004—ITU-T Rec. T.800. Information technology—JPEG2000 image coding system: core coding system. International Organization for Standardization
5. Bradley J, Brislawn C (1994) The wavelet/scalar quantization compression standard for digital fingerprint images. In: Circuits and systems, 1994. ISCAS '94, 1994 IEEE international symposium on, vol 3, pp 205–208. doi:10.1109/ISCAS.1994.409142
6. ISO/IEC (2011) JTC1 SC37 biometrics: ISO/IEC 19794–4:2011 information technology—biometric data interchange formats—part 4: finger image data. International Organization for Standardization
7. ISO/IEC (2011) JTC1 SC37 biometrics: ISO/IEC 19794–5:2011. Information technology—biometric data interchange formats—part 5: face image data. International Organization for Standardization
8. ISO/IEC (2012) JTC1 SC37 biometrics: ISO/IEC 2382–37 harmonized biometric vocabulary. International Organization for Standardization
9. ISO/IEC (2012) JTC1 SC37 biometrics: ISO/IEC 2382–37 harmonized biometric vocabulary. http://www.christoph-busch.de/standards.html
10. ISO/IEC (2008) JTC1 SC37 biometrics: ISO/IEC SC37 SD11 general biometric system. International Organization for Standardization

11. ISO/IEC (2006) TC JTC1 SC37 biometrics: ISO/IEC 19784-1:2006. Information technology—biometric application programming interface—part 1: BioAPI specification. International Organization for Standardization
12. Zwiesele A, Munde A, Busch C, Daum H (2000) Biois study—comparative study of biometric identification systems. In: 34th annual 2000 IEEE international carnahan conference on security technology (CCST), IEEE Computer Society, pp 60–63
13. Matsumoto T, Matsumoto H, Yamada K, Yoshino S (2002) Impact of artificial "Gummy" fingers on fingerprint systems. SPIE conference on optical security and counterfeit deterrence techniques IV 4677:275–289
14. Schuckers SAC (2002) Spoofing and anti-spoofing measures. Inf secur tech rep 7:56–62
15. ISO/IEC (2013) JTC1 SC37 biometrics: 5th WD ISO/IEC 30107. Information technology—biometrics—presentation attack detection. International Organization for Standardization
16. Cummins H (1935) Attempts to alter and obliterate finger-prints. J Crim Law Criminol 25:982–991
17. ISO/IEC (2009) JTC1 SC37 biometrics: ISO/IEC 29794-1:2009 information technology—biometric sample quality—part 1: framework. International Organization for Standardization
18. ISO/IEC (2006) TC JTC1 SC37 biometrics: ISO/IEC 19795-1:2006. Information technology—biometric performance testing and reporting—part 1: principles and framework. International Organization for Standardization and International Electrotechnical Committee
19. Mansfield T, Wayman J (2002) Best practices in testing and reporting performance of biometric devices. CMSC 14/02 Version 2.01, NPL
20. Criteria C (2012) Common methodology for information technology security evaluation—evaluation methodology. http://www.commoncriteriaportal.org/cc/

# Chapter 12
# Legal Aspects: Biometric Data, Evidence Rules and Trusted Identities

Els J. Kindt

> *In the near future many transactions will no longer be performed by traditional methods, like face-to-face contacts or regular mail. Instead, computer networks will be the new vehicles. As persons are physically separated, new and secure methods of identification and authentication are required*
> Peter J. Hustinx
> Preface in "At face value On biometrical identification and privacy", 1999.

**Abstract** Biometric characteristics could play an increasing role as means for binding electronic documents and transactions to a person and for identifying that person. However, one of the conditions for biometric methods to be used as an electronic signature is that spoofing vulnerabilities are adequately assessed and appropriate solutions are developed. Anti-spoofing measures are also crucial in electronic identity schemes which may include biometric characteristics. For these schemes, privacy and data protection issues remain to be solved as well.

## 12.1 Introduction

Biometric data are used to verify claims of individuals in various scenarios, for example, for (border) access control, but also for online transactions. For this purpose, an individual provides his or her biometric characteristics for making his or

E.J. Kindt (✉)
KU Leuven, Leuven, Belgium
e-mail: els.kindt@law.kuleuven.be

her claim "authentic".[1] These claims are subsequently relied upon by third parties, for example, an access control (border) guard or a bank for an online transaction. Under which conditions may these third parties trust these claims augmented with biometric data ? It is clear that our Internet economy faces the challenge to develop urgently an appropriate digital identity management framework for both the private and public sector. This is not only recognized by the OECD [1] but also by the fact that numerous national and international initiatives are currently exploring the development of digital identity management schemes and strategies.

This chapter aims to contribute to these discussions. First, we review how biometric data fit in the present legal framework in relation to evidence and electronic signatures in the European Union. We aim to identify whether methods using biometric data could qualify as electronic signatures. Specific attention is hereby paid to the need and importance of anti-spoofing measures.

We also review the proposed EU Commission Regulation on electronic identification of 2012 and whether and under which conditions biometric data could play a role in this proposed framework for trusted identities. Besides the need for solutions for biometric vulnerabilities, we expect that privacy and data protection issues as well need to be solved for the use of biometric data in trusted identity schemes.

## 12.2 Biometric Data and Evidence in the Information Society

Legal transactions in civil and commercial matters pass in today's society increasingly through electronic communication networks. The legislative framework had to follow this evolution and adopted new rules on the evidence value of electronic documents and electronic signatures.

Pursuant to Article 9 of the E-Commerce Directive 2000/31/EC, the Member States of the Union were required to ensure that their legal systems allow contracts to be concluded by electronic means [2]. More specifically, the Member States had to ensure that the legal requirements applicable to the contractual process would neither create obstacles for the use of electronic contracts nor deprive them for legal effectiveness and validity. Only for some specific categories of contracts, an exception could be made by the Member States, such as for contracts for the creation or the

---

[1] The verb "to authenticate" can be described as "making authentic, legally valid." "Authentic" has several meanings, including "1. written or made by own handwriting, not falsified, (...) real, originating in reality from whom it is attributed, 2. corresponding with the original and therefore authoritative (...) 5. of which the reliability is guaranteed (...) 6. carrying an own characteristic (...)" (Van Dale, general dictionary of the Dutch language, 13th edition (1999) at the terms "authentiseren" and "authentiek"; the term "authentication" ("authenticatie") in Dutch is therein not mentioned, but has been added in the 14th edition (2005); in this edition, the meaning of "to authenticate" is now completed with "to establish the identity of"). For a definition of authentication, see also Article 3(4) of the Proposal of Regulation on electronic identification and trust services, mentioned in Sect. 12.4.1

transfer of rights in real estate (except for rental rights), contracts requiring by law the involvement of courts or public authority, contracts on suretyship and collateral securities by persons other than professionals and contracts governed by family or succession law (see Article 9, al. 2 E-Commerce Directive 2000/31/EC).

As a result, and generally speaking, writings of parties used as evidence of a contract were no longer required to be on paper but could also be in electronic form. Electronic documents will hence also qualify as a "writing" ("geschrift"/"écrit"), subject to the national rules on evidence, after the implementation of the E-Commerce Directive 2000/31/EC. The Directive could be implemented in various ways. In Belgium, for example, the equivalence between paper and electronic documents was established by disconnecting the requirements for a "writing" from the carrier (e.g., paper) and connecting requirements to the conditions for the content. The equivalence of electronic documents with paper documents was thus established on the level of the requirements for documents. For a "writing," it is now sufficient that there "is a sequence of understandable signs which are accessible[2] for later consultation, whatever the carrier and the transmission modalities."

For a "writing" to have a strong evidence value, it will in many cases however be required that the document contains a signature. Such requirement may be imposed by a legal provision or by case law.[3] In Belgium, for example, such "acts with signature"("onderhandse akte"/"acte sous seing privé") are presently required according to the evidence rules in civil matters as evidence for transactions with a value above 375 euro. Writings without signature only count as presumptions or as a start of documentary evidence. In commercial matters, professionals are free to prove the existence and the content of commercial obligations, although writings with signature will remain important for commercial transactions (see the Articles 1341 of the (Belgian) Civil Code and Article 25 of the (Belgian) Commercial Code). To meet the requirement of a writing by someone who is binding him- or herself, it shall (only) be ensured and guaranteed that it originates from that person notwithstanding any support or the transmission modalities used.[4] Non-repudiation or the lack of deniability is an important aspect and requirement. To prove a signature, the integrity of the act with signature shall also be demonstrated. In France, the legal provisions of the Civil Code require for writings in electronic form for being accepted as evidence that the

---

[2] This should be accessible for human persons, whether directly or indirectly (e.g., with the use of computers and other technical tools). About electronic signatures, see also e.g., J. Dumortier and P. Van Eecke, "De nieuwe wetgeving over digitale en elektronische handtekening," in J. Dumortier (ed.), Recente ontwikkelingen in informatica- en telecommunicatierecht, Brugge, Die Keure, 1999, pp. 1–26; P. Van Eecke, De handtekening in het recht: van pennentrek tot elektronische handtekening, Brussel, De Boeck/Larcier, 2004, 608 p.

[3] For example, for Germany, see section 126 of the German Civil Code. In Belgium, the need for a signature is imposed by case law, as approved unanonymously by the legal scholars. See also P. Van Eecke, "De elektronische handtekening in het recht," T.B.H. 2009, (322), p. 325 ("Van Eecke, Elektronisch handtekening, 2009").

[4] Article 16 Section 2 al. 1 and 3 of the (Belgian) Act of 11 March 2003 relating to some legal aspects of information society services (B.S., 17.03.2003), implementing E-Commerce Directive 2000/31/EC ("Act of 11 March 2003").

integrity of the document is assured and that the person establishing the document is known.[5] To summarize, in order to evaluate whether a document has the value of a writing or of an act with signature, one will have to verify whether the functionalities of a writing and of a (handwritten) signature are fulfilled.[6] Other aspects, such as the carrier (whether on paper, tape, optical disk, chipcard, etc) and any technologies used are in principle not relevant.

This brings us to the question of the role of biometric data in the establishment of evidence in electronic commerce, in particular of electronic documents. Several biometric characteristics are accepted to be unique to individuals, such as fingerprint or iris. Could such biometric characteristics play a role in the establishment of electronic documents and could this be enforced under the current legal framework?

Biometric data has already been used since long to indicate that a particular object or document, whether electronic or not, originates from a particular person because of the unique link with that person. In ancient times, biometric characteristics were used to bind, for example, texts in a clay tablet or images (e.g., paintings in caves) to the author. Finger prints in ink have been used on documents as well.[7]

Biometric data are now however increasingly used in automated processing operations. Could the use of biometric data guarantee the origin of a writing, i.e., a sequence of understandable signs which are accessible for later consultation as belonging to a particular person? Could the automated processing of biometric data belonging to a particular individual be used to produce an electronic document guaranteeing the origin of the writing and its integrity? In other words, could biometric data be used for an electronic signature? We will explore this in the next section.

## 12.3 Biometric Data for Establishing Electronic Signatures?

### 12.3.1 Legal Rules on the Use of e-Signatures

We explained that an (electronic) document should preferably contain a signature to have a stronger evidentiary value. Such signature can also be an electronic sig-

---

[5] See Article 1316 1 (French) Civil Code: "L'écrit sous forme électronique est admis en preuve au même titre que l, écrit sur support papier, sous réserve que puisse être dûment identifiée la personne dont il émane et qu, il soit établi et conservé dans des conditions de nature á en garantir l' intégrité". and Article 1316 3 (French) Civil Code: "L'écritsur support électronique a la même force probante que l' écrit sur support papier. For the introduction of the concept of electronic documents and signature, further to the forementioned Directives in Germany, see A. Albrecht, Biometric Authentication from a Legal Point of View A European and German Perspective, in W. Sloan Coats (ed.), The Practitioner's Guide to Biometrics, Chicago, ABA, 2007, (87), pp. 118–119 (referring in particular to Article 126a German Civil Code (BGB)).

[6] See also Article 16 Section 1 of the (Belgian) Act of 11 March 2003.

[7] Under Belgian law, however, the use of fingerprints on a document is generally not accepted as a valid (handwritten) signature. See also Van Eecke, Elektronisch handtekening, 2009, p. 327 and the various references cited in the footnotes. The reason is that according to old case law, a (handwritten) signature should consist of letter signs, and not of symbols or other signs, such as a cross.

nature. Electronic signatures however are used in a large variety of circumstances and applications. Therefore, the E-Signature Directive 1999/93/EC was adopted and was aimed at harmonizing the legal rules on the use of electronic signatures [3]. EU Member States have adopted legislation on electronic signatures based on this E-Signature Directive 1999/93/EC.

An electronic signature is defined in Article 2.1 of this Directive as "(1) data in electronic form (2) which are attached to or logically associated with other electronic data and (3) which serve as a method of authentication" (numbers added). There are many forms and types of electronic signatures. For example, name and other identifying data attached to an email message could be considered as a form of electronic signature. The E-Signature Directive 1999/93/EC imposes upon Member States to not deny legal effectiveness and admissibility of electronic signatures as evidence in legal proceedings solely because they are in electronic form or do not comply with additional requirements mentioned in this Directive.

Such additional requirements are imposed for "advanced electronic signatures" and "qualified electronic signatures" as defined in this Directive. The "advanced electronic signature" is a signature which "(a) is uniquely linked to the signatory, (b) is capable of identifying the signatory, (c) is created using means that the signatory can maintain under his sole control, and (d) is linked to the data to which it relates in such a manner that any subsequent change of the data is detectable' (Article 2.2 E-Signature Directive 1999/93/EC). A "qualified electronic signature" is an advanced electronic signature combined with a qualified certificate and a secure-signature-creation device meeting respectively the requirements of Annex I and II and the requirements of Annex III of this Directive. These types of signature refer mainly to the use of digital signatures based on public key cryptography and infrastructure (PKI). The Belgian eID, for example, includes identity and signature keys and certificates, allowing for a qualified electronic signature. The card however does not deploy biometric data for these purposes.

The Member States adopted national legislation recognizing these types of electronic signatures and these signatures were given legal effects. Article 5 of the E-Signature Directive 1999/93/EC requires that the third type of electronic signature, the qualified electronic signature, is treated equally as a handwritten signature.[8] However, judges may not reject electronic signatures as evidence or refuse them because they are not based on a qualified certificate or created with a secure means (See Article 5.2 E-Signature Directive 1999/93/EC). To conclude, one shall retain that rather than the form of the signature, it is of importance for any signature that the required functionalities as explained above are fulfilled.

---

[8] See also, e.g., Belgium, Article 1322, al. 2 Civil Code, specifying that "a set of electronic data which may be attributed to a specific person and which demonstrates a guarantee for the integrity of the content of the document" may be sufficient for the requirement of a signature for purposes of attributing the evidence value of an act with signature to a writing.

## 12.3.2 Could Biometric Data and Methods Allow for an e-Signature?

The question now raises whether biometric data and methods allow to make an electronic signature with legal effect. We are more particularly interested in the question whether the use of (particular) biometric characteristics or methods would enable the making of an electronic signature, an "advanced electronic signature" or even a "qualified electronic signature" which confers to a writing the status of an "act with signature."

As explained above, an advanced electronic signature requires that the signature is uniquely linked to the signatory and is capable of identifying the signatory (conditions (a) and (b) for this type of signature). The fact that the signature shall in principle identify the signatory is interesting as it makes biometric data that are based on the unique biological and/or behavioral characteristics of human beings in particular useful because of its unique link to and its identification capabilities of the creator of an electronic signatory. Several biometric characteristics and biometric data derived thereof are capable of identifying the signatory. Biometric data are in principle also uniquely linked to the individual to whom they belong, even for identical (monozygotic) twins, who have distinguished unique fingerprints.[9] Biometric data based on the unique biological and/or behavioral characteristics of human beings would hence in principle meet the first two requirements for an advanced electronic signature.

An advanced electronic signature however requires in addition that the signature is created using means that the signatory can maintain under his sole control (condition (c) for this type of signature). It can be argued that biometric characteristics uniquely belong to individuals and are part of their body and are therefore also under the sole control of the individual. Biometric data would therefore meet this requirement of being means that is kept under the sole control of the signatory. Is this control affected if individuals from time to time agree to have their characteristics registered and stored for particular applications, such as for example for registered traveler's (frequent flyer) programmes ? One could say that this does not necessarily imply loss of control. It may be compared with the fact that individuals also from time to time put handwritten signatures, which could be copied (for example, by fax), without any originally placed handwritten signatures losing evidentiary evidence. To evaluate the evidentiary value, judges will have to check whether the individual to whom the biometric data belong, the genuine "owner" of the biometric data, was involved. An important risk of the use of biometric data, however, is the unwanted (and often unnoticed) capturing of biometric characteristics and its reuse by impostors for spoofing purposes [4] (p. 18, 30 and 32). Spoofing is a broad term referring to situations where someone or somewhat pretends to be someone or something else, often for purposes of criminal activities. In the context of biometric data processing,

---

[9] We do not include DNA in the concept of biometric data. For biometric data, the use or fitness for use by automated means is in our view essential and we include therefore DNA data at present not in the concept and definition of biometric data.

it is described as "the presentation of an artifact designed to imitate a legitimate biometric so as to defeat or circumvent a biometric system or process" [5]. It could be argued in court that the use of biometric characteristics, since they (potentially all [6] pp. 446–448) leave traces and therefore could be "stolen," does not guarantee that the owner of the characteristics was actually involved in the establishment of the written evidence and the transaction. Because of various abuses, including, for example, the unwanted identification of individuals in public places, such as by face recognition, we have already pleaded for legal provisions because of privacy and data protection reasons, restricting the collection of biometric data of others, in particular the hidden collection [6] (pp. 644–645). But biometric systems are also vulnerable for numerous types of attacks against various components of the biometric system itself. The biometric data can be captured for several purposes, including for spoofing and identity theft. There is evidence from various sources that several attempts to use forged or stolen biometric data to fool biometric systems have been successful. Such endeavors were made in relation with fingerprint, but also for other characteristics, such as face and iris. For this reason, an individual could also deny that he or she agreed with a particular transaction or that the writing originates from him or her. This is also referred to as repudiation. For biometric data processing, this is a particular challenge, not only in criminal, but also in civil matters.[10] Legislative initiatives limiting the (hidden) collection of biometric data of individuals would hence also be beneficial, not only from a privacy and data protection perspective, but also for the further consideration of biometric data as means for evidence and for enabling electronic commerce.

It remains, however, difficult for nonspecialists to assess these vulnerabilities. The research project Biometrics Evaluation and Testing (BEAT)[11] aims to develop and to describe metrics that allow to measure the resistance of biometric systems against known direct attacks based on spoofed characteristics and also against indirect attacks. Additional research about the vulnerabilities of biometric data, such as in the project BEAT, and also as presented in this book, is hence not only important because of the obligation under the data protection regulation to implement appropriate technical and organizational security measures upon the processing of personal (biometric) data to secure the data, but also crucial for evaluating and for assessing to what extent particular biometric data may remain under the sole control of the persons to whom they belong. This research should also allow to develop and test effective anti-spoofing measures. Making an adequate evaluation of and finding the appropriate solutions for biometric vulnerabilities are thus crucial for the further use of biometric data as means for enforcing evidence and electronic signatures.

---

[10] See BWG, Biometric Security Concerns, V.1.0, September 2003, 27 p.; see also A. Schumacher and K. Unverricht, "Rechtliche und gesellschaftliche empfehlungen zur Gestaltung Biometrischer Systeme. Gemss ISO/IEC Technical Report TR 24714-1", Datenschutz und Datensicherheit 2009, (308), p. 309.

[11] BEAT is a EU research project under the 7th Framework programme. For the homepage, see http://www.beat-eu.org/.

At the same time, one should acknowledge that even if sufficient anti-spoofing measures can be implemented, the increasing enrolment of individuals in various biometric applications should also be taken into account when evaluating the evidence value of biometric data. Biometric characteristics can be stored on objects kept under the control of the data subjects for verification purposes or in databases. The more biometric characteristics are stored, not only on objects that the individuals can keep under their sole control, but in particular in centralized databases, the more it becomes unlikely that biometric characteristics could be considered to be under the sole control of the individuals any longer and hence as means for an (advanced and even qualified) electronic signature. Storage on an object under the control of the individual concerned, for example on a smart card or token, is therefore not only for data protection but also for evidence reasons preferred as well. At the same time, additional technical measures for ensuring the control over centrally stored data remain relevant and need to be further explored. The protection of stored biometric information, enabling to limit the use of the biometric information to particular contexts and requiring the presence of the individual when using the stored protected biometric data is hereby an important measure.[12] The protection as mentioned of the centrally stored biometric information remains hereby in particular relevant. Other solutions have been proposed as well.[13] To enhance the link between the individual and the biometric data and the control, additional means which guarantee that the biometric data were deployed by the "owner" (data subject) of the biometric data only are recommended or even required for evidence purposes, for example, by the use of information only known to the data subject (e.g., the use of a PIN) and other challenge-response methods. While control of the individuals, also data subjects, over their biometric data is from a privacy and data protection (and even ethical) perspective generally considered as very important because of the special nature of the biometric data, we emphasize that such control is hence also important for the use of biometric data for evidence purposes.

For a qualified electronic signature, it is in addition necessary that the signature is based upon a "qualified certificate" and generated with a "secure-signature-creation device." A qualified certificate needs to meet specific requirements, but shall also be issued by a certification-service-provider. These providers need to respect the Annex II conditions. As for other biometric enrolments, it will hereby be very important that, especially for evidence purposes, the identity of the person to whom the certificate will be issued is adequately verified. This is also explicitly mentioned in Annex II to the Directive. A "secure-signature-creation device" is defined as "soft- or hardware

---

[12] About these new technical measures, restricting interconnections and unchecked disclosures, see also Article 29 Data Protection Working Party, Opinion 3/2012 on developments in biometric technologies, WP193, 27 April 2012, pp. 32–33.

[13] See, e.g., H. Biermann, M. Bromba, C. Busch, G. Hornung, M. Meints, and G. Quiring-Kock, (eds.) White Paper zum Datenschutz in der Biometrie, 2008. In this paper, it was suggested that use of such centralized biometric data would depend upon submission of one or more specific key(s) exclusively stored on a token kept by the data subject. In case of decentralized or centralized storage, the system design would allow the data subject to influence the disclosure and use of the biometric data.

which are used to implement the data used for making the signature and which meet the requirements set forth in the Annex III to the Directive." Further to Article 5 of the E-Signature Directive 1999/93/EC, the "data used for creating the signature" is also defined as "unique data, such as codes or cryptographic private keys, which are used by the signatory to make an electronic signature." If these additional conditions are fulfilled, the electronic signature can be considered as a handwritten signature. The use of biometric data for a qualified electronic signature requires that the conditions for an advanced electronic signature are fulfilled first, including that the signature is created using means that the signatory can maintain under his sole control. Even in case the creation device would meet the specification of Annex III to the Directive, and a qualified certificate could, after appropriate identity check, be issued, the control of the individual may remain problematic for the same reasons as we mentioned above.

The above does not mean that biometric data would not allow to make any other electronic signature with legal effect.

In case of failure of a biometric method of meeting the requirements for the creation of an advanced or qualified electronic signature, in particular, because one would not accept that tools are used which remain under the control of the signatory, biometric data captured for expressing consent could still be and qualify for an electronic signature under the E-signature Directive. The reason is that biometric data can be used for authentication. For example, providing fingerprint captured through a sensor to express agreement with some electronic text on a website (e.g., general terms) could be considered as providing an electronic signature attached to this text. Banking transactions could also be "signed" by biometric data used as a method of authentication of the originator of the order or banking transaction. For that purpose, the result of the biometric comparison need to be attached or logically associated with the data of the banking transaction. Because of the problem of control, the vulnerability of biometric systems and the increased (central) storage of biometric data, banks could limit the risks of spoofing by deploying biometric data only in combination with, for example, a PIN or the private key of the customer kept under the sole control of the customer, for example, to unlock the private key [7] (p. 15 *et seq.*). This combination allows to argue that the individual remains in control of the deployment of his biometric characteristics. This method however will in the first place be considered a third factor authentication increasing the security of the transaction, while the use of the private key kept under the control of the customer may allow for a qualified electronic signature subject to fulfilment of the requirements.

It will be further up to the courts how much weight shall be given to a particular biometric signature process. It is likely that courts would take the existence of appropriate anti-spoofing mechanisms into account in their evaluation. In case of dispute, experts will be called upon to advise on whether these measures are sufficient and the requirements of electronic signature are met. In the Proposal for Regulation on electronic identification and trust services, mentioned in Sect. 4.1, the proposed new definition of an advanced electronic signature now requires that the signature '(...) (c) is created using *electronic signature data* that the signatory can, *with high level of confidence*, *use* under his sole control (...)' (Article. 3(7)). It is the question whether this will allow better the use of biometric data for an advanced electronic signature.

As explained, the vulnerability of biometric data and biometric systems, the degree to which particular biometric can be spoofed but also increasing (central) storage, and the biometric method used, will play an important role therein.

From the above, we can conclude that biometric data and methods used for authentication purposes may qualify as an electronic signature and will be admissible as evidence, including in legal proceedings. The type of electronic signature (simple, advanced, or qualified) however will depend to an important extent upon the degree of control that the data subjects can retain over their biometric data. For evaluating this requirement, the degree that anti-spoofing measures are effective will play a role. The control is also affected by the central storage of biometric data. The increasing central storages of biometric data may hence, besides the many privacy and data protection reason, also be to the detriment of the further development and use of biometric data as electronic signature.

In the next section, we turn to the role of biometric data processing in electronic identification applications.

## 12.4 Biometric Data and Electronic Identification

### 12.4.1 The Proposal for a Regulation on Electronic Identification and Trust Services for Electronic Transactions

The European Commission has understood that the authentication of electronic identities is essential in the information society and in particular for transactions on the Internet, and this for both the private and public sector. The concern of the Commission is hereby that the solutions for the authentication of electronic identities, for example, an eID solution of a particular country, are interoperable and recognized cross-border in all Member States, as set forth in its "Digital Agenda" in 2010 [8] (p. 11).

With that objective in mind, the Commission proposed in 2012 a Regulation on electronic identification and trust services. The proposed Regulation addresses electronic identification schemes, containing clarifications and amendments to the existing electronic signature regulation, and suggests a general legal framework for the use of various so-called electronic trust services (e.g., electronic time stamping, electronic delivery services, web site authentication, ...) [9]. The Proposal will repeal the E-Signature Directive 1999/93/EC. For the electronic identification schemes, the Commission has services in mind accessible with notified electronic identification means in both the public sector (e.g., eGovernment services, eHealth, ...) and the private sector (e.g., online banking services, eCommerce services, ...). The Proposal for Regulation however only targets schemes where electronic identification is required for public services and accepted in one jurisdiction and electronic identification means which are issued by, on behalf or at least under the responsibility of a Member State.

Article 5 of the Proposal provides for the mutual recognition and acceptance of such means falling under such a scheme which—subjects to specific conditions—is eligible for notification to the Commission. An example of an electronic identification means issued by a Member State is the Belgian electronic identity card, which is also equipped and can be used to authenticate the owner online, for example, to file a tax return (Tax on Web). Important is that Member States must accept liability for the unambiguity of the link between the identification data attributed to a particular person (or legal person)(see Article 6.1 (c) and (e)). They shall also ensure the availability of the authentication possibility online, at any time and free of charge.

Is there any role for biometric data in the electronic identification schemes envisaged in this Proposal ?

### 12.4.2 Biometric Data and Electronic Identification

Article 3 (1) defines "electronic identification" as the process of using person identification data in electronic form unambiguously representing a natural or legal person. While one of the main conditions for the schemes and their notification is that the Member States must ensure an unambiguous link between the electronic identification data and the person concerned and take liability for such unambiguous attribution, it does not mean that a person cannot have multiple electronic identification means. In that case, however, they must all link to the same person.

Biometric data are not mentioned in this Proposal of Regulation on electronic identification and trust services. One of the reasons could be the continued debates about the use of biometric data for citizens in the Union and in some countries, in particular, in the electronic passports and subsequent national centralized databases.[14] Article 3 (2) defines "electronic identification means" as a material or immaterial unit containing person identification data in electronic form unambiguously representing a natural or legal person, and which is used to access services online where electronic identification using an electronic identification means and authentication is required under national legislation or administrative practice to access the service. Any technical means which meets the requirements obtains the legal effects of this Regulation. The Proposal aims to be technology-neutral.

But how will Member States guarantee such link unambiguously? Presently, Member States take various initiatives in the domain of eGovernment to ensure that data processed by services are correctly attributed to particular persons, such as by using "authentic sources" [10] (pp. 251–282). However, mistakes are often made, which shall not surprise. In Belgium, for example, only 55, 1 % of the citizens have a unique name, and 0.7 % has a name shared by 100 persons or more. On 1.01.2006,

---

[14] About these debates and pending court proceedings, see e.g., also Kindt [6].

1, 299 persons carry the name "Maria Peeters" and "Maria Janssens" is the name of 907 persons.[15]

Biometric data combined with the alphanumerical data of the person concerned may provide with an unambiguously link with a particular person. But combining biometric data with alphanumerical data requires in the first place that due organizational measures are in place to collect biometric data with good quality from the right persons to establish the required unambiguous link. For schemes which also require the collection of biometric data, such as for the European e-passport, in particular face and fingerprint, this has proven to be already quite a challenge. Members of the European Parliament, for example, questioned early 2012 the level of confidence in the process of collecting biometric data. They referred to allegations that a high number of the biometric passports in circulation in France were false, having been obtained on the basis of fraudulent documents. They also referred to tests conducted in the Netherlands, revealing that in 21 % of 448 cases, the fingerprints were non-verifiable and therefore useless. It is therefore clear that the procedures of issuance of such electronic identity will require a profound analysis of the organizational and technical procedures for the issuance of such identity. For the e-passport, the research in the project "Fast and trustworthy identity delivery and check with e-Passports leveraging traveller privacy" (Fidelity) investigates the security of the whole chain of the use of the e-passport, starting with its issuance. It is hereby recognized that it is essential that a reliable link is created between the passport holder and the passport, especially at the time of the issuance of the e-passport. The project reviews various issuance procedures, including the documents submitted to provide evidence of identity and studies the possibilities to enhance their security as well as their use. Several principles are hereby applied, such as that it shall be verified at the time of the issuance whether the identity exists (and for example, that the identity is not a fiction) and that the identity claimant is linked to the identity (and is the sole claimant of the identity). Since biometric characteristics could play a role in enhancing the identity verification, it is essential that when using biometric data at the moment of the issuance of the credentials, spoofing attacks are taken into account as well.

In addition, biometric data could be considered sensitive or are at least "of a special nature." Since several risks exist for the data subjects, the collection and use of biometric data, especially in identity schemes, have to be fair, lawful, and legitimate and not infringe the fundamental rights of the data subjects. It would include that it is demonstrated that the use of the data for such electronic identification scheme is "a pressing social need," while the biometric methods shall at the same time be relevant and sufficient (including, for example with acceptable error rates), without alternative solutions which are less infringing with the privacy and data protection rights of the data subjects. Biometric anti-spoofing measures will play a role for the required relevancy as well. The scheme should, for example, include adequate

---

[15] 5.8 miljoen Belgen dragen een unieke naam, Brussel, FOD Economie, K.M.O., Middenstand en Energie, 1.04.2011, available on http://statbel.fgov.be/nl/statistieken/organisatie/adsei/informatie/statbel/in_de_kijker_archief/in_de_kijker_2011/.

solutions for the risk that someone uses fake biometric characteristics for applying for an identity credential such as an eID or an e-passport. Finally, appropriate safeguards to protect the rights of the data subjects will be required. Because of the particular risks of the use of biometric data, including reuse and (unknown) identification, the necessity for using biometric data would hence have to be proven combined with safeguards.

The use of biometric data in electronic identification schemes for public services and schemes issued by, on behalf of or at least under the responsibility of Member States raises therefore other questions as well. For trusted identities in eCommerce and in the digital world in general, privacy and data protection is a key issue. The impact on privacy and data protection shall be carefully assessed. System wide privacy and data protection requirements are hence a must. If such schemes would imply the further collection of biometric data by governmental authorities, such as is, for example, planned in France under the newly proposed Act relating to the protection of identity, as adopted by the parliament on 6 March 2012, the use of biometric data by the government for such schemes is problematic and even requires additional attention. This is probably not sufficiently addressed in the Proposed Regulation on electronic identification. One of the problems is that biometric characteristics and hence the data, because of their uniqueness and also their persistence, can be used as a key to combine information stored in various systems about a particular person (for example, someone's use of a particular service, the crossing of a border, ...). The Article 29 Data Protection Working Party and various reports have pointed since some time to this issue of the use and possible misuse of biometric data as unique identifiers.[16] The ubiquitous use of the same unique identifier, such as biometric data, renders the assembly and the accumulation of information relating to a particular person possible and facilitates its use. The risks lay in the potential combination of the information stored in various places, but also in the ability to use the biometric identifiers to trace and survey persons. In the worst case, biometric characteristics can be used for omnipresent surveillance as an important enabler of a global surveillance infrastructure. Although the General Data Protection Directive 95/46/EC mandates Member States to determine the conditions under which an identifier of general application, as for example biometric data, may be processed, very few Member States have taken initiatives in this regard.

By decision of 22 March 2012, the Constitutional Court declared several provisions of this newly proposed French Act mentioned above, including the provisions for central storage of biometric data collected for both the French EID and E-passport, unconstitutional because of lack of safeguards. Moreover, the risks, in particular the scale, the collection and central storage of fingerprints, the technical and access specifications, and the use of the central biometric data collection for other purposes were considered not proportionate to the aims pursued.

---

[16] WP 29 Opinion on Biometrics 2003 (WP80), p. 10; CNIL, "Homo informaticus en 2005 entre servitude et liberté. L'homo informaticus biomaîtrisé", 26e Rapport d'Activité 2005, p. 49; Hes, Hooghiemstra and Borking, At Face Value, 1999, pp. 43–44.

While biometric data could remain interesting to ensure that identification data are attributed unambiguously to a natural person, several gaps in the legal protection of these personal data remain to be solved. At the same time, the deployment of technical measures, in particular the use of biometric data in protected form could provide some guarantees to the data subjects, i.e., that the biometric data are irreversible, unlinkable, and revocable. The development of effective anti-spoofing measures is another challenge [4, 6] (pp. 606–619).

## 12.5 Conclusions

We analyzed above under which conditions and to what extent biometric data and methods are fit to play a (more important) role in eCommerce and electronic identity schemes.

Biometric characteristics could play an increasing role in written evidence and as means for an electronic signature, provided spoofing vulnerabilities are adequately assessed and solutions developed. As a result thereof, biometric data could be considered as (more) under the sole control of the signatory. This is one of the basic conditions for electronic signatures to be qualified and having the value of an advanced or even qualified electronic signature. At the same time, we mention the central storage of biometric data as an additional factor which could influence the evaluation whether biometric data are under the sole control of the individuals placing a signature. Anti-spoofing measures are also crucial for biometric characteristics to play a role in electronic identity schemes, also cross-border. At the same time, including biometric data in electronic identity schemes should also provide a solution for specific risks posed by biometric data processing, such as the risks of their use as unique identifiers, as well as other risks specified. For both scenario's, the use of protected templates may limit the risks.

**Acknowledgments** This chapter was made possible thanks to the funding and work performed for the BEAT project (EU FP7, grant agreement number 284989), the Fidelity project (EU FP7, grant agreement number 284862) and the B-CCENTRE project (Prevention of and Fight against Crime Programme of the EU, European Commission, DG Home Affairs). The author further thanks prof. dr. P. Van Eecke for the review and his comments to this chapter.

## References

1. OECD (2011) Digital identity management: enabling innovation and trust in the internet economy. http://www.oecd.org/sti/ieconomy/49338380.pdf
2. EC (2000) Directive 2000/31/EC of the European parliament and of the council of 8 Jun 2000 on certain legal aspects of information society services, in particular electronic commerce, in the internal market (O.J. L 178), pp 1–16
3. EC (2000) Directive 1999/93/EC of the European parliament and of the council of 13 Dec 1999 on a community framework for electronic signatures (O.J. L 13), pp 12–20

4. Article 29 Data Protection Working Party (2012) opinion 3/2012 on developments in biometric technologies WP193
5. Li S (ed) (2009) Encyclopedia of Biometrics, Springer, p 1296, at the term "Spoofing", also available at http://www.springer.com/computer/image+processing/book/978-0-387-73002-8
6. Kindt E (2012) The processing of biometric data. A comparative legal analysis with a focus on the proportionality principle and recommendations for a legal framework. Ph.D. thesis, KU Leuven. KU Leuven Law Library
7. Cavoukian A, Stoianov A (2007) Biometric encryption: a positive-sum technology that achieves strong authentication, security and privacy. http://www.ipc.on.ca/images/resources/bio-encryp.pdf
8. EC (2010) A digital agenda for Europe (COM(2010) 245 final/2). Communication from the Commission to the European Parliament, the Council, the Economic and Social Committee and the Committee of the Regions
9. EC (2012) Proposal for a regulation to the European parliament and of the council on electronic identification and trust services for electronic transactions in the internal market (COM(2012) 238 final), p 56
10. Alsenoy B, Kindt E, Dumortier J (2011) Privacy and data protection aspects of e-government identity management. In: van der Hof S, Groothuis MM (eds) Innovating Government, Information Technology and Law Series, vol 20, pp 251–282. T. M. C. Asser Press doi:10.1007/978-90-6704-731-9_15. http://dx.doi.org/10.1007/978-90-6704-731-9_15

# Chapter 13
# Ethical Issues in Anti-spoofing

Andrew P. Rebera

**Abstract** The increasingly widespread and high-profile use of biometrics has attracted a good deal of attention from ethicists. While the ethics of biometrics in general has been widely discussed, technical features of biometric systems have understandably attracted less attention. Yet the societal acceptability of certain biometric modalities, the status of anonymised templates vis-à-vis data protection legislation, and the impact of template-ageing-induced performance degradation in rapidly ageing societies, all show that, in addition to broad ethical questions, biometrics poses more specific ethical challenges. Among these are difficulties presented by countermeasures developed to combat spoofing attacks. This chapter identifies and discusses the main ethical issues arising from the development and deployment of anti-spoofing technologies.

## 13.1 Introduction

The ethical implications of the use of biometrics for identifying, authenticating, profiling, and categorising people have attracted a good deal of critical attention. Several themes are recurrent. In the policy field, biometrics raises difficult questions regarding data protection. More directly philosophical questions concern the conceptualisation of persons implicit in the development and use of biometrics, as well as the role of biometrics in various sociopolitical and economic settings. Irma van der Ploeg, for instance, has explored the societal and ethical implications of the "informatisation" and "digitisation" of the body which is associated with biometrics: the creation of "machine-readable bodies".[1]

---

[1] See, e.g. [1]. Further critiques include that of philosopher Giorgio Agamben, who has argued that the routine biometric identification of citizens is dehumanising and demeaning, casts citizens as inherently suspect, and in so-doing dangerously distorts biopolitical power relations: "What is at stake here is none other than the new and 'normal' biopolitical relation between citizens and the State. This relation no longer has to do with free and active participation in the public sphere, but instead concerns the routine inscription and registration of the most private and most incommunicable element of subjectivity—the biopolitical life of the body" [2], p 202.

A.P. Rebera (✉)
Independent Scholar,
71 Albert Road, Keynsham, UK
e-mail: andrewrebera@gmail.com

© Springer-Verlag London 2014
S. Marcel et al. (eds.), *Handbook of Biometric Anti-Spoofing*,
Advances in Computer Vision and Pattern Recognition,
DOI: 10.1007/978-1-4471-6524-8_13

In addition to the broad ethical questions it poses, biometrics throws up more specific ethical challenges. Individual modalities, for instance, raise individual issues (e.g. fingerprinting is sometimes held to have a negative association with criminality, facial recognition raises the possibility of profiling on the basis of emotion-detection, etc.); and specific societal contexts may raise context-specific questions (e.g. concerning the use of biometrics in ageing societies).[2]

More specific challenges include those presented by countermeasures to spoofing attacks. Spoofing is a form of sensor-level attack on a biometric system, in which the perpetrator attempts to have a system erroneously identify or authenticate him by presenting a fake biometric feature to the scanner. All physiological modalities can be spoofed, though some may be easier to spoof than others. Researchers in the TABULA RASA project have demonstrated the efficacy of spoofing attacks against different modalities (face, iris, fingerprint, voice, gait, and electrophysiological modalities)[3]; and the issue of spoofing has come public attention in the recent controversy concerning Apple's iPhone 5S—the fingerprint sensor of which was spoofed within two days of the phone's going on sale. This chapter identifies and discusses the main ethical issues arising from the development and deployment of anti-spoofing countermeasures. The following summaries of different "families" of countermeasures will suffice to ground discussion in this chapter (for further details the reader should consult other chapters of this book).

- *Liveness detection* techniques mobilise physiological indications of liveness to distinguish real (living) biometric features from fake ones. Dedicated scanners can detect characteristics peculiar to living features (e.g. perspiration from a genuine fingerprint); alternatively, the original signal derived from a feature can be analysed to detect patterns distinguishing fakes (e.g. skin exhibits different reflectance patterns to representations of skin, such as photographs).
- *Challenge-response* techniques are, in a sense, a form of liveness detection. The user is challenged to perform an action deemed to distinguish their genuine feature from a fake. Using a facial recognition system, for instance, a person may have to blink a certain number of times (distinguishing them from, e.g., a photograph).
- Combining biometric modalities—*Multi-modality*—increases the number of features a spoofer must replicate: the more modalities, the more difficult a successful attack becomes (to spoof two or more modalities requires more resources, wider know-how, etc.).
- Some modalities may be *inherently robust to spoofing attacks*. For instance, electrophysiological modalities (EEG, ECG) are difficult to spoof because the patterns on which they rely are inaccessible without specialist equipment. Such modalities

---

[2] On the societal and ethical impact of biometrics in ageing societies see [3].

[3] TABULA RASA—"Trusted Biometrics Under Spoofing Attacks"—is funded by the European Commission under the Seventh Framework Programme (Grant Agreement no. 257289; http://www.tabularasa-euproject.org/). It aims to: address the need for a draft set of standards to examine the problem of spoofing; propose countermeasures to spoofing attacks; and to examine novel biometrics that may be inherently robust to direct attacks.

are not impossible to spoof, but the "barriers to entry" for the spoofer are higher than with some other modalities.

It is interesting to note that the latter two techniques can be considered "countermeasures" only by taking that word in a broad sense (one might justifiably consider them as of interest simply in terms of their use as reliable identifiers). That they are currently considered countermeasures tells us something interesting about the history and development of biometrics and anti-spoofing—and about its possible future.[4] As the field develops, it is possible that anti-spoofing countermeasures will achieve the status of entirely unremarkable, standard components of biometric systems. If that happens, what it *means* to use a biometric will change from (putting it crudely) *comparing two representations of a feature* to a more complicated process involving forms of feature verification such as, say, liveness detection. This theme is not our focus here, yet it is worth highlighting because of its connection with much of the discussion to follow.

## 13.2 Ethical Issues Raised by Anti-spoofing Countermeasures

Anti-spoofing techniques raise ethical questions that, while undoubtedly related, are independent of those raised by biometrics in general. This chapter is concerned with ethical issues raised by anti-spoofing countermeasures, rather than by biometrics per se.

### *13.2.1 Privacy, Intimacy and Integrity*

This section addresses issues arising from the capacity of anti-spoofing techniques to capture and process data which may be considered—in two senses to be articulated below—"intimate". As a preliminary, however, two clarifications are in order.

Our topic in this section is, broadly, *privacy*. The scholarly literature on privacy is wide, interdisciplinary and complex. It features disagreement as to what privacy-protection measures are in order, but also on the foundational matter of what privacy *is*. Legal scholar Daniel Solove has written:

> Privacy [...] is a concept in disarray. Nobody can articulate what it means. [It] is a sweeping concept, encompassing (among other things) freedom of thought, control over one's body, solitude in one's home, control over personal information, freedom from surveillance, protection of one's reputation and protection from searches and interrogation [5], p. 1.

For present purposes, we may bypass much of this uncertainty. Our scope is considerably more focussed. Thus, the first clarification serves to narrow our focus from privacy in general to specific aspects concerning, in particular, intimacy.

---

[4] Anti-spoofing research is not in itself new (e.g. [4]). The increasing prominence of the field is presumably connected with more widespread use of biometric systems, and the increasingly serious consequences of identity fraud.

The second clarification serves, by contrast, to caution against too restricted focus: while this section is concerned with instances of data processing, it in no way follows that the questions at stake relate solely to data protection. The question of data protection with respect to biometric systems is interesting, and anti-spoofing techniques can certainly aggravate those issues.[5] Yet the focus of this section (indeed of the chapter as a whole) is more encompassing. When discussing intimacy, the question will not be of whether there is a (potential) breach of data protection legislation, but of *if*, *when* and *how* the gathering of intimate data may be ethically acceptable.

Clarifications in place, let's turn to the question of intimacy. The word "intimate" (in its adjectival sense) stems from the Latin *intimus* (meaning "inmost"), from whence we derive its contemporary meaning (or one of them) of *deeply personal*. A potential problem with some anti-spoofing techniques then, is that they rely for their efficacy on the exploitation of data which could be considered intimate in that sense.

Data might be considered deeply personal if they get to (or approach) the heart of who or how someone is.[6] Data potentially revealing of medical information are deeply personal in this way: generally speaking, if others inquire too closely after your medical information, they do you a harm. Similarly, data revealing of certain lifestyle choices are, for the most part, protected by ethical and legal norms: except in certain specific circumstances (a court of law perhaps), one's sex life, dietary habits and so on, are nobody else's business. This is partly motivated by the attempt to prevent discrimination, but is also motivated by the very personal nature of such data.

There are two senses in which these kinds of information are intimate. In one sense, their intimate nature stems from a natural concern a person may have for the kind information others may know about them. The thought that information about one's sex life (say) is no one else's business is based on the premise that others do not have a legitimate claim to access that information. In another sense, however, intimacy can be based on norms concerning the kind of physical access a person is prepared to allow others. The wearing of certain clothes, the drawing of curtains and the closing of doors all protect intimacy by imposing a physical barrier between an intimate thing and those who would otherwise see, touch or access it. These two senses concern, respectively, ways in which *psychological* and *physical* integrity can be violated.

With this distinction in mind, it is clear that anti-spoofing raises issues of intimacy. Countermeasures may well exploit intimate data and information. Liveness detection techniques may process data which, even if not directly revealing of one's medical status, is nonetheless related to it. (After all, techniques such as pulse oximetry derive from medical techniques.) Now, to reiterate, the point is not to do with the nature of medical data in itself. It is rather that persons may well consider such information intimate, and hence hold that its use constitutes an alarming deviation from a broadly acceptable status quo. The data is intimate both in the sense that others do not

---

[5] In the Europe Union, the Data Protection Directive (95/46/EC) sets the legal framework for the processing of personal data. Data protection with respect to anti-spoofing is discussed in [6].

[6] Or of *what* someone is. The above-mentioned critiques of van der Ploeg and Agamben raise, in different ways, this question.

(except in specific circumstances) normally have a legitimate claim to access it; and in the sense that it derives from normally inaccessible (e.g. subdermal) parts of the body. Accessing such data could constitute an affront to a person's psychological and/or physical integrity (quite independently of the status of such data with respect to data protection legislation).

Similar concerns attend all anti-spoofing techniques. For some challenge-response techniques—namely those involving actions provoking a physiological reaction (e.g. whitening of the finger)—the critique is the same. For challenge-response techniques based intentional behavioural responses (e.g. blinking on demand) there is a possibility of revealing of an abnormality. Some abnormalities—particularly, but not only, medical conditions—are liable to be considered intimate. Note that this is irrespective of whether those conditions are physically apparent. In cases such as some forms of arthritis or nystagmus, it is not the fact that others can know of the condition that is ethically relevant, but rather the fact that the data on which such knowledge would be based is the specific focus of—i.e. is singled out by—the challenge-response procedure. Hence the point of such medical examples is not to promote special measures *in such cases*, but to demonstrate that intimacy and integrity are at issue *in all cases* (whether medical conditions or other abnormalities are involved or not).

Arguments of these kinds apply to countermeasures exploiting modalities considered inherently robust to spoofing attacks. Behavioural modalities (e.g. gait) are potentially indicative of unusual mobility or agility; modalities based on internal physiology (e.g. vein or electrophysiological patterns) are intimate in that others cannot normally physically access them and, even if they could, do not have a legitimate claim to be able to (other things being equal).

The use of multi-modality raises a variation on the arguments above. Multi-modal biometrics may cause an affront to intimacy and integrity by gathering *too much* data (what constitutes "too much" is likely to be contentious.) A problem of proportionality raises its head here: processing a great deal of data may be a disproportionate response to the challenges posed by a particular context of deployment.[7] Once again, the ethical problem is not so much amount of data processing per se, but the fact that in interrogating several modalities, a biometric system is liable to be felt by an individual (or more generally by a group) as examining them unacceptably closely—as constituting an unwanted and unwarranted intrusion into a person's sphere of intimacy. To violate that sphere is to violate a person's integrity (physical, psychological or both).

Not all entries into one's personal, private sphere are threats to integrity. After all, as a noun, the word "intimate" denotes those whom we welcome into our private lives. Intimacy is an integral part of personhood (the inability to foster it is pathological). We also invite other persons (not normally described as "intimates") into our private spheres for quite specific reasons: most obviously in relation to healthcare, but also

---

[7] Whether the question of proportionality is considered from the perspectives of ethics or (as is commonplace) data protection, what is at stake is the proportionality of the identification system *as a whole* (rather than of the anti-spoofing component in isolation). On this see [6].

in the fields of finance, legal matters and education (to pick up an earlier example, a doctor's directing her full attention to one's arthritis or nystagmus does not undermine one's integrity). Thus we manage intimacy, integrity, and privacy through norms of appropriate behaviour which are responsive to two major factors: context and consent.[8] These major factors are open to change and development: consent can be revoked; *context*—particularly, but not only, insofar as it concerns sociocultural interactions among individuals and larger groups — is an extremely dynamic concept. The ways in which technologies are experienced within a community can change, as can that community itself as technologies become embedded in its ways of life. As anti-spoofing technologies become more commonplace, it will be necessary to regularly revisit their role and acceptability in society. This is a very complex but necessary task.

## *13.2.2 Autonomy and Choice*

Autonomy is, broadly speaking, the capacity of an individual to make decisions of their own, free from coercion. More specifically, those decisions should be both free and *informed*. Here we focus on the latter condition.

The basic of the shape of the problem is this: to identify a person is to perform an operation affecting them in certain ways. Respect for autonomy demands that the administrators of an identification system should provide the person with sufficient information that they can make a reasonable assessment of the potential consequences, and on that basis decide whether to go ahead with the identification. A number of problems arise. First, consequences can never be known with complete comprehensiveness or precision; hence there are limits to how well the administrator could possibly inform a person or target group. Second, the administrator cannot reasonably be held responsible for all possible consequences; hence their responsibility to inform target groups of those consequences is diminished. Third, various background factors are present, including legal requirements. These may differ from case to case (e.g. legal requirements are different in different jurisdictions; requirements are different in civil, medical, military, law-enforcement and aviation contexts). Fourth, the level of information required to sufficiently inform one target group may differ—possibly wildly—from that required to sufficiently inform another. Fifth, an effective means of communicating information to one target group may be not be an effective means of informing another.

Since these issues concern all identification systems (biometric or not), our focus here is only on the question of how much information administrators or vendors should be expected to provide in relation to anti-spoofing techniques.

Information provided to data subjects cannot be too technical. Currently, most people have no expertise in biometrics, hence to provide them with technical details

---

[8] On the relationship between privacy and context see the work of Helen Nissenbaum, notably [7].

would be overwhelming, probably uninteresting, and possibly counterproductive. Giving too little information is problematic, but so is giving too much. Efforts should therefore be made to identify, for each modality, what we might call "core information", which can be easily communicated and understood, and which explains the process of being identified by that modality. For example, with respect to fingerprint, there is no real need to provide details about ridge patterns or particular algorithms: that level of precision will not increase people's understanding so markedly as to offset the difficulty of the explanation. The "core information" to be given in relation to fingerprint might include, instead, some simple facts about the procedure for scanning a finger and the matching of fingerprints.[9] Once the core information relating to a modality has been established, it can be judged whether the addition of an anti-spoofing measure would involve the use of data, or activities, which are not adequately explained by the core information. For example, suppose a liveness detection procedure involves detecting a pulse. If it is deemed (a) that information concerning this kind of procedure should in principle be communicated to users, and (b) it is not already part of the core information, then users should be provided with additional information. Or again, if a challenge-response measure involves an activity not normally considered part of engaging with a particular sensor, then if the requirement that the user performing that action is not already covered by the core information, users ought to be given further information.

As spoofing becomes an increasingly prominent issue, it will be necessary to reconsider what kinds of procedures are considered "standard" in the use of any particular modality (and hence what the "core information" provided to users should be). After all, anti-spoofing need not only be seen as a security-enhancing measure: it can also be seen as aimed at improving system performance.[10] This is particularly clear for multi-modality and inherently robust modalities: the line between data processing specifically aimed at identification and aimed at security is almost—if not completely—indistinguishable. Anti-spoofing measures—particularly those that are "invisible" to the user (e.g. liveness detection, which requires no user cooperation)—may well, over time, come to appear as "normal" steps in the process of biometric identification. Developments of this kind touch on the way in which a society—and groups and individuals within it—*understand* biometrics, anti-spoofing, and what it *means* to live with those technologies. In considering such developments, it is essential to attempt to understand what is (and what is perceived, at the societal level) a "normal" engagement with a biometric system, and how anti-spoofing technologies possibly upset that status quo. It is then necessary to find an appropriate compromise between the need to not overload users with technical information and the necessity of informing users if sensitive (e.g. private or intimate) data is used.

---

[9] Efforts towards standardisation in this area would be valuable.

[10] Referring to anti-spoofing only as a security measure reflects, and contributes to, important societal narratives concerning security, suspicion, risk and so on. This is discussed in [6].

## 13.2.3 Acceptability, Fairness and Non-discrimination

This section concerns the societal acceptability of anti-spoofing technologies. Two sorts of cases will detain us: the acceptability of countermeasures in particular cultural contexts; and the potential of countermeasures to be unfair to, or to discriminate against, particular groups.

A biometric system's societal acceptability is a function of many factors—the authors of [8] (to take just one example) identify several, including how accustomed users are to biometric technologies and whether there is a human in attendance overseeing use of the system. They write that "Different biometrics are acceptable in applications deployed in different demographics depending on the cultural, ethical, social, religious, and hygienic standards of that society" (p. 17). Such considerations obviously apply also in the case of anti-spoofing. In some instances, a countermeasure may be presumed societally acceptable on the assumption that the system of which it is a component is acceptable. If an already acceptable deployment of a fingerprint scanner (for an ATM machine, say) incorporates liveness detection measures that place no further burden on the user—the user experience is effectively the same—the countermeasure is likely to be acceptable.[11] Yet the implementation of multimodal systems, or those based on inherently robust modalities, should be carefully assessed.[12] Consider also that acceptability may increase or decrease over time.

The related problems of fairness and discrimination concern instances where a system leaves particular users either un- or less able to use it. This poses a challenge to anti-spoofing technologies (though by no means a unique one[13]): as far as possible, countermeasures should rely only on data or abilities that all people can provide or carry out. In some cases this will require that, say, an inherently robust modality is not deployed on its own—or that if it is, reasonable alternatives, which are unlikely to single out those partaking of them as unusual, should be provided. Or it may require that challenge-response measures are deployed with sensitivity to the capacities of those likely to encounter them. Requesting a blink as a countermeasure for either facial recognition or iris systems is likely to be a good fit for a laptop-login: most users will be able to use that system, and those who cannot will typically have other options (e.g. traditional passwords, voice-recognition options, etc.). But that same technique would likely be an unsuitable countermeasure for a system managing access to a service for the visually impaired.

This suggests a general mitigation strategy: namely, close attention to contextual details. When a biometric system is deployed in a given scenario, that scenario should be carefully analysed to identify any factors that may influence the system's acceptability. In particular, it must be considered whether the anti-spoofing countermeasures

---

[11] Depending on whether and what further data processing is involved.

[12] Users may deem new modalities unacceptable or unpalatable if they are unfamiliar, or simply not a good fit for that society. Fingerprint may be acceptable in a society, but enhancing robustness by adding face as a second modality may be unacceptable (e.g. in societies where many people routinely cover their faces).

[13] It occurs with any biometric system because no modality is 100 in ageing societies, see [3, 9].

raise any issues or tensions not raised by the biometric system itself. If so, other anti-spoofing measures may be more suitable.

### 13.2.4 Openness, Convenience and Security

How open should stakeholders in the biometrics community—academic researchers, industrial and commercial researchers, vendors of systems, organisations and individuals deploying systems—be about vulnerabilities to spoofing, and the effectiveness of countermeasures?

Transparency and openness are, for the most part, positive (as discussed above, they can promote autonomy in decision-making). It is important to distinguish openness and honesty. Naturally, all pronouncements about spoofing and countermeasures should be honest—lies are unacceptable.[14] But none of this implies any prima facie obligation to *actively* reveal *all* information about vulnerabilities, or about the effectiveness of countermeasures. The right sort of information should be made available to the appropriate stakeholders.

Vendors of systems and countermeasures have a duty to be openned about the vulnerabilities of systems they sell. Research in the TABULA RASA project arrived at the following suggestion:

> Vendors should make available to customers sufficient information regarding security and vulnerabilities that the customer is able to make a well-informed judgment as to whether the system in question is a good fit for the specific context(s) in which they intend to deploy it.[15]

This implies a dual responsibility. The vendor must provide sufficient information to the customer. But the customer also needs a very clear understanding of their actual requirements. Measuring the vulnerability of a biometric device—or the effectiveness of a countermeasure—is extremely difficult due to the importance of contextual factors (particularly considering that such factors are not static, but change over time). Thus, the customer must identify relevant factors: the amount of human supervision expected, other (non-biometric) relevant security measures, cultural norms influencing acceptability and so on.

Commercial researchers may have legitimate reasons for not advertising their findings. Perhaps revealing the vulnerabilities and poor performance of an emerging modality would undermine its potential market. There are ethically legitimate economic justifications for not releasing such findings (e.g. consequentialist analyses of long-term implications) *so long as* the systems or devices in question are not yet on the market or otherwise in use. Similar considerations may apply to academic researchers, although they may strike a different balance between the commercial implications of publishing findings and the potential benefit to the scientific

---

[14] Whether lying is always and everywhere unacceptable—whether, were it so, this would apply also to spoofing—is addressed in [6].

[15] See TABULA RASA's "Ethical Guidelines" (Deliverable D7.5; Sect. 9.3), Rebera and Mordini [3] at: http://www.tabularasa-euproject.org/.

community. The guiding and underlying principle is this: if a biometric system or anti-spoofing countermeasure is at the stage at which it is likely to affect people (i.e. by being used), then:

1. those people affected by it ought to have the means of discovering how it is likely to impact them;
2. those people or organisations deploying it ought to have access to details concerning its vulnerabilities and the effectiveness of any countermeasures.

The two points above have the form of claim rights and, as such, impose corresponding duties upon researchers, vendors and deployers of systems and countermeasures to make the appropriate information available to the appropriate stakeholders.

As discussed above, it must be understood that quantifying system vulnerabilities and countermeasure effectiveness are *extremely* complicated. Absolute precision is impossible. Hence suitable standards for comparing countermeasures are urgently needed.

## 13.3 Conclusion: Should Anti-spoofing Countermeasures be Compulsory?

Identity theft and fraud are widespread problems with serious consequences. This being so, one might suppose that, since anti-spoofing countermeasures enhance security against identity fraud, such measures should be mandatory, at least in some circumstances.

As a blanket measure, the above suggestion is incorrect. There is no need to demand the routine inclusion of countermeasures in *all* biometric systems. To aid discussion, it may help to have an example in mind. The recent controversy over Apple's iPhone 5S—the fingerprint sensor of which was spoofed within two days of the phone's going on sale—will serve.

Like any other mobile phone, the iPhone requires security measures to ensure that only the owner is able to access its applications and content. A standard security feature is a numerical code, chosen by the owner, which they key in to unlock the phone. Some versions of the iPhone 5S come equipped with "Touch ID", a fingerprint sensor managing user authentication. Users can enrol up to five fingerprints, which can then be used to access to the phone itself and the user's iTunes account (for purchasing music, films, etc.). All fingerprint data is stored on the phone itself and, according to Apple's head of software, cannot be retrieved from it. Two days after the worldwide release of the iPhone 5S, a German group called the *Chaos Computer Club* announced that they had successfully spoofed their way into an iPhone 5S, using a fingerprint lifted from a glass surface and transposed onto a cover that could be worn over another person's finger.[16]

---

[16] Details of this story can be found across the media. The comment from Apple's head of software is taken from: http://www.theguardian.com/technology/2013/sep/22/apple-iphone-fingerprint-scanner-hacked.

The spoofing of the iPhone 5S's fingerprint sensor caused a media furore; but, in the end, it is difficult to conclude from the episode that the fingerprint sensor is any less secure than the traditional numerical code logon. The procedure for spoofing a fingerprint is one of the simplest spoofing methods, yet it is considerably more complicated, and requires far greater technical know-how, than the most likely form of "spoofing" to which a numerical code logon is vulnerable (namely, surreptitious observation of the user's code[17]). Additionally—and this is the issue with which this chapter will close—the episode again shows something about the importance of *context* in anti-spoofing and, consequently, that responsibility for security lies not only with technology providers, but also partly with every other actor in a given scenario.

It is difficult to overestimate the importance of contextual factors in assessing a countermeasure's suitability. In terms of security, to decide on the most fitting countermeasure, at a minimum the person or organisation deploying the biometric system should understand:

- what asset the system manages access to, and what value that asset has;
- what would be the consequences of illegitimate access to the asset;
- who might have an interest in gaining illegitimate access to the asset;
- how difficult (in general) it would be to gain illegitimate access to the asset;
- what other security features are in place in the scenarios (e.g. physical locks and blocks, human supervision, etc.).

And with respect to ethics, in addition to the above, the following should be understood:

- the balance of proportionality between the sensitivity of the data gathered and the value of the asset (i.e. does the nature of the asset justify the use of the countermeasures involved?);
- what ethical, legal or policy standards and frameworks are in place in the envisaged scenario, and how are they to be complied with;
- which groups are likely to use the system and which if any of them are likely to be singled out by it (e.g. minors, people with disabilities, etc.);
- background sociopolitical, cultural or historical factors—in particular those liable to influence the perceived acceptability of the system and countermeasure (e.g. a history of political opposition to a certain form of identification system).[18]

From all these factors, it is clear that in some cases a person or organisation deploying a biometric system would be (to some extent) morally culpable if they failed to provide reasonable anti-spoofing protection.[19] For example, a system managing access to a critical infrastructure facility (a nuclear plant, say) requires very

---

[17] Consider also that if one loses one's phone, the person finding it could, in theory, guess a numerical code (supposing they cannot hack into the phone), but they cannot guess a fingerprint.

[18] These contextual factors are discussed in the TABULA RASA project's "Ethical Guidelines" (Deliverable D7.5).

[19] Primary responsibility presumably resides with the spoofer.

robust anti-spoofing protection because the consequences of illegitimate access are potentially massive. In that scenario, it would be enormously irresponsible to deploy a system vulnerable to relatively low-cost, low-tech spoofing attacks.[20] On the other hand, in many cases security requirements are far lower. As we move down that scale, it becomes increasingly apparent that users are themselves (partly) responsible for using technology in ways that do not place themselves or others at risk.[21]

Mobile phone users need secure devices to prevent unauthorised access and, more particularly, because they store (or access) private information on them.[22] But phones are used very frequently. From the beginning then, users have two requirements: security and convenience. Phone providers will aim to provide, as default, a balance between the two.

For smartphones, arguably an appropriate balance would be somewhat as follows. Primary access should be secure, but not at a significant cost to convenience (either by slowing access time or sapping processing power). But if that is the case, then other features within the phone which could be abused should be given additional protection. Sometimes this is standard: you can use your smartphone to access a bank account but access is subjected to further security checks (administered by the bank). In other cases, further security is not standard (e.g. accessing contact lists, or, in the iPhone 5S case, accessing the iTunes store).[23] As mentioned above, users must take some responsibility for their own security behaviour—by, for example, ensuring that any sensitive data (e.g. a professional email account) is suitably protected. Thus, when attributing moral responsibility and liability for the consequences of fraud or other malicious acts resulting from spoofing, key issues will always include:

- whether the provider provided a system adequately robust to spoofing attacks (the concept of "adequacy" is to be analysed through examination of relevant contextual factors, including as realistic as possible a vulnerability assessment);
- whether the user could reasonably has been expected to understand the threat from spoofing and its potential consequences. In some cases, such an understanding should be actively promoted by the provider: in others it falls under "common sense" (but this is an *extremely* difficult matter, particularly with respect to new and emerging technologies);
- whether the user brought additional vulnerability upon themselves through the way they used the system (or the tool or asset the system managed access to).

---

[20] Of course matters are more complicated than this. To take just one very simple example, it would be irresponsible to deploy an extremely secure system without adequately training people in its correct operation.

[21] Compare personal responsibility for online safety: regulators, ISPs and website administrators all have some responsibility—but so do individuals.

[22] This shows how societal understanding of technologies evolves. Mobiles are no longer mere communication devices, but can be used for computing, storing data, accessing services, mobile payments and more.

[23] An important further consideration is that access to one service or data set can often result in access to others. For example, access to an online store account could yield a great deal of personal and financial information.

This chapter surveyed ethical issues arising from the development and deployment of anti-spoofing countermeasures. It focused on issues of: privacy, intimacy and integrity; autonomy and choice; acceptability, fairness and non-discrimination; openness, convenience and security. A key and recurrent factor has been the importance of the background contexts into which anti-spoofing technologies are introduced. Understanding which countermeasures are most appropriate in a given case, and what are the ethical risks associated, is a matter of close attention to those contexts. Of course contexts are complicated things. They are dynamic and different threads within them unravel at different speeds. Significantly, researchers attempting to analyse contexts are no more independent of those contexts than are the technologies which provoke the analyses in the first place.

Anti-spoofing raises several ethical issues in addition to those raised by biometrics in general. Perhaps one of the most difficult, intriguing and important of these concerns the relationship between countermeasures and systems. Are countermeasures additional complements to systems, or integral components? How will that relationship evolve? Will anti-spoofing become standard in biometric identification? And, most importantly, what does all of this mean for the people and groups that have to live with biometric technologies? The first step in addressing ethical issues raised by anti-spoofing technologies is to identify the live issues affecting us all at present. This chapter has been a contribution to that task. The second step is to identify, track and solve the ethical issues that may and will appear in the future. That very difficult task is ongoing.

**Acknowledgments** This work has been partly funded through the European Commission Framework Programme 7 (FP7) project TABULA RASA: Trusted Biometrics under Spoofing Attacks (Grant Agreement no. 257289).

# References

1. van der Ploeg I (2003) Biometrics and the body as information: Normative issues in the socio-technical coding of the body. In: Lyon D (ed) Surveillance as social sorting: privacy, risk, and automated discrimination. Routledge, London, pp 57–73
2. Agamben G (2008) No to biopolitical tattooing. Commun Crit/Cult Stud 5(2):201–202
3. Rebera AP, Mordini E (2013) Biometrics and ageing: social and ethical considerations. In: Fairhurst M (ed) Age factors in biometric processing. The Institute of Engineering and Technology, London, pp 37–62
4. Lummis RC, Rosenberg AE (1972) Test of an automatic speaker verification method with intensively trained mimics (a). J Acoust Soc America 51(1A):131–132
5. Solove DJ (2008) Understanding privacy. Harvard University Press, Cambridge
6. Andrew P, Rebera Matteo E, Bonfanti SV (2013) Societal and ethical implications of anti-spoofing technologies in biometrics. Sci Eng Ethics . doi: 10.1007/s11948-013-9440-9(In press)
7. Nissenbaum H (2010) Privacy in context: technology, policy, and the integrity of social life. Stanford Law Books, Stanford
8. Anil K Jain, Ruud Bolle SP (1999) Introduction to biometrics. In: Jain K , Ruud Bolle SP (ed.) Biometrics: Personal Identification in Networked Society, Springer, New York, pp 1–42
9. Rebera AP, Guihen B (2012) Biometrics for an ageing society. In: Brömme CBA (ed) BIOSIG 2012 proceedings. Gesellschaft fr Informatik, Bonn, pp 409–416

# Appendix A
# Evaluation Databases

Stan Z Li, Javier Galbally, André Anjos and Sébastien Marcel

## A.1 Introduction

"*In God we trust; all others must bring data*". This quote commonly attributed to William Edwards Deming[1] may be applied to any machine learning or pattern recognition problem, however, it is specially true for the biometric technology due to the variety of knowledge areas that it covers, which require large amounts of data and specific evaluation protocols.

Certainly, one of the key challenges faced nowadays by this rapidly evolving technology is the need for new public standard datasets that permit the objective and statistical evaluation of the different aspects related to biometric recognition systems (e.g., performance, security, interoperability or privacy). This is particularly relevant for the assessment of spoofing attacks and their corresponding anti-spoofing protection methodologies.

In the field of spoofing, only quite recently the biometric community has started to devote some important efforts to the acquisition of large and statistically meaningful anti-spoofing databases. In most cases, these datasets have been captured in the

---

[1] (W.E.D, 1900–1993). On the Web, this quote has been widely attributed to Deming, however, as stated in the introduction of [1].

S.Z. Li
Center for Biometrics and Security Research and National Laboratory
of Pattern Recognition, Institute of Automation, Chinese Academy
of Sciences, Shanghai, China
e-mail: szli@nlpr.ia.ac.cn

J. Galbally
Biometric Recognition Group—ATVS, Universidad Autonoma
de Madrid, Madrid, Spain
e-mail: javier.galbally@uam.es

A. Anjos · S. Marcel
Idiap Research Institute, rue Marconi 19, 1920 Martigny, Switzerland
e-mail: marcel@idiap.ch

© Springer-Verlag London 2014
S. Marcel et al. (eds.), *Handbook of Biometric Anti-Spoofing*,
Advances in Computer Vision and Pattern Recognition,
DOI: 10.1007/978-1-4471-6524-8

framework of international competitions such as the series of Fingerprint Liveness Detection Competitions, LivDet, held biannually since 2009, or the more recent 2-D Face Anti-Spoofing contests that started in 2011. These, and a few others, are very valuable examples of the way to proceed in order to further develop the security capabilities of biometric systems, since they provide a public and common benchmark where developers and researchers can objectively evaluate their proposed anti-spoofing solutions and compare them in a fair manner to other existing approaches.

However, in spite of the patent interest that the biometric community has shown over the last recent years in the study of the vulnerabilities of this technology to spoofing attacks, the availability of such anti-spoofing databases is still scarce. These lack of data may be explained both from a technical and a legal point of view: (i) From a technical perspective, the acquisition of spoofing-related data presents an added challenge to the usual difficulties encountered in the acquisition of standard biometric databases (i.e., time-consuming, expensive, human resources needed, cooperation from the donors...): the generation of a large amount of fake artifacts which are in many cases tedious and slow to generate on large scale (e.g., gummy finger, printed iris lenses, face videos); (ii) The legal issues related to data protection are controversial and make the sharing and distribution of biometric databases among different research groups or industries very tedious and difficult. These legal restrictions have forced most laboratories working in the field of spoofing to acquire their own proprietary (and usually small) datasets on which to evaluate their protection methods. Although these are very valuable efforts, they have a limited impact, since the results may not be compared or reproduced by other institutions.

The present appendix is a summary of the current publicly available anti-spoofing databases that may be used for the development of new and efficient protection measures against direct attacks. Only the fingerprint, face and iris traits are considered in the chapter since, for the other modalities, although different studies related to spoofing can be found in the literatures, to the best of our knowledge no public datasets have been released.

## A.2 Fingerprint Anti-spoofing Databases

### A.2.1 Fake Fingerprint Generation

Before describing the most widely used fake fingerprint databases which are publicly available, and in order to help to understand their structure, we believe it is useful to present here a brief summary of the most common techniques used for the generation of gummy fingers.

The creation of fake fingers is in almost all cases carried out following one of three procedures depending on the starting point of the manufacturing process:

- *Starting from the user's finger* This method is also known as "cooperative" and further reading may be found for instance in [2, 3]. In this case, the legitimate user

Appendix A: Evaluation Databases

is asked to place his finger on a moldable and stable material in order to obtain the negative of the fingerprint. In a posterior step the gummy finger is recovered from the negative mold. The different typical steps performed in the generation process are depicted in Fig. A.1.

- *Starting from a latent fingerprint* This method is also referred to in many publications as "non-cooperative" and was first introduced in [4]. In this case the first step is to recover a latent fingerprint that the user has unnoticedly left behind (e.g., on a CD). The latent fingerprint is lifted using a specialized fingerprint development toolkit and then digitalized with a scanner. The scanned image is then enhanced through image processing and finally printed on a PCB from which the gummy finger is generated. The typical main steps of this non-cooperative process are depicted in Fig. A.2.
- *Starting from a minutiae template* This possibility was studied for the first time in [5]. In this case the first step is to reconstruct the fingerprint image from a compromised minutiae template of the user following one of the algorithms described in the literature [6, 7]. Once the digital image has been reconstructed, the gummy finger is generated using a PCB in an analogue way to the non-cooperative method described above.

Currently we can find four large fingerprint anti-spoofing databases where most of the attacks cited above may be found for a variety of sensors and for different materials of the gummy fingers: the ATVS-FFp DB and the three databases corresponding to the series of Fingerprint Liveness Detection competitions (LivDet) held in 2009, 2011 and 2013.

## A.2.2 ATVS-FFp DB

The ATVS-FFp DB [3] is publicly available at the ATVS-Biometric Recognition Group website.[2]

It comprises real and fake fingerprint images coming from the index and middle fingers of both hands of 17 users ($17 \times 4 = 68$ different fingers). For each real finger, two gummy fingers were created with modeling silicone following a cooperative and non-cooperative process as described in Sect. A.2.1.

Four samples of each fingerprint (fake and real) were captured in one acquisition session with three different sensors of the most widely spread acquisition technologies currently available:

- Flat optical sensor Biometrika FX2000 (569 dpi, image size $312 \times 372$).
- Flat capacitive sensor by Precise Biometrics model Precise 100 SC (500 dpi, image size $300 \times 300$).
- Sweeping thermal sensor by Yubee with Atmel's Fingerchip (500 dpi, image size $232 \times 412$).

---

[2] http://atvs.ii.uam.es/.

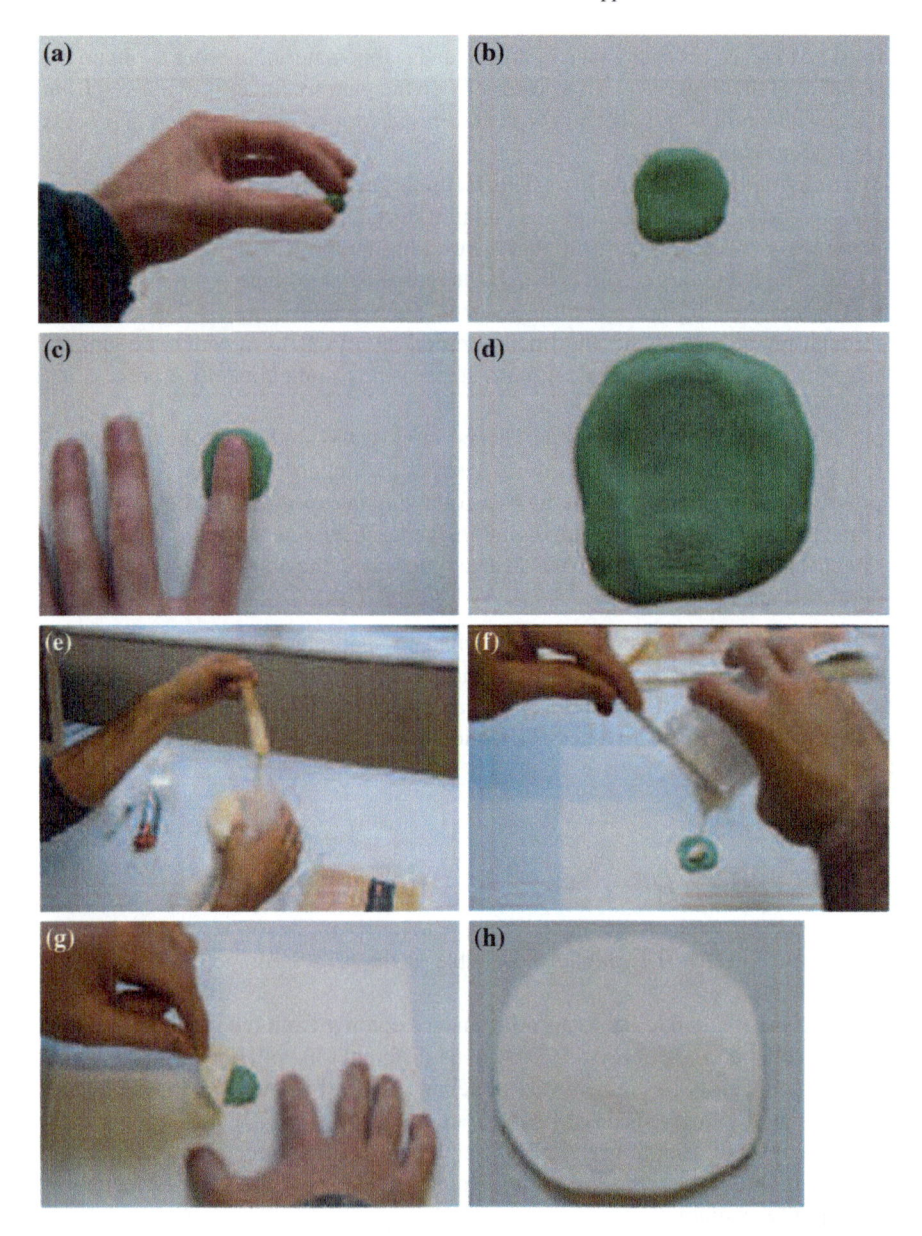

**Fig. A.1** Typical process followed to generate silicone fake fingerprints with the cooperation of the user: select the amount of moldable material (**a**), spread it on a piece of paper (**b**), place the finger on it and press (**c**), negative of the fingerprint (**d**). Mix the silicone and the catalyst (**e**), pour it on the negative (**f**), wait for it to harden and lift it (**g**), fake fingerprint (**h**)

Appendix A: Evaluation Databases 251

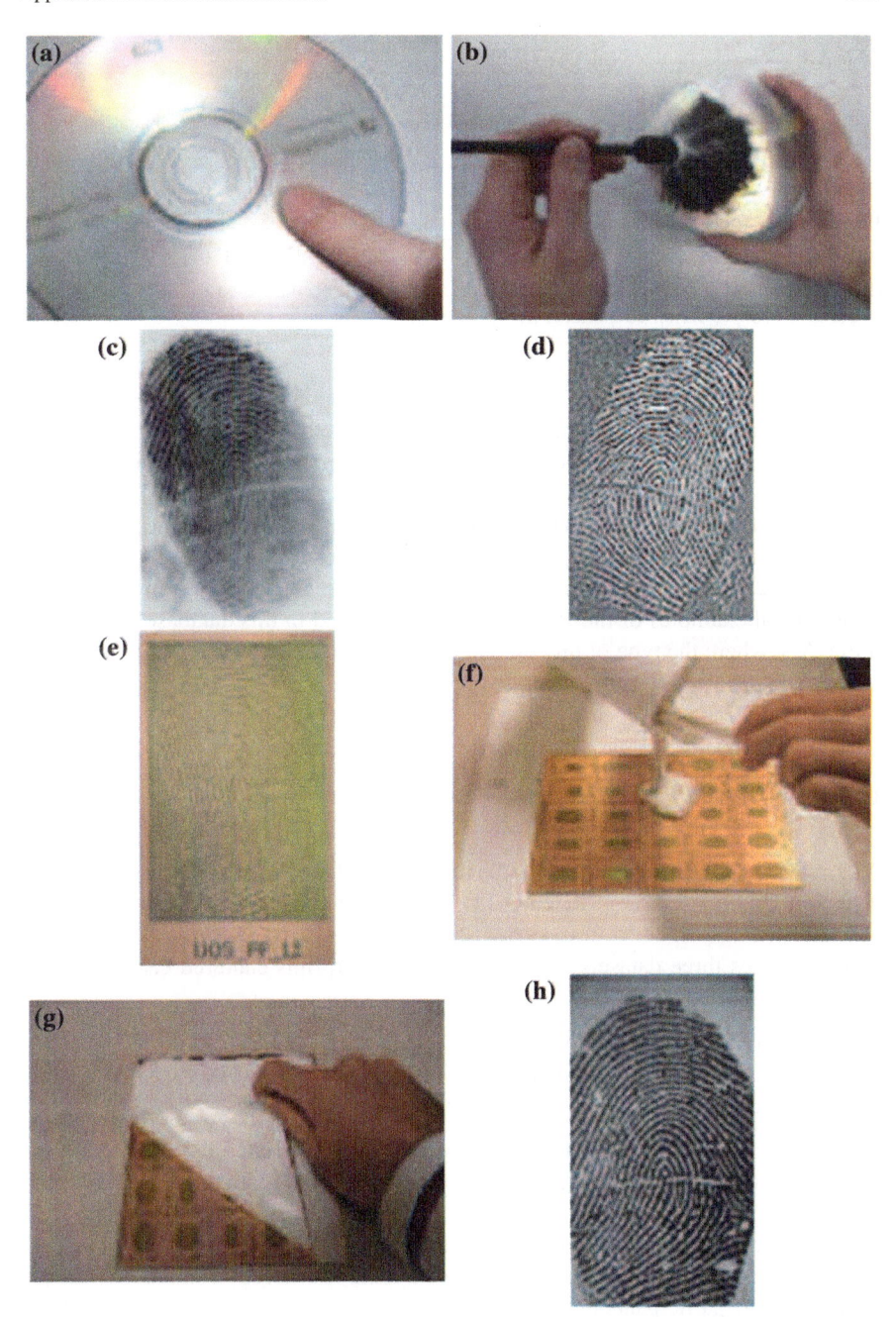

**Fig. A.2** Typical process followed to generate silicone fake fingerprints without the cooperation of the user: latent fingerprint left on a CD (**a**), lift the latent fingerprint (**b**), scan the lifted fingerprint (**c**), enhance the scanned image (**d**), print fingerprint on PCB (**e**), pour the silicone and catalyst mixture on the PCB (**f**), wait for it to harden and lift it (**g**), fake fingerprint image acquired with the resulting gummy finger on an optical sensor (**h**)

**Table A.1** General structure of the ATVS-FFp DB

|  | ATVS-FFp DB |  |  |  |
|---|---|---|---|---|
|  | Real/Fake (#Train = #Test) |  | Fakes generation |  |
|  | # Fingers | # Samples | *Coop* | *No-Coop* |
| Biometrika FX2000 (569 dpi) | 68/68 | 272/272 | 136 | 136 |
| Precise SC100 (500 dpi) | 68/68 | 272/272 | 136 | 136 |
| Yubee (500 dpi) | 68/68 | 272/272 | 136 | 136 |

The distribution of the fake images is given in terms of the procedure used for their generation: cooperative (*Coop*), or non-cooperative (*No-Coop*).

Thus, the database comprises 68 fingers ×4 samples ×3 sensors = 816 real image samples and as many fake images for each scenario (with and without cooperation). In order to ensure inter- and intra-class variability, samples of the same finger were not captured consecutively.

The database is divided into a train and test set which contain half of the fingerprint images with no overlap between them (i.e., samples corresponding to each user are just included in one of the sets), and their general structure is given in Table A.1. Some typical examples of the images that can be found in this database are shown in Fig. A.3, where the type of process used for the generation of the gummy fingers is given (cooperative or non-cooperative).

## A.2.3 LivDet 2009 DB

The LivDet 2009 DB was acquired in the framework of the First Fingerprint Liveness Detection Competition held in 2009 [8], and is publicly available at the contest website.[3]

It comprises three datasets of real and fake fingerprints captured each of them with a different flat optical sensor:

- Flat optical, Biometrika FX2000 (569 dpi, image size 312 × 372).
- Flat optical, CrossMatch Verifier 300CL (500 dpi, image size 480 × 640).
- Flat optical, Identix DFR2100 (686 dpi, image size 720 × 720).

The gummy fingers were generated using three different materials: gelatine, play-doh and silicone, following always a consensual procedure (with the cooperation of the user).

The train and test sets of this database are the same as the ones used in the LivDet 2009 competition so that the results achieved on it may be directly compared to those obtained by the participants in the contest.

The train and test sets comprise over 5,000 samples coming from around 100 different fingers (depending on the dataset). The general distribution of the fingerprint

---

[3] http://prag.diee.unica.it/LivDet09/.

Appendix A: Evaluation Databases 253

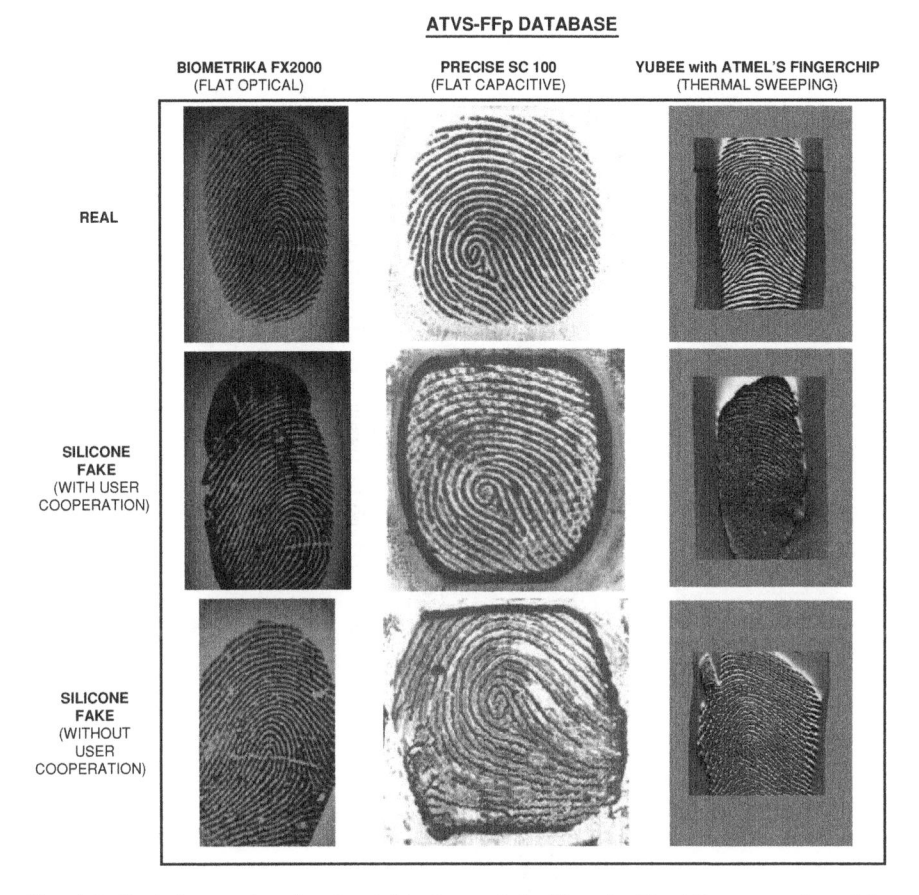

**Fig. A.3** Typical examples of real and fake (generated with and without the cooperation of the user) fingerprint images that can be found in the public ATVS-FFp DB

images between both sets is given in Table A.2, where the number of real and fake fingers/samples and the material used for the generation of the gummy fingers are specified.

Some typical examples of the images that can be found in this database are shown in Fig. A.4, where the material used for the generation of the fake fingers is given (gelatine, playdoh or silicone).

## A.2.4 *LivDet 2011 DB*

The second Fingerprint Liveness Detection Competition was held in 2011 [9]. For this competition a new database, the LivDet 2011 DB, was acquired as extension of

**Table A.2** General structure of the LivDet 2009 DB

|  | LivDet 2009 DB | | | | | |
|---|---|---|---|---|---|---|
|  | Train (Real/Fake) | | | Test (Real/Fake) | | |
|  | # Fingers | # Samples | | # Fingers | # Samples | |
| Biometrika FX2000 (569 dpi) | 13/13 | 520/520s | | 39/13 | 1473/1480s | |
| CrossMatch Verifier 300CL (500 dpi) | 35/35 | 1000/1000 (344g+346p+310s) | | 100/35 | 3000/3000 (1036g+1034p+930s) | |
| Identix DFR2100 (686 dpi) | 63/35 | 750/750 (250g+250p+250s) | | 100/35 | 2250/2250 (750g+750p+750s) | |

The distribution of the fake samples is given in terms of the materials used for their generation: $g$ stands for gelatin, $p$ for playdoh and $s$ for silicone

Appendix A: Evaluation Databases 255

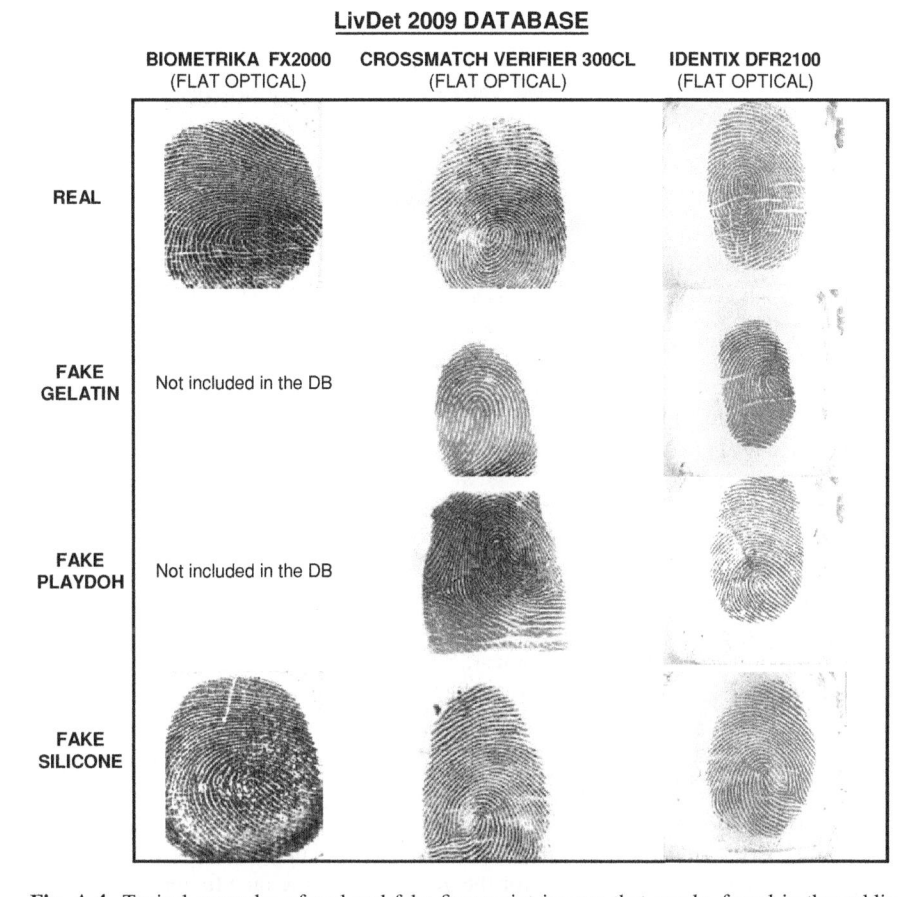

**Fig. A.4** Typical examples of real and fake fingerprint images that can be found in the public LivDet 2009 DB. A *blank space* in the figure means that the corresponding fake type is not present in the database

the previous LivDet 2009 DB (see Sect. A.2.3), and is currently publicly available through the competition website.[4]

The LivDet 2011 DB comprises four datasets of real and fake fingerprints captured each of them with a different flat optical sensor. The resolution of some of the sensors (Biometrika and Digital Parsona) was slightly modified in order to have the same value across all four datasets (500 dpi). This way, the impact of the variation of the fingerprint image size on the performance of the tested anti-spoofing algorithms may be estimated:

- Flat optical, Biometrika FX2000 (569 dpi → 500 dpi, image size 312 × 372).
- Flat optical, Digital Persona 4000B (512 dpi → 500 dpi, image size 355 × 391).

---

[4] http://people.clarkson.edu/projects/biosal/fingerprint/index.php.

**Table A.3** General structure of the LivDet 2011 DB (# denotes "number of")

| | LivDet 2011 DB | | | | | | | |
|---|---|---|---|---|---|---|---|---|
| | Real/Fake (#train = #test) | | Material fakes (#train = #test) | | | | | |
| | # Fingers | # Samples | e | g | l | p | s | w |
| Biometrika FX2000 (500 dpi) | 100/20 | 1,000/1,000 | 200 | 200 | 200 | | 200 | 200 |
| Digital Persona 4000B (500 dpi) | 100/20 | 1,000/1,000 | | 200 | 200 | 200 | 200 | 200 |
| ItalData ET10 (500 dpi) | 100/20 | 1,000/1,000 | 200 | 200 | 200 | | 200 | 200 |
| Sagem MSO300 (500 dpi) | 56/40 | 1,000/1,000 | | 200 | 200 | 200 | 200 | 200 |

The distribution of the fake samples is given in terms of the materials used for their generation: $e$ stands for ecoflex, $g$ for gelatin, $l$ for latex, $p$ for playdoh, $s$ for silicone and $w$ for wood glue

- Flat optical, Italdata ET10 (500 dpi, image size 640 × 480).
- Flat optical, Sagem MSO300 (500 dpi, image size 352 × 384).

The gummy fingers were generated following a consensual procedure using six different materials: ecoflex (platinum-catalysed silicone) gelatine, latex, playdoh, silicone and wood glue.

The train and test sets of this database are the same as the ones used in the LivDet 2011 competition so that the results achieved on it may be directly compared to those obtained by the participants in the contest.

The train and test sets comprise over 8,000 samples coming from around 200 different fingers (depending on the dataset). The general distribution of the fingerprint images between both sets is given in Table A.3, where the number of real and fake fingers/samples and the material used for the generation of the gummy fingers are specified.

Some typical examples of the images that can be found in this database are shown in Fig. A.5, where the material used for the generation of the fake fingers is given.

## A.2.5 LivDet 2013 DB

During the writing of this book the LivDet 2013 edition was being held. The DB used in the evaluation will be made public on the website of the competition once the final results are published.[5] Although part of the information may not be fully accurate (especially that related to the test set which has still not been released), we present here a summary of the most important features of the database.

The LivDet 2013 DB comprises four datasets of real and fake fingerprints captured with three different flat optical sensors and a thermal sweeping scanner:

- Flat optical, Biometrika FX2000 (569 dpi, image size 312 × 372).
- Flat optical, Italdata ET10 (500 dpi, image size 640 × 480).

---
[5] http://prag.diee.unica.it/fldc/.

Appendix A: Evaluation Databases 257

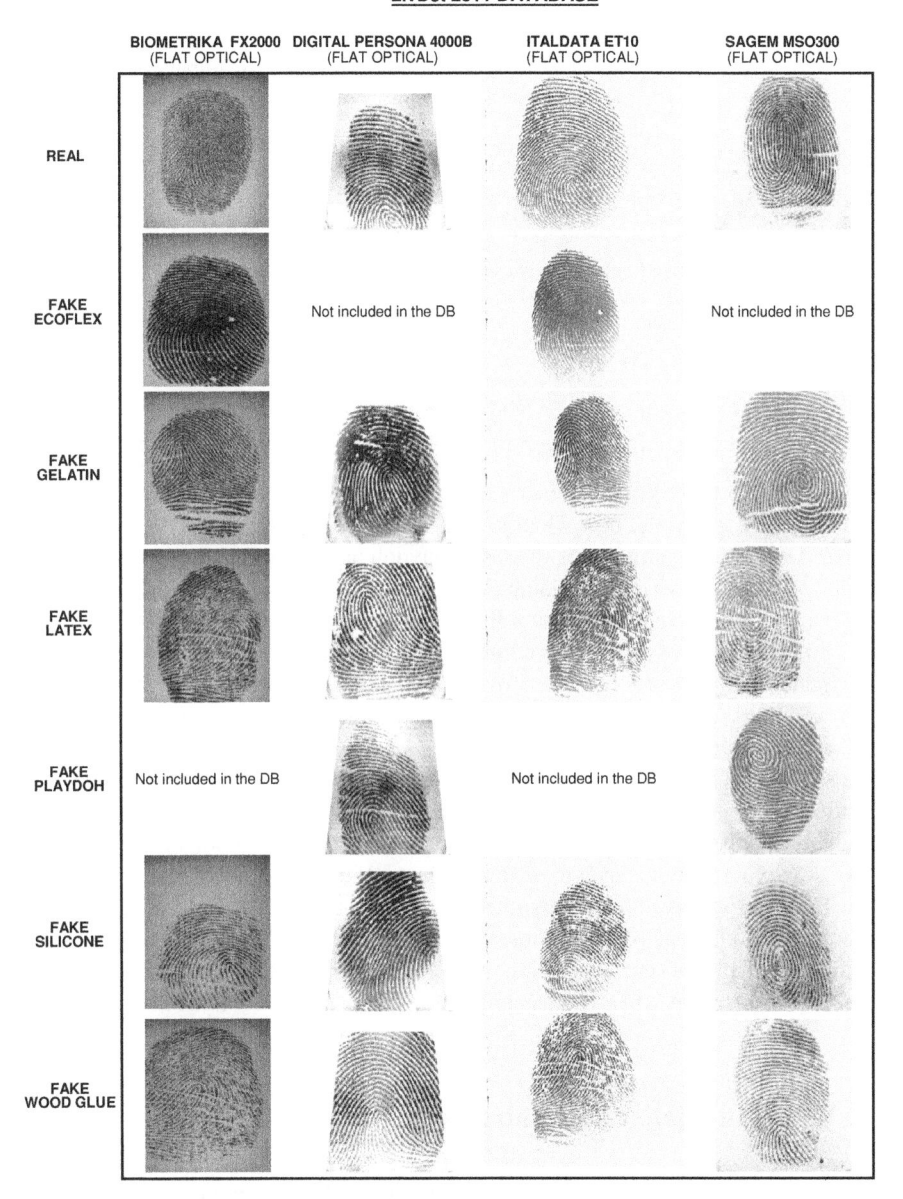

**Fig. A.5** Typical examples of real and fake fingerprint images that can be found in the public LivDet 2011 DB. A *blank space* in the figure means that the corresponding fake type is not present in the database

**Table A.4** General structure of the LivDet 2013 DB (# denotes "number of")

| | LivDet 2013 DB | | | | | | | |
|---|---|---|---|---|---|---|---|---|
| | Real/Fake (#train = #test) | | Material fakes (#train = #test) | | | | | |
| | # Fingers | # Samples | b | e | g | l | m | p | w |
| Biometrika FX2000 (569 dpi) | 200/50 | 1,000/1,000 | | 200 | 200 | 200 | | 200 | 200 |
| ItalData ET10 (500 dpi) | 500/125 | 1,250/1,000 | 250 | | 250 | | 250 | 250 | |
| CrossMatch L SCAN (500 dpi) | 200/50 | 1,000/1,000 | | 200 | 200 | 200 | | 200 | 200 |
| Atmel Fingerchip (96 dpi) | 250/125 | 1,250/1,000 | 250 | | 250 | | 250 | 250 | |

The distribution of the fake samples is given in terms of the materials used for their generation: *b* stands for body-double silicone, *e* for ecoflex silicone, *g* for gelatin, *l* for latex, *m* for modasil, *p* for playdoh and *w* for wood glue

- Flat optical, CrossMatch L SCAN Guardian (500 dpi, image size 640 × 480).
- Thermal sweeping, Atmel Fingerchip (96 dpi, image size not available).

The gummy fingers were generated following a consensual procedure using seven different materials: body-double skin-safe silicone rubber, ecoflex platinum-catalysed silicone, gelatin, latex, modasil, playdoh and wood glue.

The train and test sets of this database are the same as the ones used in the LivDet 2013 competition so that the results achieved on it may be directly compared to those obtained by the participants in the contest.

The train and test sets comprise over 8,000 samples coming from around 200 different fingers (depending on the dataset). The general distribution of the fingerprint images between both sets is given in Table A.4, where the number of real and fake fingers/samples and the material used for the generation of the gummy fingers are specified.

Some typical examples of the images that can be found in this database are shown in Fig. A.6, where the material used for the generation of the fake fingers is given.

In Table A.5 we present a comparative of the most important features of the four fingerprint spoofing databases previously presented: the ATVS-FFp DB (Sect. A.2.2), and the three databases corresponding to the series of Fingerprint Liveness Detection Competitions, LivDet 2009, 2011 and 2013 (Sects. A.2.3, A.2.4 and A.2.5).

## A.3 Face Anti-spoofing Databases

As in the previous section we will present here a very brief summary of the studied most common direct attacks to face recognition systems, which may help to understand the rationale behind the design and structure of the presented face anti-spoofing databases.

The vast majority of face spoofing attacks may be classified in one of three groups:

- *Photo-Attacks* These fraudulent access attempts are carried out presenting to the recognition system a photograph of the genuine user. This image may be printed

Appendix A: Evaluation Databases

**LivDet 2013 DATABASE**

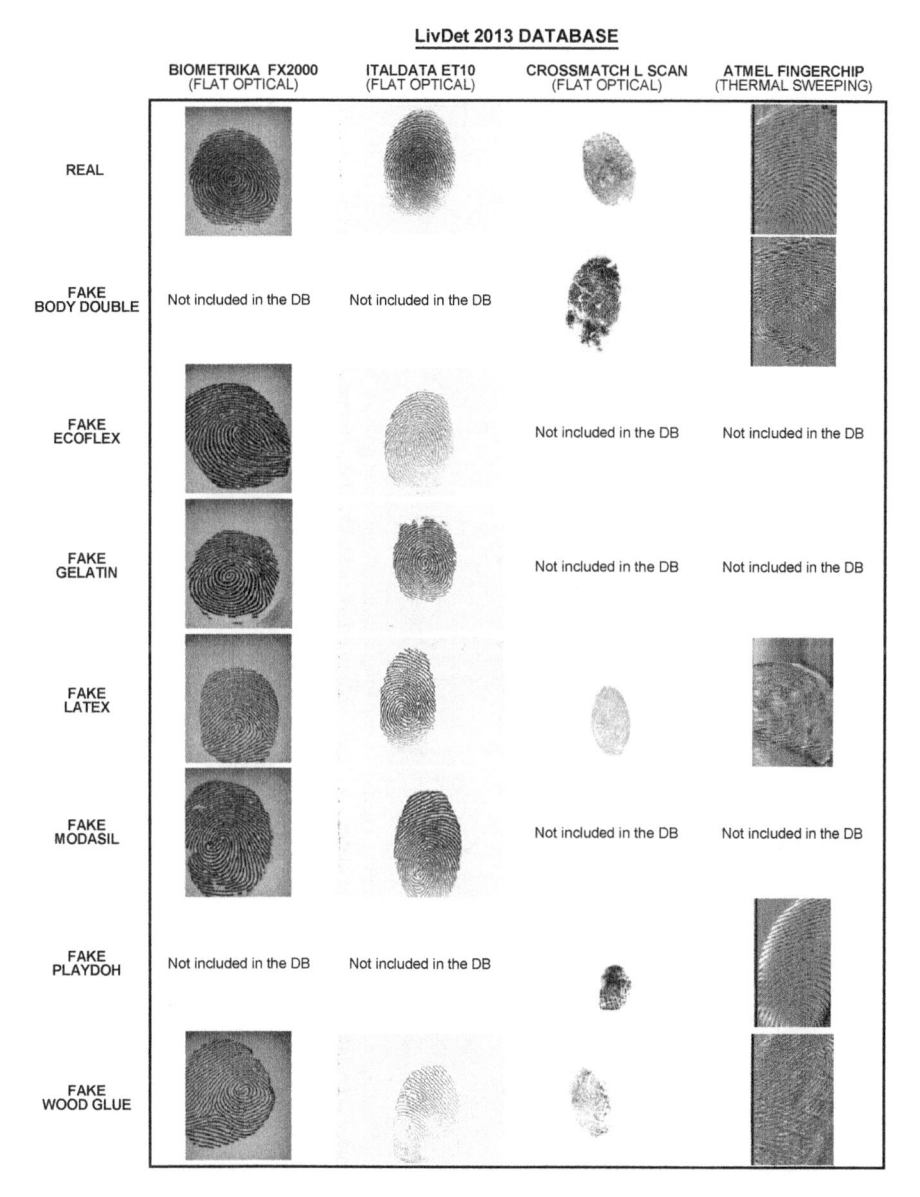

**Fig. A.6** Typical examples of real and fake fingerprint images that can be found in the public LivDet 2013 DB. A *blank space* in the figure means that the corresponding fake type is not present in the database

**Table A.5** Comparative of the most relevant features corresponding to the four fingerprint spoofing databases described in the present Annex

| | Overall Info. (Real/Fake) | | Sensor Info. | | | | Fakes Generation | | Fakes Material | | | | | | | |
|---|---|---|---|---|---|---|---|---|---|---|---|---|---|---|---|---|
| | # Fingers | # Samples | # Sensors | FO | FC | ST | Coop | N-Coop | b | e | g | l | m | p | s | w |
| ATVS-FFp DB | 68/68 | 816/816 | 3 | ✓ | ✓ | ✓ | ✓ | ✓ | | | | | | | ✓ | |
| LivDet 2009 DB | 100/35 | 5,500/5,500 | 3 | ✓ | | | ✓ | | | | ✓ | | | | ✓ | |
| LivDet 2011 DB | 200/50 | 8,000/8,000 | 4 | ✓ | | | ✓ | | | ✓ | ✓ | ✓ | | | ✓ | ✓ |
| LivDet 2013 DB | 500/125 | 9,000/8,000 | 4 | | | ✓ | ✓ | | ✓ | ✓ | ✓ | ✓ | ✓ | ✓ | | ✓ |

*FO* stands for Flat Optical, *FC* for Flat Capacitive, *ST* for Sweeping Thermal, *Coop* for cooperative generation process, *N-Coop* for non-cooperative generation process, *b* for body-double silicone, *e* for ecoflex silicone, *g* for gelatin, *l* for latex, *m* for modasil, *p* for playdoh, *s* for non-specific silicone and *w* for wood glue

Appendix A: Evaluation Databases                                                                                                       261

on a paper (i.e., print attacks) or may be displayed on the screen of a digital device such as a mobile phone or a tablet (i.e., digital-photograph attacks) [10, 11].

- *Video-Attacks* Also referred to in some cases as *replay-attacks*. In these type of spoofing attempts the attacker, instead of using a still image, he replays a video of the genuine client using a digital device (e.g., mobile phone, tablet or laptop)[12, 13].
- *Mask-Attacks* These are far less common than the previous two types and are only starting to be systematically studied. In these cases the spoofing artifact is a 3-D mask (e.g., self crafted with silicone) of the genuine client face [14]. Although there are some companies where you can get such a face 3-D model for a reasonable price,[6] self-manufacturing this type of masks is in general fairly difficult and time consuming. An alternative that has also been studied is the use of photographic-masks, which are high resolution printed photographs where the eyes and the mouth have been cut out, and the impostor is placed behind [15].

In addition, all the previous types of attacks have a number of variants depending on the resolution (quality) of the attack device, the type of support used to present the fake copy (e.g., handheld or fixed support), or the type of external variability allowed (e.g., illumination or background). Currently there are four large public face anti-spooofing databases. They are: the NUAA Photo Imposter database, the Replay (Photo, Print) Attack databases, the CASIA Face Anti-Spoofing database and the 3D Mask Attack (3DMAD) database.

### A.3.1 NUAA PI DB

The NUAA Photo Imposter Database[7] is available from on request through the corresponding author's of [11]. The database was built using a generic unspecified webcam that captured photo attacks and real-accesses to 15 different identities. The database is divided in three sesssions with different illumination conditions, as shown in Fig. A.7. The amount of data among sessions is unbalanced as not all the subjects participated in the three acquisition campaigns.

In all sessions, participants were asked to look frontally to the web camera, posing a neutral expression and avoiding eye blinks or head movements so that it resembles a photo as much as possible. The webcam would then record for about 25 s at 20 fps from which a set of frames is hand-picked for the database. The original video sequence is not distributed with the database. Bitmap images are available instead of each of the hand-picked frames from the database.

Attacks were generated by first collecting high (unspecified) definition photos for each subject using a Canon camera of unspecified model, in such a way that the face would take about 2/3 of whole photograph area available. Photos were then printed on photographic paper with dimensions 6.8 cm x 10.2 cm (small) and 8.9 cm

---

[6] http://www.thatsmyface.com/.
[7] http://parnec.nuaa.edu.cn/xtan/NUAAImposterDB_download.html.

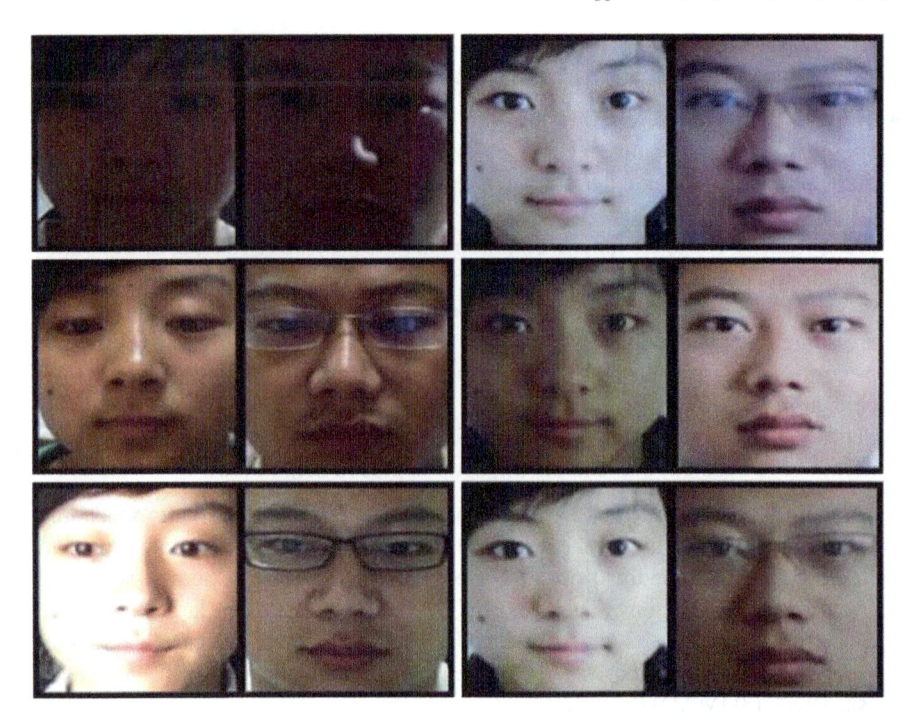

**Fig. A.7** Samples from the NUAA Photo Imposter Database, extracted from [11]. In each column (from *top to bottom*) samples are respectively from *session 1*, *session 2* and *session 3*. In each row, the *left pair* are from a live human and the *right* from a photo. Note that it contains variability commonly encountered by a face recognition system (e.g., gender, illumination or glasses). All original images in the database are color pictures with the same definition of 640×480 pixels

x 12.7 cm (bigger) using a traditional development method or on a 70 g white A4 paper using an unspecified Hewlet-Packard color printer. The three samples are then used to create photo attacks by moving the photo during the capture, as indicated on Fig. A.8. Table A.6 summarizes the number of images and main characteristics per session.

### A.3.1.1 Protocols

The NUAA Photo Imposter Database is decomposed into two sets, one for training and another for testing. Images for the training set are those coming from Sessions 1 and 2 exclusively, which contains data for the first nine clients. A total of 3,491 images are available from which 1,743 represent real-accesses while 1,748, photo attacks containing different warping. The test set makes use of the remaining 9,123 images from Session 3 and therefore, does not overlap with the training set. The test set contains real-access data (3,362 images) from the other remaing six clients, but also for some clients from the training set. The attack data for the test set contains

Appendix A: Evaluation Databases

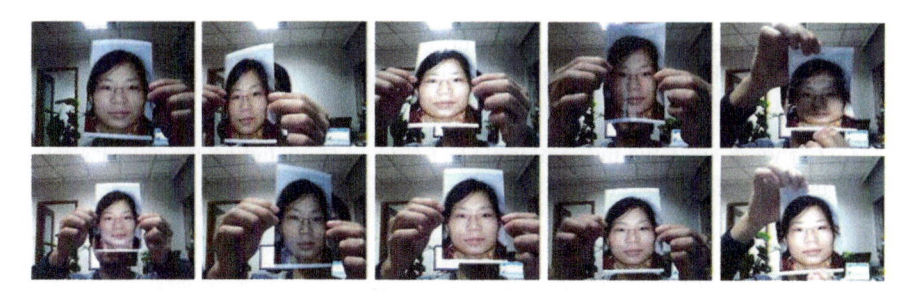

**Fig. A.8** Attack samples from the NUAA Photo Imposter Database, extracted from [11]. From *left* to *right*, we show examples of attacks generated by: (*1*) moving the photo *horizontally*, *vertically*, *back* and *front*; (*2*) rotating the photo in depth along the *vertical axis*; (*3*) the same as (*2*) but along the *horizontal axis*; (*4*) bending the photo *inward* and *outward* along the *vertical axis*; (*5*) the same as (*4*) but along the *horizontal axis*

**Table A.6** General structure of the NUAA PI DB

|  | NUAA PI DB |  |  |  |  |
|---|---|---|---|---|---|
|  | Overall Info. (train/test) |  | # Images per session (train/test) |  |  |
|  | # Users | # Images | Session 1 | Session 2 | Session 3 |
| Real accesses | 15 (9/9) | 5,105 (1,743/3,362) | 889 (889/0) | 854 (854/0) | 3,362 (0/3,362) |
| Print-Attacks | 15 (9/15) | 7,509 (1,748/5,761) | 855 (855/0) | 893 (893/0) | 5,761 (0/5,761) |

5,761 images with an even larger mix of data from clients also available in the training set.

No development set is available on this database, which makes comparative tunning of machine learning algorithms difficult. Prior work [12, 16, 17] overcame this limitation by implementing cross-validation based only on the training data. To do so, the training data is divided into (almost) equally sized subsets and classifiers are trained by grouping together four of the subsets and leaving one out, that is finally used to tune and evaluate the classification performance. The classifier that achieves the best classification performance on the folded training set is then selected and finally evaluated on the test set.

Performance characterisation using the NUAA Photo Imposter Database is not imposed as part of the training and testing protocol, though database proponents reported results using the Area Under the ROC Curve (AUC) obtained while evaluating classification schemes *uniquely* on the test set.

The data is distributed in three folders which contain:

1. the raw picture (in JPEG format), with size 640 × 480 pixels as output by the webcam;
2. the face cropped by the author's own Viola-Jones face detector (also in JPEG format), with variable bounding-box size; and, finally

3. the face cropped (as above), but also normalized to a size of 64 × 64 in which detected eyes have a fixed position (in Bitmap format). The resulting crops are also gray-scaled to eight bits precision.

Most of work available in literature [11, 12, 16, 17], including the author's reference use the pre-cropped data.

## A.3.2 The Replay Attack Database Family

The Replay-Attack Database[8] [12] and its subsets (the Print-Attack Database [18] and the Photo-Attack Database [19]) are face anti-spoofing databases consisting of short video recordings of about 10 s of both real-access and spoofing attacks to a face recognition system. This was the first database to support the study of motion-based antispoofing techniques. This database was used on the 2011 and 2013 Competition on Countermeasures to 2-D Facial Spoofing Attacks [20, 21].

Samples were recorded from 50 different identities. The full database contains spoofing attempts encompassing three major categories of most intuitive attacks to face recognition systems:

- Print-Attacks: attacks with photograps printed on a paper;
- Photo attacks: digital photographs displayed on a screen of an electronic device;
- Video attacks: video clips replayed on a screen of an electronical device.

Depending on the subset utilized, one has access to the three types of attacks, the first one (Print-Attack subset) or the first two (Photo-Attack subset). To create the real accesses available in the database each person recorded three video clips at two different stationary conditions:

- controlled: In this case the background of the scene is uniform and the light of a fluorescent lamp illuminates the scene;
- adverse: In this case the background of the scene is non-uniform and day-light illuminates the scene.

Under these two different conditions, people were asked to sit down in front of a custom acquisition system built on an Apple 13-inch MacBook laptop and capture two video sequences with a resolution of 320 by 240 pixels (QVGA), at 25 fps and of 15 s each (375 frames). Videos were recorded using Apple's Quicktime format (MOV files).

The laptop was positioned on the top of a small support (approx. 15 cm in height, like shown in Fig. A.9) so that faces are captured as they look up-front. The acquisition operator launches the capturing program and asks the person to look into the laptop camera as they would normally do waiting for a recognition system to do its task. The program shows a reproduction of the current image being captured and, overlaid, the

---

[8] http://www.idiap.ch/dataset/replayattack.

Appendix A: Evaluation Databases

**Fig. A.9** Setup used for the acquisition of real-accesses for the Replay-Attack database

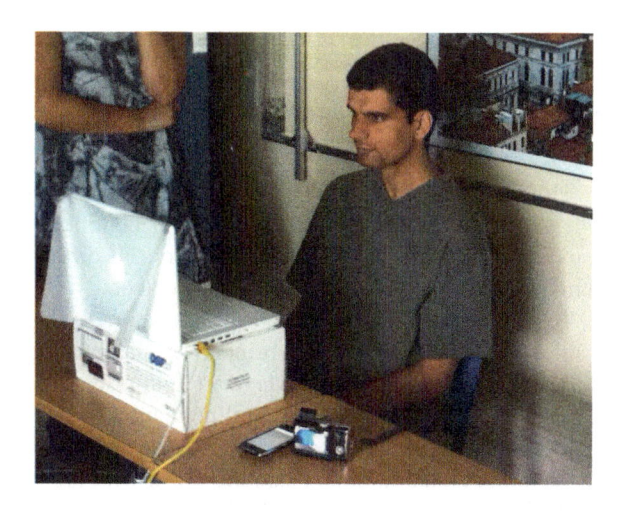

output of a face-detector used to guide the person during the session. In this particular setup, faces are detected using a cascade of classifiers based on a variant of Local Binary Patterns (LBP) [22] referred as Modified Census Transform (MCT) [23]. The face-detector helps the user self-adjusting the distance from the laptop camera and making sure that a face can be detected at most times during the acquisition. After acquisition was finished, the operator would still verify the videos did not contain problems by visual inspection and proceed to acquire the next video. This procedure is repeated three times for each of the stationary conditions described above, making up a total number of six real accesses (videos) per client.

In order to create the attacks, photographs and video clips needed to be recorded. The photographs were used as a basis for generating print and photo attacks, while the videos were used as a basis for preparing the video attacks. To record this extra data to prepare the attacks, the acquisition operator took two photographs and two video clips of each person in each of the two illumination and background settings used for recording the real accesses. The first photograph/video clip was recorded using iPhone 3GS (3.1 megapixel camera) and the second using a high-resolution 12.1 megapixel Canon PowerShot SX200 IS camera. People were asked to cooperate in this process so as to maximize the chances of an attack to succeed. They were asked to look up-front like in the acquisition of the real-access attempts. Finally, attacks were generated by displaying the taken photographs and video clips on a particular attack media in front of the aquisition system. The aquisition system for recording the spoofing attacks is identical to the one used for recording the real accesses.

The forged attacks are executed so that the border of the display media is not visible in the final video clips of spoofing attacks. This was done to avoid any bias on frame detection for algorithms that are developed and tested with this database. Furthermore, each spoofing attack video clip is recorded for about 10 s in two different attack modes:

- hand-based attacks: in this mode, the operator holds the attack media using their own hands;
- fixed-support attacks: the operator sets the attack media on a fixed support so they don't do involuntary movements during the spoof attempt.

The first set of (hand-based) attacks show a shaking behavior that can be observed when people hold photographs of spoofed identities in front of cameras and that, sometimes, can trick eye-blinking detectors. It differs from the second set that is completely static and should be easier to detect.

To generate the print attacks, the operator displays hard copies of the high-resolution digital photographs printed on plain A4 paper using a Triumph-Adler DCC 2520 color laser printer. There are four print-attacks per client, corresponding to two tries under the two different illumination conditions. Digital photo and video attacks are generated by displaying either the iPhone sample on the iPhone screen or the high-resolution digital samples taken with the 12.1 megapixel camera using an iPad screen with resolution (1,024 by 768 pixels). Figure A.10 shows examples of attacks in the different conditions explored by the Replay Attack Database.

#### A.3.2.1 Protocols

A total of 1,300 video clips is distributed with the database. From those, 300 correspond to real-accesses (3 trials in two different conditions for each of the 50 clients). The first trial for every client and condition is put apart to train, tune and evaluate face verification systems. The remaining 200 real-accesses and 1,000 attack video clips are arranged into different protocols that can be used to train, tune and evaluate binary anti-spoofing classifiers. Identities for each subset were chosen randomly but do not overlap, i.e. people that are on one of the subsets do not appear in any other set. This choice guarantees that specific behavior (such as eye-blinking patterns or head-poses) are not picked up by detectors and final systems can generalize

**Fig. A.10** Example attacks in different scenarios and with different lighting conditions. On the *top* row, attacks in the controlled scenario. At the *bottom*, attacks with samples from the adverse scenario. Columns from *left* to *right* show examples of real accesses, hard-print, photo and video attacks

Appendix A: Evaluation Databases

better. Identities between the verification protocol and anti-spoofing protocols match —i.e., identities on available on the training set of the verification protocol match the ones available on a training set in any of the anti-spoofing protocols available with the dataset. The same is true for any other subset. This feature is an important characteristic of the Replay Attack Database, allowing it to be used for the combined operation of anti-spoofing and face verification systems [21] (see also Chap. 12 "Evaluation Methodologies").

One of six so-called "Anti-spoofing Protocols" can be used when simple binary classification of spoofing attacks is required. The protocols are associated with specific conditions, specific type of attack, specific devices used to perform the attack or different types of support for the attacks. Each anti-spoofing protocol in the database contains the 200 videos of real-accesses plus different types of attacks as indicated on Table A.7.

Face annotations (bounding-boxes) automatically annotated by a cascade of classifiers based on a variant of Local Binary Patterns (LBP) referred as Modified Census Transform (MCT) [23] are also provided. The automatic face localisation procedure works detects faces in more than 99 % of the total number of frames acquired.

In the case developed counter-measures requires training, it is recommended that training and development samples are used to train classifiers how to discriminate. One trivial example is to use the training set for training the classifier itself and the development data to estimate when to stop training. A second possibility, which may generalize less well, is to merge both training and development sets, using the merged set as training data and to formulate a stop criteria. Finally, the test set should be **solely** used to report error rates and performance curves. If a single number is desired, a threshold $\tau$ should be chosen at the development set and the Half-Total Error Rate (HTER) reported using the test set data. As means of uniformizing reports, we recommend choosing the threshold $\tau$ on the Equal Error Rate (EER) at the development set.

Table A.7 Number of attack videos in the six different anti-spoofing protocols provided by the Replay-Attack database

| Protocol | Hand attack (train/dev/test) | Fixed support (train/dev/test) | All supports (train/dev/test) | References |
|---|---|---|---|---|
| Print | 30/30/40 | 30/30/40 | 60/60/80 | [18] |
| Mobile | 60/60/80 | 60/60/80 | 120/120/160 | |
| Highdef | 60/60/80 | 60/60/80 | 120/120/160 | |
| Photo | 90/90/120 | 90/90/120 | 180/180/240 | [19] |
| Video | 60/60/80 | 60/60/80 | 120/120/160 | |
| Grantest | 150/150/200 | 150/150/200 | 300/300/400 | [12] |

On the right of the table, references to prior work that introduced specific studies with those protocols

## A.3.3 The CASIA Face Anti-spoofing Database

The CASIA Face Anti-Spoofing Database[9] [13] (CASIA-FASD) introduces face attacks with a varying degree of imaging quality. It is a database that poses the spoofing detection as a binary classification task like the NUAA Photo Imposter Database described on Sect. A.3.1. Contrary to the later, this database provides video files allowing for the exploration of texture, motion or fusion techniques for anti-spoofing.

As indicated by the authors, quality is a factor that may influence the quality of anti-spoofing, especially facial texture analysis based methods. The database contains data from 50 real clients, collected through three different devices with varying quality as shown in Fig. A.11:

- low quality: captured using an old USB camera of unspecified brand, which acquires low quality videos with a resolution of $640 \times 480$ pixels;
- normal quality: captured using a new USB camera of unspecified brand with a better image quality (but also with a resolution of $640 \times 480$ pixels;
- high quality: captured using a Sony NEX-5 with a resolution of $1{,}920 \times 180$ pixels.

Real-accesses (genuine) videos are captured in natural scenes with no artificial environment unification. Subjects are required to blink during data taking as authors indicate that facial motion is crucial for liveness detection as in [18, 19]. Spoofing attacks are generated following 3 different strategies as shown in Fig. A.12:

- Warped photo attacks: one frame is hand-picked from the high resolution videos collected with the Sony camera for every subject and printed on copper paper, keeping a better quality than that which can be obtained on A4 printing paper, avoiding print marks that can be seen on [18]. In this type of attack, the attacker

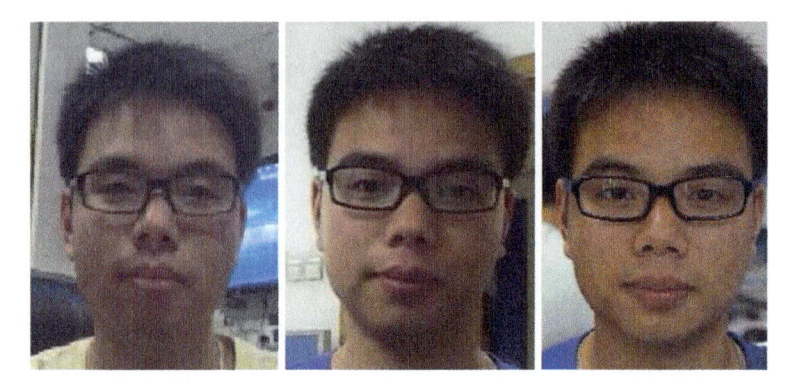

**Fig. A.11** Samples showing low, normal and high quality, from *left* to *right*, captured used to create the attacks and real-accesses for the CASIA-FASD, from [13]

---

[9] http://www.cbsr.ia.ac.cn/english/FaceAntiSpoofDatabases.asp.

Appendix A: Evaluation Databases

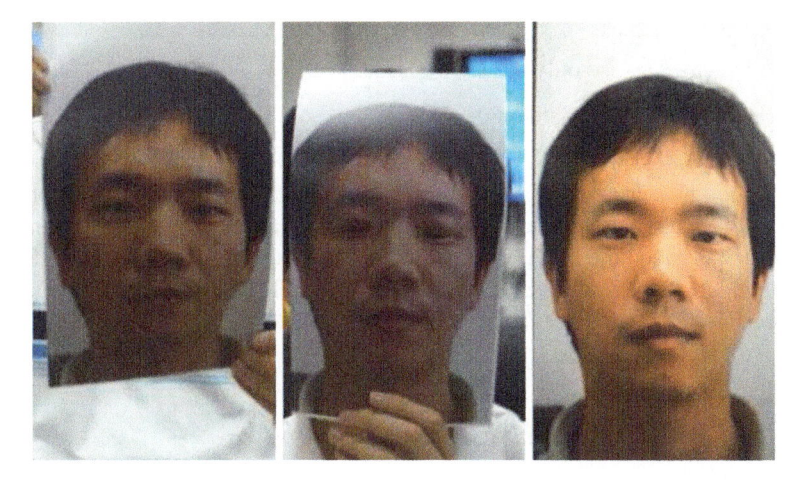

**Fig. A.12** Samples showing the three types of attacks present in the CASIA-FASD. From *left* to *right* warped photo, cut photo and video attacks, from [13]

warps the printed photo in front of the camera trying to simulate facial motion. The photo is cut around the face region;
- Cut photo attacks: the same prints as above undergo some trimming so that the attacker only preserve the face region available on the printed photo. The eye regions are also trimmed so that the attacker can also try to fake eye blinking by laying this improvised mask over their own face or with the support of a second piece of paper that remains moveable;
- Video attacks: in this case the attacker displays the high-resolution videos using an iPad with a screen resolution of $1,280 \times 768$ pixels.

#### A.3.3.1 Protocols

The data from the CASIA-FASD can be used through seven different anti-spoofing protocols, split into two subsets for training and testing spoofing classifiers. No development set is available for tunning counter-measures. In total, 12 videos of about 10 s are available for each identity: 3 real-accesses, three warped photo-attacks, three cut photo-attacks and three video attacks produced using each of devices with variable quality described before. Authors recommend that algorithms are thoroughly tested for each of the seven protocols in the three different test scenarios:

1. Quality Test
    - Low: Use only the low-quality images;
    - Normal: Use only the normal-quality images;
    - High: Use only the high-quality images.
2. Attack Test
    - Warped photo attacks: Use only the warped photo attacks;

- Cut photo attacks: Use only the cut photo attacks;
- Video attacks: Use only the iPad attacks.

3. Overal Test: use all available videos.

The Detection-Error Trade-off (DET) curve as in [18] should be used to evaluate the anti-spoofing accuracy. From DET curves, the point where the False Acceptance Rate (FAR) equals False Rejection Rate (FRR) is located, and the corresponding value, which is called the Equal Error Rate (EER), should also be reported. For any evaluating algorithm, seven DET curves and seven EER results should be reported corresponding to the above seven protocols.

### A.3.4 The 3D Mask Attack (3DMAD) Database

The 3D Mask Attack Database (3DMAD)[10] [24] is composed of real-accesses and mask attack videos to 17 different identities. Data was recorded using Microsoft Kinect sensor and therefore includes 2D visual spectra and depth information. This database represents the first controlled assessement of mask attacks to 2D face recognition systems. To create the database, masks in hard resine for each of the 17 individuals were ordered from the website thatsmyface.com. To do so, the company requires photos from the front and the person's profile out of which they prepare and print a 3D model of the person's face. The authors argue that this type of mask attacks is more realistic than those in [25] for example, since they can be articulated from non-consentual images of clients instead of full 3D models that require user cooperation. Out of the original set of images for each client, the authors ordered life-size wearable masks and also paper-cut ones. The original frontal and profile images of each client and the paper-cut masks are made available with the database download. The masks used to create the attacks on this database are shown in Fig. A.13.

As indicated before, all recordings in the database are performed using a Microsoft Kinect device for Xbox 360. The sensor provides both RGB (8-bit per color channel) and depth data (11-bit, single channel) with a size of 640 × 480 pixels at a constant acquisition speed of 30 fps. The depth data can be used to explore the vulnerability of 3D face recognition systems to mask attacks. The 2D RGB data is useful for visual spectra two-dimensional face recognition, which is the subject of this chapter. Images of real-accesses and mask attacks as captured by the Kinect sensor can be seen at Fig. A.14.

The videos are collected in three different sessions encompassing two real-access sessions two weeks apart from each other and one spoofing session performed by a single attacker. Each session records five videos of exactly 10 s for each client, which are stored in uncompressed format (HDF5). With these settings, 255 color and depth videos containing 300 frames each are available in the database. The conditions for each session are well-controlled: the scene background is uniform and lighting is

---

[10] http://www.idiap.ch/dataset/replayattack.

Appendix A: Evaluation Databases

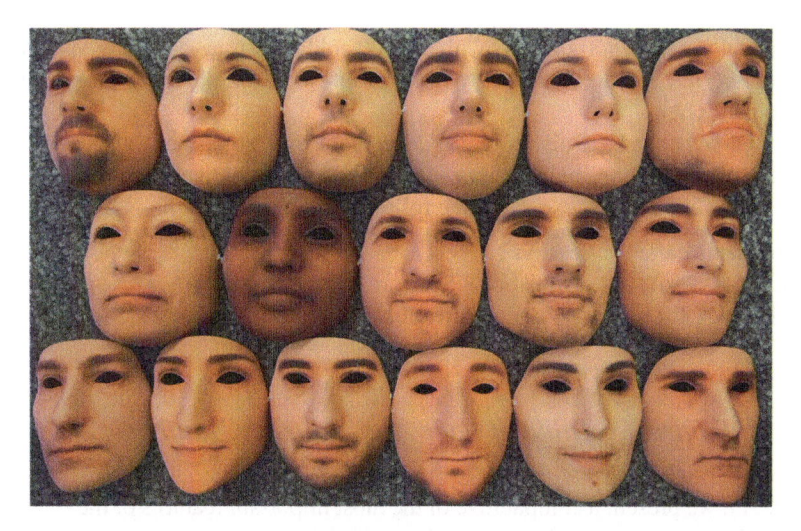

**Fig. A.13** The 17 hard-resin facial masks used to create the 3DMAD dataset, from [24]

**Fig. A.14** Examples of real accesses (*columns 1 and 3*) and mask attacks, (*columns 2 and 4*) available in the 3DMAD dataset. The *first row* represents data captured using the Kinect's 2D visual spectra camera, while the *second*, the depth camera. From [24]

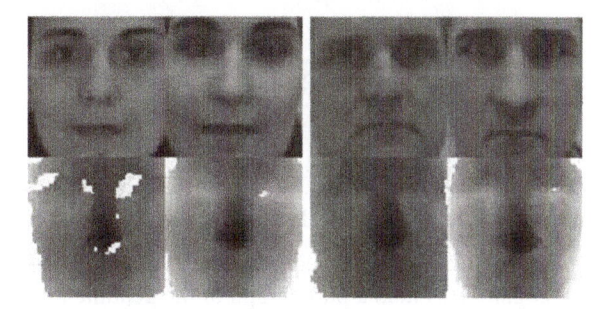

adjusted to minimize shadows cast on the face. The database is also distributed with annotations of eye positions for every 60th frame in all videos, linearly interpolated so that all frames have valid key points.

### A.3.4.1 Protocols

The 17 subjects in the database are divided into three groups allowing for antispoofing and face verification systems to be trained and evaluated with minimal bias. The number of identities in each subset is 7 (training), 5 (development) and 5 (test). Training of counter-measures to spoofing attacks should be done only using data from the training and development subsets while the test set should be solely used to report final performances.

In practice, because of the short number of video sequences in the database, authors recommend the use of cross-validation for the evaluation of anti-spoofing classifiers. To create the folds, one should select randomly, but without repetition, the clients for each subset respecting the size conditions described above (7-5-5).

The original article reports results with a 1,000-fold leave-one-out cross-validation, by averaging the HTER obtained by fixing a threshold on the EER estimated the development set.

The 3DMAD database also provides a protocol for testing face verification systems. To make that possible, authors subdivide the development and test sets into gallery and probe videos respecting the following protocol:

- Enrollment (gallery): Session 1
- Real access Probing (verification): Session 2
- Mask-attack Probing (spoofed verification): Session 3

### A.3.5 Comparative Table of Face Anti-spoofing Databases

In Table A.8 we present a comparative of the most important features of the four face spoofing databases previously presented.

## A.4 Iris Anti-spoofing Databases

Although some works have presented very sophisticated spoofing artifacts such as the use of multilayered 3-D artificial irises [26]. Almost all the iris spoofing attacks reported in the literature follow one of two trends:

- *Photo-Attacks* These fraudulent access attempts are carried out presenting to the recognition system a photograph of the genuine iris. In the vast majority of cases this image is printed on a paper (i.e., print attacks) although it may also be displayed on the screen of a digital device such as a mobile phone or a tablet (i.e., digital-photograph attacks) [27].
- *Contact Lens-Attacks* In this case the pattern of the genuine iris is printed on a contact lens that the attacker wears at the moment of the fraudulent access attempt [28].

Although the iris is one of the most analyzed traits in terms of its vulnerabilities to spoofing attacks, to the best of our knowledge, there is only one publicly available database which contains real and fake iris images: the ATVS-FIr DB.

### A.4.1 ATVS-FIr DB

The ATVS-FIr DB [29, 30] is publicly available at the ATVS-Biometric Recognition Group website.[11]

---

[11] http://atvs.ii.uam.es/.

# Appendix A: Evaluation Databases

**Table A.8** Comparative of the most relevant features corresponding to the three face spoofing databases described in in the present Annex

| | Overall Info. (Real/Fake) | | | Sensor Info. (quality) | | | | Attack Info. (types) | | | | Attack Info. (support) | | Attack Info. (Illumination) | |
|---|---|---|---|---|---|---|---|---|---|---|---|---|---|---|---|
| | # Users | # Samples | Type | # Sensors | LQ | SQ | HQ | Print | Mobile | Tablet | Mask | Held | Fixed | Controlled | Uncontrolled |
| NUAA PI | 15/15 | 5,105/7,509 | Images | 1 | | ✓ | | ✓ | | | | ✓ | | | ✓ |
| Replay-Attack | 50/50 | 200/1000 | Videos | 1 | | ✓ | | ✓ | ✓ | | | ✓ | ✓ | ✓ | ✓ |
| CASIA FAS | 50/50 | 150/450 | Videos | 3 | ✓ | ✓ | ✓ | ✓ | | ✓ | | ✓ | | | ✓ |
| 3D Mask Attack | 17/17 | 170/85 | Videos | 2 | | ✓ | | | | | ✓ | ✓ | | ✓ | |

*LQ* stands for Low Quality, *SQ* for standard Quality and *HQ* for High Quality

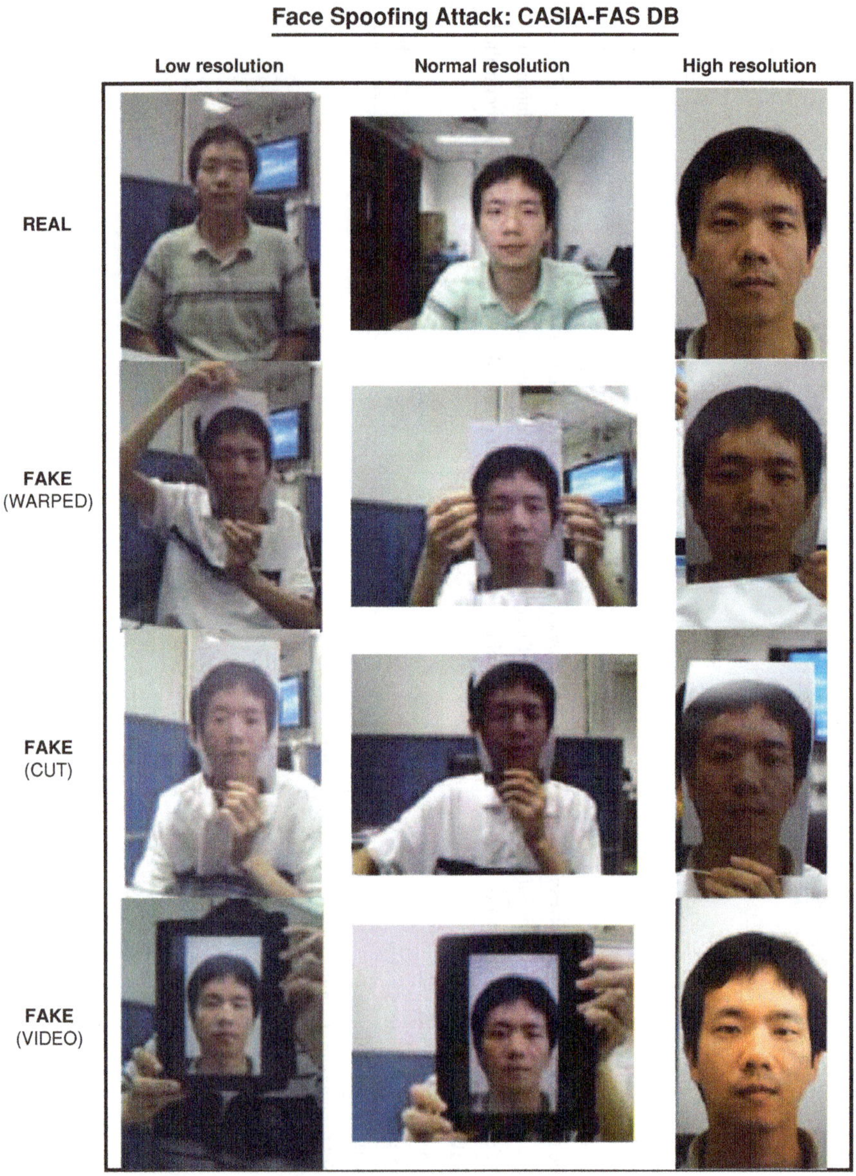

**Fig. A.15** Typical examples of real and fake (warped, cut and video) face images that can be found in the public CASIA FAS DB. Images were extracted from videos acquired with the three capturing devices used: low, normal and high resolution

The database comprises real and fake iris images (printed on paper) of 50 users randomly selected from the BioSec baseline corpus [31]. It follows the same structure as the original BioSec dataset, therefore, it comprises 50 users × 2 eyes × 4 images

Appendix A: Evaluation Databases

× 2 sessions = 800 fake iris images and its corresponding original samples. The acquisition of both real and fake samples was carried out using the LG IrisAccess EOU3000 sensor with infrared illumination which captures bmp grey-scale images of size 640 × 480 pixels.

The fake samples were acquired following a three step process which is further detailed in [29]: (i) first original images were processed to improve the final quality of the fake irises, (ii) then they were printed using a high-quality commercial printer, and last (iii) the printed images were presented to the iris sensor in order to obtain the fake image.

Although the database does not have an official protocol, in the experiments described in [30] the database was divided into a: train set, comprising 400 real images and their corresponding fake samples of the first 50 eyes; and a test set with the remaining 400 real and fake samples coming from the other 50 eyes available in the dataset.

In Fig. A.16 we show some typical real and fake iris images that may be found in the dataset.

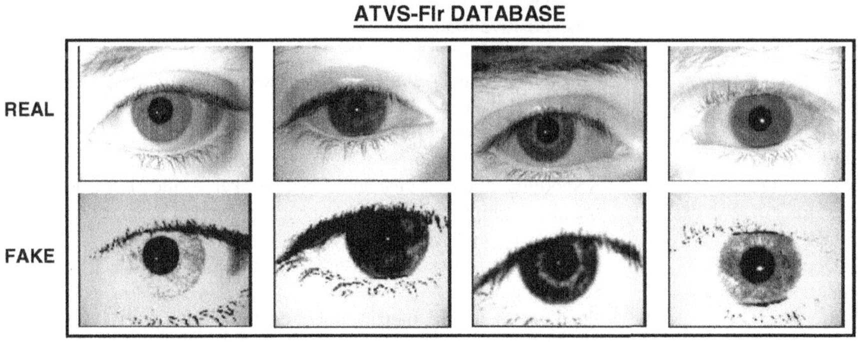

**ATVS-FIr DATABASE**

**Fig. A.16** Typical real iris images (*top row*) and their corresponding fake samples (*bottom row*) that may be found in the ATVS-Fir DB

**Table A.9** General structure of the ATVS-FIr DB

|                | ATVS-FIr DB   |           |                      |      |
|----------------|---------------|-----------|----------------------|------|
|                | Overall Info. |           | # Samples per subset |      |
|                | # Users       | # Samples | Train                | Test |
| Real-Accesses  | 50            | 800       | 400                  | 400  |
| Print-Attacks  | 50            | 800       | 400                  | 400  |

The distribution of the train and test set is given according to the protocol followed in [30]

## A.5 Glossary

| | |
|---|---|
| anti-spoofing: | Countermeasure to an spoofing attack, see presentation attack detection |
| ASV: | Automatic Speaker Verification |
| AUC: | Area Under ROC |
| DET: | Detection-Error Tradeoff |
| EER: | Equal Error Rate |
| EPC: | Expected Performance Curve |
| EPSC: | Expected Performance and Spoofability Curve |
| FAR: | False Accept Rate |
| FFR: | False Fake Rate |
| FLR: | False Living Rate |
| FMR: | False Match Rate |
| FN: | False Negative |
| FNMR: | False Non-Match Rate |
| FNR: | False Negative Rate |
| FNSPD: | False Non-Suspicious Presentation Detection |
| FP: | False Positive |
| FPR: | False Positive Rate |
| FRR: | False Reject Rate |
| FSPD: | False Suspicious Presentation Detection |
| GFAR: | Global False Accept Rate |
| GFRR: | Global False Reject Rate |
| HTER: | Half Total Error Rate |
| impersonation: | A spoofing attack against automatic speaker verification whereby a speaker attempts to imitate the speech of another speaker |
| LFAR: | Liveness False Accept Rate |
| LivDet: | Fingerprint Liveness Detection Competitions |
| liveness detection: | See anti-spoofing |
| obfuscation: | Changing his/her biometric characteristic in order to evade identification. |
| PA-NDR: | Presentation Attack Non-Detection Rate |
| PADR: | Presentation Attack Detection Rate |
| PCB: | Printed Circuit Board |
| presentation attack detection: | See anti-spoofing |
| presentation attack: | See spoofing attack |
| replay: | A spoofing attack against automatic speaker verification with the replaying of pre-recorded utterances of the target speaker |
| ROC: | Receiver Operating Characteristic |
| SFAR: | Spoof False Accept Rate |
| speech synthesis: | A spoofing attack against automatic speaker verification using automatically synthesised speech signals generated from arbitrary text |
| spoof detection: | See anti-spoofing |
| spoofing attack: | Outwitting a biometric sensor by presenting a counterfeit biometric evidence of a valid user. see presentation attacks spoofing, see spoofing attack see presentation attack |

Appendix A: Evaluation Databases

TABULA RASA: Is the accronym of the European project "Trusted Biometrics under Spoofing Attacks" funded under the 7th Framework Programme of the European Union (EU) (grant agreement number 257289) www.tabularasa-euproject.org.
TPR: True Positive Rate
voice conversion: A spoofing attack against automatic speaker verification using an attackers natural voice which is converted towards that of the target
WER: Weighted Error Rate

**Acknowledgments** This work has been partially supported by projects Contexts (S2009/TIC-1485) from CAM, Bio-Shield (TEC2012-34881) from Spanish MECD, TABULA RASA (FP7-ICT-257289) and BEAT (FP7-SEC-284989) from EU, and *Cátedra UAM-Telefónica*.

# References

1. Hastie T, Tibshirani R, Friedman J (2001) The elements of statistical learning. Springer, New York
2. Matsumoto T, Matsumoto H, Yamada K, Hoshino S (2002) Impact of artificial gummy fingers on fingerprint systems. Proceedings of SPIE optical security and counterfeit deterrence techniques IV 4677:275–289
3. Galbally J, Fierrez J, Alonso-Fernandez F, Martinez-Diaz M (2011) Evaluation of direct attacks to fingerprint verification systems. J Telecommun Syst Spec Issue of Biometrics Syst Appl 47:243–254
4. van der Putte T, Keuning J (2000) Biometrical fingerprint recognition: don't get your fingers burned. In: Proceedings of IFIP conference on smart card research and advanced applications, pp 289–303
5. Galbally J, Cappelli R, Lumini A, de Rivera GG, Maltoni D, Fierrez J, Ortega-Garcia J, Maio D (2010) An evaluation of direct and indirect attacks using fake fingers generated from ISO templates. Pattern Recogn Lett 31:725–732
6. Cappelli R, Maio D, Lumini A, Maltoni D (2007) Fingerprint image reconstruction from standard templates. IEEE Trans Pattern Anal Mach Intell 29:1489–1503
7. Ross A, Shah J, Jain AK (2007) From template to image: reconstructing fingerprints from minutiae points. IEEE Trans Pattern Anal Mach Intell 29:544–560
8. Marcialis GL, Lewicke A, Tan B, Coli P, Grimberg D, Congiu A, Tidu A, Roli F, Schuckers S (2009) First international fingerprint liveness detection competition–livdet 2009. In: Proceedings of IAPR international conference on image analysis and processing (ICIAP), LNCS, vol 5716, pp 12–23
9. Yambay D, Ghiani L, Denti P, Marcialis GL, Roli F, Schuckers S (2012) LivDet2011–Fingerprint liveness detection competition 2011. In: Proceedings of 5th international conference of biometrics (ICB)
10. Duc N, Minh B (2009) your face is not your password. In: Proceedings of US black hat conference
11. Tan X, Li Y, Liu J, Jiang L (2010) Face liveness detection from a single image with sparse low rank bilinear discriminative model. In: Proceedings of European conference on computer vision (ECCV), LNCS, Springer, vol 6316, pp 504–517
12. Chingovska I, Anjos A, Marcel S (2012) On the effectiveness of local binary patterns in face anti-spoofing. In: IEEE BIOSIG 2012
13. Zhiwei Z, Yan J, Liu S, Lei Z, Yi D, Li SZ (2012) A face antispoofing database with diverse attacks. In: Proc IAPR Int Conf Biometrics (ICB), pp 26–31

14. Kim Y, Na J, Yoon S, Yi J (2009) Masked fake face detection using radiance measurements. J Opt Soc Am 26:760–766
15. Kollreider K, Fronthaler H, Bigun J (2008) Verifying liveness by multiple experts in face biometrics. In: Proceedings IEEE international conference on computer vision and pattern recognition (CVPR)
16. Määttä J, Hadid A, Pietikäinen M (2011) Face spoofing detection from single images using micro-texture analysis. In: Proceedings of IAPR IEEE international joint conference on biometrics (IJCB), Washington DC, USA
17. Määttä J, Hadid A, Pietikäinen M (2012) Face spoofing detection from single images using texture and local shape analysis. IET Biometrics 1(1):3–10
18. Anjos A, Marcel S (2011) Counter-measures to photo attacks in face recognition: a public database and a baseline. In: Proceedings of IAPR IEEE international joint conference on biometrics (IJCB), Washington DC, USA
19. Chakka MM, Anjos A, Marcel S (2013) Motion-based counter-measures to photo attacks in face recognition, IET Biometrics. doi:10.1049/iet-bmt.2012.0071
20. Chakka MM, Anjos A, Marcel S, Tronci R, Muntoni B, Fadda G, Pili M, Sirena N, Murgia G, Ristri M, Roli F, Yan J, Yi D, Lei Z, Zhang Z, Li SZ, Schwartz WR, Rocha A, Pedrini H, Lorenzo-Navarro J, Castrillon-Santana M, Maatta J, Hadid A, Pietikainen M (2011) Competition on countermeasures to 2-d facial spoofing attacks. In: International joint conference biometrics (IJCB)
21. Chingovska I, Anjos A, Marcel S (2013) Anti-spoofing in action: joint operation with a verification system. In: Proceedings of IEEE conference on computer vision and pattern recognition, workshop on biometrics
22. Ahonen T, Hadid A, Pietikäinen M (2010) Face recognition with local binary patterns. In: European conference on computer vision (ECCV), pp 469–481
23. Froba B, Ernst A (2004) Face detection with the modified census transform. In: IEEE international conference on automatic face and gesture recognition, pp 91–96
24. Erdogmus N, Marcel S (2013) Spoofing in 2d face recognition with 3d masks and anti-spoofing with kinect. In: Biometrics: theory applications and systems conference (BTAS'13)
25. Kose N, Dugelay JL (2013) Countermeasure for the protection of face recognition systems against mask attacks. In: IEEE international conference on automatic face and gesture recognition
26. Lefohn A, Budge B, Shirley P, Caruso R, Reinhard E (2003) An ocularist's approach to human iris synthesis. IEEE Trans Comput Graphics Appl 23:70–75
27. Matsumoto T (2004) Artificial irises: importance of vulnerability analysis. In: Proceedings Asian biometrics workshop (AWB), vol 45
28. Wei Z, Qiu X, Sun Z, Tan T (2008) Counterfeit iris detection based on texture analysis. In: Proceedings IAPR ICPR
29. Ruiz-Albacete V, Tome-Gonzalez P, Alonso-Fernandez F, Galbally J, Fierrez J, Ortega-Garcia J (2008) Direct attacks using fake images in iris verification. In: Proceedings COST 2101 workshop on biometrics and identity management (BioID), pp 181–190 Springer LNCS-5372
30. Galbally J, Ortiz-Lopez J, Fierrez J, Ortega-Garcia J (2012) Iris liveness detection based on quality related features. In: Proceedings international conference on biometrics (ICB), pp 271–276
31. Fierrez J, Ortega-Garcia J, Torre-Toledano D, Gonzalez-Rodriguez J (2007) BioSec baseline corpus: a multimodal biometric database. Pattern Recogn 40:1389–1392

# Index

**A**
Anti-spoofing, 1, 184
Area under ROC, 192
Artefact, 207
Artefact species, 207
Artefact type, 207
Artificial eyeball, 103
Attack, 5
Attack success rate, 195

**B**
Biometric capture process, 207
Biometric capture subject, 207
Biometric characteristic, 207
Biometric feature, 207
Biometric security, 1
Blink, 8
Blood pressure, 8
Blueprint, 22

**C**
Challenge-response, 71
Clothing impersonation, 147
Common criteria, 211
Contact lens, 103
Corneal reflex, 8
Cosmetic contact lens, 105

**D**
3D attack, 66
Data interchange formats, 205
Data protection, 216
Detection-error tradeoff, 192
Direct attack, 1, 5

**E**
Ecoflex, 40
Equal error rate, 191
Ethics, 231
Evaluation, 184
Expected performance and spoofability curve, 199
Expected performance curve, 192
Eye blinking, 71, 105

**F**
Face recognition, 66, 84
False accept rate, 193, 211
False alarm rate, 193
False fake rate, 193
False live rejection rate, 193
False living rate, 193
False match rate, 194, 211
False negative, 191
False negative rate, 191
False non-match rate, 194, 211
False non-suspicious presentation detection, 193
False positive, 191
False positive rate, 191
False reject rate, 193, 211
False spoof accept rate, 193
False suspicious presentation detection, 193
Fingermark, 14
Fingerprint, 14, 35
Fingerprint lifting, 25
Forensic science, 14
Forgeries, 9, 13
Friction ridge skin, 14

## G
Gait, 146
Gelatine, 40
General biometric system, 204
Glass eye, 105
Global false accept rate, 195
Global false reject rate, 195

## H
Hacking, 5
Half total error rate, 191
Harmonized biometric vocabulary, 204
Hippus, 8, 105

## I
Identity concealer, 207
Impersonation, 124
Impostor, 5, 207
Indirect attack, 5
Iris recognition, 103

## L
Latex, 40
Legal framework, 216
Licit scenario, 188
Lip reading, 78
Liveness, 6, 208
Liveness detection, 6, 36
Liveness false accept rate, 195
Local binary patterns (LBP), 74, 112

## M
Mask attack, 68
Metal plate etching, 24
Mobile phone, 70
Motion, 71, 85
Multi-spectral, 84, 107
Multimodal, 164

## N
Near-infrared, 89

## O
Obfuscation, 5
Optical flow, 72

## P
Papillary lines, 14

Patellar reflex, 8
Perspiration, 8
Photo engraving, 24
Photograph attack, 66
Plastic eye, 105
Playdoh, 40
Presentation attack, 1, 207
Presentation attack detection, 1, 208
Presentation attack detection rate, 211
Presentation attack non-detection Rate, 211
Printed circuit board, 24
Printed iris, 103
Privacy, 215, 233
Pulse, 8
Pupil constriction, 105
Pupillary light reflex, 105

## Q
Quality measures, 37

## R
Receiver operating characteristic, 192
Red-eye effect, 106
Reflectance, 73
Replay, 124

## S
Silhouette, 149
Silicone, 40
Speaker recognition/verification, 123
Speech synthesis, 124
Spoof detection, 6
Spoof false accept rate, 195
Spoof scenario, 189
Spoofing, 1, 184
Spoofing databases, 245
Standard, 204
Subversive biometric capture subject, 207
Subversive user, 207
Success rate, 195

## T
Tablet, 70
TABULA RASA, 10
Targeted attack, 147
Texture, 74, 85, 107, 147
True positive rate, 191

## U
Uncooperative biometric capture subject, 207
Uncooperative presentation, 207

## V
Video attack, 66
Voice conversion, 124
Vulnerability, 1

## W
Wavelet scalar quantization, 204
Weighted error rate, 191
Wood glue, 40

## Z
Zero-effort attack, 5